Implementing Cisco Collaboration Applications (CAPPS) Foundation Learning Guide

Chris Olsen

Cisco Press

800 East 96th Street

Indianapolis, Indiana 46240 USA

Implementing Cisco Collaboration Applications (CAPPS) Foundation Learning Guide

Chris Olsen

Published by:
Cisco Press
800 East 96th Street
Indianapolis, IN 46240 USA

Printed in the United States of America

First Printing December 2015

Library of Congress Control Number: 2015956440

ISBN-13: 978-1-58714-447-9

ISBN-10: 1-58714-447-6

Warning and Disclaimer

This book is designed to provide information about Implementing Cisco Collaboration Applications (CAPPS) for the Cisco CCNP Collaboration certification exam 300-085. Every effort has been made to make this book as complete and as accurate as possible, but no warranty or fitness is implied.

The information is provided on an "as is" basis. The authors, Cisco Press, and Cisco Systems, Inc. shall have neither liability nor responsibility to any person or entity with respect to any loss or damages arising from the information contained in this book or from the use of the discs or programs that may accompany it.

The opinions expressed in this book belong to the author and are not necessarily those of Cisco Systems, Inc.

Trademark Acknowledgments

All terms mentioned in this book that are known to be trademarks or service marks have been appropriately capitalized. Cisco Press or Cisco Systems, Inc., cannot attest to the accuracy of this information. Use of a term in this book should not be regarded as affecting the validity of any trademark or service mark.

Special Sales

For information about buying this title in bulk quantities, or for special sales opportunities (which may include electronic versions; custom cover designs; and content particular to your business, training goals, marketing focus, or branding interests), please contact our corporate sales department at corpsales@pearsoned.com or (800) 382-3419.

For government sales inquiries, please contact governmentsales@pearsoned.com.

For questions about sales outside the U.S., please contact international@pearsoned.com.

Feedback Information

At Cisco Press, our goal is to create in-depth technical books of the highest quality and value. Each book is crafted with care and precision, undergoing rigorous development that involves the unique expertise of members from the professional technical community.

Readers' feedback is a natural continuation of this process. If you have any comments regarding how we could improve the quality of this book, or otherwise alter it to better suit your needs, you can contact us through e-mail at feedback@ciscopress.com. Please make sure to include the book title and ISBN in your message.

We greatly appreciate your assistance.

Publisher: Paul Boger

Associate Publisher: Dave Dusthimer

Business Operation Manager, Cisco Press: Jan Cornelssen

Acquisitions Editor: Brett Bartow

Managing Editor: Sandra Schroeder

Development Editor: Ellie Bru

Project Editor: Mandie Frank

Copy Editor: Keith Cline

Technical Editors: James "Mac" McInvaille, R. J. Neill Craven

Editorial Assistant: Vanessa Evans

Designer: Mark Shirar

Composition: codeMantra

Indexer: Erika Millen

Proofreader: Box Twelve Communications

About the Author

Chris Olsen, CCSI, CCNP, along with numerous other Cisco voice and data center specializations (in addition to Microsoft, VMware, and Novell certifications), has been an independent IT and telephony trainer, consultant, author, and technical editor for more than 22 years. He earned his Bachelor of Science in Mechanical Engineering and Master of Science in Mechanical Engineering at Bradley University in the 1980s. Chris has been a technical trainer for more than 22 years and has taught more than 60 different courses in Cisco, Microsoft, VMware, and Novell. For the past nine years, he has specialized in Cisco and Microsoft Unified Communications, along with VMware virtualization and Cisco data center technologies. He has done a wide array of IT and telephony consulting for many different companies. Chris and his wife, Antonia, live in Chicago and Mapleton, Illinois.

About the Technical Reviewers

James "Mac" McInvaille CCSI #31293, CCNP Voice, JNCIP-SP #297, is a Certified Cisco Systems Instructor and a network consulting engineer for Cisco Systems with a large multinational corporation in the financial sector. He is a subject matter expert with the Unified Communications product line for Cisco Systems, as a CCNP Voice consultant and certified instructor. Previously, Mac was a solutions engineer for HP-EDS for the Bank of America voice-transformation project. Prior to HP-EDS, Mac was the lead technical consultant for the Carolinas Region of Dimension Data, NA. His responsibilities included the support and guidance of a team of engineers and technologists involved in the consultation, implementation, delivery, and training of VoIP and other Unified Communications products, as well as high-level routing and switching designs. All of this started with a 12-year distinguished military career in the U.S. Air Force that gave him the confidence and experience to be where he is today. He enjoys his leisure time with his high school sweetheart, Crystal, traveling and visiting family around the Carolinas and East Coast.

R. J. Neill Craven, CCIE #1755, CCSI #93014, CCDP, CCVP, has more than 35 years of experience in the telecommunications and computer industries. His management experience and extensive practical knowledge make him a highly regarded and competent professional, experienced in the design, planning, implementation, and support of major integrated networks.

Dedications

This book is dedicated to my wonderful wife, Antonia, whose constant love and tireless commitment to making my life better gave me the time to write this book. I am forever grateful.

Acknowledgments

I would like to thank all my good friends and colleagues at Global Knowledge and NterOne for their excellent support over the years.

I want to give special recognition to Neill Craven and James "Mac" McInvaille for their great guidance along the way on this book.

The production team at Pearson of Brett Bartow, Ellie Bru, and Mandie Frank are real pros and made my third Cisco Press book a most rewarding experience.

Contents at a Glance

Contents

Introduction

Cisco Unity Connection, Cisco Unity Express, Cisco Instant Message and Presence, Cisco TelePresence Video Communication Server, and the Cisco TelePresence Management Suite provide valuable technologies to a Cisco Unified Communications design. This book was designed with the focus on utilizing these technologies in a production environment as effectively as possible. Industry leaders were consulted for technical accuracy throughout this book.

Who Should Read This Book?

This book is designed for those Unified Communications engineers and technologists who want to implement Cisco Unity Connection, Cisco Unity Express, Cisco Instant Message and Presence, Cisco TelePresence Video Communication Server, and the Cisco TelePresence Management Suite in a Unified Communication design.

How This Book Is Organized

Chapter 1, "Designing and Deploying Cisco Unity Connection": The book starts by providing an overview of the technical requirements and functionality of Cisco Unity Connection. The required essentials of VMware storage and networking are discussed to ensure a successful Unity Connection installation.

Chapter 2, "Integrating Cisco Unity Connection with Cisco Unified Communications Manager": The product Cisco Unity Connection cannot function on its own. This chapter provides the details of an integration with Cisco Unified Communications Manager or other private branch exchange products. The requirements for Unity Licensing in the Prime License Manager tool are outlined.

Chapter 3, "Configuring Cisco Unity Connection User, Templates, and Class of Service": Once Unity Connection is installed, users and user settings must be configured to enable voice mail. This chapter describes the creation of users with class of service settings to provision the best services for each user within the organizational design.

Chapter 4, "Configuring the Cisco Unity Connection System": This chapter gives the foundation of common configurations of Cisco Unity Connection such as distribution lists, security settings, and Lightweight Directory Access Protocol.

Chapter 5, "Implementing Cisco Unity Connection Dial Plan and Call Management": This chapter explains the Cisco Unity Connection dial plan components of partitions and search spaces. Partitions, group objects, and search spaces comprise the search rights for objects in the included partitions. Call handlers are used to build auto-attendant functionality with Cisco Unity Connection.

Chapter 6, "Configuring Unified Messaging": This chapter explains the single inbox feature of unified messaging. Single inbox allows users to receive their voice messages in the company mail inbox with the proper message waiting indicator synchronization when users are reading the e-mail on a PC or listening to the messages on the phone.

Chapter 7, "Troubleshooting Cisco Unity Connection": This chapter explains how to resolve common issues with Cisco Unity Connection integrations and operations. In addition, the chapter presents the Cisco Unified Real Time Monitoring Tool to monitor Cisco Unity Connection and explains micro and macro traces for Cisco Unity Connection.

Chapter 8, "Deploying Voice-Mail Redundancy in Branch Offices": This chapter describes the deployment of Cisco Unity Connection Survivable Remote Site Voicemail and its features and limitations. This chapter also describes the configuration process of the branch and the headquarters, or central, sites.

Chapter 9, "Designing and Deploying Cisco Unity Express": Cisco Unity Express provides a feature-rich messaging solution that is ideal for the requirements of branch locations or small to medium-sized businesses. This chapter describes the features and characteristics of Cisco Unity Express.

Chapter 10, "Integrating Cisco Unity Express with Cisco Unified Communications Manager Express": This chapter describes how to integrate Cisco Unity Express with Cisco Unified Communications Manager Express using Session Initiation Protocol. Sections that are covered include the setup of the Cisco Unity Express service module and the IP routing for Cisco Unity Express access. The various message waiting indicators and dual-tone multifrequency options are also discussed.

Chapter 11, "Configuring Cisco Unity Express User Accounts and Features": This chapter describes the Cisco Unity Express system settings. The configuration of mailboxes and distribution lists is also covered. Cisco Unity Express time-based schedules and other features such as integrated messaging are also discussed.

Chapter 12, "Configuring Call Routing with Cisco Unity Express Auto-Attendant": This chapter describes the Cisco Unity Express auto-attendant applications and options. Many businesses require an automated system for processing inbound calls. For example, when customers call the business number, they hear a welcome message and are prompted to press telephone buttons for different services. This type of service is referred to as an automatic attendant or auto-attendant.

Chapter 13, "Troubleshooting Cisco Unity Express": This chapter describes how to troubleshoot issues within a Cisco Unity Express voice-mail solution using Cisco Unified Communications Manager Express as the call-processing system.

Chapter 14, "Designing and Deploying Cisco Unified IM and Presence": This chapter describes the Cisco Unified Communications IM and Presence architecture and design. Native presence in Cisco Unified Communications Manager is presented, and the different Cisco Unified Communications IM and Presence approaches are described. Cisco Unified Communications IM and Presence can be configured to peer with another Cisco Unified Communications IM and Presence cluster in the same domain or can be federated with Cisco Unified Communications IM and Presence clusters in a different domain.

Chapter 15, "Describing Cisco Unified Communications IM and Presence Components and Communications Flows": This chapter describes the Cisco Unified Communications IM and Presence architecture, protocols, interfaces, and call flows.

Chapter 16, "Integrating Cisco Unified Communications IM and Presence": This chapter describes the integration of Cisco Unified Communications Manager and Cisco Unified Communications IM and Presence. First, Cisco Unified Communications Manager is prepared for integration with Cisco Unified Communications IM and Presence. Cisco Unified Communications IM and Presence is then set up to connect with Cisco Unified Communications Manager and system settings are modified. Network services are then established so that Cisco Jabber can discover its domain and services. Finally, the chapter discusses the Cisco Jabber installation options.

Chapter 17, "Configuring Cisco Unified Communications IM and Presence Features and Implementing Cisco Jabber": This chapter describes how Cisco Jabber can be used in phone-only mode as compared to Cisco Jabber in softphone mode. The chapter explains the profiles that must be used (for example, the profiles for voice messaging) and how deskphone mode is implemented to control desk phones.

Chapter 18, "Configuring Cisco Jabber Mobile and Integrating Directory Servers": This chapter describes how to configure and deploy Cisco Jabber Mobile and how the client accesses the directory for contact search and number resolution.

Chapter 19, "Verifying and Troubleshooting Tools for Cisco Unified IM and Presence Components": This chapter covers the Cisco Unified Communications IM and Presence system troubleshooter and the Cisco Jabber Connection Status tool, which help the administrator resolve presence issues quickly. Some common issues for Cisco Jabber are presented and resolved. Finally, tracing is introduced.

Chapter 20, "Deploying Cisco Collaboration Systems Applications with Cisco Prime Collaboration": This chapter introduces the Cisco Prime Collaboration modules and focuses on provisioning. Day 1 and Day 2 activities are described. The use of the design and deployment options in Cisco Prime Collaboration are discussed, and the Cisco Prime Collaboration telephone self-care portal is covered.

Chapter 21, "Describing Video Infrastructure": This chapter describes the layers of the collaboration infrastructure for video integrated solutions and explains the differences between Cisco Unified Communications Manager and Cisco TelePresence Virtual Communications Server as the call-processing system. Cisco Jabber Video for TelePresence is described as a client that can be automatically provisioned and register to the Cisco TelePresence Virtual Communications Server only.

Chapter 22, "Describing Cisco TMS": This chapter provides a detailed description of the Cisco TelePresence Management Suite (Cisco TMS) capabilities and scheduling options. Exchange extension and web scheduling are also explained in detail.

Chapter 1

Designing and Deploying Cisco Unity Connection

Upon completing this chapter, you will be able to do the following:

- Describe the hardware options to deploy a virtualized voice-messaging solution
- Describe the different versions of ESXi and the available licensing options
- Show a physical architecture and compare it with the virtual architecture of a server including the operating system and applications
- Describe the VM on a host system and its associated files
- Describe the options for creating custom-based VMs and illustrate the simplicity of using Cisco OVA files for virtualization
- Describe how Cisco guarantees the performance of Cisco Unity Connection in a VM using shares and reservations
- Describe the virtual switch, which is set up by default with every ESXi installation and how physical NICs can be teamed for redundancy
- Describe the different storage options for virtualization
- Describe the parameters that affect the sizing and design of a Cisco Unity Connection solution
- Describe the Cisco Unity Connection high-availability options
- Describe traffic patterns for voice messaging and how these change when voice messaging is centralized
- Describe Cisco Unity Connection networking and VPIM options
- Describe the virtualization of Cisco MediaSense for Cisco Unity Connection video greetings, and how to deploy the platform

- Describe the hardware and resource guidelines for planning and sizing Cisco Unity Connection video greetings
- Describe the call flows in voice messaging and the purpose of the Cisco Unity Connection ports

This chapter introduces the server platforms and Cisco Unity Connection overlays, which are the basis for all designs and integration of Cisco Unity Connection with Cisco Prime License Manager (PLM), design scenarios with single, multiple, and linked sites, as well as backup voice-mail solutions during a WAN outage.

Physical Server Choices for Cisco Collaboration System Applications

You have multiple options to deploy Cisco Unity Connection:

- Cisco TRC servers are optimized for Cisco Collaboration System solutions for Cisco Business Edition 6000 or 7000 or for Cisco Collaboration System on the Cisco Unified Computing System (UCS).
- Cisco SRE or Cisco UCS Express is a network module that you install in a router. You can run VMware ESXi on this module to host Cisco Unity Connection for Survivable Remote Site Voice Mail (SRSV). For more information about Cisco Collaboration System on Cisco UCS Express go to: http://docwiki.cisco.com/wiki/Cisco_Unity_Connection_on_UCSE.
- You can use any existing server (specification-based) if the server matches the Cisco-specified requirements for speed and capacity for the main virtual resources: CPU, memory, and storage. If 1 Gbps or faster interfaces are used, NIC interfaces are not the limiting factor in a virtualized Cisco Collaboration System environment.

In a traditional physical server platform, one server hosts one operating system. When using virtualization, the servers that run each individual application are called VMs, and they run on one host server (for example, a DNS server, web server, or Cisco Unity Connection). According to Gartner research results, a normal server has an average utilization of 10 percent. Virtualization allows you to increase server utilization and efficiency and optimize the physical footprint of the data center. A better physical footprint leads to fewer servers, fewer cables, and a better green footprint with less power and cooling.

Note With Cisco Collaboration System Release 10.x, the installation of Cisco Collaboration System applications has to be done in a VM. Bare-metal installations are not supported anymore.

VMware vSphere ESXi Virtualization

VMware vSphere ESXi is a specialized operating system known as a hypervisor that you install on the physical server, which is called the host system. The ESXi hypervisor runs on top of it one or more guest systems (virtual machines or VMs), for example, Cisco Unified Communications Manager (CUCM) and Cisco Unity Connection. Only VMware ESXi is supported for Cisco Collaboration System virtualization.

VMware vSphere ESXi 5.5 comes in three editions: Standard Edition, Enterprise Edition, and Enterprise Plus Edition. There were Advanced and ESX offerings in Version 4.x, which are not available in Version 5.0+.

For hardware support, go to the *VMware Compatibility Guide at* http://www.vmware.com/go/hcl.

The three versions editions differ in their supported features and list prices. The prices can be easily viewed at http://www.vmware.com/products/vsphere/pricing.html. The prices are based on the features that are required. For example, if you want to deploy Cisco Nexus 1000V series switches, you must use the Enterprise Plus license. The Enterprise Plus license is required because you must deploy the distributed switch feature. VMware vCenter is also required for management and administration. In most small or medium-sized companies with two Cisco UCS C-series servers with DAS, the Standard version will be enough. However, if you need extra features, you might have to license the Enterprise or Enterprise Plus version.

For more details, product comparison, and a short description of the features in the different editions, go to VMware vSphere with Operations Management at http://www.vmware.com/products/vsphere/compare.html.

If you use Cisco Business Edition 6000, VMware vCenter is not supported. On the other hand, if you run servers other than Cisco TRC servers for Cisco Collaboration System virtualization, you must use VMware vCenter. All of these considerations will guide you in selecting the right ESXi edition.

Note that if you buy ESXi licenses from Cisco, the Cisco TAC takes care of issues that are related to the hypervisor.

Note The predecessor VMware hypervisor product to ESXi is ESX. ESX is end of life from VMware and is not supported on Cisco Unified Communications products.

For more information about Cisco Collaboration System VMware requirements, review the *Unified Communications VMware Requirements* document at http://docwiki.cisco.com/wiki/Unified_Communications_VMware_Requirements.

Physical and Virtual Architecture Comparison

This section shows a physical architecture and compares it with the virtual architecture of a server, including the operating system and applications. Figure 1-1 shows the comparison between traditional servers on the left running one operating system and many operating systems in the form of virtual machines running on a single hypervisor on the right.

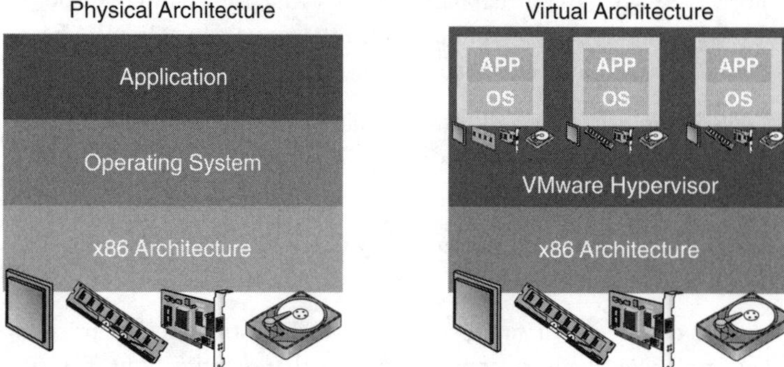

Figure 1-1 *Physical Versus Virtual Server Comparison*

A physical server is defined by its CPUs, RAM, network interface cards, and hard disks. Even if there are different motherboards, chipsets, etc., these four components are the main server parameters that are important for Cisco Collaboration System virtualization.

The operating system (for example, Red Hat Linux for Cisco Collaboration System) is installed, and the drivers are selected according to the hardware components in the physical server.

In the virtual architecture, this setup is basically the same. The hypervisor is the operating system and will install drivers for the NICs, hard disk controllers, and other components.

The significant advantage of the virtual architecture is that the virtual machines (VMs) are installed with an operating system using virtual drivers that do not depend on the physical hardware. This advantage allows you to easily move the VMs to any other host server.

Another significant advantage is that the VMs are isolated. An error in any VM does not bring down other VMs on the same physical server.

If you change the hardware in the server (for example, by replacing a NIC), the hypervisor must adjust the software drivers accordingly, but the VMs are not affected at all.

Virtual Machine Encapsulation and Files

This section describes the VM on a host system and its associated files. Figure 1-2 illustrates that different VMs have their own folders with their own files. Cisco Unity Connection would be an example of one or two of these VMs.

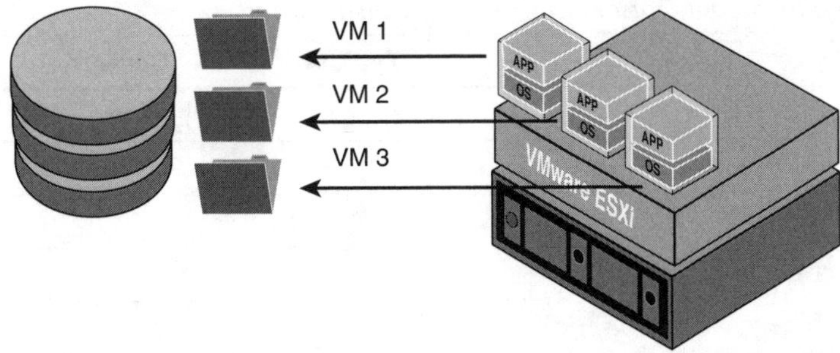

Figure 1-2 *Virtual Machines File Storage*

A VM is software and consists of many files. The data store with the VMware File System (VMFS) stores all these files in one directory.

Encapsulation of VM files allows the folder to easily become part of the business continuity or disaster recovery solution. The diagram presents a host server with three VMs that are each stored in one folder. The file structure of VMFS is similar to Linux or UNIX. Each data store is mounted to a folder and contains subdirectories with the files of a VM. VMFS is also optimized to support large files and to perform many concurrent writes.

A folder of a single VM contains, for example, the following files: Other files may exist as well based on the actions done on the VM:

- *.vmx configuration files with the hardware settings
- *.vswp swap files
- *.nvram BIOS files
- *.log log files
- *.vmdk disk files

Typical Versus Custom Virtual Machine Creation

This section describes the options for creating custom-based VMs and illustrates the simplicity of using Cisco OVA files for virtualization. An OVA file is an Open Virtualization Archive that contains a compressed, "installable" version of a virtual machine. When you open an OVA file it extracts the VM and imports it into whatever virtualization software you have installed on your computer. Table 1-1 compares the typical versus custom options when creating a new VM.

VMs can be manually created within VMware. As you can see in the table, you may not have all of the required information for the Cisco Collaboration System applications VM. This is why manually creating VMs for Cisco Collaboration System is not supported. You must use preconfigured Cisco Collaboration System OVA templates.

Table 1-1 *Typical Versus Custom Options During a VM Installation*

Option	Typical	Custom
VM name	x	x
Data store selection	x	x
VM version		x
Operating system selection	x	x
Number of sockets and cores		x/x
Memory size		x
Number of NICs and network adapters	x/x	x/x
SCSI adapter		x
Create/reuse disk/RDM/diskless		x/x/x/x
Disk size and mode	x/x	x/x
Disk location		x
Virtual device node—SCSI/IDE		x/x

x represents a choice or required information to be entered during the VM creation.

To be TAC-supported, VMs for Cisco Unified Communications applications must use a VM configuration from the OVA file provided by that application.

An OVA ensures that a VM installation is standardized and simplified:

- The OVA templates represent what the UC applications have been validated with.
- It is the only way to ensure UC applications are deployed on "aligned" disks for storage-area network (SAN) deployments (that is, pre-aligned file system disk partitions for the VM's vDisks).

OVA templates are preconfigured settings that help you deploy a virtual machine as follows:

- Virtual machine Version 10 is used with ESXi 5.5
- Guest operating system is Red Hat Enterprise Linux Version 6
- Number of cores with reservation
- Memory with reservation
- Number of NICs and network adapters
- SCSI controller
- New disk with extended partition alignment
- Disk capacity and provisioning mode
- Virtual device node

Cisco creates the OVA template for every Cisco Collaboration System application and selects the right parameter for you. These templates are smaller files, usually a couple of 100 kilobytes. After the VM is created from the OVA template, you need to mount the Cisco Collaboration System applications ISO installer file. This step can be compared to inserting a CD or DVD to run the installation process.

There are also OVA files (for example, for Cisco Prime Collaboration Provisioning). The download size depends on the application. These OVF files are imported and simply started. There is no installation necessary. When starting the VMs for the first time, you must enter the IP address and login credentials. Depending on the Cisco Collaboration System applications, you may have to add some additional parameters.

Note Open Virtualization Format (OVF) is an open standard for packaging and distributing virtual appliances or, more generally, software to be run in virtual machines.

On all Cisco Collaboration VM installations, you must download the corresponding OVA file for a successful installation.

Note VM hardware Version 10 is used in VMware vSphere ESXi 5.5, VM Version 9 is used in VMware vSphere ESXi 5.1, and VM Version 8 is used in VMware vSphere ESXi 5.0. VMware vSphere ESXi 5.5 is backward-compatible, so, for example, VM Version 8 can be used with a VMware vSphere ESXi 5.5 host as well.

OVA Template for Cisco Unity Connection

This section describes the characteristics of the Cisco Unity Connection OVA templates and the required physical resources. Table 1-2 illustrates the different OVA options when deploying Unity Connection as a VM.

Table 1-2 *Cisco Unity Connection OVA Installation Options*

User Capacity	vCPUs	Memory	vDisk	vNIC
100	1	4	1 × 160 GB	1
1000	1	4	1 × 160 GB	1
5000	2	6	1 × 200 GB	1
10000	4	6	2 × 146 GB or 2 × 300 GB or 2 × 500 GB	1
20000	7	8	2 × 300 GB or 2 × 500 GB	1

Cisco Unity Connection requires one idle CPU per server where Cisco Unity Connection is hosted to guarantee voice quality.

Note With ESXi Version 5.5 and Unity Connection Version 10.5.2, the extra core is not required if the Unity Connection latency sensitivity feature is enabled and the value is set to high.

Table 1-2 presents the available VM overlays for Cisco Unity Connection installations. The 100-user OVA template is only supported on Cisco UCS Express.

Another important factor is the number of ports. When using G.711 or G.729, the following numbers of ports are supported:

- 100 users and 8 ports
- 1000 users and 24 ports
- 5000 users and 100 ports
- 10,000 users and 150 ports
- 20,000 users and 250 ports

These templates may be adjusted and optimized with new versions of Cisco Collaboration System or ESXi. When running Cisco Unity Connection on a virtualized platform, one more idle core must be reserved for Cisco Unity Connection to guarantee the quality of call recording.

A Cisco Unity Connection cluster consists of two servers. Two servers do not double the number of users, but a cluster does double the number of voice-mail ports. So, the largest Cisco Unity Connection cluster with two servers can support 20,000 users with 500 voice-mail ports.

For current information about supported platforms please visit the Virtualization for Cisco Unity Connection page, available at http://docwiki.cisco.com/wiki/Virtualization_for_Cisco_Unity_Connection#Version_10.5.28x.29.

Resizing Virtual Machine Resources

This section describes the virtual resources that can be modified in a VM after the Cisco Collaboration System application is already installed.

The sizing and allocation of virtual resources is done with the OVA templates. Software upgrades might require a change in the virtual resource allocation.

Generally, virtual resources can be added. However, for Cisco Collaboration System applications, the VM must be shut down to add vCPUs and vRAM. Resizing of the hard disk leads to repartitioning, and the content of the disk is destroyed. For vNICs, the application must support multiple interfaces and an IP address. The NIC redundancy is provided by the hypervisor and is transparent to the Cisco Collaboration System application.

Note VM changes that result in an unsupported OVA configuration are not allowed. Check the latest Cisco Collaboration System virtualization guidelines for resizing VMs.

If you need to resize a VM for a Cisco Collaboration System application upgrade, deploy a new VM with the new hardware specification. Then do a fresh installation, backup and restore the application, and upgrade the Cisco Collaboration System application.

Shares and Reservations

This section describes how Cisco guarantees the performance of Cisco Unity Connection in a VM using shares and reservations. Figure 1-3 illustrates the option in VMware vCenter for changing the shares and reservations for a VM.

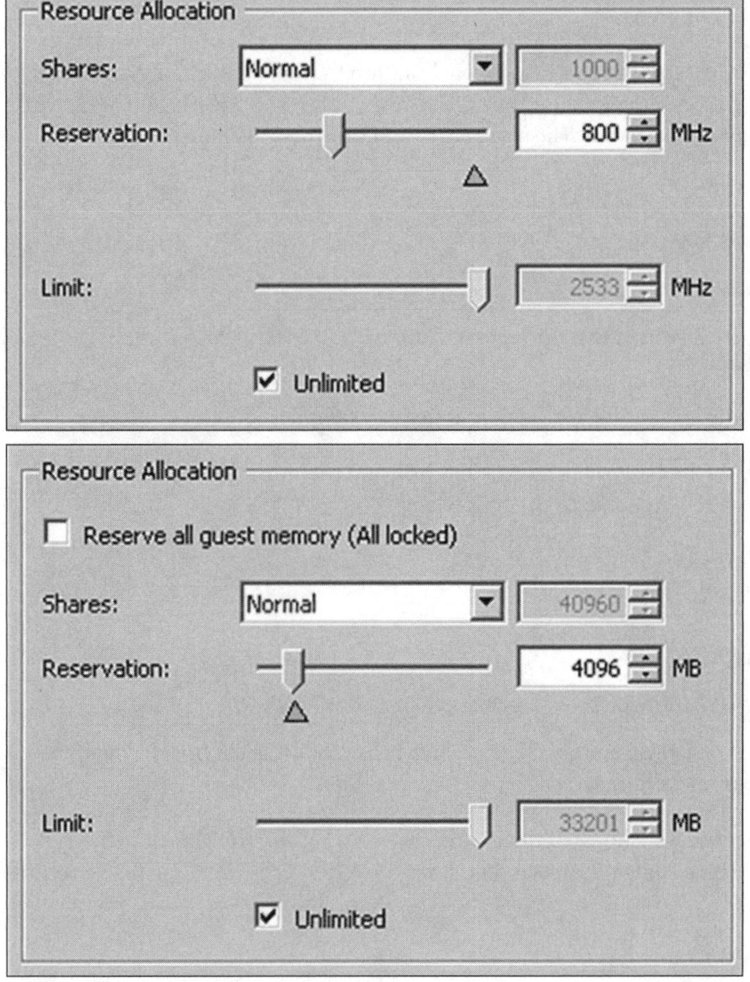

Figure 1-3 *VM Resource Allocation*

Figure 1-3 shows how to control resource utilization for CPUs and memory with shares, reservations, and limits. Cisco Collaboration System applications OVAs are configured with reservations to guarantee the Cisco Collaboration System quality and experience.

Three parameters can be configured for CPU, memory, and I/O control for VM access to resources:

- **Limit:** This value cannot be exceeded, but is limited by the physical resources.
- **Reservation:** This limit must be available for the VM to be started successfully. If this amount of resources is not available when starting the VM, the VM is not powered on.
- **Shares:** A share controls the access to resources and can be compared with weights that you assign to a VM.

The figure shows the settings for a Cisco Collaboration System application VM that is deployed with an OVA template. For the CPU, the default reservation is 800 MHz with a normal share and no limitation. The shares can be set to the following:

- Low equals 500.
- Normal equals 1000.
- High equals 2000.
- For custom user-defined shares, the maximum is 2533 MHz, which is the speed of the physical core.
- 2533 MHz equals the value for unlimited in this example.

For the memory, the reservation is set to 4096 MB, and the normal share is 40,960. The shares can be set in this example to the following:

- Low equals 20,480.
- Normal equals 40,960.
- High equals 81,920.
- For custom user-defined shares, the maximum is 4096 MB.
- The value for unlimited equals 33,201, which is the total capacity of the memory pool in this example host server.

For completeness, but not shown in the figure, the value for the I/O allocation is, by default, Normal with a share of 1000 and no limit for IOPS. The shares can be set to the following:

- Low equals 500.
- Normal equals 1000.

- High equals 2000.
- For custom user-defined shares, the value is between 200 and 4000.

Changing any of these parameters leads to an unsupported Cisco Collaboration System deployment. However, all necessary settings are included in the OVA template.

Virtual Switch and NIC Teaming

This section describes the vSwitch, which is set up by default with every ESXi installation, and how physical NICs can be teamed for redundancy. Figure 1-4 is a representation of the default VMware standard switch.

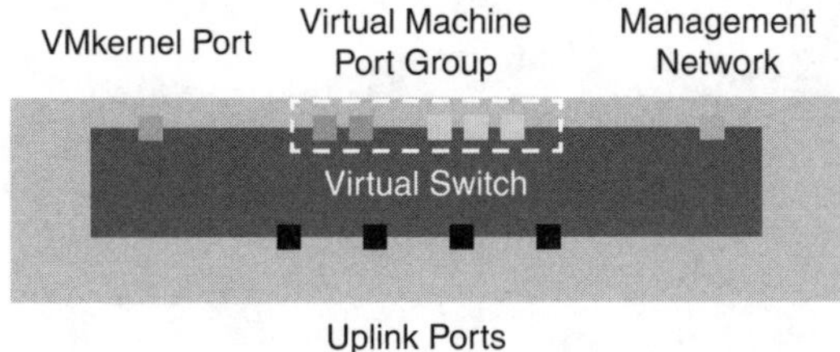

Figure 1-4 *VMware Standard vSwitch*

Virtual networking in a host server is provided by the vNetwork. The main component of this vNetwork is the vSwitch. The vSwitch is a software switch that is implemented in the VMkernel. A host server can be configured to have one or more vSwitches. The VM traffic must pass through one of the vSwitches to reach another VM on the same host server or any other device in the network. However, a vSwitch cannot communicate with another vSwitch in the same host server. For example, in addition to a network for Cisco Collaboration System, you might run a management or storage network on the same host server.

The switches work on Layer 2 of the OSI model, but do not offer the same features that a physical switch provides. For example, there is no Telnet access to the vSwitch. If you want to configure additional switch features, such as access lists, you can implement the Cisco Nexus 1000V Distributed Virtual Switch.

Every vSwitch must be mapped to its own physical NIC. However, a vSwitch can be connected to more than one physical NIC. You can place multiple interfaces into a channel group to communicate with the network and load-balance the traffic on the network interfaces.

When connecting two VMs to the same vSwitch, the traffic can be routed directly between the VMs. Network administrators might be concerned because the traffic is not visible to the network, so you cannot apply policies, for example. With Cisco Data Center VM-FEX (http://www.cisco.com/en/US/netsol/ns1124/index.html), you can eliminate this behavior and make the traffic visible to the network.

In the standard setup, vSwitch0 is created. The vSwitch comprises a VM port group, named VM Network, and the VM kernel, named Management Port.

NIC Teaming

Figure 1-5 is an example of a VMware virtual switch named vSwitch0 in ESXi represented in the blue box connected to the physical switches on the bottom.

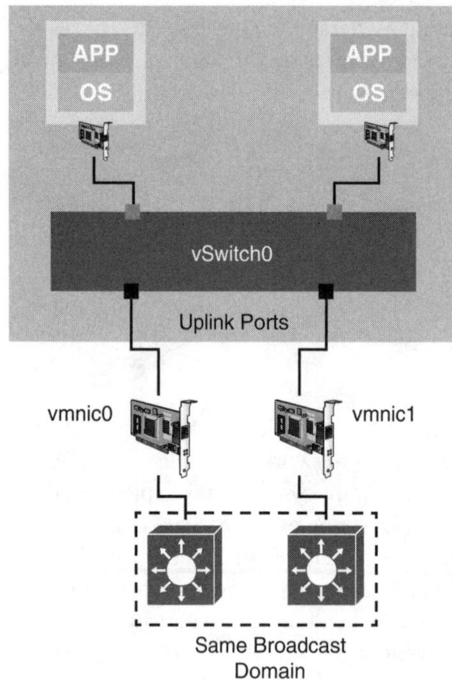

Figure 1-5 *VMware vSwitch Uplinks*

Figure 1-6 illustrates NIC Teaming on a virtual switch in VMware vCenter. VMware software controls which vmnic is used for outbound communication.

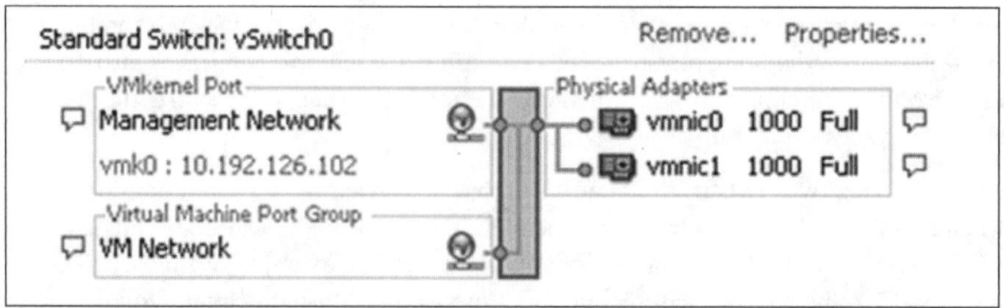

Figure 1-6 *VMware vSwitch NIC Teaming*

Figure 1-6 shows an ESXi host with a standard virtual switch labeled as vSwitch0 connected via NIC teaming to network switches that belong to the same broadcast domain.

When building a NIC team to avoid a single point of failure, use a NIC on the motherboard and a NIC that is based on the PCI architecture, if possible. Go to the vSwitch properties and add a second NIC to the vSwitch0. After adding the second NIC, the result should look the way it is presented in the figure. With a standby adapter, only the active NIC interface is used at any time to transfer data.

Note Most of Cisco Collaboration System applications that run in VMs support only a single vNIC and a single IP address. Cisco Unity Connection also supports only one vNIC.

Storage Overview

This section describes the different storage options for virtualization.

Figure 1-7 shows the different types of storage supported by VMware to hold VM files.

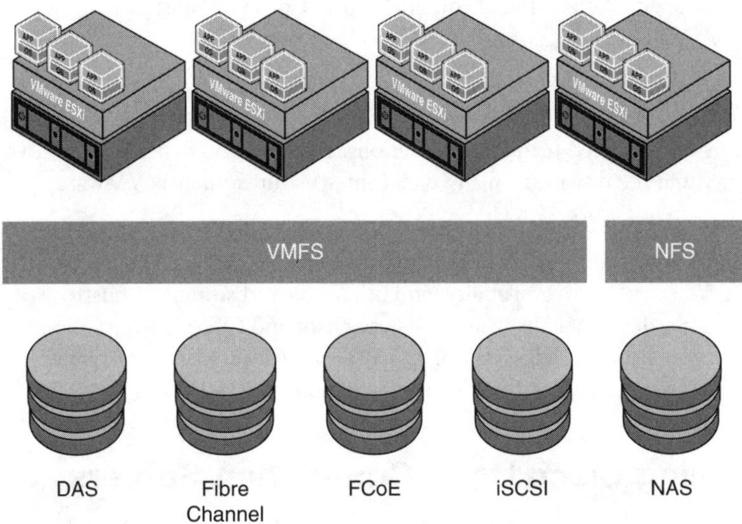

Figure 1-7 *VMware Supported VM Storage Technologies*

Data stores are used to store the VM files. The data store provides a uniform model to store files and hides the specifics of the storage device. The data store format is VMFS, an operating system native file system, or a storage device using NFS.

VMware vSphere ESXi supports the following storage technologies:

- **DAS:** Direct-attached storage (DAS) is a storage disk or storage array that is directly attached to the host server.

- **Fibre Channel:** The host server can be connected to a Fibre Channel switch that is also connected to a storage array. Fibre Channel is a lossless network protocol that transports SCSI commands in the upper layer of the protocol stack. Often, people talk about SAN and Fibre Channel in the same way, which is incorrect. SAN is a network topology, and Fibre Channel is a protocol, just like iSCSI or FCoE are protocols.
- **FCoE:** Fibre Channel over Ethernet accesses basically the same target device as Fibre Channel. The only difference is that from the host server to the fabric switch, the path is Ethernet where Fibre Channel frames are encapsulated into Ethernet frames. Be aware that Ethernet is not a lossless network like Fibre Channel. Discussions of unified fabric, unified ports, or converged networks usually involve FCoE.
- **iSCSI:** With iSCSI, you also put SCSI commands into another protocol, in this case TCP/IP. iSCSI is an IP storage solution.
- **NAS:** Network-attached storage (NAS) is also accessed via TCP/IP at the file system level. NFS is used for the data store, but NFS does not support SCSI commands.

Storage technologies are based on 1-Gbps or 10-Gbps Ethernet. For Cisco Collaboration System specifications-based solutions with FCoE, you must use 10-Gbps interfaces.

DAS is mostly found in Cisco UCS C-series deployments, where the hypervisor and Cisco Collaboration System application are installed locally on the server. For small data center environments or dedicated technology solutions, DAS is a good choice to remove the SAN complexity. On the downside, many data center features, such as VMware vMotion and others, do not work with DAS.

Shared storage can be accessed by many host servers, which allows features such as VMware vMotion, VMware High Availability, and others. Shared storage is mostly used with Cisco UCS B-Series deployments, where the hypervisor and Cisco Collaboration System applications are installed on SANs, which is also called a *diskless deployment*. Shared storage can be used as a central repository for templates or VM files.

Sizing and Scaling Cisco Unity Connection Servers

This section describes the parameters that affect the sizing and design of a Cisco Unity Connection solution.

A call in any audio codec format that Cisco Unity Connection SCCP or Session Initiation Protocol (SIP) signaling supports is transcoded to linear pulse code modulation (LPCM). Supported codecs in Cisco Unity Connection are, for example, G.711 mu-law, G.711 a-law, G.722, G.729, and iLBC.

Note iLBC (Internet Low Bitrate Codec) is a free speech codec suitable for robust voice communication over IP

From LPCM, the recording is encoded in the recording format that is specified in Cisco Unity Connection Administration. The recordings can be encoded in LPCM, G.711 mu-law, G.711 A-law, G.729A, G.726, or GSM 06.10; G.711 mu-law is the default.

Because transcoding occurs in every connection, there can be a difference in system impact when the line codec differs from the recording codec. For example, using G.729A as the line codec and G.711 mu-law as the recording codec does not place additional load on the Cisco Unity Connection server for transcoding. However, the ILBC and G.722 codecs require more computation to transcode and therefore place additional load on the Cisco Unity Connection server. Selecting one of these codecs reduces the available voice-mail ports on a Cisco Unity Connection server by about 75 percent. For more details, refer to the "Notes on 20,000-User VM Configuration" section of the *Virtualization for Cisco Unity Connection* document at http://docwiki.cisco.com/wiki/Virtualization_for_Cisco_Unity_Connection#Notes_on_20000_user_VM_configuration.

To determine the number and configuration of voice-messaging ports that are required, consider the following factors:

- **The existing voice-messaging system:** Evaluate how well the existing voice-messaging system functions, if applicable. This evaluation might give the designer some idea of how many ports are needed for taking voice messages, for turning message waiting indicators (MWIs) on and off, and for message notification.
- **Use of Cisco Unity Inbox or Cisco Unity Connection ViewMail for Microsoft Outlook:** Cisco Unity Connection uses Telephony Record and Playback (TRAP). to allow users of the Cisco Unity Inbox web client or Cisco Unity Connection ViewMail for Microsoft Outlook client to play and record voice messages by phone rather than by using speakers and a microphone. This feature is especially helpful for users who work in cubicles, where there is a lack of privacy. However, when a user uses TRAP to play or record a message, a port on the Cisco Unity Connection server is used. No port is used when a user uses speakers and a microphone to play and record messages. If the customer wants users to use TRAP, calculations for the total number of required voice ports will need to take this need into account.
- **Cisco Unity Connection cluster:** In some cases, an existing voice-messaging system has more voice-messaging ports than Cisco Unity Connection supports. When configured as a two-node Cisco Unity Connection cluster (an active-active, high-availability Cisco Unity Connection server pair), the Cisco Unity Connection system can support twice the number of voice-messaging ports, which are compared to a single-server deployment.

Note This deployment option does not double the number of users

- **Cisco Unity Connection networking:** You can purchase additional Cisco Unity Connection servers or Cisco Unity Connection cluster pairs and then use links to connect these pairs and increase the number of supported voice ports.

For Cisco Unity Connection systems that are configured to store voice mails only (not e-mails or faxes), base the server requirements on the total number of voice-storage minutes that are required for each user. A supported Cisco Unity Connection server generally provides storage for at least 20 to 30 minutes of voice messages per user, for the maximum number of supported users on that server.

Note You configure the storage equivalent of the minutes. That is, you don't configure the number of minutes per mailbox, you configure the storage.

Active-Active, High-Availability Deployment

This section describes the Cisco Unity Connection cluster using two servers that are active-active.

Figure 1-8 shows Cisco Unity Connection in an active-active, high-availability deployment. Note that two, and only two, Unity Connection servers can exist in a HA deployment. The content of voice mail is replicated to both the publisher and subscriber; so if either server becomes unavailable, voice mail remains available.

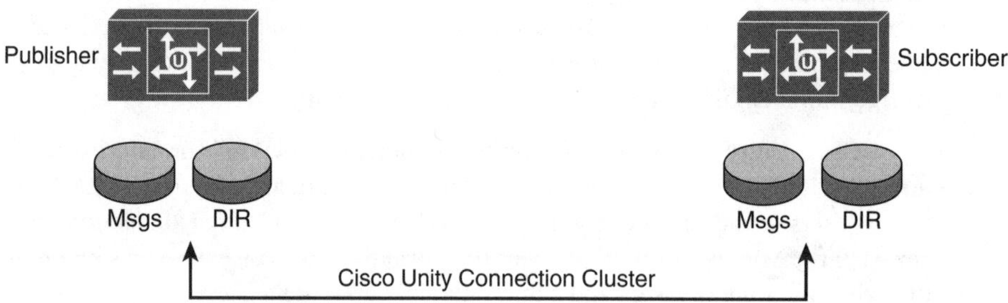

Figure 1-8 *Unity Connection High Availability Deployment*

High availability and disaster recovery are two primary customer requirements for preserving voice-mail services in the event of a Cisco Unity Connection system outage or disaster.

Cisco Unity Connection supports a two-server, active-active, high-availability solution to provide high availability for voice messaging within a LAN site. Both servers in the active-active pair run Cisco Unity Connection; both accept calls, as well as HTTP and IMAP requests. If only one server in the server pair is active, Cisco Unity Connection preserves most of the end-user functionality, including voice calls, HTTP requests, and IMAP requests. When one cluster server is down, the port capacity is reduced by 50 percent.

One Cisco Unity Connection server is designated as the publisher node in the server pair. The other Cisco Unity Connection server is designated as the subscriber node in the server pair. The role separation is consistent with the CUCM clustering scheme, in which there is always one publisher and multiple subscribers. However, in Cisco Unity Connection, only two servers are supported for active-active, high availability.

To store the incoming voice messages, a message store on a Cisco Unity Connection server must be chosen for the users. The database is shared and synchronized between both servers. If a caller leaves a message, the message is synchronized to the second server. If one of the servers fails in a Cisco Unity Connection cluster, the user can still retrieve the messages.

Cisco Unity Connection Deployment Options

This section describes different Cisco Unity Connection single-site and multiple-site deployment options.

> **Note** In the context of Unity Connection, the term *site* refers to a digital network of up to ten "locations." Therefore, a single-site deployment is a single digital network and a multisite deployment is a pair of digital networks connected by an intersite link.

Single-Site Deployment

A single-site deployment is the simplest form of a Cisco Unity Connection deployment. Cisco Unity Connection can also be deployed as a standalone server in a Cisco Collaboration System solution.

Cisco Unity Connection implementations range from a 1000-user integration in Cisco Business Edition 6000 up to a Cisco Unity Connection server cluster that supports as many as 20,000 voice-mail users. A second Cisco Unity Connection server does not increase the number of users, but it doubles the number of available voice-mail ports from 250 per server to 500 per cluster. A failing Cisco Unity Connection server halves the number of voice-mail ports, but is still fully functional.

Figure 1-9 shows Cisco Unity Connection in a single site deployment.

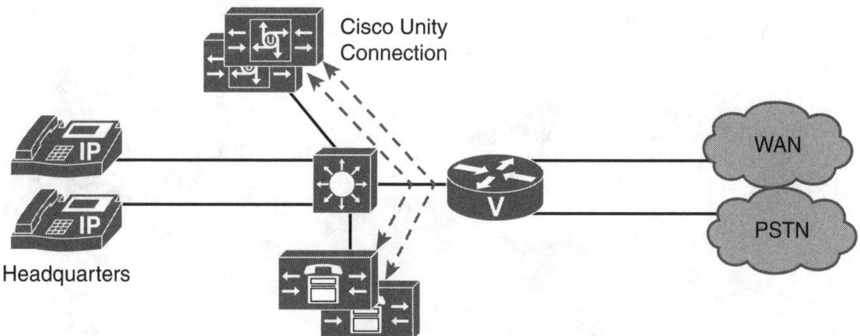

Figure 1-9 *Unity Connection Single Site Deployment*

In a single-site deployment, typically only one G.711 codec is used. CAC or transcoders are unnecessary because no additional branches are connected via WAN connections, which typically use the G.729 codec.

The platform overlay is a collection of hardware and software options that determines the capacity, capabilities, and number of users that are supported. When high availability are needed or when multiple locations are expected, another deployment model might better meet the needs of your organization.

Traffic patterns do not need to be evaluated when Cisco Unity Connection is used in a single-site solution. One G.711 call requires 80 kbps on Layer 3. A Cisco Unity Connection server that offers as many as 250 voice ports requires only 20 Mbps (250 calls * 80 kbps per call) on Layer 3.

However, the following specifies the Cisco Unity Connection requirements when the servers in a cluster are installed in the same site:

- For a cluster with two virtual machines, both must have the same virtual platform overlay.
- A minimum of 7 Mbps bandwidth is required for every 50 ports.

Centralized Multisite Deployment

In a centralized Cisco Unity Connection solution, a single Cisco Unity Connection server, and the WAN are single points of failure. For high availability, use a Cisco Unity Connection cluster with two Cisco Unity Connection servers in active-active mode. A service level agreement (SLA) is a contract between a service provider (either internal or external) and the end user that defines the level of service expected from the service provider. The WAN SLAs should offer highly available and redundant WAN connections from the headquarters to the branches. Despite such precautions, a failure could prevent the Cisco Unity Connection branch users from using the centralized voice-messaging system (similar to call-processing issues during a WAN failure).

Figure 1-10 shows Cisco Unity Connection in a centralized multisite site deployment.

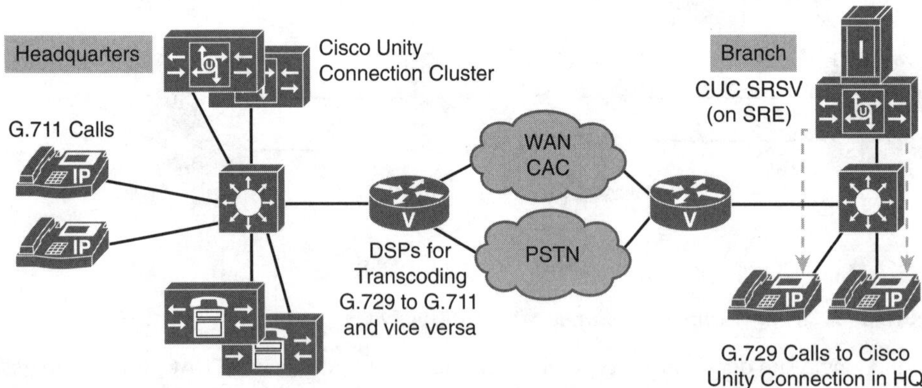

Figure 1-10 *Unity Connection Centralized Multisite Site Deployment*

In the case of a failure, Cisco Unity Connection SRSV takes over the voice-messaging functionality for branch users and offers local voice-mail and auto-attendant features. After the WAN has recovered, Unity Connection SRSV synchronizes with Cisco Unity Connection and changes back to passive mode, like SRST, which requires a Cisco IOS router to function.

When centralized applications are used, traffic patterns constantly change and must be evaluated. For example, suppose that a customer with 250 voice-messaging users replaces a private branch exchange (PBX) and local voice-mail system with a centralized Cisco Collaboration System solution. If 10 percent of the branch employees use the centralized voice-mail system simultaneously, voice messaging brings 25 additional connections (25 calls * 24 kbps on Layer 3 = 600 kbps) to the voice-traffic pattern for the Cisco Unity Connection application where QoS is required. Quality of service (QoS) refers to the capability of a network to provide better service to selected network traffic.

A digital signal processor (DSP) is a specialized microprocessor within a Cisco voice gateway with its architecture optimized for the operational needs of digital signal processing. The goal of DSPs is usually to measure, filter and/or compress continuous real-world analog signals. Calls also may need to be transcoded at the headquarters site, which might require additional DSP resources. Carefully design centralized Cisco Collaboration System solutions, and consider the traffic pattern for voice mail, auto-attendant, and transcoders.

Decentralized Multisite Deployment

In a decentralized Cisco Unity Connection solution, the Cisco Unity Connection clusters are networked through intersite links.

> **Note** Intersite links can be used only between identical voice-messaging systems, connecting Cisco Unity Connection to Cisco Unity Connection.

If you want to connect Cisco Unity Express, for example, you must configure Voice Profile for Internet Mail (VPIM). The linked sites are called a *Cisco Voicemail Organization*. The gateways exchange directory synchronization information by using HTTP or HTTPS; voice messages are exchanged between the sites by using SMTP.

Figure 1-11 shows Cisco Unity Connection in a decentralized multisite site deployment.

Traffic patterns in these deployments also change constantly (for example, as messages are sent to or received from users on the remote voice-messaging system). However, these messages, which are sent via HTTPS, are not real-time streams, so these messages do not require QoS. Calls via the phone to users at the remote site need to be calculated and the proper bandwidth needs to be reserved. WAN bandwidth usage is the same whether a user places a call or leaves a message over the WAN. Still, transcoders are required when using G.729 in the WAN.

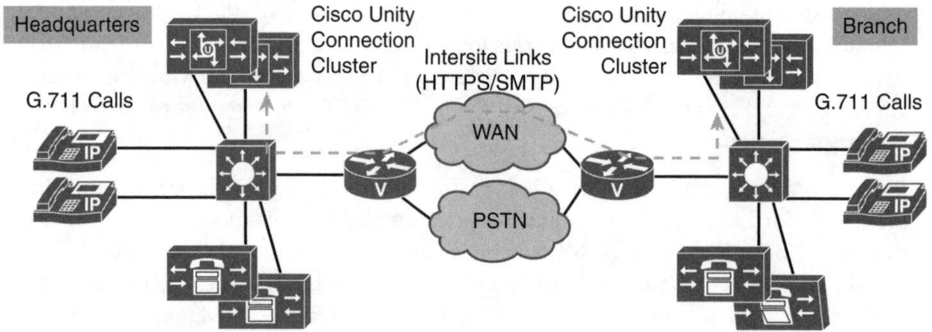

Figure 1-11 *Unity Connection Decentralized Multisite Site Deployment*

During a WAN failure, calls are rerouted automatically over the public switched telephone network (PSTN), and voice messages are left via PSTN. In a deployment of two clusters with, for example, 15,000 users, a lot of calls (and therefore voice-messaging traffic) can occur between the locations. This situation is especially true in companies that work with virtual or distributed teams in many locations.

You can separate the two Cisco Unity Connection servers in a cluster. The following describes the requirements for a cluster over the WAN:

- Depending on the number of voice-messaging ports on each Unity Connection server, the path of connectivity must have the following guaranteed bandwidth with no steady-state congestion: 7 Mbps for every 50 voice-messaging ports on each server.
- When both the subscriber and publisher are taking calls, the maximum round-trip latency must be no more than 60 ms. When only the publisher is taking calls and the subscriber is idle but replicating with the publisher, the maximum round-trip latency must be no more than 150 ms.

The bandwidth numbers above are intended as guidelines to ensure proper operation of an active-active cluster regarding synchronization traffic between the two servers. Additional conditions such as network congestion, CPU utilization, and message size may contribute to lower throughput than expected.

Traffic-Pattern Evaluation Example

This section describes traffic patterns for voice messaging and how these patterns change when voice messaging is centralized.

A customer wants to migrate from an existing PBX network to a Cisco Collaboration System, including centralized voice messaging. The current PBXs each include a voice-mail system with a mailbox for every user. The call logger shows that a peak for voice messaging exists after lunch breaks on Monday and Thursday, with 4 percent concurrency. The customer wants to maintain this concurrency factor after migrating to a centralized voice-mail solution that uses the WAN for voice connections, using the G.729 codec.

Figure 1-12 shows an example of traditional PBX and voice-mail systems that will be migrated to Cisco Unity Connection.

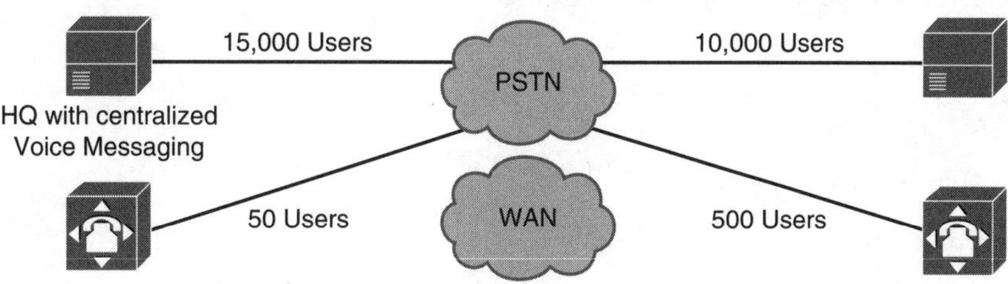

Figure 1-12 *Unity Connection Migration Example*

Centralized Cisco Unity Connection System Example

Figure 1-13 shows an example of a centralized voice-messaging solution. The bandwidths given are just an example. Three Cisco Unity Connection clusters with five Cisco Unity Connection servers are required; 25,550 / 5 = 5110 users per Cisco Unity Connection server, so the concurrency factor is (25500 + (5 * 250)) / 25550 = 4.89 percent. If only four Cisco Unity Connection servers are used, the concurrency factor will fall to (25550 + (4 * 250)) / 25550 = 3.92 percent (6387 users per Cisco Unity Connection server). However, you might advise the customer to use Unified Messaging where the company mail is used to send voice messages. Feature selection might also change the traffic pattern. Because Unified Messaging does not require real-time traffic and no Cisco Unity Connection ports, four servers might be enough when implementing a centralized voice-messaging solution.

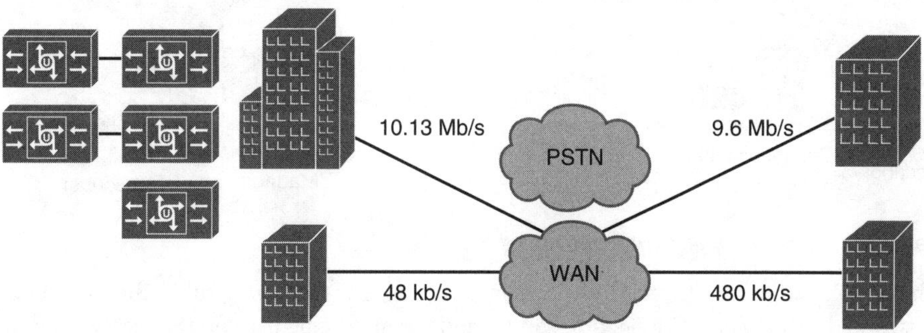

Figure 1-13 *Centralized Unity Connection Example*

Cisco Unity Connection Networking

This section describes networking, where Cisco Unity Connection servers or clusters in different sites are logically linked together.

In voice-messaging networking, the systems in different locations are logically networked together to present a single messaging system to both inside and outside users.

Cisco Unity Connection supports the following:

- Digital networking
- Intersite networking
- VPIM networking
- HTTPS networking

Note The SMTP protocol is used for directory synchronization within a network.

Voice-mail networking allows messaging among multiple Cisco Unity Connection servers. Networked Cisco Unity Connection systems automatically exchange directory information. Therefore, a user on one Cisco Unity Connection system can dial out to or address messages to a user on any other system by name or extension, if the target user is reachable in the search scope of the originating user. The networked systems function as though they share a single directory. Users do not need to know where another user is located. They need only the name or extension number to address a message to any user or system distribution list in the directory.

Figure 1-14 shows an example of connecting two different sites with Unity Connection.

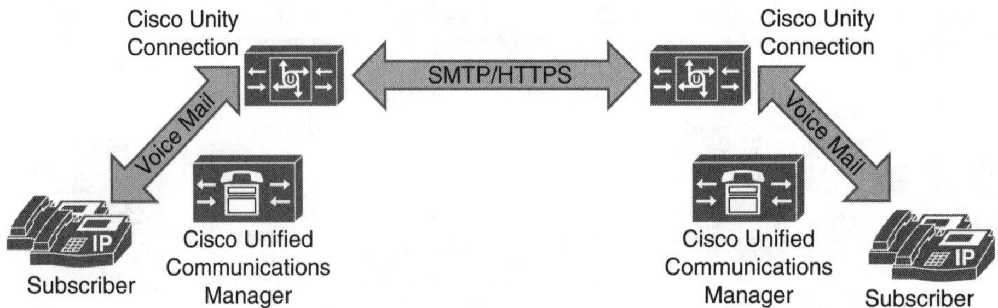

Figure 1-14 *Unity Connection Connecting Sites*

The user uses the same Cisco Unity Connection tools for messaging subscribers on other networked Cisco Unity Connection servers and for messaging user on the same server. If your organization also has the fax mail and Text-To-Speech (TTS) e-mail features, users can use the phone to forward fax and e-mail messages to any user in the organization.

Objects such as those in the following list are replicated in a Cisco Unity Connection digital voice-mail network:

- Users
- System distribution lists (including membership)

- Partitions
- Search spaces
- Recorded voice names

Note Unity Connection uses partitions and search spaces similar to CUCM to allow control of where calls are allowed and denied.

Cisco Unity Connection Links

Administrators can join two or more Cisco Unity Connection servers or clusters (up to a maximum of ten clusters) to form a well-connected network, referred to as a Cisco Unity Connection site. The servers that are joined to the site are referred to as locations. When a Cisco Unity Connection cluster is configured, the cluster counts as one location in the site.

Figure 1-15 shows Unity Connection Links with site gateways.

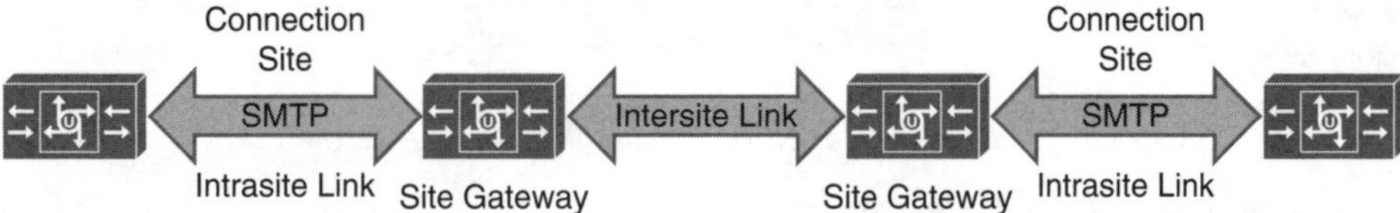

Figure 1-15 *Unity Connection Links*

When a user addresses a message, Cisco Unity Connection searches for a matching extension on the local Cisco Unity Connection server first. If a match is found, Cisco Unity Connection ends the search and never looks for a matching extension at another location.

Additionally, if required, two Cisco Unity Connection sites can be joined to support a maximum of 20 locations for businesses that need more than 10 locations. Only one intersite link is supported per site, so you can link a single Cisco Unity Connection site to another Cisco Unity Connection site.

To create an intersite link, choose a single location from each site to act as a gateway to the other site. All directory synchronization communications pass between the two site gateways, which limit the connectivity requirements and bandwidth usage to the link between those two site gateway locations.

When using a Cisco Unity Connection cluster as a site gateway, only the publisher server in the cluster participates in directory synchronization over the intersite link. However, the subscriber server continues to provide message exchange over the intersite link if the publisher server is down.

Digital Networking with Active-Active Pairs

Legacy networked systems use SMTP transport for message transport and HTTPS for directory replication. Cisco Unity Connection locations can be deployed across geographic boundaries. Each server that joined the network must be able to access all other servers on the network directly through the SMTP and HTTPS ports. Alternatively, SMTP messages can be routed through an SMTP smart host.

Figure 1-16 shows Unity Connection digital networking with active-active pairs.

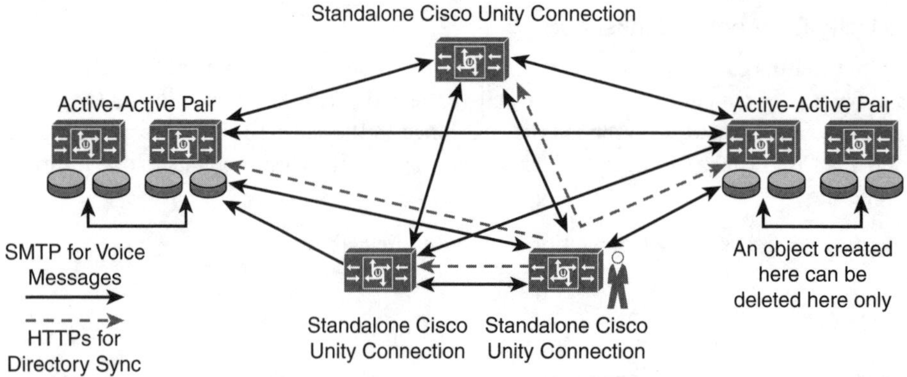

Figure 1-16 *Unity Connection Digital Networking with Active-Active Pairs*

In a network, each Cisco Unity Connection object is created and homed on a single Cisco Unity Connection system, which is known as a Cisco Unity Connection location. An object can be modified or deleted only on the Cisco Unity Connection system on which it was created. Each location in a Unity Connection site or Cisco Voicemail Organization has its own directory of users and other objects that were created on the location and are said to be "homed" on that location. The collection of objects and object properties that are replicated among locations and sites is referred to as the global directory.

Note Cisco Unity Connection networking is not supported for use with Cisco Business Edition 5000 and is supported only with Cisco Business Edition 6000/7000.

Voice Profile for Internet Mail

Cisco Unity Connection supports the VPIM protocol, which is an industry standard that allows different voice-messaging systems to exchange voice and text messages over the Internet or any TCP/IP network. VPIM is based on the SMTP and MIME protocols. VPIM networking is supported for use with Cisco Business Edition 6000.

Cisco Unity Connection supports up to 100 VPIM locations and 150,000 VPIM and system contacts in the Cisco Unity Connection directory. These limits apply either to the directory of a single Cisco Unity Connection server, a cluster pair, or the global directory in a network.

Figure 1-17 shows Unity Connection VPIM.

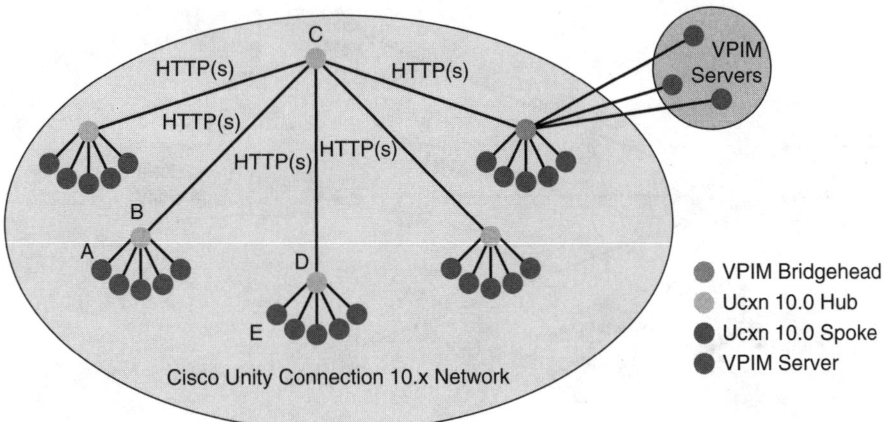

Figure 1-17 *Unity Connection VPIM*

If you deploy VPIM in an HTTPS network, you can designate one or more Cisco Unity Connection locations in the network as VPIM bridgehead servers. The Cisco Unity Connection server that is configured for VPIM networking is referred to as the bridgehead server. This server handles the configuration of VPIM locations and contacts, depending upon your requirements. The VPIM location data and all contacts at the VPIM location (including automatically created contacts) are replicated from the bridgehead to other locations within the network. When a VPIM message is sent by a user who is homed on a Cisco Unity Connection location other than the bridgehead, the message first passes to the bridgehead, which forwards the message to the destination server. Similarly, the messages from VPIM contacts are received by the bridgehead and relayed to the home server of the Cisco Unity Connection recipient.

HTTPS Networking

In Cisco Unity Connection Version 10.x, legacy networking is supported to connect multiple Cisco Unity Connection servers in a network. However, it is recommended to deploy a new network using HTTPS networking. Legacy networking includes both intrasite (digital) and intersite networking. The legacy and HTTPS networking are not supported simultaneously in the same network.

The main objective of introducing HTTPS networking is to increase the scalability and security of Cisco Unity Connection deployments. The architecture of HTTPS networking is scalable both in terms of the number of Cisco Unity Connection locations and the total directory size.

Within a network, each location uses HTTPS protocol to exchange directory information and SMTP protocol to exchange voice messages with each other.

Figure 1-18 shows Unity Connection HTTPS networking.

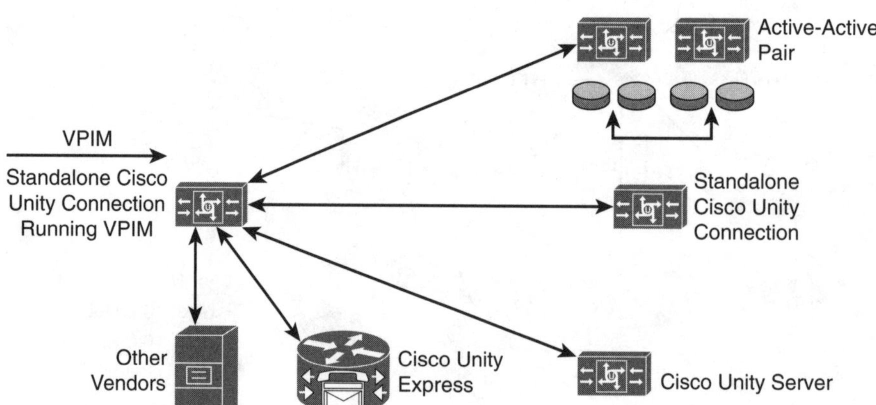

Figure 1-18 *Unity Connection HTTPS Networking*

The locations in an HTTPS network are linked together through an HTTPS link. The topology that is used in HTTPS networking is hub-and-spoke topology, which plays an important role in increasing the scalability of directory size and number of Cisco Unity Connection locations. In a hub-and-spoke topology, there are two types of locations: the hub location and the spoke location. The Cisco Unity Connection location that has more than one HTTPS link is known as the hub location. The Cisco Unity Connection location that has only one HTTPS link is known as the spoke location. The figure shows a network of multiple Unity Connection locations joined by HTTPS links.

In a hub-and-spoke topology, all the directory information among the spokes is shared through the hub or hubs that connect the spokes. For example, in the figure, if spoke A needs to synchronize directory information with spoke E, the directory information will flow from spoke A to hub B, hub B to hub C, hub C to hub D, and then from hub D to spoke E.

> **Note** The maximum number of Cisco Unity Connection locations that you can connect in an HTTPS network is 25.

A single HTTPS network system supports a single site, and each site can have a maximum of 25 nodes; however, multiple HTTPS network systems can be joined using VPIM.

> **Note** VPIM Networking is the only form of networking supported on the Cisco Business Edition 6000/7000.

If you deploy VPIM in a Unity Connection networking site, each Cisco Unity Connection digital or HTTPS network must have one server defined as the bridgehead or site gateway. The bridgehead or site gateway is used to communicate with other digital or HTTP(S) networks. The Cisco Unity Connection global directory (the entire collection of local and replicated objects and object properties) is subject to certain size limits. However, it also generates a Cisco Unified Real-Time Monitoring Tool (RTMT) alert so that the administrator can take appropriate action. In Cisco Unity Connection Version 10.x, there are separate limits on the number of users, the number of contacts, and the number of system distribution lists. The size limits at the time of the 10.x release are as follows:

- 100,000 users
- 150,000 contacts
- 100,000 system distribution lists
- 25,000 users per system distribution list:
    - 1.5 million total list members across all system distribution lists
    - 20 levels of nesting (where one system distribution list is included as a member of another list)

Cisco MediaSense Overview

Businesses and organizations need to record calls for various reasons, including regulatory compliance, quality management, legal discovery, employee education, business intelligence, and customer service optimization. Unfortunately, traditional recording solutions can make recording difficult and expensive to implement. Cisco MediaSense solves these challenges by recording audio and video on the network, simplifying the architecture, lowering costs, and providing optimum scalability across various scenarios such as selective recording, call transfers, site-based recording, and multiparty conferences.

The network-based architecture of Cisco MediaSense allows for quick availability of the captured media for different applications, regardless of location, through simple application programming interfaces (APIs). These interfaces implement open web standards, enabling a rich ecosystem of applications from Cisco technology partners, including quality management and advanced quality management solutions.

The new features and benefits of Cisco MediaSense as of Version 10.x are as follows:

- Recording with Cisco Unified Contact Center Express
- VoH (video on hold)
- ViQ (video in queue) with Cisco Remote Expert
- vCisco Unity Connection video greeting
- Search and play enhancements

Cisco MediaSense is a Session Initiation Protocol (SIP)-based, network-level service that provides voice and video media recording capabilities for other network devices. Fully integrated into Cisco's Unified Communications architecture, MediaSense automatically captures and stores every VoIP conversation which traverses appropriately configured Unified Communications Manager IP phones or Cisco Unified Border Element devices. In addition, an IP phone user or SIP endpoint device may call the MediaSense system directly in order to leave a recording consisting of media generated only by that user. Such recordings can include video as well as audio—offering a simple and easy method for recording video blogs and podcasts.

No matter how they are captured, recordings may be accessed in several ways. While a recording is still in progress, it can be streamed live ("monitored") through a computer which is equipped with a media player such as VLC or RealPlayer, or one provided by a partner or third party. Once completed, recordings may be played back in the same way, or downloaded in raw form via HTTP. They may also be converted into .mp4 or .wav files and downloaded in that format. All access to recordings, either in progress or completed, is through web-friendly URIs. MediaSense also offers a web-based Search and Play application with a built-in media player. This allows authorized users to select individual calls to monitor, playback, or download directly from a supported web browser. In addition to its primary media recording functionality, MediaSense offers these other capabilities:

- It can play back specific video media files on demand on video phones or supported players. This capability supports ViQ, VoD, or VoH use cases in which a separate call controller invites MediaSense into an existing video call in order to play a previously designated recording.
- Integrate with Cisco Unity Connection to provide video voice-mail greetings. Videos are recorded on MediaSense directly by Unity Connection users and are then played back to their video-capable callers before they leave their messages.
- The following are important design considerations:
- Media recordings can occupy a large amount of disk space, so space management is a significant concern.
- MediaSense also maintains a metadata database where information about all recordings is maintained. A comprehensive Web 2.0 API is provided that allows client equipment to query and search the metadata in various ways, to control recordings that are in progress, to stream or download recordings, to bulk-delete recordings that meet certain criteria, and to apply custom tags to individual recording sessions.

Cisco MediaSense Five-Server Deployment

In a Cisco MediaSense deployment, a cluster contains a set of servers, with each server containing a set of services. Cluster architecture provides high availability (for recording but not for playback) and failover (if the primary server fails, there is automatic failover to the secondary server). High-availability servers must be in the same LAN network.

Figure 1-19 shows the maximum five-server option in a Cisco MediaSense deployment.

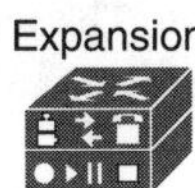

Figure 1-19 *Cisco Five-Server MediaSense Deployment*

Cisco MediaSense functions only within LANs. WANs are not supported. All Cisco MediaSense servers and CUCM servers must be located in the same LAN. Within a LAN, the maximum round-trip delay between any two servers must be less than 2 ms.

The primary and secondary servers in a Cisco MediaSense deployment are synchronized when administrative changes are made on either server. Database replication copies the data automatically from the primary server to the secondary server, and vice versa.

There are three types of servers:

- **Primary (required):** Supports all database operations as well as media operations.
- **Secondary (optional):** Supports all database operations as well as media operations. Provides high-availability for the database.
- **Expansion (optional):** Provides additional capacity for media operations, but not for database operations. Expansion servers are only used in seven-vCPU deployments, and are never used in UCS-E module deployments.

The primary and secondary servers in a Cisco MediaSense deployment are synchronized when administrative changes are made on either server. Database replication copies the data automatically from the primary server to the secondary server, and vice versa.

Cisco MediaSense supports any of the following combinations of servers:

- One primary server
- One primary server and one secondary server
- One primary, one secondary server, and from one to three expansion servers

A single-server deployment has one Cisco MediaSense server on the Cisco Collaboration System operating system platform. All network services are enabled by default. Each single-server deployment supports a maximum of 300 simultaneous sessions and a Busy Hour Call Completion (BHCC) rate of 9000 sessions per hour (with a two-minute average call duration). Single-service deployments enable you to add more servers later to address redundancy issues, to provide high availability, to increase storage capacity, and to increase simultaneous recording capacity.

A dual-server deployment has two Cisco MediaSense servers on the Cisco Collaboration System operating system platform. The first server is called the primary server. The second server is called the secondary server. All network services are enabled on both servers. Dual-server deployments provide high availability. The recording load is automatically balanced across the primary and secondary servers because all services are always active on both servers.

Three-server deployments have a primary server, a secondary server, and one expansion server. All network services are enabled by default on all servers in the cluster. The three-server model provides redundancy and increases storage capacity and simultaneous recording and playback capacity. The recording load is automatically balanced across the servers.

Four-server and five-server deployments have one primary server, one secondary server, and two or three expansion servers. This deployment model provides redundancy, increases storage capacity, and increases capacity for simultaneous recording and playback sessions. The recording load is automatically balanced across the servers because services are always active on their respective servers.

Cisco MediaSense Virtualization and Platform Overlays

This section describes the virtualization of Cisco MediaSense and the limitations per platform overlay. Table 1-3 shows the different Cisco MediaSense platform overlays for virtualization.

Table 1-3 *Cisco MediaSense Platform Overlays*

<table>
<tr><th></th><th>Node Type</th><th>vCPU</th><th>vRAM (GB)</th><th>vDisk</th><th>Audio Media Streams</th><th>Nodes per Cluster</th></tr>
<tr><td>2vCPU Configuration</td><td>Primary and secondary node</td><td>2</td><td>6</td><td rowspan="3">Disk 1 – 80 GB for OS
Disk 2 – 80 (600) GB for Database and working storage
Disk 3 – 210 GB Minimum
Can be expanded to 12 TB</td><td>40</td><td>2</td></tr>
<tr><td>4vCPU Configuration</td><td>Primary and secondary node</td><td>4</td><td>8</td><td>200</td><td>2</td></tr>
<tr><td>7vCPU Configuration</td><td>Primary, secondary, or expansion node</td><td>7</td><td>16</td><td>400</td><td>5</td></tr>
</table>

Cisco MediaSense can be virtualized as well. The table shows the virtual resource requirements and some selected system limitations per OVA template.

The node type can be primary, secondary, or expansion node. Only the seven-vCPU template can be used as an expansion node. Calculate the number of video streams that are required to select the right OVA template size. The Cisco MediaSense server has three hard disks for the operating system, the database, and the storage of the recordings. The number of vCPUs has a direct impact on the number of available audio or video streams.

Video Compatibility Matrix and Network Topology

This section describes the requirements for video greetings in Cisco Unity Connection and the network topology.

Video greetings are available as of Cisco Unity Connection Version 10.0(1). To record or play video greetings, you need to integrate video endpoints, CUCM, and Cisco MediaSense into one video-enabled voice-messaging solution.

The requirements for video greetings are as follows:

- Video endpoints with SIP (for example, Cisco Unified IP Phone 9971 or Cisco Jabber for Desktop)
- Video-enabled endpoints with SCCP (for example, Cisco Unified IP Phone 8945)
- Cisco Unity Connection Version 10.0(1)
- Cisco MediaSense Version 10.0(1)
- CUCM Version 8.5(1) and later

The supported version combinations are determined by testing. While other combinations may provide acceptable results to customers, Cisco must test or approve these combinations before they are supported.

Video Network Topology

Figure 1-20 shows the integration protocol requirements for Cisco Unity Connection video greetings.

If your voice-messaging solution is integrated with SCCP, you need to reconfigure the integration to use SIP. Cisco Unity Connection and Cisco MediaSense can both run as standalone or in a cluster.

Note that the Cisco Unity Connection video greeting feature needs a dedicated Cisco MediaSense server. The Cisco MediaSense server cannot be shared for any other Cisco MediaSense features.

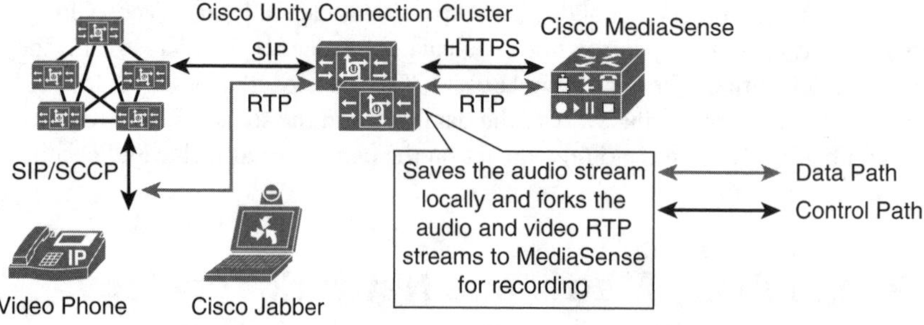

Figure 1-20 *Cisco Video Network Topology*

Only user accounts can be enabled for video greetings, and all forms of call handlers remain audio-only. Using user accounts as call handlers is the only way to enable a video-enabled call handler. User accounts have many options that are similar to call handlers, and can use input to route calls to other user greetings or to transfer outside of the Cisco Unity Connection system. Each branch in a user-based video-enabled call handler represents one user account. For example, if a root video greeting is built with three options and each of those three options have two sub-options, a total of six video-enabled user accounts would be required to facilitate that call handler structure.

Design Guidelines for Video Greetings

The Cisco Unity Connection video greeting feature is currently only supported using the seven-vCPU OVA template. Each server in a Cisco Unity Connection cluster can support up to 20 concurrent video calls for a total of 40 video calls within the cluster. For a single Unity Connection server, 35 concurrent video calls are supported.

Cisco MediaSense must also be deployed using the larger seven-vCPU OVA template. Smaller OVAs will be tested and the design guide will be updated as the testing is completed. This Cisco MediaSense instance must be a single server, cannot be part of a Cisco MediaSense cluster, and Cisco MediaSense must be dedicated to the Unity Connection video greeting feature. Only one Cisco Unity Connection high-availability pair or single server can be integrated per Cisco MediaSense server.

Cisco MediaSense must be colocated with Cisco Unity Connection with 1-Gbps connectivity between the servers and less than 10-ms round-trip time (RTT) latency.

Video Greetings Operation

Video greetings are only supported using SIP trunk integrations. Cisco Unity Connection 10.5.(2) supports the use of 360p (640 × 360), 480p (720 × 480), 720p (1280 × 720) and 1080p (1920 × 1080) video greetings. Cisco MediaSense and Cisco Unity Connection allow the recording of video greetings up to 1080p (1920 × 1080). This situation offers limited compatibility across the video-enabled phone portfolio and is not a supported configuration because Cisco MediaSense does not support transcoding video to reduce the resolution for non-1080p video devices. To restrict video greetings to 360p, Cisco Unity Connection leverages CUCM Region configurations. When using video greetings in Cisco Unity Connection 10.x only G.711 mu-law codec is supported for audio and H.264 codec is supported for video. The Cisco Unity Connection SIP trunks must be put in a region that has the following relationship settings, with all other regions containing video-enabled devices that might call Cisco Unity Connection and expect video greetings:

- **Audio Codec Preference List:** (Default or preference of the administrator)
- **Maximum Audio Bit Rate:** 64 kbps
- **Maximum Session Bit Rate for Video Calls:** 600 kbps
- **Maximum Session Bit Rate for Immersive Video Calls:** 600 kbps

These settings will ensure maximum compatibility across the Cisco video-enabled phone portfolio and provide the best possible experience for using video greetings.

When recording a video greeting, the audio and video RTP streams are both sent directly to Cisco Unity Connection. Cisco Unity Connection saves the audio RTP stream locally as an audio-only version of the video greeting and forks the audio and video RTP streams to Cisco MediaSense for recording. For playback, if the device is video-enabled, Cisco Unity Connection will instruct Cisco MediaSense to stream the video greeting to Cisco Unity Connection to be forked to the device. If Cisco MediaSense is not available or unable to play back the video greetings or if the device calling Cisco Unity Connection is not video-enabled, Cisco Unity Connection will play the audio-only portion of the video greeting that it recorded. The audio-only greeting is the audio track from the video greeting. It is possible to have different greetings for audio-only callers and video-enabled callers.

Call Flows

This section describes the call flows in voice messaging and the purpose of the Cisco Unity Connection ports.

Leaving or Retrieving a Message

In Figure 1-21, a PSTN caller dials the number 408 555-1001. The called party has set a Call Forward All (CFA) to send calls to voice mail. The call is extended to the Cisco Unity Connection system which utilizes a Unity Connection port.

The user of IP phone 1001 presses the Messages button to receive the voice messages which again utilizes a Unity Connection port. Alternatively, the user can dial, from any phone, the voice-messaging number 408 5552100. After a message is recorded, the Unity Connection system will request the CUCM to enable the message waiting light (MWI).

Cisco Unity Connection can notify users when new messages are recorded. The Cisco Unity Connection system starts a call to the notification device, which requires the voice-mail port to have the CSS to call the PSTN.

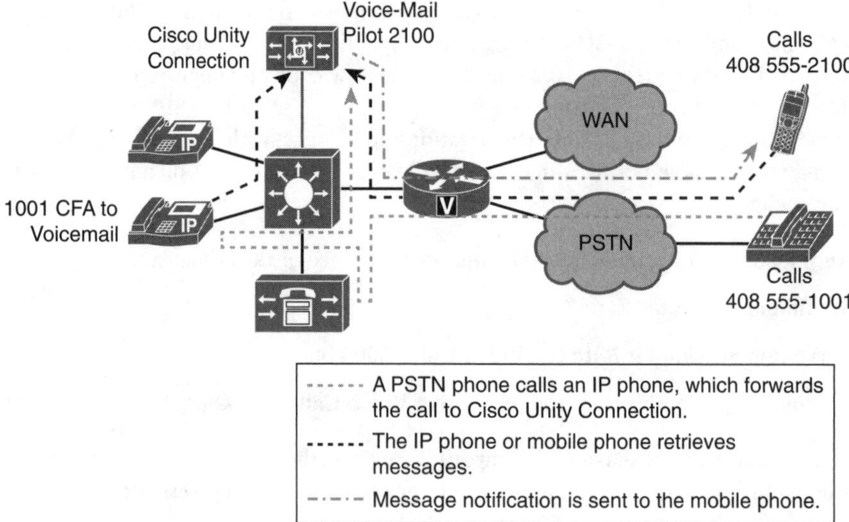

Figure 1-21 *Leaving or Retrieving a Message in Cisco Unity Connection*

Additional Call-Flow Options

You can add new Unity Connection ports, per server, in an active-active Cisco Unity Connection cluster. Figure 1-22 shows two ports that are dedicated for MWI dial-out (turn MWI on and MWI off) and six ports that are used to perform message notification and to answer calls so that the calls can be dropped or retrieved.

Voice-mail ports can offer different functionalities, and a port can be enabled to support whichever of the following function(s) are required of it:

- Answer call
- Perform message notification
- Send MWI requests
- Allow TRAP connections

The voice-mail port of the SIP trunk calling search space (CSS) determines whether calls can be made, in general.

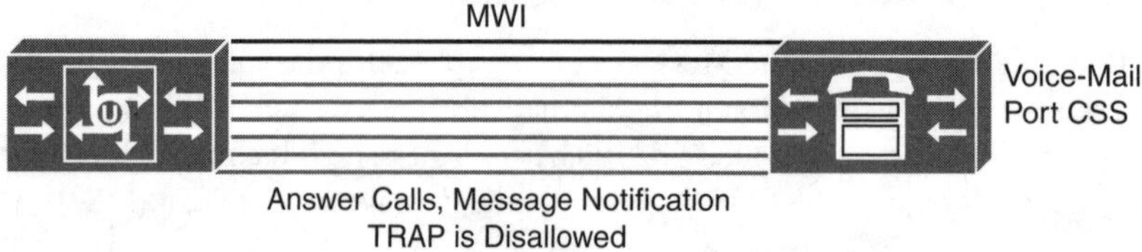

Figure 1-22 *Unity Connection Voice Port Utilization*

The ports can be used and dedicated to the four events that are listed in Figure 1-22.

Voice-Messaging Call Flows in SRST and AAR Mode

This topic shows the call flow when the WAN is unavailable or call access control (CAC) blocks the call.

SRST and Cisco Unity Connection

When the WAN is unavailable, IP phones register with the SRST router. Figure 1-23 shows how voice messaging is processed in SRST mode through the PSTN along the dashed line instead of the WAN connection.

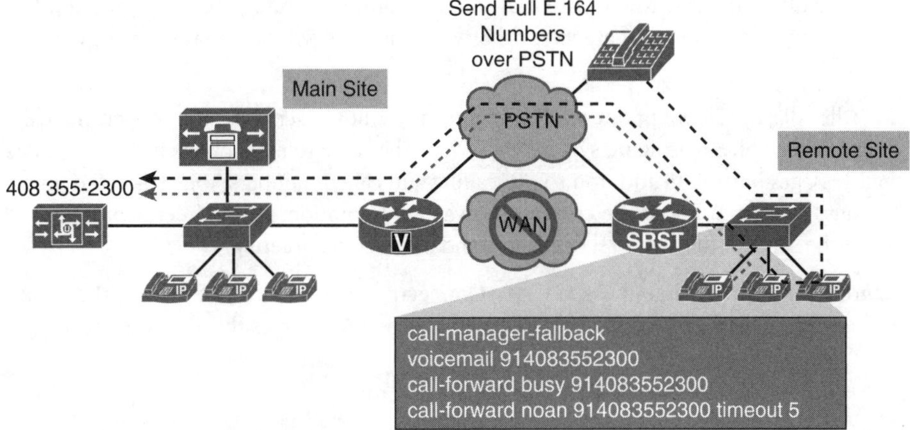

Figure 1-23 *SRST and Cisco Unity Connection*

By default, there is no activity when a user presses the Messages button after the IP phones have registered with the SRST router. When configured through the following commands, the IP phones can reach the mailbox in case of SRST fallback. Users can leave a message if the called user does not answer or is busy. The following commands need to be configured on the SRST router to offer voice messaging over PSTN as a backup during a WAN failure:

```
call-manager-fallback
 voicemail 914083552300
 call-forward busy 914083552300
 call-forward noan 914083552300 timeout 5
```

Actual numbers used must be within your dial plan. The numbers shown here for SRST are just an example. When dialing out, voice translation rules on the voice gateway modify the calling number to the E.164 format for all Cisco Unity Connection users. Therefore, add the alternate number (E.164) for all Cisco Unity Connection users in the centralized voice-mail system. Voice translation rules might also modify the redirected number, either outgoing or incoming.

AAR and Cisco Unity Connection

When the WAN is busy and the AAR process takes over call processing, the AAR process rebuilds the voice-mail number. This process combines the AAR group, external phone-number mask, and directory number; for example, 91 + 408355XXXX + 2300 = 914083552300. Make sure that you configure the AAR CSS in the inbound call section on the remote gateway; otherwise, the calls will not be rerouted over the PSTN.

If a caller dials a remote phone via PSTN, and the remote user does not answer, the call is sent to the voice-messaging system via PSTN. The same thing happens if a user presses the Messages button. In addition to the calling and called numbers, the redirected number must be sent. Without the correct gateway configuration, the redirected number cannot be sent, so the caller reaches the standard opening greeting.

Figure 1-24 shows AAR and Cisco Unity Connection working together where the voice mail calls go over the PSTN in the dashed line when CAC denies the WAN usage.

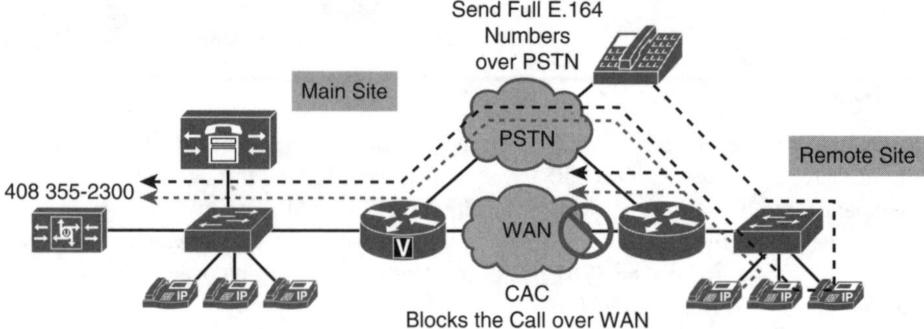

Figure 1-24 *AAR and Unity Connection*

If the redirected number is sent as an E.164 number, configure an alternate extension on Cisco Unity Connection. For a call via the PSTN, the calling and redirected numbers are sent in E.164 format. Unless an alternate extension is configured, the standard opening greeting is played instead of the user greeting. Again, redirected numbers can be modified via voice translation rules.

Summary

This section summarizes the key points that were discussed in this lesson:

- The OVA templates are preconfigured to use the correct amount of virtual resources with resource reservation. The main virtual resources for a Cisco Collaboration System application are vCPU, vRAM, storage, and the vNIC.
- The installation of ESXi (operating system or hypervisor) presents the host system, which itself hosts the guest systems. Every ESXi installation creates by default a virtual switch which is connected to the first physical interface. Enable NIC teaming for hardware redundancy.
- Deploy Cisco Unity Connection in single or multiple sites. In centralized multisites, you can use Cisco Unity Connection SRSV to offer local voice messaging functionality when the WAN is down. Evaluate the traffic pattern in multisite deployments and adapt the bandwidth and QoS to the new requirements.
- Cisco Unity Connection can be connected with intersite links, and different voice messaging systems can be connected with VPIM.
- Cisco MediaSense can be used for recordings. When implementing video greetings, Cisco MediaSense is required, since it records and plays the video greetings to the caller.

Review Questions

Answer the following questions, and then see Appendix A, "Answers to Review Questions," for the answers.

1. **Which Linux distribution is used for the Cisco Unity Connection appliance as an operating system?**

   a. CentOS

   b. Red Hat Enterprise Linux

   c. Rocks Cluster Distribution

   d. Suse Linux Enterprise

   e. Ubuntu

2. **Which storage system is not based on VMFS?**

   a. DAS

   b. Fibre Channel

   c. FCoE

   d. NAS

   e. iSCSI

3. Cisco Unity Connection requires one additional reserved core CPU per Cisco Unity Connection VM in VMware vSphere ESXi.

a. true

b. false

4. How many servers are supported in a Cisco Unity Connection cluster?

a. 2

b. 4

c. 6

d. 8

e. 12

5. Digital networking can be used to connect Cisco Unity Connection to other voice messaging systems (for example, Cisco Unity Express or third-party voice-messaging systems).

a. true

b. false

6. Which option is not a Cisco Unity Connection v10.x voice-mail port functionality?

a. Answer calls

b. Perform message notification

c. Enable unified messaging functionality

d. Send MWI requests

e. Allow TRAP connections

Chapter 2

Integrating Cisco Unity Connection with Cisco Unified Communications Manager

Upon completing this chapter, you will be able to do the following:

- Describe the Cisco Unity Connection GUI interface options and the main Cisco Unity Connection menu
- Introduce the Cisco Unified RTMT, which can be used for multiple Cisco Collaboration System applications
- Explain Cisco PLM installation and usage options
- Explain how to add Cisco Unity Connection in Cisco PLM
- Describe the integration options for Cisco Unity Connection
- Describe the integration of Cisco Unity Connection with Cisco Unified Communications Manager using SCCP
- Describe the integration of Cisco Unity Connection with Cisco Unified Communications Manager using SIP
- Describe the Cisco Unity Connection troubleshooting tools to test the integration for any issues
- Describe on-net and off-net calls and where you can classify the calls
- Show how call forward can be configured and how call classification is used to control the call routing behavior when forwarding calls
- Describe how directed and forwarded calls are routed in Cisco Unity Connection
- Show the capabilities of the Port Monitor to monitor the caller, called, and redirected numbers
- Describe the default call-routing behavior for directed and forwarded calls
- List some considerations for integrating with Cisco Unified Communications Manager and describe how to secure Cisco Unity Connection to prevent toll fraud

This chapter introduces the Cisco Unity Connection administration interfaces and explains how to integrate Cisco Unity Connection with Cisco Unified Communications Manager (CUCM).

Cisco Unity Connection Administration

This section describes the Cisco Unity Connection graphical user interface (GUI) interface options and shows the main Cisco Unity Connection menu.

Cisco Unity Connection can be administered via a GUI. Browse to Cisco Unity Connection using **https://*<CUC-IP-address>*/cuadmin** to administer these Cisco Unity Connection systems:

- **Cisco Unity Connection Administration:** Configure users, call handlers, mailboxes, system settings, and so on.
- **Cisco Unified Serviceability:** Configure traces, activate services, set control center and Simple Network Management Protocol (SNMP) parameters, and so on.
- **Cisco Unified Operating System Administration:** Set the parameters for IP, Network Time Protocol (NTP), and time; change the server version or reboot the server; access security settings (such as IPsec); upgrade software; and so on.
- **Cisco Unified Connection Serviceability:** Start macro and micro traces, and manage the cluster, reporting, and so on.
- **Cisco Unity Connection Disaster Recovery System:** Back up and restore the Cisco Unity Connection system.

If GUI access is not working properly, additional maintenance tasks can be performed via the command-line interface (CLI) using Secure Shell (SSH). With Cisco Prime Collaboration Provisioning, you can also do daily maintenance tasks activities in an automated way.

The primary administration work in Cisco Unity Connection happens in Cisco Unity Connection Administration. You can add and manage users, user templates, configure dial plans, and so on. Cisco Unity Connection logically groups configuration items in menu sections. The Users menu, for example, allows you to create, import, or synchronize users.

Cisco Unified RTMT

The Cisco Unified Real Time Monitoring Tool (RTMT) can be used for multiple Cisco Collaboration System applications such as Cisco Unity Connection (UC) and CUCM. It is a valuable tool to validate the UC and CUCM integration.

Install the Cisco Unified RTMT from the **System Settings > Plugins** section, found in the Navigation pane in Cisco Unity Connection Administration. The Cisco Unified RTMT tool can be used to connect to CUCM, as well. You may have to update missing modules when accessing an application for the first time.

Figure 2-1 shows the layout of the Cisco Unity Connection RTMT tool. You can use the tool to view Cisco Unity Connection information for the system, server, performance, and tools. The Port Monitor is helpful during troubleshooting. The Port Monitor shows the calling, called, and redirected numbers of the caller, in real time. It also shows the current played greeting for remote troubleshooting.

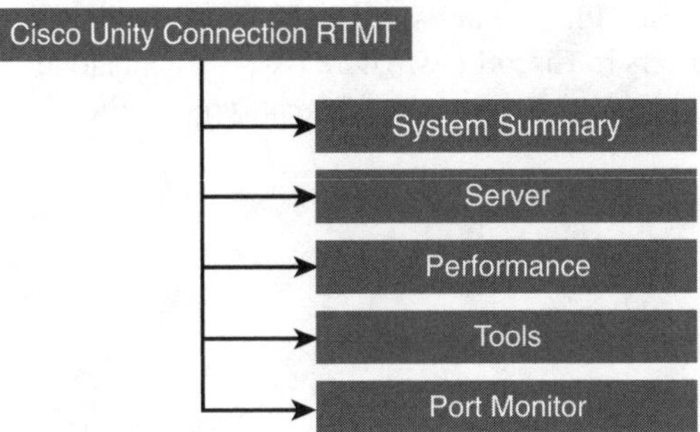

Figure 2-1 *Cisco Unity Connection RTMT Layout*

Cisco Prime Licensing for Voice Messaging

This section explains Cisco Prime License Manager (PLM) installation and usage options. Adding licensing is critical in Cisco Unified Communications products for version 10. You have a 60-day initial grace period, after which voice mail will fail to function without a valid license installation.

Follow these steps to begin using Cisco PLM:

1. Cisco PLM can be installed standalone on a single server or collocated as a service on CUCM and Cisco Unity Connection.
2. Log in to Cisco PLM via https://<ip-address>/plm-admin.
3. Add the product instances.
4. Use the dashboard or the License Usage page to determine which licenses are required for your product.
5. Migrate existing licenses or perform new license fulfillment if you have Cisco PLM installed on a new standalone system.

Cisco PLM (previously called Cisco ELM) enables you to perform these tasks:

- Add, edit, or delete a product instance.
- View system status information.
- Use the dashboard or license usage view to evaluate license fulfillment requirements.
- Migrate licenses using the Upgrade Licenses Wizard.

- Use the Add Licenses wizard to determine new licensing requirements.
- Generate a license request.
- Install a license.

Cisco PLM can be collocated as a service that is usually done on the CUCM server. Alternatively, you can add a standalone Cisco PLM, which is a good choice when connecting multiple applications and clusters to Cisco PLM. There is also a standalone Cisco PLM Open Virtualization Archive (OVA) template available that requires the following resources:

- 1 vCPU
- 4 GB vRAM
- 50 GB storage
- 1 vNIC

The initial login to Cisco PLM requires the application username and password that you created as part of the installation. After the initial login, Cisco PLM allows you to add additional administrator accounts.

Add Cisco Unity Connection in Cisco PLM

This section explains how to add Cisco Unity Connection in Cisco PLM. Cisco Unity Connection must be licensed in PLM.

When adding a product instance, start with the CUCM and the installed applications (for example, Cisco Unity Connection). The following information is mandatory when adding products:

- Name (The hostname of the Cisco Collaboration System application can be obtained by navigating to Cisco Unified Operating System Administration and choosing **Show > System**.)
- Product type (CUCM, Cisco Unity Connection, or Cisco Emergency Responder)
- Hostname or IP address
- Username (operating system administration username of the product)
- Password (system administrator password of the product)

On the Product Instances page, click **Synchronize Now** to extract the licensing information from the new products. If you do not synchronize, the current product instance information will not appear in Cisco PLM.

Cisco Unity Connection Integration Options

This section describes the integration options for Cisco Unity Connection.

Cisco Unity Connection integrates messaging and voice-recognition components to provide global access to calls and voice messages, as illustrated in Figure 2-2. Cisco Unity Connection advanced communication services offer voice commands to place calls or listen to messages in hands-free mode. These services also offer commands to check messages over the telephone or from a desktop, through an e-mail inbox or a web browser.

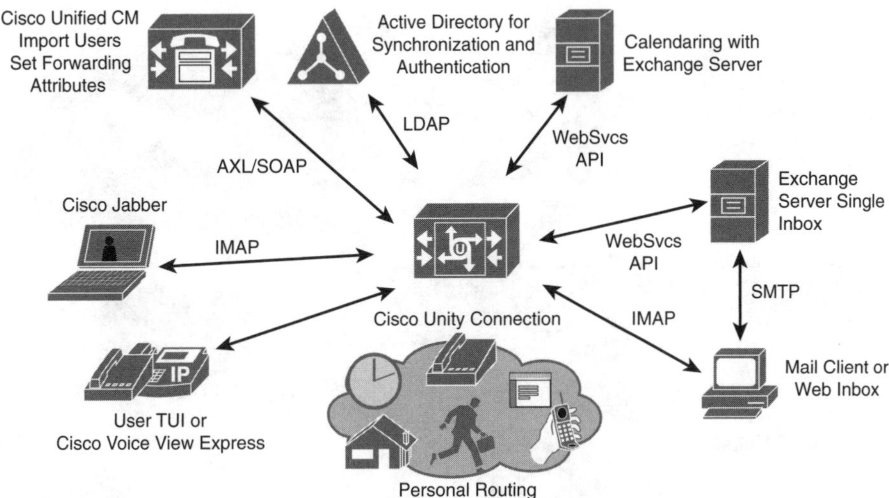

Figure 2-2 *Cisco Unity Connection Integration Options*

Running on a Linux-based network appliance platform as a virtual machine (VM), Cisco Unity Connection has its own integrated message and data stores. Cisco Unity Connection can integrate with CUCM, CUCM Express, or traditional private branch exchanges (PBXs). Cisco Unity Connection can be configured to import a user database from CUCM by using Administrative XML (AXL) and Simple Object Access Protocol (SOAP). AXL is a SOAP-based application programming interface (API) that enables remote provisioning of CUCM.

Cisco Unity Connection can integrate with Microsoft Exchange Server to deliver voice messages to an Internet Message Access Protocol (IMAP) e-mail inbox. Exchange Web Services (EWS) provides the functionality to enable client applications to communicate with the Exchange server. EWS provides access to much of the same data that is made available through Microsoft Office Outlook. EWS allows users to import calendaring information from Microsoft Exchange, for personal transfer rules. With Single Inbox (Unified Messaging), the users can receive their voice messages via the company Exchange mailbox. In addition, calendaring integration can be done with Microsoft Exchange Server.

Microsoft Active Directory integration is available by using the Lightweight Directory Access Protocol (LDAP) to synchronize Cisco Unity Connection usernames and passwords to Active Directory. Authentication for web-based application access is an optional feature of Active Directory integration.

Cisco Unity Connection provides a telephone user interface (TUI) and a voice user interface (VUI). By using an IP phone and visual voice mail, users can visually check and browse their mailboxes.

Cisco Unity Connection can integrate with CUCM or other PBXs through gateways, as shown in Figure 2-3.

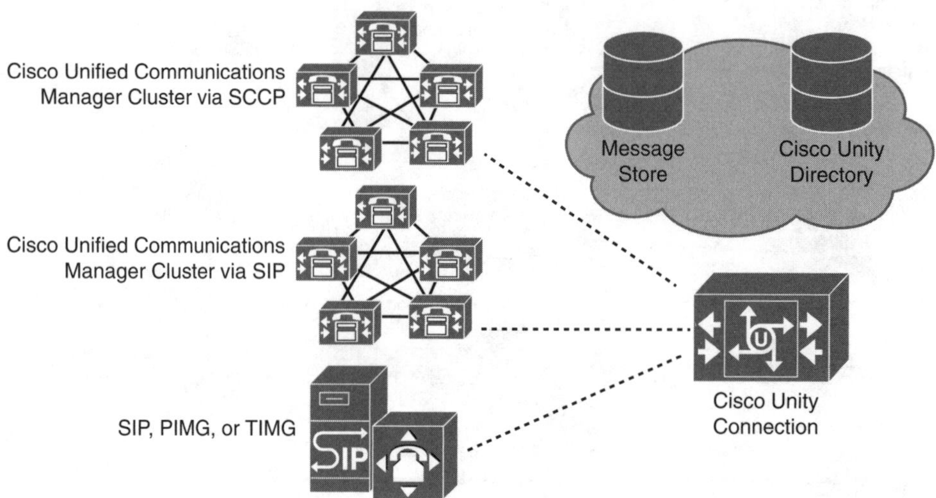

Figure 2-3 *Cisco Unity Connection Telephone System Integration Options*

Cisco Unity Connection supports simultaneous integrations with multiple telephone systems such as CUCM (using Skinny Client Control Protocol [SCCP] or Session Initiation Protocol [SIP]), CUCM Express (using SIP), and third-party PBX solutions. Third-party PBX solutions that support SIP may integrate directly with Unity Connection.

Circuit-switched phone system integrations can be accomplished through the Cisco Unity PBX IP Media Gateway (PIMG) or Cisco TDM IP Media Gateway (TIMG) and a SIP trunk. When using, for example, a digital integration with digital PIMG units, the phone system sends call information, MWI requests, and voice connections through the digital lines, which connect the phone system to the PIMG units (media gateways). The PIMG units communicate with the Cisco Unity Connection server through the LAN or WAN by using SIP.

Cisco Unity Connection SCCP Integration

When integrating CUCM with Cisco Unity Connection via SCCP, use the Voice Mail Port Wizard in CUCM Administration. The Voice Mail Port Wizard asks for parameters (such as number of voice-mail ports), automatically generates the voice-mail ports, and puts the ports into the line group. The hunt list and hunt pilot need to be configured manually. Figure 2-4 illustrates the logical software components required for a CUCM to Unity Connection SCCP integration.

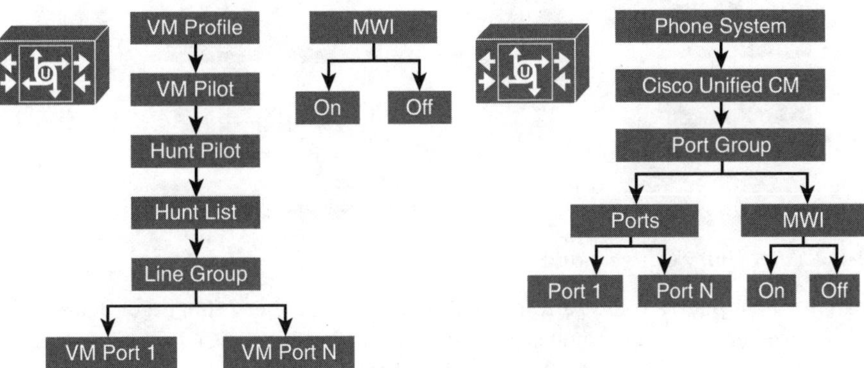

Figure 2-4 *Cisco Unity Connection SCCP Integration*

When a user presses the Messages button on a Cisco IP phone, CUCM looks up the voice-mail profile and voice-mail pilot. For example, if the voice-mail pilot is configured with the number 2100, the CUCM searches for a hunt pilot that has the number 2100. The hunt pilot looks up its configured hunt list, which then looks up the line group. The voice-mail ports are then used as defined in the line-group parameter distribution mechanism (for example, round robin).

On the Cisco Unity Connection system, the call enters via the ports that are the counterparts of the CUCM voice-mail ports. The Cisco Unity Connection ports can be configured for a specific use, such as taking e-mails, setting the MWI, and so on.

You can control call routing by how calls come in and leave the Cisco Unity Connection system via the port group or phone system.

Also, MWI must be configured with the same numbers (for example, 2110 for MWI on and 2111 for MWI off), on both the CUCM and Unity Connection. Cisco Unity Connection dials out the MWI number. The call is extended to the CUCM, which then communicates with the IP phone. The MWI is turned on or off. You can also manually dial numbers to test whether the MWI numbers can reach the IP phones. Class of service (CoS) with calling search spaces and partitions in CUCM can be used to prevent this behavior.

The standard SCCP integration uses TCP port 2000. IP phones also use TCP port 2000 to communicate with CUCM. The communication between the IP phone and Cisco Unity Connection can be secured on port 2448, which requires the use of digital certificates.

Cisco Unity Connection SIP Integration

This section describes the integration of CUCM and Cisco Unity Connection using SIP. Figure 2-5 illustrates the logical components required for a CUCM to Unity Connection SIP integration.

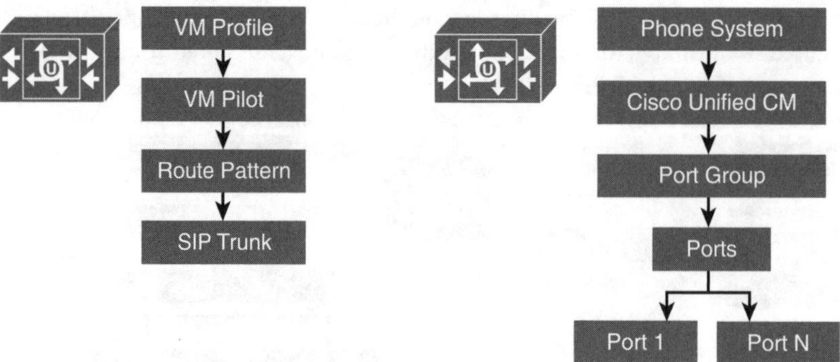

Figure 2-5 *Cisco Unity Connection SIP Integration*

Instead of a hunt pilot, a route pattern (for example, the number 2100) is configured. The voice-mail profile and voice-mail pilot are used as they are in SCCP integration. When a user presses the Messages button on the IP phone, CUCM takes the number that is configured in the voice-mail pilot (for example, 2100), and then searches for a route pattern that has that number. CUCM then reaches Cisco Unity Connection via the SIP trunk. The number of ports is undefined in CUCM.

On the Cisco Unity Connection system, the elements that are used for SIP integration are more or less the same, compared to the elements that are used for SCCP integration. The ports are configured to register with a SIP server, which is the CUCM. The number of ports is specified in the Cisco Unity Connection system only.

MWI handling is different between SCCP and SIP integrations. SIP integration does not use explicit numbers for MWI on or MWI off.

SIP integration uses port 5060, which is the standard SIP port. IP phones also use this port, for example, to communicate with CUCM. The communication between the IP phone and Cisco Unity Connection can be secured by using port 5061.

When you intend to use video greetings, you have to use SIP when integrating Cisco Unity Connection with CUCM.

Cisco Unity Connection Integration Troubleshooting Tools

This section describes the Cisco Unity Connection troubleshooting tools to test the integration for any issues.

Within Cisco Unity Connection Administration, use the Check Telephony Configuration tool to confirm the phone system integration settings. If the test is not successful, the Task Execution Results list displays one or more messages with troubleshooting steps. After correcting the problems, check the configuration again.

When setting up the ports, choose **Test Port** in the Related Links list. The port test is done on a port basis. If there is an issue with a single port, the Test Port application will list details and recommend the next steps.

The example port test output in Figure 2-6 shows a mismatch in the number of ports on CUCM and Cisco Unity Connection. There are more ports on Cisco Unity Connection than on CUCM, and therefore the port cannot register with the CUCM.

⊗	Port PhoneSystem-1-010: Failed registering as CiscoUM1-VI10 to 10.1.5.12:2000	Verify the port's settings, including security mode, match the configuration of voice mail device CiscoUM1-VI10 on 10.1.5.12.	Failure reason: ErrorReceivedSkinnyRegisterRejectMessage. SCCP message = [StationRegisterRejectMessage (36 bytes) text="Security Error"]

Figure 2-6 *Cisco Unity Connection Executed Test with Port Count Mismatch*

On CUCM, go to the Cisco Voice Mail Port overview and verify that the ports show as registered with CUCM.

To verify that the ports and the integration are working on both systems, press the Messages button on any phone using the default voice-mail profile. If no users are configured, the standard opening greeting is played. If the standard opening greeting is played, Cisco Unity Connection is successfully integrated with CUCM.

On-Net and Off-Net Calls

At the route-pattern level in CUCM, calls can be classified as on-net or off-net only in the outbound direction. For trunks and gateways, calls can be classified in either the outbound or inbound direction. Calls cannot be classified in translation patterns. Figure 2-7 illustrates the call classifications within CUCM.

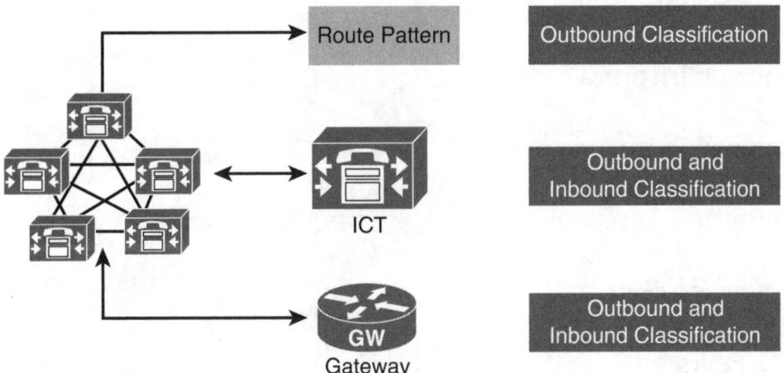

Figure 2-7 *CUCM On-Net and Off-Net Calls*

The default call classification is as follows:

- Route patterns are set to off-net.
- Trunks are set to the system default.
- Gateways are set to the system default.
- IP phones are always on-net and cannot be changed.

The call classification service parameter (system default) is set to off-net by default.

When configuring route patterns, you can configure the Allow Device Override parameter. This check box is unchecked by default. When you check the check box, CUCM uses the call classification setting that is configured on the associated gateway or trunk instead of using the route pattern call classification setting.

Call Forward Options

Figure 2-8 shows the Call Forward options to configure for the directory numbers in CUCM for an IP phone.

Call Forward and Call Pickup Settings

	Voice Mail
Calling Search Space Activation Policy	
Forward All	☐ or
Secondary Calling Search Space for Forward All	
Forward Busy Internal	☑ or
Forward Busy External	☑ or
Forward No Answer Internal	☑ or
Forward No Answer External	☑ or
Forward No Coverage Internal	☐ or
Forward No Coverage External	☐ or
Forward on CTI Failure	☐ or
Forward Unregistered Internal	☑ or
Forward Unregistered External	☑ or

Figure 2-8 *CUCM IP Phone Call Forwarding Options*

For many call forward options, internal and external callers can be treated differently. Call Forward All (CFA) cannot distinguish between internal and external callers.

However, call classification allows you to forward internal callers to a mobile phone and external callers to a voice mailbox.

Unless a calling search space (CSS) is set (in other words, if there are no route patterns in the <None> partition), a destination cannot be entered. Consequently, a call cannot extend to the configured number. For example, a number that is entered for CFA at an IP phone will not be accepted.

Cisco Unity Connection Call Routing

This section describes how directed and forwarded calls are routed in Cisco Unity Connection.

Figure 2-9 shows two examples of callers reaching Cisco Unity Connection. The difference is the number that Cisco Unity Connection uses for call routing and whether the call was direct or forwarded.

Message flows to Cisco Unity Connection:

• Internal and external directed calls use the calling number for identification.

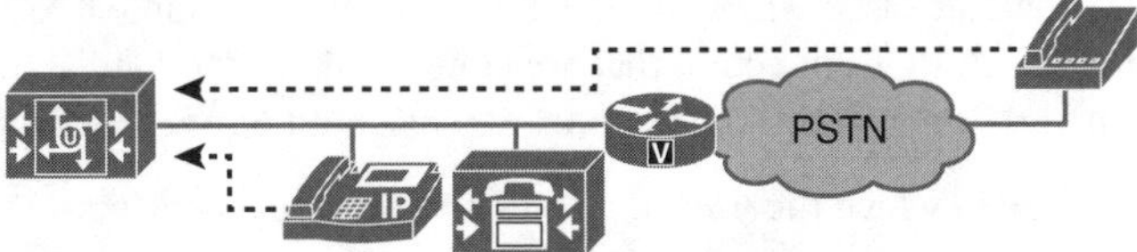

• Forwarded calls use the forwarded number for identification.

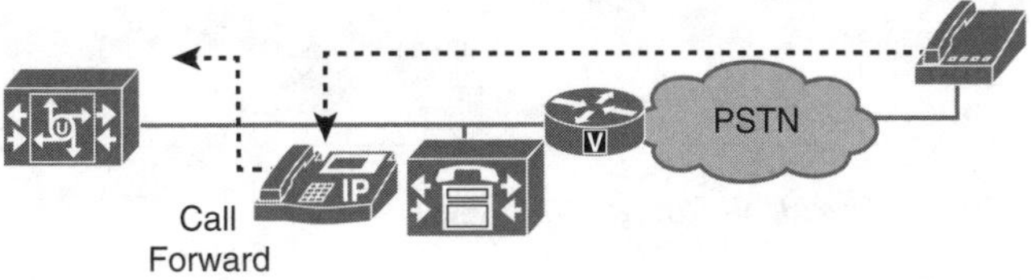

Figure 2-9 *Cisco Unity Connection Call Routing*

A directed call is initiated when, for example, the Messages button is pressed on a phone or a public switched telephone network (PSTN) caller dials the Cisco Unity Connection system pilot number. In both cases, the calling number is recognized and controls the call flow in Cisco Unity Connection:

- If the calling number is a configured extension, the mailbox answers with a personal login and asks for the PIN.
- Otherwise, the standard opening greeting is played. This action is the default for all PSTN callers.

To recognize external callers, alternate extensions, such as mobile phone or home office numbers of a user, can be configured.

A forwarded call is defined through an internal or external caller that dials the directory number 2001, for example. A call forward—such as Call Forward All (CFA), Call Forward Busy (CFB), or Call Forward No Answer (CFNA)—can be configured on the directory number 2001, to send calls to voice mail. Some other call forwards exist (for example, in case a device is unregistered). In this example, the incoming call to 2001 is forwarded to Cisco Unity Connection. The forwarding number is responsible for the selection of the mailbox with the extension 2001. If the extension 2001 exists in Cisco Unity Connection, the caller can leave a message.

If a forwarded call reaches Cisco Unity Connection and the forwarded number is not preserved, the call is directed the opening greeting.

Port Monitor

This section shows the capabilities of the port monitor to monitor the caller, called, and redirected number.

The Port Monitor can be started in Cisco Unified RTMT, by selecting menu option **Unity Connection > Port Monitor.**

The Port Monitor shows all Cisco Unity Connection ports. In this example, there are four ports on Cisco Unity Connection that are connected via a SIP integration to CUCM. A SCCP integration would show the port extension directory numbers (DNs).

Figure 2-10 shows a call in which the user of phone 2001 presses the Messages button and is asked to enter the PIN.

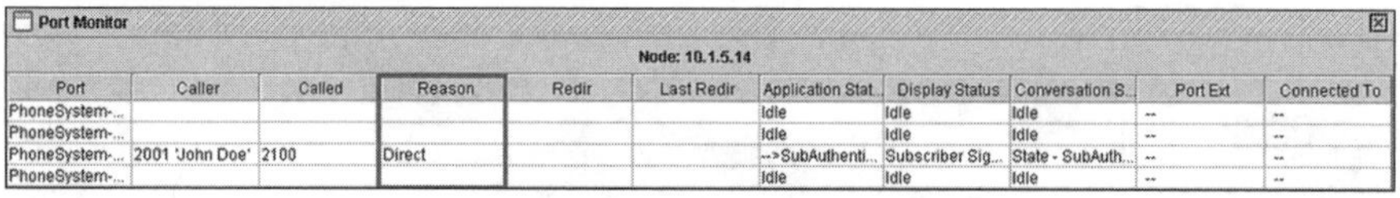

Port Monitor

Node: 10.1.5.14

Port	Caller	Called	Reason	Redir	Last Redir	Application Stat...	Display Status	Conversation S...	Port Ext	Connected To
PhoneSystem-...						Idle	Idle	Idle	--	--
PhoneSystem-...						Idle	Idle	Idle	--	--
PhoneSystem-...	2001 'John Doe'	2100	Direct			-->SubAuthenti...	Subscriber Sig...	State - SubAuth...	--	--
PhoneSystem-...						Idle	Idle	Idle	--	--

Figure 2-10 *Cisco Unity Direct Call Routing in RTMT*

Figure 2-11 shows a call in which Jane calls John. John does not answer and the call is forwarded to Cisco Unity Connection. The difference in these calls is the value of the Reason field—direct and CFNA.

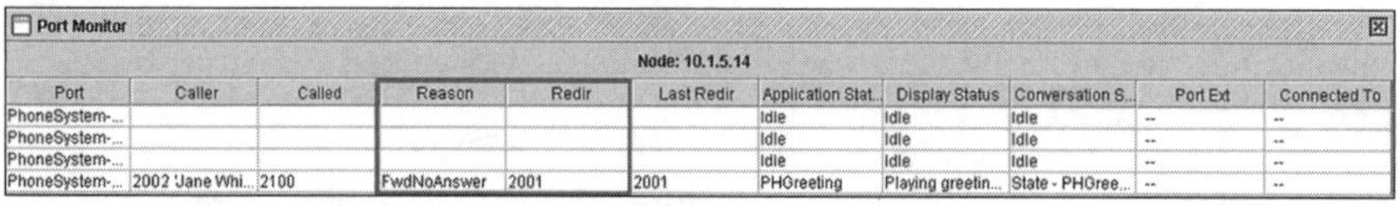

Port Monitor

Node: 10.1.5.14

Port	Caller	Called	Reason	Redir	Last Redir	Application Stat...	Display Status	Conversation S...	Port Ext	Connected To
PhoneSystem-...						Idle	Idle	Idle	--	--
PhoneSystem-...						Idle	Idle	Idle	--	--
PhoneSystem-...						Idle	Idle	Idle	--	--
PhoneSystem-...	2002 'Jane Whi...	2100	FwdNoAnswer	2001	2001	PHGreeting	Playing greetin...	State - PHGree...	--	--

Figure 2-11 *Cisco Unity CFNA in RTMT*

The following information is available:

- **Port:** This field displays the Cisco Unity Connection ports (for example, PhoneSystem-1-001).

- **Caller:** This field displays the calling number of the caller.
- **Called:** This field displays the called number (for example, the hunt pilot number).
- **Reason:** The reason is listed as Direct for a directed call or Forwarded for a forwarded call.
- **Redir:** This field displays the originally called number (the phone on which call forward is enabled).
- **Last Redir:** If a call is forwarded twice before reaching Cisco Unity Connection, this field displays the last redirected number. For example, if 2002 forwards all calls to 2001, and 2001 forwards the caller to Cisco Unity Connection, Redir displays 2002 and Last Redir displays 2001.
- **Application:** This field displays the status of the port (for example, Idle or PHGreeting).
- **Display Status:** This field displays the currently played greeting (for example, Playing Greeting for Call Handler or Opening Greeting).
- **Conversation Status:** This field displays the state of the greeting.
- **Port Ext:** This field displays the port numbers (for example, 2501 and 2502 when using SCCP integration).
- **Connected:** This field displays the connection information. The IP address of the CUCM and the port number are shown (for example, 10.2.1.1:2000 when using SCCP).

Default Call-Routing Behavior

This section describes the default call-routing behavior for directed and forwarded calls.

By default, two direct and two forwarded call-routing rules exist in Cisco Unity Connection.

For direct calls as shown in Figure 2-12, the user can log in to the mailbox by entering the PIN. If the caller has no assigned mailbox, the standard opening greeting is played.

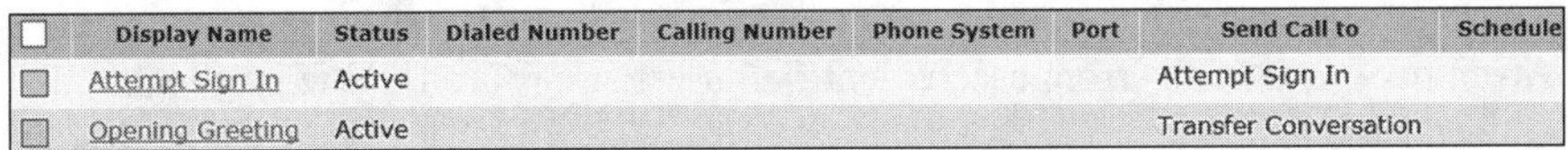

	Display Name	Status	Dialed Number	Calling Number	Phone System	Port	Send Call to	Schedule
	Attempt Sign In	Active					Attempt Sign In	
	Opening Greeting	Active					Transfer Conversation	

Figure 2-12 *Cisco Unity Direct Call Routing Behavior*

For forwarded calls illustrated in Figure 2-13, in which a caller dials an extension that is not answering, the call is forwarded to Cisco Unity Connection. If the forwarding number is a configured extension in Cisco Unity Connection, the caller can leave a message for this user. If the extension is not configured, the standard opening greeting is played to the caller.

Display Name	Status	Dialed Number	Calling Number	Forwarding Station	Phone System	Port	Send Call to	Schedule
Attempt Forward	Active						Attempt Forward	
Opening Greeting	Active						Transfer Conversation	

Figure 2-13 *Cisco Unity Forwarded Call Behavior*

Additional call-routing rules can be configured for direct and forwarded calls to manage call routing or start another auto-attendant.

Direct Call Routing

Direct call-routing rules process calls from users and unidentified callers that directly dial Cisco Unity Connection as illustrated in the options in Figure 2-14.

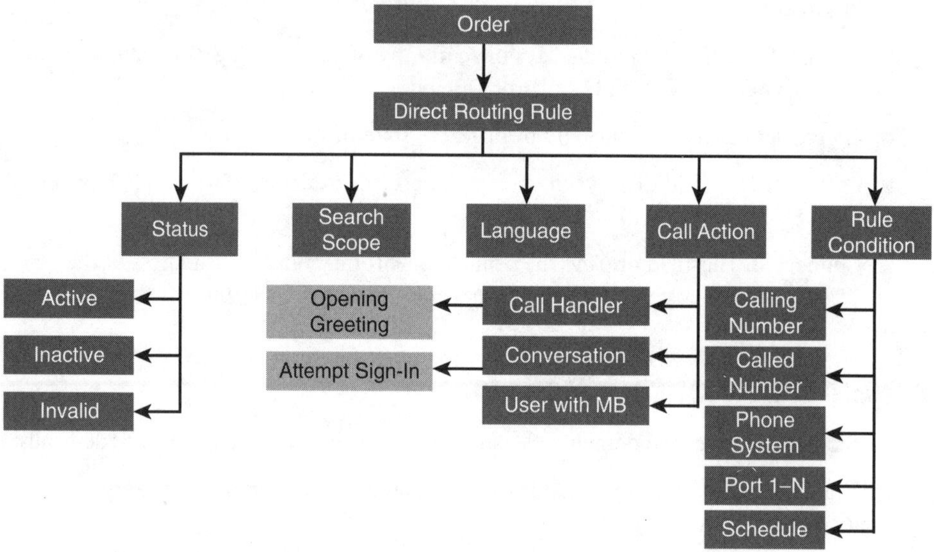

Figure 2-14 *Cisco Unity Direct Call Routing Options*

The following are the predefined rules in the default direct call-routing rules:

- **Attempt Sign-In:** Calls from users (identified users) are routed to the user login conversation.
- **Opening Greeting:** Calls from unidentified callers (users without a mailbox) are routed to the opening greeting.

The order of the Attempt Sign-In rule can be changed. Rules that are added in the direct call-routing table can also be changed. The Opening Greeting rule is always the last entry in the call-routing table.

When a direct call-routing rule is used, calls can be filtered and an action can be applied. Callers can be sent to the following options:

- **Calling Number:** The rule is applied for specified calling number, such as 2001, or 123* for all calls starting with 123.
- **Dialed Number:** The rule is applied for specified dialed number, such as the number of a call handler.
- **Port:** The rule is applied for specified incoming port (1 to n).
- **Phone System:** The rule is applied for specified phone system that delivers the call. This condition can be selected if more than one phone system exists.
- **Schedule:** The rule is applied for the selected schedule, such as all hours, weekdays, or any customized schedule.

Call actions can be used in combination with rule conditions. For example, all calls that come from the phone number of a particular customer can be transferred directly to the user, or all calls that come to an outdated company number can get an informational message about the new number and then be transferred to the company auto-attendant.

You can specify the following call-routing rule conditions:

- **Calling Number:** The rule reacts according to the calling number, such as 2001, or 123* for all calls starting with 123.
- **Dialed Number:** The rule reacts according to the dialed number, such as the number of a call handler.
- **Port:** The rule reacts according to the incoming port (1 to n).
- **Phone System:** The rule reacts according to the phone system that delivers the call. This condition can be selected if more than one phone system exists.
- **Schedule:** The rule reacts according to a selected schedule, such as all hours, weekdays, or any customized schedule.

When combined with the call action, such rule conditions can, for example, transfer all calls from the area code 123 to a certain user, or process in a specific way, all calls from 2001.

A call-routing rule can be configured with one or more rule conditions. If all rule conditions match, the call action is executed.

Forwarded Call Routing

Forwarded call-routing rules process calls that are forwarded to Cisco Unity Connection. Forwarded calls are either from a user extension or from an extension that is not associated with a user account, such as a conference room. Figure 2-15 illustrates the call forwarding options.

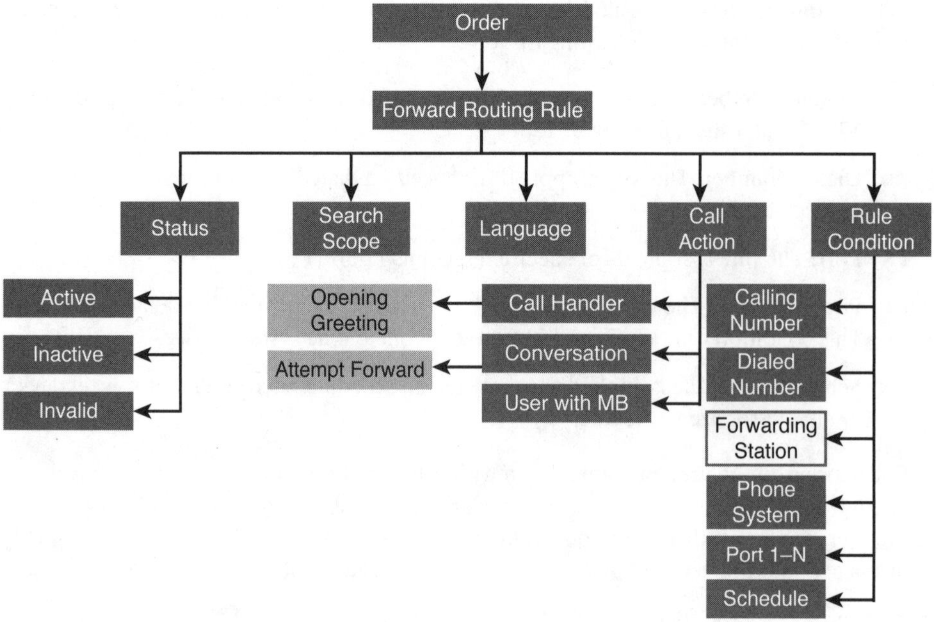

Figure 2-15 *Cisco Unity Forward Call Routing Options*

The following forwarded routing rules are predefined:

- **Attempt Forward:** All calls that are forwarded from a Cisco Unity Connection user with a mailbox are routed to the user greeting. The caller can leave a message.
- **Opening Greeting:** Calls that are forwarded from an extension that is not associated with a user account are routed to the opening greeting.

The difference between direct routing and forward routing is the origin of the call:

- Direct call
- Forwarded call

An additional rule condition is available for forwarded calls compared to directed calls. This rule is the Forwarding Station rule condition, which reacts according to the number of the phone that is configured with a call forward.

Forwarding routing rules can be used, for example, to process all calls that go to a conference station and to send these calls to an operator.

Integration Considerations

The section lists some considerations related to integrating Cisco Unity Connection with CUCM and to securing Cisco Unity Connection to prevent toll fraud.

If the extension number for the user in Unity Connection does not match the directory number for the user in CUCM, MWI is not turned on for new voice messages.

To prevent toll fraud, configure the CSS on the voicemail ports or SIP trunk to disallow, for example, international calls. This restriction can be combined with restriction tables in Cisco Unity Connection.

In addition, you can prevent the misuse of voice mailboxes by hardening the PINs. Brute-force attacks may allow hackers to transfer themselves to international or premium numbers, generating high phone bills. Define security policies in your company for PIN and password selection. Use mailbox locking after the PIN is entered incorrectly three times, for example. When LDAP authentication is used, the LDAP server security policies apply for the password instead of the Cisco Unity Connection password policies.

Summary

This section summarizes the key points that were discussed in this chapter:

- Cisco Unity Connection can be integrated using SCCP and SIP. When you want to use video greetings, you need to use SIP for the integration.
- Cisco Unity Connection must be integrated with Cisco PLM for centralized licensing.
- You can use call classification to control which forwarding option is allowed to send callers to voice mail or a mobile phone, for example.
- Install the Cisco Unified RTMT to use the Port Monitor. The Port Monitor shows you the called, calling, and redirected numbers in real time with an easy-to-use GUI.
- Call routing distinguishes between direct calls and forwarded calls. Direct calls are, for example, calls where the user presses the Messages button on the phone. When a call in not answered, the call in sent to Cisco Unity Connection and is marked as a forwarded call.
- If the caller in known in Cisco Unity Connection (an identified user), the mailbox can be accessed or a message can be left. Otherwise, the Cisco Unity Connection opening greeting is played.

Review Questions

Answer the following questions, and then see Appendix A, "Answers to Review Questions," for the answers.

1. **Which two types of call forward have no option for internal and external call coverage?**

   a. Forward All

   b. Forward No Answer

   c. Forward No Coverage

d. Forward on CTI failure

e. ward Unregistered

2. Using Cisco Unified RTMT, which of the following is not a valid field in the Port Monitor?

a. Port

b. Caller

c. Called

d. Reason

e. Redir

f. First Redir

Chapter 3

Configuring Cisco Unity Connection Users, Templates, and Class of Service

Upon completing this chapter, you will be able to do the following:

- Describe the concept of using CoS to assign additional features to users
- Describe the user templates in Cisco Unity Connection and how they can be used in different scenarios
- Provide an overview of how users are created in Cisco Unity Connection
- Describe the main Cisco Unity Connection user parameters and how a user account can be individualized
- Describe the settings for the PINs and passwords and the predefined roles in Cisco Unity Connection
- Transfer a call to another extension
- Describe the different greeting options that a user can set up
- Describe how the TUI experience can be modified for a caller and for a Cisco Unity Connection user
- Provide scenarios in which alternate extensions are required in the user configuration
- Describe the initial setup of a user's voice mailbox
- Describe the mailbox store and how the mailbox access is managed in a Cisco Unity Connection cluster
- Describe how messages are stored and the options that are available to optimize storage space
- Explain the use of distribution lists, which can be created on a user or system level
- Describe how users can be notified about new voice messages

This chapter explains Cisco Unity Connection CoS and the features that Cisco Unity Connection users can access when enabled in class of service (CoS). User templates help you to efficiently create users who are based on standardized templates. Creating new users manually using predefined CoS and templates helps you to quickly establish new users and deploy a defined feature set.

Cisco Unity Connection Class of Service

In Cisco Unity Connection, CoS determines the features that each user can use. There are two default classes of service: the system CoS and the voice-mail user CoS. The system CoS cannot be deleted and only some of the parameters can be changed. Figure 3-1 illustrates the Unity Connection CoS options.

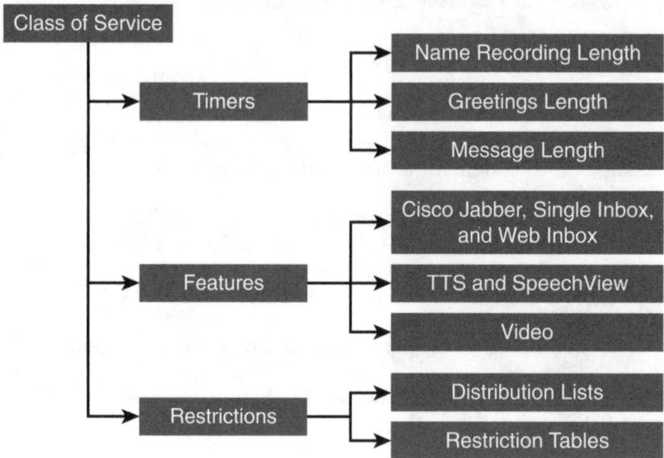

Figure 3-1 *Cisco Unity Connection CoS*

The voice-mail user CoS supports the following features:

- Timers define the allowed recording length, and are available for names (the maximum length is 30 seconds), greetings (the maximum length for a greeting is 90 seconds), and messages (the maximum message length is 300 seconds).
- Users are listed in the directory so that, for example, a directory handler can search for and find all users. You may allow users to delist themselves. A directory handler is a phone number a user can call which will allow them to look up other users within Unity Connection.
- Allow users to access e-mail messages over the phone using the Text-to-Speech (TTS) feature.
- The Cisco SpeechView feature converts voice messages to text up to 500 characters and delivers the text version of the voice message to your e-mail inbox, allowing you to read your voice messages and take immediate action.

- Video is disabled by default for greeting recording and outside callers.
- Only the administrator can set alternate extension behavior by default; you may allow users to view and manage their alternate extensions.
- The number of private distribution lists (25) and members per private distribution list (99) is limited by default.
- Call transfer for outgoing or transferred calls can be restricted.

Additional features that may need to be licensed are disabled by default (for example, access to voice mail using an Internet Message Access Protocol (IMAP) client or single inbox). Other features, such as Cisco Jabber access to voice messages, are also disabled by default. These restricted features are primarily those that could generate additional costs, for instance transfer rules for the company or the ability to disregard security policies.

User Access to Features

You can use CoS to give users access to certain features. The following are the most commonly used features that can be enabled or modified in the voice-mail user CoS.

User access to certain features can be allowed with CoS:

- Record the name of the user.
- Choose to be listed in the directory.
- Enable video greetings.
- View or manage alternate extensions.
- Change call-screening or holding options.
- Set Advanced features:
  - Allow Cisco Jabber to access voice messages.
  - Enable unified messaging.
- Provide transcriptions of voice messages (Cisco SpeechView).

Cisco Unity Connection User Templates

Templates must be created before any user is created, because templates are applied only once when adding or importing a user to Cisco Unity Connection. Figure 3-2 shows a few of the User Template Options.

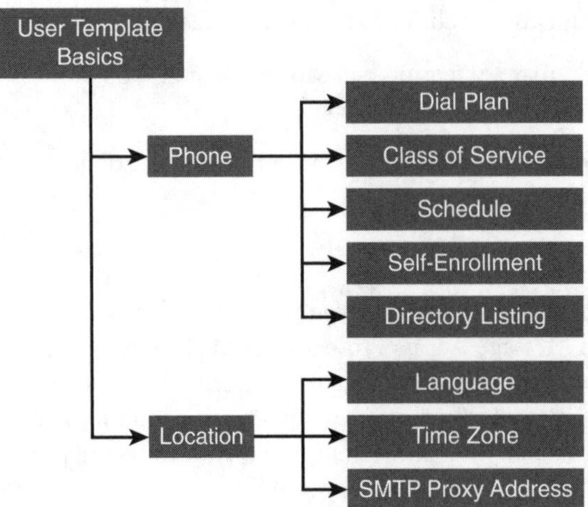

Figure 3-2 *Cisco Unity Connection User Template Options*

These are the most important settings in the user template:

- Add a name for the template that describes (for example, the user function, such as employee or manager).
- The dial plan is set under the phone section and defines which partition the user belongs to and in which search space the user can search when sending messages. After the Cisco Unity Connection installation, there are one default partition and one search space, which are named after the Cisco Unity Connection system hostname. These partition and search space elements form the dial plan, and are associated with the default voice-mail user template. The default voice-mail user CoS is assigned with the default user template.

The schedule is set, by default, to Weekdays. The schedule should be changed to All Hours so that the individual greeting of the end user is always played. You can disable the listing of users in the directory depending on the company policies.

- The language is set in the location section. This setting is important in a multinational deployment as well as in a single-location deployment, in which different groups might expect callers from only certain countries.
- The time zone is used for generating time stamps for voice messages. Setting a proper time stamp helps users to get correct information about when a message was received, by using the time zone of the user location.

User Template Example

User templates enable you to work more efficiently on recurring tasks. General parameters that are the same for all users or groups of users can be predefined. Then, all new users that are added in Cisco Unity Connection will have the same preselected settings (for example, the same language or time zone settings). If the user template is changed at any time, the new settings will affect only users that are created after the template change. To change parameters for a group of existing users, use the Bulk Administration Tool (BAT) in Cisco Unity Connection. Figure 3-3 illustrates some options of a user template. Future changes can easily be made to users created by a template.

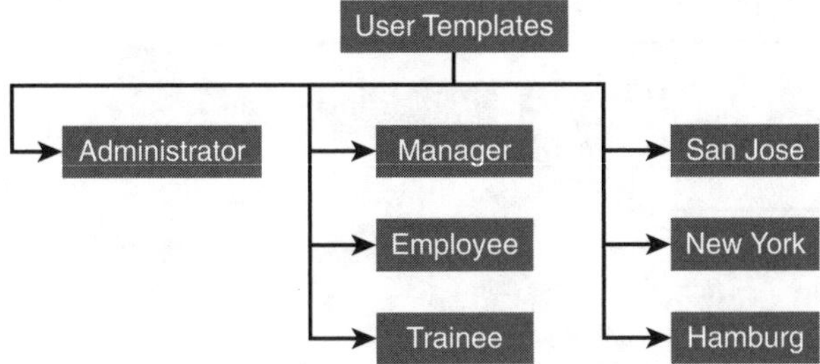

Figure 3-3 *Cisco Unity Connection User Template Example*

There are two default user templates: an administrator template and a voice-mail user template. These templates cannot be deleted and cannot be modified. The administrator template has only limited options compared to the user templates. An administrator can, for example, build a user template model in which settings are preconfigured for managers, employees, or trainees. Managers may have mailboxes with more space for voice messages, or they can be notified via mobile phone when a new message arrives. Employees may have preconfigured message actions. Trainees may be limited to listening to their voice messages. User templates can also be based on locations and can specify which language to use. User templates can have time zones that are defined for a location so that messages are recorded with the correct time stamp.

When creating a new user, choose the appropriate user template. By doing so, the user template entries are applied to the newly created user accounts.

Note User templates are applied only to newly created user accounts. Any changes to a user template have no effect on existing user accounts.

User-Creation Options

User templates facilitate manual configuration of new users. You can create multiple users in bulk by importing data from a .csv file. Alternatively, you can import users from a supported Lightweight Directory Access Protocol (LDAP) directory such as Microsoft Active Directory or a Cisco Unified Communications Manager (CUCM) server. Figure 3-4 shows the user-creation options.

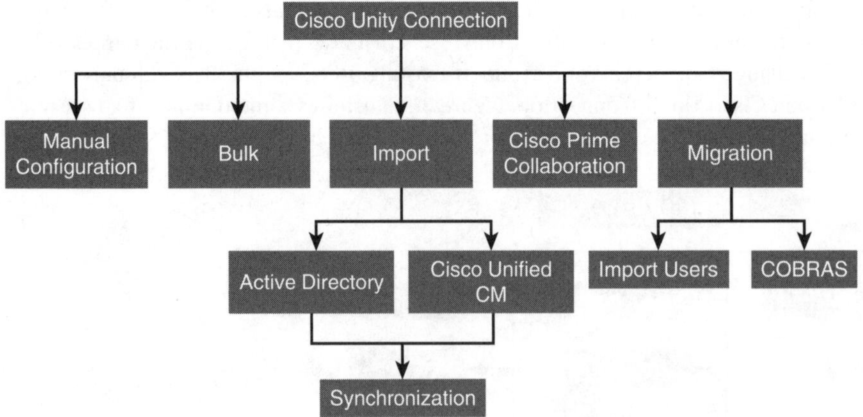

Figure 3-4 *Cisco Unity Connection User-Creation Options*

When using Cisco Prime Collaboration Provisioning, the users are imported from the LDAP server to Cisco Prime Collaboration Provisioning. You can then provision end users in CUCM and Cisco Unity Connection based on the imported user database.

Users can also be migrated from Cisco Unity when migrating to Cisco Unity Connection. Administrators can use the COBRAS to migrate users, with or without their messages, from a Cisco Unity system to a Cisco Unity Connection system.

COBRAS is a set of tools that administrators can use to back up all subscriber, call-handler, public distribution list, schedule, and routing-rule information in Cisco Unity. Administrators can use COBRAS to restore some or all of that information to Cisco Unity Connection. For information about supported versions of COBRAS, go to http://www.ciscounitytools.com.

Cisco Unity Connection User

This section describes the main Cisco Unity Connection user parameters and how an end user account can be individualized, as illustrated in Figure 3-5.

If CoS and user templates are predefined, only a few individual selections and settings are required. When creating a user account, select a user template (for example, a customized employee user template). The individual user parameters are a unique alias (ID), first and last name, and the extension (directory number on CUCM). The two minimum parameters are the alias and the extension. You cannot create a new user account without specifying these two parameters. The first and last name is optional for Cisco Unity Connection, but entering a first and a last name automatically generates the display name. If you do not create a display name, users of voice recognition will not be able to address messages to this user or call this user by name. In addition, you can configure alternate extensions and names for a user.

The alternate extension is not required but increases the productivity and improves user experience; for example, set up the mobile and home phone numbers as alternate

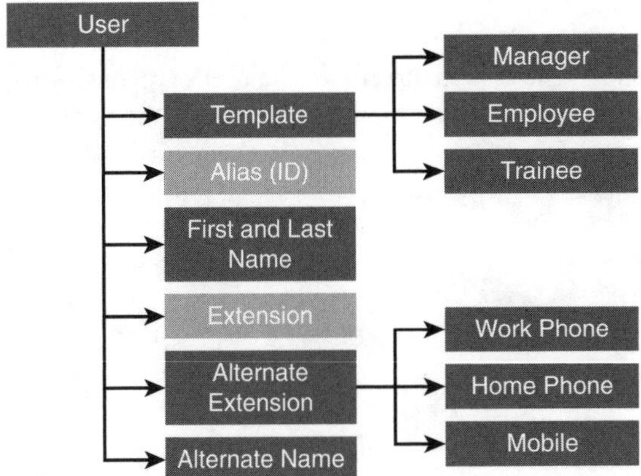

Figure 3-5 *Cisco Unity Connection End User-Creation Options*

extensions. With this approach, a user can use alternate devices to dial the Cisco Unity Connection pilot number and get the personal login, which requires only PIN entry. If an undefined extension calls into Cisco Unity Connection, the standard opening greeting is played by default.

Password Settings and Roles

Passwords for telephone user interface (TUI) and graphical user interface (GUI) access observe the system authentication rules. For example, an authentication rule might define a minimum credential length of three digits or characters and might allow trivial passwords for a lab environment. With this authentication rule, the password for all new users can be set to 123. In addition, you can specify that users must change the password at the next login. Adjust these settings to comply with the company policies.

For security reasons, disable the use of trivial passwords and specify a minimum length of eight digits for the PIN in the authentication rule. PINs are used for TUI access, to receive voice messages. The web-application password is used to access the Cisco Unity Connection Personal Options pages (Cisco Personal Communications Assistant). However, if you use Lightweight Directory Access Protocol (LDAP) authentication, the user domain password is used and the domain security settings are applied.

When calling the Cisco Unity Connection system pilot number, Cisco Unity Connection might ask the caller for a password—which is actually the PIN. For security reasons, do not enable the Does Not Expire check box. Passwords will then need to be changed on a regular basis. However, a PIN must be administered in Cisco Unity Connection Administration; the PIN cannot be defined in the LDAP server.

A user can be assigned to an administrator group by using roles (for example, the predefined User Administrator role). With such access rights assigned, the user can create new user accounts. By default, no administrator role is assigned to the users.

User Transfer Rules

Transfer rules allow Unity Connection to send callers directly to the user's greeting or to transfer the caller to the user's extension or some other number specified in the transfer rules These options are shown in Figure 3-6.

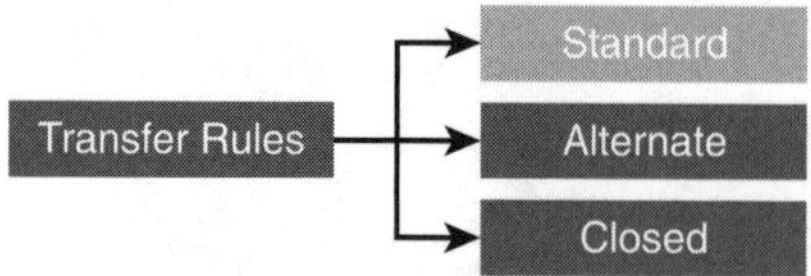

Figure 3-6 *Cisco Unity Connection Transfer Rules*

The following three transfer rules are predefined:

- The standard transfer rule is enabled without an end date (always active) and cannot be modified.
- The alternate transfer rule may replace the standard transfer rule. For example, the alternate transfer rule can customize the time for which the transfer rules should be enabled. During vacation, an alternative transfer rule could be used instead of the standard transfer rule.
- If the schedule of the user is set to weekdays only, the closed transfer rule is used during the weekends and after business hours.

Call transfer settings determine how Cisco Unity Connection handles the transferred calls:

- **Release to Switch:** Unity Connection puts the caller on hold, dials the extension, and releases the call to the phone system. When the line is busy or is not answered, the phone system—not Unity Connection—forwards the call to the user or handler greeting. This transfer type allows Unity Connection to process incoming calls more quickly.
- **Supervise Transfer:** Unity Connection acts as a receptionist and manages the transfer. If the line is busy or the call is not answered, Unity Connection—not the phone system—forwards the call to the user or handler greeting.

When Unity Connection is set to supervise transfers, it can provide additional call control with call holding and call screening. Call screening offers these options:

- Tell Me When the Call Is Connected
- Tell Me Who the Call Is For
- Ask Me If I Want to Take the Call
- Ask for Caller's Name

Greetings

Only the standard and error greetings are set up and enabled by default. Figure 3-7 shows how the different greetings take precedence over the others. There is also an error greeting if a caller dials a number that cannot be routed.

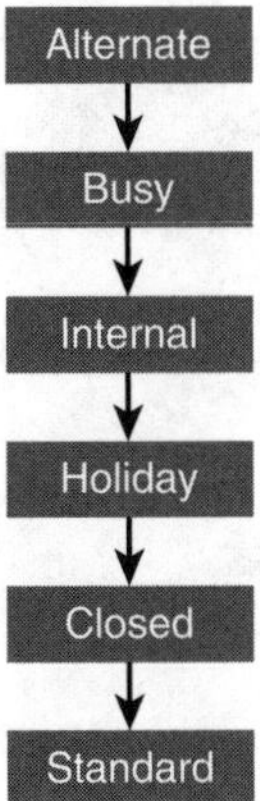

Figure 3-7 *Cisco Unity Connection Greetings*

Greetings enable users to individualize their greetings in different ways:

- If not recorded by the user, Cisco Unity Connection automatically generates the standard greeting, from the display name. This greeting plays at all times, unless it is overridden by another greeting.
- An alternate greeting can be used for various special situations, such as vacations or a leave of absence (for example, "I will be out of the office until...)." An alternate greeting overrides all other greetings.
- A closed greeting can be played on weekends, if the schedule is set to weekdays.
- A holiday greeting allows users to have a personalized greeting on holidays (for example, Christmas).
- In addition, three rarely used system greetings exist: busy, error, and internal.

These greetings can be configured by the end user via the Cisco Personal Communications Assistant.

Other parameters that can be defined in the greeting configuration include what callers hear before, during, and after the greeting, or the language of the prompts.

With Cisco Unity Connection 10.x, users can record a video greeting that can be shown to internal and external callers. The Cisco Unity Connection 10.5 still does not support leaving video messages. Cisco Media Sense is required for video integration.

TUI Experience

This section describes how the TUI experience can be modified for a caller and for a Cisco Unity Connection user.

The following parameters can be changed in the Phone menu:

- Conversation volume, from low to high, with a default of medium
- Conversation speed, slow to fastest, with a default of normal
- Time format, with a default of 12 hours
- Timers for entering digits (for example, how long to wait for the next digit when a name is being entered)

The following parameters can be modified for message playback:

- Set volume and speed for message playback
- Enable counter announcements for new voice, fax, or e-mail messages
- Set the order for playing new or saved messages (urgent first, followed by order of incoming time)
- Enable playback of information from the sender: extension, message number, time of sending the message, and so on
- Confirm deletions of new and saved messages

Alternate Extensions

When the WAN link is congested from the CAC definitions, as shown in Figure 3-8, a rerouting over the public switched telephone network (PSTN) is required with CUCM Automated Alternate Routing (AAR) for calls to Cisco Unity Connection.

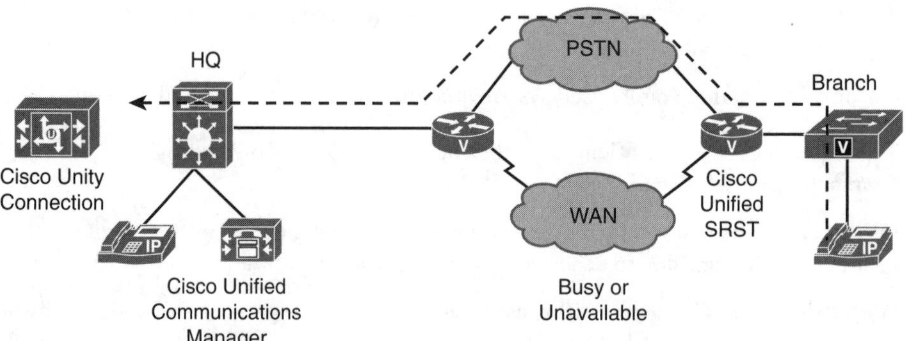

Figure 3-8 *Cisco Unity Connection Alternate Extensions*

A Cisco Unified SRST router sends the call with its complete E.164 number as the calling number (for example, 408 555-2001) to Cisco Unity Connection. Many installations use the four digit number as the Cisco Unity Connection extension. The number 408 555-2001 can be configured as an alternate extension for the user that has extension 2001 in Cisco Unity Connection.

There are other options. Instead of using alternate numbers, a number transformation can be configured on the hunt pilot or Session Initiation Protocol (SIP) trunk, or voice translation rules can be configured to modify the calling numbers for incoming calls.

If the WAN is busy, AAR also reroutes the call over the PSTN. Depending on the number-modification configuration, the calling or forwarded number can be sent as the complete E.164 number.

You can also add mobile numbers or home office numbers as alternate extensions, so that users who call in from any alternate extension are identified and only need to enter the PIN to access the voice-mail services.

Voice Mailbox

This section describes the initial setup of a user's voice mailbox.

During the user account creation process, a Cisco Unity Connection administrator can enable or disable the self-enrollment feature for the voice mailbox of the new user, as illustrated in Figure 3-9.

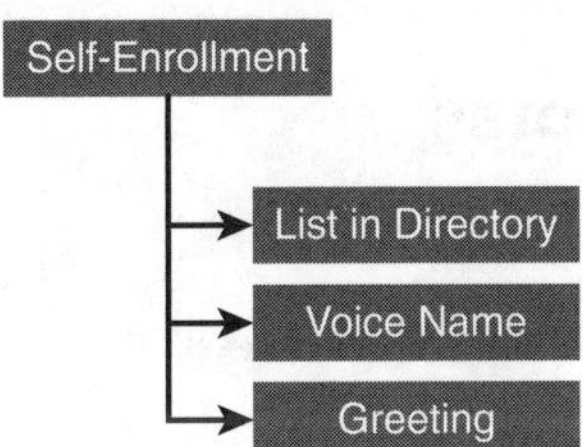

Figure 3-9 *Cisco Unity Connection Voice Mailbox Self-Enrollment Options*

Users can decide to list their extension in the Cisco Unity Connection directory. If a caller chooses to search by name, the directory handler searches the directory list for directory list-enabled users.

The voice name can be rerecorded; for example, instead of the greeting "2001 is not available," Cisco Unity Connection announces "John Doe is not available." By default, Cisco Unity Connection generates the spoken name from the display name.

Optionally, the greeting can be changed from a standard greeting to an alternate personalized greeting.

Mailbox Stores and Membership

Figure 3-10 illustrates the use of different mailbox stores and user membership in a mailbox store. Unity Connection can store all e-mails in an active arrangement over two Unity Connection virtual machines (VMs).

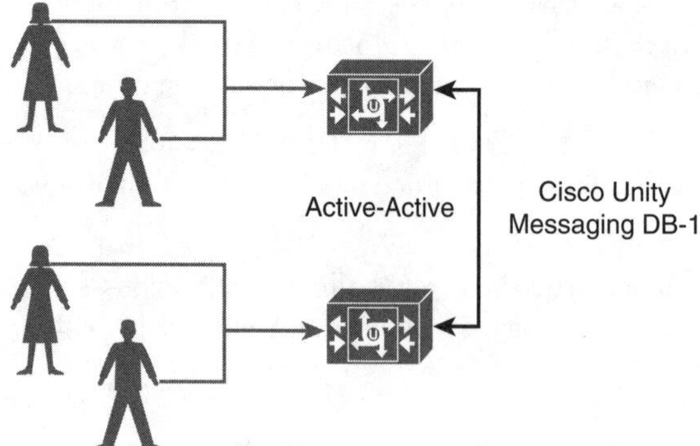

Figure 3-10 *Cisco Unity Connection Mailbox Stores and Membership*

A voice mailbox belongs to a user. To store the incoming voice messages, a message store on a Cisco Unity Connection server must be chosen. The database is shared and synchronized between both servers. If a caller leaves a message, the message is synchronized to the other server. If one of the servers fails in a Cisco Unity Connection cluster, the user can still retrieve the messages via the other server.

Message Aging Policy and Mailbox Quotas

In Unity Connection Unified messaging has the following features:

- Synchronization of voice messages in Unity Connection and Microsoft Exchange mailboxes (also known as single inbox)
- TTS access to Exchange e-mail
- Access to Exchange calendars, which allows users to do meeting-related tasks by phone (for example, hear a list of upcoming meetings, or accept or decline meeting invitations)
- Access to Exchange contacts, which allows users to import Exchange contacts and use the contact information in personal call transfer rules and when placing outgoing calls using voice commands
- Notification of upcoming Cisco Unified MeetingPlace meetings on the phone
- Scheduling and joining of MeetingPlace meetings
- Transcription of Unity Connection voice messages (SpeechView)

Optimizing message storage is important when a high number of users are enabled for unified messaging. Because all messages would be copied to the Exchange server as well, the required message storage space on external systems increases.

Message aging policy and mailbox quotas can be defined on a system level, in user templates, or on a user account level. Alert texts can be defined to be sent as a message when quotas are reached or messages are moved or deleted by the system.

To ensure that the hard disk where voice messages are stored does not fill up, aging rules can be configured in Cisco Unity Connection. These rules automate the message deletion process. Read messages can be moved to the Deleted Items folder after a specified number of days (disabled by default). Messages in the Deleted Items folder can be permanently deleted after a number of days (15 by default).

The mailbox quotas warn users that the mailbox is reaching the maximum allowed size (at 11 MB by default), prevent the user from sending voice messages to other users (at 12 MB by default), or prevent the user from sending or receiving voice messages (at 14 MB by default).

For reference, 12 MB translates to approximately 200 minutes of recording with the G.729 codec, and approximately 25 minutes of recording with the G.711 codec.

Private Distribution Lists

All users in Cisco Unity Connection can use system distribution lists. Administrators can create system distribution lists for general usage. In addition, users can manage and use their own private distribution lists.

As an example in Figure 3-11, a sales manager is responsible for three teams: voice, security, and network.

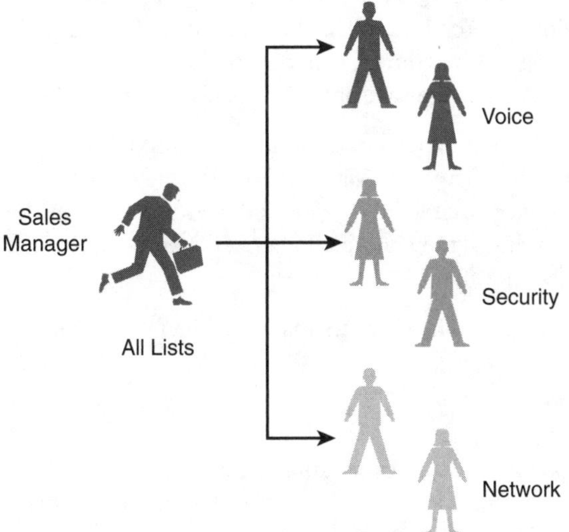

Figure 3-11 *Cisco Unity Connection Private Distribution List Example*

To leave them individual news and information, the sales manager creates three private distribution lists. To manage all three groups at the same time, the sales manager can create an additional private distribution list (called All Lists) that includes the three private distribution lists. The sales manager can distribute a message to all three groups via the private distribution list All Lists. Any user that is included in any of the three teams receives such a message.

Notification Devices

This section describes how users can be notified about new voice messages.

The MWI on an IP phone is the default standard notification on Cisco Unity Connection for all users.

Additional notification devices can be set up for mobile users, as shown in Figure 3-12.

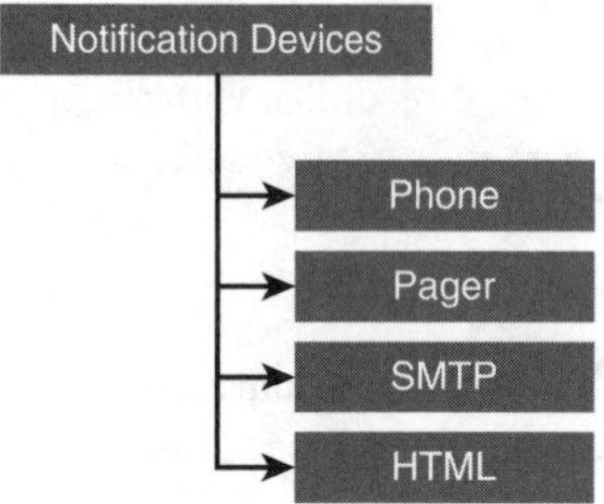

Figure 3-12 *Cisco Unity Connection Notification Devices Options*

Notification devices are phones, pagers, or e-mail addresses. As many as three phone devices can be defined per Cisco Unity Connection user. As soon as a voice message is left for a user, Cisco Unity Connection can, for example, call the mobile number of the user for whom the caller left the message. When the user answers the phone, Cisco Unity Connection informs the user of the new voice message and asks the user to enter a PIN.

An e-mail with the voice message can be sent to any e-mail address using SMTP or HTML, but if the user listens to a message that is sent via e-mail, MWI cannot be synchronized with the IP phone. However, if integrated or unified messaging is used, MWI is synchronized after the user listens to the message. Integrated messaging is voice messaging that is integrated at the client level.

Restriction tables allow you to control the phone numbers that subscribers and administrators can use for:

- Transferring calls.
- Recording and playback by phone from Cisco Unity applications when the phone is the designated recording and playback device in the Media Master. (The Media Master is available in the Cisco Unity Administrator, the Cisco Unity Assistant, the Cisco Unity Inbox, and ViewMail.)

- Delivering faxes to a fax machine.
- Sending message notifications.

User templates allow enabling of the notification devices, in general. However, users or administrators need to configure the notification device addresses. These devices addresses are, for example, the mobile phone numbers or external e-mail addresses of the users. To disallow calling, for example, to international numbers, set up the restriction table to block cost-intensive calls.

Summary

This section summarizes the key points that were discussed in this chapter:

- CoS allows administrators to control which features users can access. CoS also defines additional options that, if enabled, can be set by users and consequently reduce the work of administrators.
- User templates enable you to set parameters for new user accounts, based on their group or location. User template parameters are simply copied to a new user. Changes in a user template do not affect existing user accounts.
- Create single user accounts manually and use CoS and user templates to efficiently and quickly deploy new user accounts for voice messaging.

Review Questions

Answer the following questions, and then see Appendix A, "Answers to Review Questions," for the answers.

1. **Which two greetings are not valid in Cisco Unity Connection? (Choose two.)**
   a. Standard
   b. Alternate
   c. External
   d. Error
   e. Vacation
   f. Busy

2. **Which mailbox quota option is not valid?**
   a. Informational quota
   b. Warning quota
   c. Send quota
   d. Send/receive quota

3. If the user does not record a spoken name, which parameter is used to generate a spoken name?

a. Spoken names must be recorded when setting up the mailbox.

b. Display name

c. First and last name

d. Name announcement

4. How many members can users add by default to their private distribution list?

a. 25

b. 50

c. 99

d. 100

e. 200

Chapter 4

Configuring the Cisco Unity Connection System

Upon completing this chapter, you will be able to do the following:

- Describe the Cisco Unity Connection system settings
- Explain the inheritance and precedence of settings when configuring user or call handler settings
- Describe the Cisco Unity Connection general settings, including time and localization settings
- Describe a scenario where time zones are used in different locations of a centralized voice-messaging solution
- Explain the system distribution lists in Cisco Unity Connection and how they are used to send voice messages to multiple users
- Describe the authentication rules that are used to secure access to Cisco Unity Connection
- Describe the roles that can be assigned to users in Cisco Unity Connection to give them administrator access rights for limited parts of the system
- Describe the restriction tables that can be used to prevent calls such as calls to long-distance or international phone numbers
- Describe the components of LDAP integration: LDAP synchronization and LDAP authentication
- Explain how to import users from an LDAP server
- Describe how to automatically convert the synchronized extension of LDAP users
- Explain the search base for the user selection and synchronization
- Explain how an LDAP filter is used to optimize the user selection and synchronization results

This chapter explains Cisco Unity Connection system settings, which contain many configuration options. The chapter also discusses schedules and holiday schedules and their effect on greetings, announcements and so on. System distribution lists and authentication rules are described in more detail, followed by roles and restriction tables to restrict calls for message notification or caller transfer. User templates help you to efficiently create user accounts that are based on standardized templates. Users can be imported from the Lightweight Directory Access Protocol (LDAP) server or Cisco Unified Communications Manager.

Cisco Unity Connection System Settings Overview

This section describes the Cisco Unity Connection system settings.

The system settings in Cisco Unity Connection enable the administrator to modify the default system behavior. Figure 4-1 lists several examples and shows the system settings menu options.

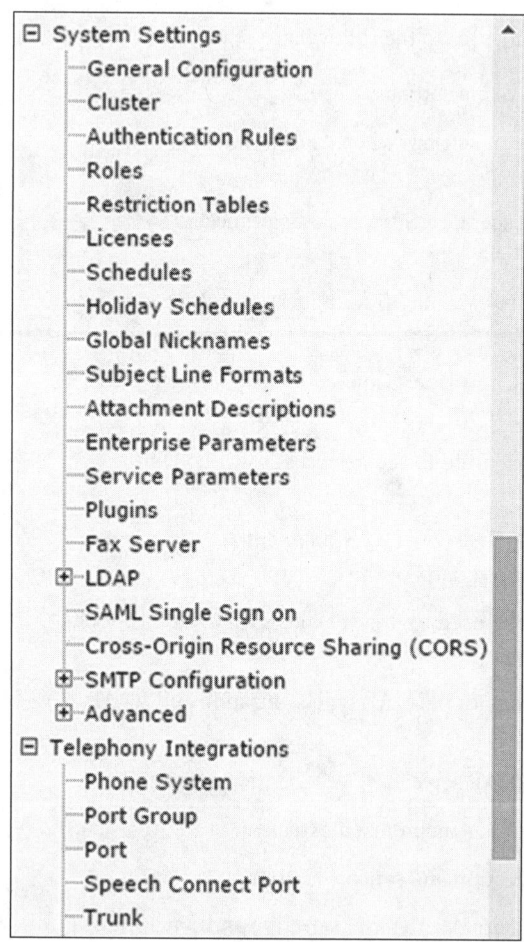

Figure 4-1 *Cisco Unity Connection Administration*

The predefined roles can be used to limit the graphical user interface (GUI) access to certain configuration areas or to limit the telephony user interface (TUI) options for different kinds of administrators.

The enterprise and service parameters in Cisco Unity Connection are like the Cisco Unified Communications Manager (CUCM) enterprise parameters and service parameters. For instance, there are the parameters that allow you to change quality of service (QoS) settings and so on.

LDAP can be integrated and allows the use of the LDAP directory and LDAP authentication. With the use of LDAP authentication, a single password login can be provided to the users.

General Settings Versus User Settings

This section explains the inheritance and precedence of settings when configuring user or call handler settings.

As in CUCM, parameters can be set in the enterprise or service parameters, which are valid for all entities in the Cisco Unity Connection system. A change in the enterprise or service parameters immediately affects all entities. Default parameters, such as a default partition, are preselected for all new objects that contain that parameter field. Figure 4-2 illustrates the inheritance and precedence of settings.

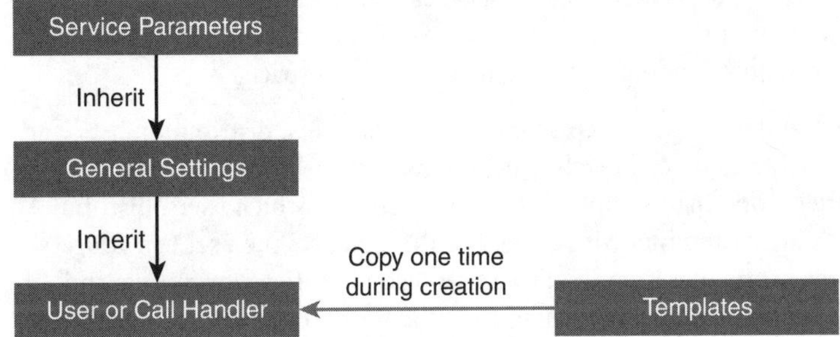

Figure 4-2 *Cisco Unity Connection Inheritance and Precedence of Settings.*

The next level of parameter settings is the general settings, which can alter system settings. A change at this level immediately affects all entities.

A call handler answer calls and can take messages and provide menus of options (for example, "For customer service press 1, for sales press 2"), route calls to users and to other call handlers, and play audiotext (prerecorded information).

The user, call handler, and contact templates can override the general settings, applicable to new objects, because parameters are copied from the template during the creation of a new object, which is called *initial mode*. A change to a template does not affect existing objects.

On the user account, call handler, and contact level, a configuration parameter overrides the general settings and takes precedence. If, for instance, a manager needs additional mailbox space for voice messages, the mailbox quota setting can be modified on the user account level for the manager account only.

General Configuration

This section describes the Cisco Unity Connection general settings, including time and localization settings. Table 4-1 shows the Unity Connection general configuration and the time zone options.

Table 4-1 *Cisco Unity Connection General Configuration*

	Description
General Configuration	System language, recording format, greeting length, default partition, and search scope IP addressing mode (IPv4).
Time Zone	Set during installation. Network Time Protocol (NTP) server may be changed via GUI. Time zone may be changed via command-line interface (CLI).

In Unity Connection, you create partitions as a way to group together objects to which callers and users can address messages or place calls while interacting with Unity Connection. One or more partitions can be grouped together as members of a search space, and a partition can be a member of more than one search space.

Search spaces are used to define the search scope of objects (users, distribution lists, and so on) that a user or outside caller can reach while interacting with Unity Connection. For example, the search scope that is applied to a user identifies which users, distribution lists, or Voice Profile for Internet Messaging (VPIM) contacts the user can address messages to. The search scope that is applied to a user also identifies which users and contacts the user can call by name dialing when using the voice-recognition conversation.

In Cisco Unity Connection Administration, choose **System Settings > General Configuration** to modify the following preconfigured settings:

- The default time zone setting determines when schedules are active. In addition, the default time zone is applied to users and call handlers that have the Use Default Time Zone check box checked.
- From the System Default Language drop-down list, choose the language in which system prompts are played to users and callers. Additional language files can be loaded after installation. Languages are not licensed, and Cisco Unity Connection 10.x does not enforce a limit on the number of languages you can install and use. However, the more languages you install, the less hard disk space is available for storing voice messages. For details, see the "Adding or Removing Unity Connection

Languages" section of the *Install, Upgrade, and Maintenance Guide for Cisco Unity Connection Release 10.x* document available at http://www.cisco.com/c/en/us/td/docs/voice_ip_comm/connection/10x/install_upgrade/guide/10xcuciumgx.html:

- From the Recording Format drop-down list, choose the default format (codec) for recorded messages. The default setting is G.711 mu-law. The other options are PCM linear, G.711 a-law, G.729A, G.726, and GSM 06.10.
- Enter the maximum greeting length for system call handler greetings. The range is 1 to 1200 seconds; the default setting is 90 seconds.
- If automatic gain control (AGC) is enabled, enter the average volume, in decibels, that Cisco Unity Connection automatically maintains for recording voice messages and user greetings, in the Target Decibel Level for Recordings and Messages area. The AGC decibel levels are set in negative numbers.
- From the Default Partition and Default Search drop-down lists, choose the partition and search space that Cisco Unity Connection uses as the default when creating new objects, such as users or templates. If these options are modified in a template, such as when creating a new user, the template settings will be used instead of the default settings.

The time settings are configured in Cisco Unified Operating System Administration, under **Settings > NTP Servers**. Ensure that the external server is stratum 9 or better (9 to 1). The NTP server settings can be configured only on the first node or publisher.

You must have an NTP server reachable for Unity Connection to be installed.

The time zone that is set during the Cisco Unity Connection installation can be changed only via CLI. Any change that is made to the NTP servers can take as many as 5 minutes to take effect.

To see the currently configured time zone, issue the **show timezone config** command. Use the **show timezone list** command to search for the correct time zone. Use the **set timezone** command to change the time zone; for example, use the option 152 to indicate New York time.

A reason to change the time zone could be that a Cisco Unity Connection server has moved to another location (time zone). A wrong time zone makes the time stamps in the Cisco Unity Connection system wrong, which could represent a difficulty when troubleshooting different Cisco Unified Communications systems at the same time. The time zone must be configured on Unity Connection.

Time Zone Usage

This section describes a scenario in which time zones are used at different locations of a centralized voice-messaging solution.

Figure 4-3 shows a centralized Cisco Unity Connection system with users in two locations in different time zones.

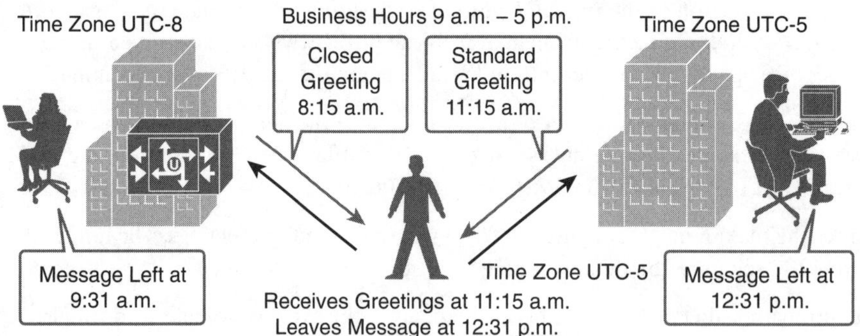

Figure 4-3 *Cisco Unity Connection Different Time Zone Example*

Mailboxes, call handlers, greetings, and other objects in Cisco Unity Connection rely on the time zone and a schedule. Users with a schedule that is set to business hours—Monday through Friday from 9:00 a.m. to 5:00 p.m. (0900 to 1700)—has an active standard transfer rule on their mailbox during this time.

For example, in combination with time zone settings, the business hours are set to eastern standard time (EST, coordinated universal time [UTC] –5 hours). A call that originates at 4:00 p.m. (1600) Pacific standard time (PST, UTC –8 hours), and that is directed to a Cisco Unity Connection system based in the EST zone, actually reaches Cisco Unity Connection at 7:00 p.m. (1900).

In the example, the business hours are set to Monday through Friday from 9:00 a.m. to 5:00 p.m. (0900 to 1700). The time zones are set to UTC –5 and to UTC –8. If a caller who is based in EST calls a local number at 11:15 a.m. (1115), Cisco Unity Connection answers the call at 11:15 a.m. (1115). If the caller dials a number that is based in PST, the call arrives at 8:15 a.m. (0815) PST and Cisco Unity Connection plays a closed greeting, according to the business hour schedule.

The time zones are used in different ways. When a call is forwarded to voice mail, the configured time zone of the called user controls the announcement, depending on the time when the message is left. The greeting (for example, standard or closed) is also chosen according to the time of the call at the called location, in combination with a schedule. The same is true for the call handlers.

Schedules are one of the variables that Cisco Unity Connection uses to manage calls. Call handler transfer rules can be varied based on a schedule, and schedules can be applied to routing rules to change call-routing patterns for different time periods. Schedules also affect when user and call handler greetings play.

Cisco Unity Connection offers three predefined schedules: All Hours, Weekdays, and Voice Recognition Update. All can be modified, but not deleted. By default, the Weekdays schedule is configured to observe standard hours from 8:00 a.m. through 5:00 p.m. (0800 through 1700), Monday through Friday. The schedule is also configured to observe the predefined holiday schedule, which does not contain any dates or times by default.

For each schedule that is created or modified, multiple ranges of hours and days make up the standard and closed hours. The definition of these ranges is as follows:

- **Standard hours:** The standard hours and days make up the normal business hours, when the organization is open. Standard hours can include multiple time ranges and different time ranges on different days. For example, standard hours for an organization might be Monday through Friday from 8:00 a.m. (0800) to noon (1200) and 1:00 p.m. to 5:00 p.m. (1300 to 1700), to accommodate a lunch break, and Saturday from 9:00 a.m. to 1:00 p.m. (0900 to 1300). Standard transfer rules are in effect during the days and time ranges that are added to the standard schedule; standard user and call handler greetings play during standard hours.
- **Closed hours:** The hours and days that are not identified as standard hours are considered nonbusiness hours, when the organization is closed. Closed user and call handler transfer rules operate at all times—including holidays—that are not specified by the standard schedule. Closed user and call handler greetings play according to the closed hours.

You can specify the holidays in advance (that is, for future years). In addition to other schedules, you can set up a holiday schedule that defines specific holiday dates and times:

- When a holiday schedule is in effect, Cisco Unity Connection plays holiday greetings (if enabled) and observes closed-hours transfer rules. Several years of holidays can be set up at one time. Because many holidays occur on different dates each year, confirm that the holiday schedule remains accurate annually.
- Holiday greetings for users and call handlers play during this period.

Cisco Unity Connection Distribution Lists

This section explains the system distribution lists in Cisco Unity Connection and how they are used to send voice messages to multiple users. Figure 4-4 illustrates the Unity Connection system and private distribution list options.

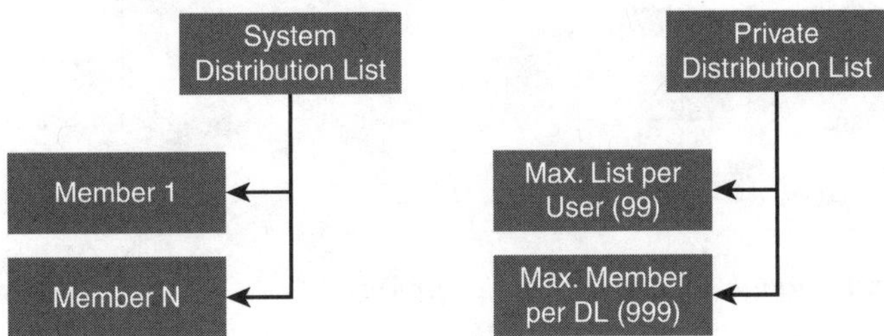

Figure 4-4 *Cisco Unity Connection Distribution Lists*

Members of a system distribution list typically are users who need the same information regularly, such as employees in a department or members of a team. The predefined system distribution lists are the following:

- Undeliverable Messages
- All Voice Mail Users
- All Voicemail-Enabled Contacts

A voicemail user can configure private distribution lists. An administrator can define a maximum of 99 private distribution lists per user; the default is 25.

Within the private distribution list, the number of members can be set to a maximum of 999; the default is 99.

Cisco Unity Connection Authentication

This section describes the authentication rules that are used to secure access to Cisco Unity Connection.

For Cisco Unity Connection users who are authenticated by an LDAP directory, this authentication rule applies only to voicemail passwords (PINs). The LDAP directory, rather than Cisco Unity Connection, manages web authentication and failed sign-in attempts. For Cisco Unity Connection users who are not linked to user data in an LDAP directory, this authentication rule applies both to voice-mail passwords and to web passwords. Figure 4-5 shows the different authentication rule options.

Edit Authentication Rule

Display Name*	Recommended Voice Mail Auther ✕
Failed Sign-In	3 Attempts ☐ No Limit for Failed Sign-Ins
Reset Every Failed Sign-In Attempts	30 Minutes
Lockout Duration	30 Minutes ☐ Administrator Must Unlock
Minimum Duration between Credential Changes	1440 Minutes
Credential Expires After	180 Days ☐ Never Expires
Expiration Warning Days	15 Days
Minimum Credential Length	6
Stored Number of Previous Credentials	5

☑ Check for Trivial Passwords

Figure 4-5 *Cisco Unity Connection Authentication Rule Options*

The following settings can be configured under **System Settings > Authentication Rules** section of the Cisco Unity Connection Administration:

- **Display Name:** Enter a descriptive name for the authentication rule.
- **Failed Sign-In:** Enter the number of failed sign in attempts that are allowed before an account is locked. When this field is set to zero, no limit is placed on the number of failed sign-in attempts, and the user will not be locked out of the account. The default setting is three attempts.
- **No Limit for Failed Sign-Ins:** Check this check box to set no limit on the number of failed sign-in attempts and prevent users from being locked out of the account.
- **Reset Every Failed Sign-In Attempts:** Enter the number of minutes after which Cisco Unity Connection will clear the count of failed sign-in attempts (unless the failed sign in limit is already reached and the account is locked). When this field is set to zero, a failed sign-in attempt will result in the user account being locked until an administrator manually unlocks it. The default setting is 30 minutes.
- **Lockout Duration:** Enter the number of minutes that a user account will remain locked after the allowed number of failed sign in attempts has been reached. While the account is locked, users cannot access Cisco Unity Connection by phone. If a value of zero is entered, the account remains locked until an administrator manually unlocks it. The default is 30 minutes.
- **Administrator Must Unlock:** Check this check box so that locked accounts will remain locked until manually unlocked by an administrator.
- **Minimum Duration Between Credential Changes:** Enter the number of minutes that must elapse between password changes. This setting does not apply when administrators change the password in Cisco Unity Connection Administration. The default is 240 minutes.
- **Credential Expires After:** The default setting is 180 days.
- **Never Expires:** Check this check box so that passwords that are based on this authentication rule never expire. Use of this check box is most applicable for low-security users or for accounts that more than one person can access. Note that when this check box is checked, users can still change passwords at any time.
- **Expiration Warning Days:** Enter the number of days before passwords expire that Cisco Unity Connection will warn users about that expiration. A value of zero means that Cisco Unity Connection will not warn users that a password is about to expire.
- **Minimum Credential Length:** Enter the required number of digits for user passwords. Enter a value between 1 and 64, where the default is 8 digits for the password and 6 digits for the PIN. In general, shorter passwords are easier to use, but longer passwords are more secure, so more than 8 characters (password) or 6 digits (PIN) are recommended. When the minimum credential length changes, users will be required to use the new length the next time that they change their passwords.

- **Stored Number of Previous Credentials:** Enter a value for the number of previous passwords that Cisco Unity Connection stores for a user. When a user enters a new password, Cisco Unity Connection compares it to the stored passwords, and rejects it if it matches a password in the history. A value of zero means that Cisco Unity Connection will not store any previous passwords for the user. The default is five passwords.
- **Check for Trivial Passwords:** Check this check box. The next section provides more information about trivial passwords.

Check for Trivial Passwords

Table 4-2 gives examples of providing unsecure trivial user passwords.

Table 4-2 *Cisco Unity Connection Trivial Password Example*

Description	Example
The digits are not all the same.	9999
The digits are not consecutive.	1234 or 4321
The password is not the same as the primary extension.	2001
The password is the reverse of the primary extension.	1002
The same digits are used more than twice.	900012
The password is a 1-digit increment of a previous password.	20185 or 20186
The password contains fewer than 3 different digits.	18181

To secure access to Cisco Unity Connection via TUI, check the **Check for Trivial Passwords** check box for the authentication rules and create a company password policy to enforce the password check. If checking for trivial passwords, Cisco Unity Connection verifies that a new password meets the system-specified criteria when user phone passwords are changed.

In addition to checking the Check for Trivial Passwords check box, consider providing users with a password policy that advises them to avoid unsupported passwords.

Roles

This section describes the roles that can be assigned to users in Cisco Unity Connection to give them administrator access rights for limited parts of the system.

Cisco Unity Connection offers levels of privileges for administrator accounts that are set according to a list of predefined roles as illustrated in Table 4-3. Roles specify which tasks administrators can execute. Before adding administrator accounts, choose the roles that are assigned to each account.

Table 4-3 *Cisco Unity Connection Predefined Roles*

Role	Description
Audio text administrator	Administers call handlers, directory handlers, and interview handlers
Audit administrator	Administers application and database auditing
Greeting administrator	Manages call handler recorded greetings via TUI
Help desk administrator	Resets user passwords and unlocks user accounts, view user settings
Mailbox access delegate account	Access to all messages via messaging APIs
Remote administrator	Administers the database using remote management tools
System administrator	Top-level Unity Connection administrator; access to all Unity Connection administrative functions, reports, and tools for server and users
Technician	Access to functions that enable management of system and phone system integration settings, viewing of all system and user settings, and can run all reports and diagnostic tools
User Administrator	Administers users; access to all user administration functions and user administrations tools

System administrator is the role of the default administrator account that the installer specified during initial setup of Unity Connection. A system administrator is the only role that has permission to create administrative accounts. There also is a tenant administrator.

To see the specific privileges for each administrator role, choose **System Settings > Roles** in Cisco Unity Connection Administration, and click the name of the role. Changes cannot be made to the permissions that are associated with each predefined role.

Cisco Unity Connection Restriction Tables

This section describes the restriction tables that can be used to prevent calls such as calls to long-distance or international phone numbers.

Cisco Unity Connection comes with predefined restriction tables, which can be modified but not deleted. By default, each of these restriction tables prevents access to long-distance phone numbers.

The following restriction tables are predefined:

- **Default Fax:** This table restricts the numbers that can be used for fax delivery.

- **Default Outdial:** This table restricts the numbers that can be used for message notifications. The table also restricts the user extensions that Cisco Unity Connection can dial when the phone is chosen as the recording and playback device in the Media Master.
- **Default System Transfer:** This table restricts the numbers that can be used for caller system transfers, which allow unidentified callers to transfer to a number that they specify. For example, callers might want to dial a lobby or conference room phone that is not associated with a Cisco Unity Connection user. By default, the table does not allow Cisco Unity Connection to dial any numbers.
- **Default Transfer:** This table restricts the numbers that can be used for call transfer.
- **User-Defined and Automatically Added Alternate Extensions:** This table restricts the numbers that can be offered as alternate extensions. For example, you can restrict a lobby or conference room extension so that users who often call Cisco Unity Connection from those shared phones are not automatically prompted to add the number as an alternate extension.

Cisco Unity Connection LDAP Integration

This section describes the components of LDAP integration: LDAP synchronization and LDAP authentication (as illustrated in Figure 4-6).

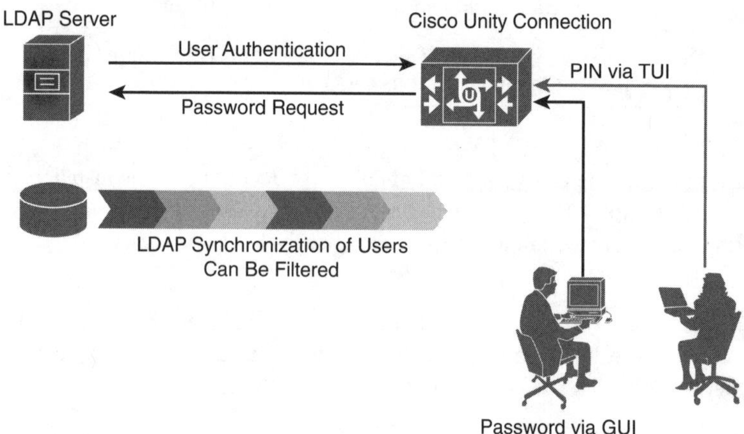

Figure 4-6 *Cisco Unity Connection LDAP Integration*

LDAP integration comprises two parts. In LDAP synchronization, users are imported from the LDAP server to Cisco Unity Connection. Cisco Unity Connection cannot copy any information to the LDAP server. In LDAP authentication, users can use the domain password to log in to Cisco Unity Connection user pages. However, the PIN is always kept local in Cisco Unity Connection.

Import of Users from LDAP Server

This section explains how to import users from an LDAP server.

To import users from LDAP, activate the Cisco DirSync service under **Tools > Service Activation** in Cisco Unified Serviceability.

To set up the LDAP system, configure the following parameters under the section **System Settings > LDAP** in the Cisco Unity Connection Administration:

- **Enable Synchronizing from LDAP Server:** Check this check box so that Cisco Unity Connection gets basic information about Cisco Unity Connection users from the LDAP directories that are specified on the LDAP Directory configuration page.
- **LDAP Server Type:** Choose the type of LDAP server from which Cisco Unity Connection will import the user data.
- **LDAP Attribute for User ID:** Choose the field in the LDAP directory that should appear in the Alias field in Cisco Unity Connection for imported LDAP users. sAMAccountName specifies, for example, jdoe as the user alias. If you want to integrate with multiple domains, use the userPrincipalName (for example, jdoe@cisco.com).

The LDAP directory configuration is like the CUCM LDAP directory configuration. The configuration requires the following LDAP directory settings:

- **LDAP Manager Distinguished Name and LDAP Password:** Enter the name and password of an LDAP directory administrator account that has access to data in the LDAP user search base that is specified in the LDAP User Search Base field.
- **LDAP User Search Base:** Enter the LDAP directory location that contains the user data that should be synchronized with Cisco Unity Connection user data. Cisco Unity Connection imports all users in the tree or subtree (domain or organizational unit) that the search base specifies.

The synchronization can be done once or on a regular basis:

- **Perform Sync Just Once:** Check this check box to resynchronize user data in the Cisco Unity Connection database and in the LDAP directory one time, rather than at regular intervals.
- **Perform a Re-Sync Every:** To resynchronize user data in the Cisco Unity Connection database with user data in the LDAP directory at regular intervals, specify the frequency with which the resynchronizations should occur. The minimum interval is 6 hours. The first resynchronization occurs on the date and time that is specified in the Next Re-Sync Time field.

These fields can be synchronized with an LDAP server:

- **User ID:** The value of the LDAP field that is listed here is stored in the Alias field in the Cisco Unity Connection database. The field that is listed here was specified on the LDAP Setup page, in the LDAP Attribute for User ID list.
- **Middle Name:** Choose which value from the LDAP directory to store here: middleName or initials.
- **Manager ID:** The value of the manager field in the LDAP directory is always stored in the Manager ID field in the Cisco Unity Connection database.

- **Phone Number:** Choose which value from the LDAP directory to store here: telephoneNumber or ipPhone.
- **Title:** Synchronize the title.
- **Mobile Number:** Synchronize the mobile number that is stored in the attribute mobile.
- **Directory URI:** Synchronize the URI from the msRTCSIP-primaryuseraddress or mail. You may select None to not synchronize this parameter.
- **First Name:** The value of the givenName field in the LDAP directory is always stored in the First Name field.
- **Last Name:** The value of the sn field (surname) in the LDAP directory is always stored in the Last Name field. Without this parameter defined in the LDAP server, the user is not listed in the import result window.
- **Department:** The value of the department field in the LDAP directory is always stored in the Department field. The value of the department field in the LDAP directory is always stored in the Department field.
- **Mail ID:** Choose which value from the LDAP directory to store here: mail or sAMAccountName.
- **Home Number:** A configured home number is synchronized.
- **Pager Number:** A configured pager number can be synchronized as well.

In addition to these parameters, you can synchronize up to five custom attributes. In the group information section, you can specify a mask to apply to synced telephone numbers to create a new line for inserted users.

Finally, set the LDAP server parameters IP address and port 389. To point to a Microsoft Global Catalog, use port 3268 instead. The connection to the LDAP server should be secured. Cisco Unity Connection uses port 636 when you choose LDAPS for the protocol used to communicate with domain controllers. If you are using Secure Sockets Layer (SSL) to encrypt data that is transmitted between the LDAP server Global Catalog and the Cisco Unity Connection server, the port 3269 is used.

To start the import process, select the LDAP server from which you want to import users. If you do not see any users, the LDAP server has not been successfully synchronized with Cisco Unity Connection. In addition, users without a last name that is configured in the LDAP server are not displayed in this import list.

When all issues are resolved, choose the voice-mail template that you want to apply. Choose the users whom you want to import and start the import process. Also, you can import all users rather than choosing individual users.

Imported User

Compared to a manually configured user, the Alias, First Name, and Last Name fields for an imported user are read-only fields. If you want to change these field parameters, you must make the change in the LDAP server.

You can also convert the LDAP integrated user to a local user as shown in Figure 4-7. This process can be reversed by integrating a local user with the LDAP server. However, both of these processes must be done manually. CUCM works differently. Local users are automatically converted to LDAP users (again) after the next LDAP synchronization.

Name
Alias* jdoe
First Name John
Last Name Doe
Display Name John Doe
SMTP Address jdoe @cuc10
Initials
Title
Employee ID

LDAP Integration Status
Integrate with LDAP Directory
Do Not Integrate with LDAP Directory

Phone
Extension* 2001

Figure 4-7 *Cisco Unity Connection LDAP Imported User*

You can modify the extension number for single users. For multiple users, you can automate this process in the advanced LDAP settings.

Phone Number Conversion

This section describes how to automatically convert the synchronized extension of LDAP users.

If you want to map phone numbers in the LDAP directory to extensions in Cisco Unity Connection but the phone numbers do not match the extensions, you can add a regular expression and a replacement pattern that together convert the phone numbers into extensions, as shown in Table 4-4.

Table 4-4 *Cisco Unity Connection Phone Number Conversion with Regular Expressions*

Regular Expression	Replacement	Example Conversion
(.*)	$1	Use the LDAP phone number as the Connection extension.
.*(\d{4})	$1	Use the last 4 digits of the LDAP phone number as the Connection extension.

Table 4-4 *Continued*

Regular Expression	Replacement	Example Conversion
(\d{4}).	$1	Use the first 4 digits of the LDAP phone number as the Connection extension.
.*(\d{4})	9$1	Prefix a 9 to the last 4 digits of the LDAP phone number.

The following are the mechanisms of regular expressions.

- The regular expression determines which phone numbers to operate on (for example, phone numbers that are ten digits long) and the portion of the phone numbers to use as a basis for the extensions (for example, the last four digits).
- The replacement pattern specifies to use either the values selected by the regular expression or to perform additional operations (for example, prefix a 9).

Cisco Unity Connection uses the regular expression package of the Java library. Table 4-4 lists some examples of the conversions that are possible with the expanded functionality.

Note the following:

- Cisco Unity Connection automatically removes nonnumeric characters from the phone number, so the regular expression does not need to account for nonnumeric characters.
- LDAP phone numbers are converted to Cisco Unity Connection extensions only once, when you first synchronize Cisco Unity Connection data with LDAP data. On subsequent, scheduled synchronizations, values in the Cisco Unity Connection Extension field are not updated with changes to the LDAP phone number. As a result, you can change the LDAP phone number as required, including specifying a completely different number, and the extension will not be overwritten the next time that Cisco Unity Connection synchronizes data with the LDAP directory.
- You can write more than one combination of a regular expression and a replacement pattern that produces the same result.

Search Base

This section explains the search base for the user selection and synchronization.

The Cisco DirSync service, which is enabled through the Cisco Unity Connection Serviceability web page, performs the synchronization. When the service is enabled, as many as five synchronization agreements can be configured in Cisco Unity Connection.

An agreement specifies a search base, which is a position in the LDAP tree where Cisco Unity Connection will begin its search for user accounts to import. Cisco Unity Connection can import only users that exist in the domain that is specified by the search base for a particular synchronization agreement. Figure 4-8 shows two synchronization agreements:

- One synchronization agreement specifies User Search Base 1 and imports users jsmith, jdoe, and jbloggs.
- The other synchronization agreement specifies User Search Base 2 and imports users jjones, bfoo, and tbrown.

The CCMDirMgr account is not imported because it does not reside below the point in the LDAP tree that the user search base specifies.

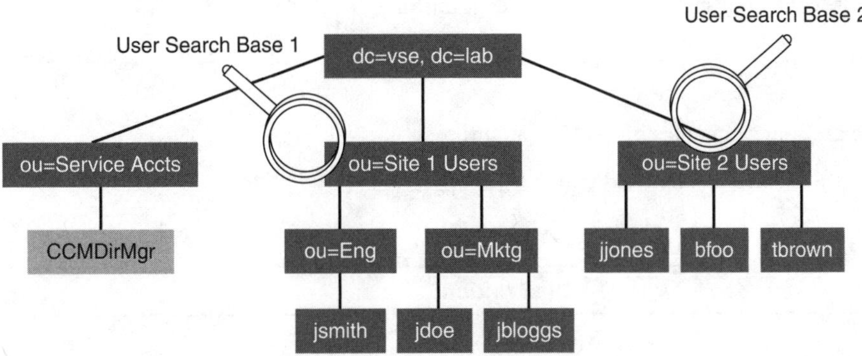

Figure 4-8 *Cisco Unity Connection LDAP Search Base Example*

When users are organized in a structure in the LDAP directory, use that structure to control which user groups are imported. In this example, a single synchronization agreement could have been used to specify the root of the domain. However, that search base would also have imported the Service Accts (except when the sn fields were empty). The search base does not need to specify the domain root; it may specify any point in the tree.

LDAP Filter

This section explains how an LDAP filter is used to optimize the user selection and synchronization results.

You can configure only five search agreements. If you need more than five search agreements, you must point the search agreement to the root domain in combination with LDAP filters. With these filters you can, for example, only import users from certain subdomains or from certain locations. Filters give you more scalability for importing users from large LDAP directories with many subdomains and organizational units.

Table 4-5 describes the search filter syntax that can be used for the LDAP filter in the LDAP directory configuration. Search filters allow the definition of search criteria and provide more efficient and effective searches. Unicode strings represent these search filters.

Table 4-5 *LDAP Filters*

Examples	Description
(objectClass=*)	All objects
(&(objectCategory=person) (objectClass=user)(!cn=john))	All user objects except john
(sn=sm*)	All objects with a surname that starts with sm
(&(objectCategory=person) (objectClass=contact) (|(sn=Smith) (sn=Johnson)))	All contacts with a surname that is equal to Smith or Johnson

These are some examples of LDAP search filters.

Table 4-6 lists frequently used search filter operators.

Table 4-6 *Search Filter Operators*

Operator	Description
=	Equal to
~=	Approximately equal to
<=	Less than or equal to
>=	Greater than or equal to
&	AND
|	OR
!	NOT

To match a part of a directory number (for example, to look for the groups in two subtrees), use a filter such as the following:

```
(&(objectClass=group)(|(ou:dn:=Chicago)(ou:dn:=Miami)))
```

This filter will find groups that have an organizational unit component in the directory number (DN), which is either Chicago or Miami.

To exclude entities that match an expression, use an exclamation point (!):

```
(&(objectClass=group)(&(ou:dn:=Chicago)(!(ou:dn:=Boston))))
```

This filter will find all Chicago groups except those that have a Boston organizational unit component. Note the extra parentheses: (!(<expression>)).

After creating the filter, apply the filter in the LDAP directory configuration. Because only one filter can be selected in the LDAP directory configuration, more organizational units or other objects must be added to the filter. The filter can contain a maximum of 2048 characters. Enclose the filter text within parentheses ( ).

The LDAP filter filters the results of LDAP searches. LDAP users that match the filter are imported into the Cisco Unity Connection database, whereas LDAP users that do not match the filter are not imported. The filter text that is entered must comply with the regular LDAP search-filter standards that are specified in RFC 4515. You should verify the LDAP search filter against the LDAP directory and search base.

Note You can test the filter with LDAP browsers; for example, you can test with Softerra LDAP Administrator at http://www.ldapadministrator.com/.

Import of Users from CUCM

This section shows the import process for users that are located on CUCM.

To import users from CUCM, activate the Cisco Administrative XML (AXL) service on CUCM. Then configure the AXL server in the phone system configuration. Add a new AXL server with the IP address of the CUCM and the port number 8443. Then enter the username and password of the CUCM application user.

Users who are not configured with a primary extension cannot be imported. Go to the end-user configuration in CUCM and set the primary extension. Then go back to Cisco Unity Connection and try the import process again. Users who are already configured in Cisco Unity Connection are not shown during the import process.

Importing users from CUCM has the advantage that all users are already synchronized and filtered from the LDAP directory. The preferred way of selecting the user source is to have the primary extension number that is configured for all users.

Imported CUCM User

Figure 4-9 shows the CUCM imported user configuration. In contrast with an LDAP synchronized user, the Extension field is also a read-only field. If you want to change these parameters, you must make the change in CUCM. CUCM imported users cannot be migrated to LDAP synchronized users. The LDAP integration status cannot be modified.

Name

Alias* jdoe

First Name John

Last Name Doe

Display Name John Doe

SMTP Address jdoe @cuc10

Initials

Title

Employee ID

LDAP Integration Status

Integrate with LDAP Directory

Do Not Integrate with LDAP Directory

Phone

Extension* 2001

Figure 4-9 *Imported CUCM User*

Summary

This section summarizes the key points that were discussed in this chapter:

- Cisco Unity Connection system settings are the core of the Cisco Unity Connection configuration. These settings control integrations, enterprise and service parameters, access rights to Cisco Unity Connection and so on.
- During the installation, the correct time zone is set. This time zone controls the schedules and holidays and which greeting or transfer rule is active.
- Use the authentication rules to secure the access to Cisco Unity Connection via GUI or TUI. Enable the check for trivial passwords. For administrator access, predefined roles are set up. The system administrator has the most powerful access.
- Restriction tables can be used to restrict caller transfer or message notification to certain numbers. By default, international and long-distance numbers are disallowed.
- By using LDAP synchronization, you can import users from an LDAP server to Cisco Unity Connection. Cisco Unity Connection cannot copy data to the LDAP server. When using LDAP authentication, users can log in to the user pages by entering the domain password.
- You can also import users from the CUCM, because you can assume that the CUCM user base is already optimized.

Review Questions

Answer the following questions, and then see Appendix A, "Answers to Review Questions," for the answers.

1. **What is the default maximum greeting length (in seconds) in Cisco Unity Connection?**

    a. 60

    b. 90

    c. 120

    d. 180

    e. 300

2. **What does the question mark (?) mean when configuring patterns in restriction tables?**

    a. Match zero or more digits

    b. Match exactly one digit

    c. Match one or more digits

    d. None of the above

3. **Which configuration is the correct LDAP user search base configuration for a default domain cisco.com?**

    a. dc=Users, dc=cisco, dc=com

    b. cn=Users, dc=cisco, dc=com

    c. cn=Users, cn=cisco, dc=com

    d. cn=Users, cn=cisco, cn=com

4. **Which option is a userPrincipalName?**

    a. jdoe

    b. cisco.com\jdoe

    c. jdoe@cisco.com

    d. None of the above

5. **Which LDAP filter would you use to filter on the last name Doe?**

    a. (sn=doe)

    b. (ln=doe)

    c. !(sn=doe)

    d. |(ln=doe)

Chapter 5

Implementing Cisco Unity Connection Dial Plan and Call Management

Upon completing this chapter, you will be able to do the following:

- Describe Cisco Unity Connection dial plan partitions and search spaces
- Show an example of a customer requirement to implement the Cisco Unity Connection dial plan
- Describe the different kinds of call handlers that are available in Cisco Unity Connection
- Show how a call handler in Cisco Unity Connection can be reached
- Show an example that combines all three call handlers into one auto-attendant
- Describe call handler templates and how they are set up
- Describe the actions you can apply to caller input that is entered by the caller
- Describe the call flow in Cisco Unity Connection with the default call handlers
- Analyze the greeting options for the opening greeting call handler
- Analyze the call action based on the caller input
- Describe the default operator call handler functionality
- Show the settings of the Goodbye call handler
- Describe the directory handler and how to limit the search scope in Cisco Unity Connection
- Describe the interview handler, which is used to interview callers and record their answers

This chapter explains the Cisco Unity Connection dial plan components: partitions and search spaces. Partitions group objects, and search spaces comprise the search rights for objects in the included partitions. Call handlers are used to build auto-attendant functionality with Cisco Unity Connection.

Cisco Unity Connection Dial Plan Components

The dial plan in Cisco Unity Connection consists of partitions and search spaces. These entities can be compared to Cisco Unified Communications Manager (CUCM) partitions and calling search spaces (CSSs). Figure 5-1 shows an example of the use of search spaces in Unity Connection.

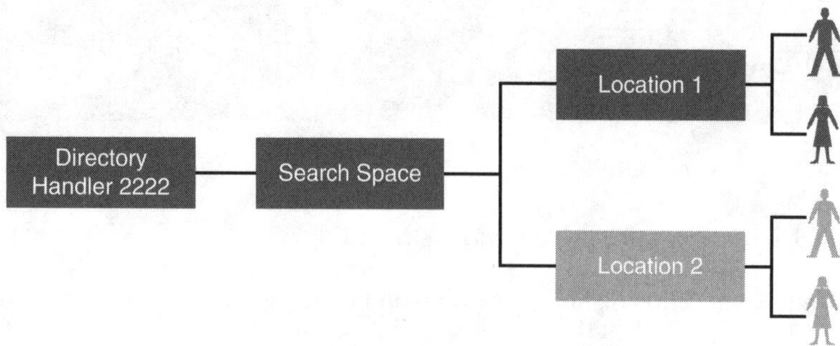

Figure 5-1 *Cisco Unity Connection Dial Plan*

- During the installation of Cisco Unity Connection, a hostname must be entered. This hostname is the default name of the preconfigured partition and search space. The partition and search space then appear as preselected components. For example, all new users or call handlers will belong to this default partition and will be assigned the default search space.
- A search space can be used to control where a directory handler—and respectively, the caller—can search for users (for example, when the caller selects the options to dial a user or send a message). A search space can limit a caller to search on the current server only, all servers, or in certain partitions or locations only.

For example, in a multisite scenario, the administrator can create one directory handler per location. These site-specific directory handlers can search for users in the current site (partition) only, not throughout the complete company directory. Another example would be to place the managers in a manager partition so that external users cannot directly search and dial the managers.

Comparing Dial Plans

The dial plan components in Cisco Unity Connection and CUCM are similar, as illustrated in Table 5-1.

Table 5-1 *Cisco Unity Connection Versus CUCM Dial Plan Comparison*

Application	Cisco Unity Connection	CUCM
Dial plan components	Partition and search space	Partition and CSS
Dial plan terminology	Dial plan	Calling privileges
Partitions assigned to	Users, contacts, distribution lists, call handlers, Voice Profile for Internet Mail (VPIM) locations	Directory number, route pattern, translation pattern, hunt pilot
Search space assigned to	Users, routing rules, call handlers, VPIM locations	Directory number, IP phone, gateway, trunk, translation pattern, (MWI) numbers

Both systems use the same elements, but the terminology differs:

- Search space in Cisco Unity Connection is referred to as *CSS* in CUCM.
- Dial plan in Cisco Unity Connection is referred to as *calling privileges* in CUCM.
- In Cisco Unity Connection, CoS describes a feature set that a user can use.

In Cisco Unity Connection, partitions are assigned to objects such as: user primary and alternate extensions, contacts, system distribution lists, call handler, or VPIM locations. In CUCM, partitions are assigned to components such as directory numbers, route and translation patters, and hunt pilots.

In Cisco Unity Connection, search spaces are assigned to objects such as: users, routing rules, call handlers, or VPIM locations. In CUCM, CSSs are assigned to directory numbers, the phone device, gateways, trunks, translation patterns, virtual machine (VM) ports, and MWI numbers.

Dial Plan Example

The company has a headquarters and a remote site with a centralized Cisco Unity Connection. Each site should offer a site-specific directory handler that can search in that specific site only using the elements that are listed in Figure 5-2.

Now, if a caller dials the number of the directory handler at headquarters (HQ), only users in the HQ partition can be called. The search is limited to the included partition—in this case, the HQ partition—in the search space that is assigned to the directory handler.

The same extension can exist in every partition. However, an alias can exist only once in Cisco Unity Connection. If you attempt to add an alias a second time, the following message appears: "The alias has already been assigned to another object in this location."

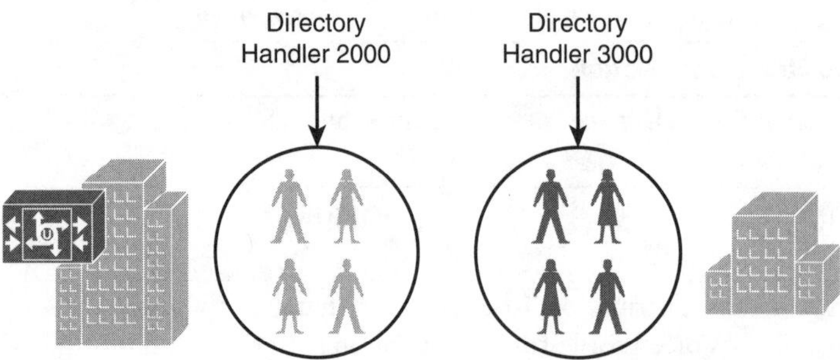

Figure 5-2 *Cisco Unity Connection Dial Plan Example*

Cisco Unity Connection Call Handler Types

In Cisco Unity Connection call management, the following three kinds of call handlers can be selected, as shown in Figure 5-3.

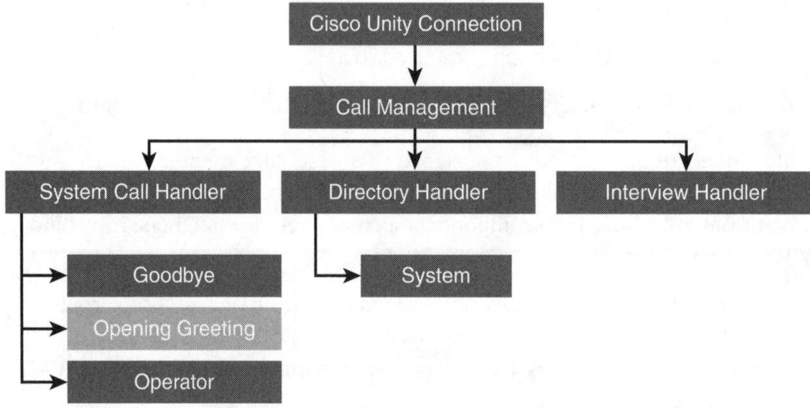

Figure 5-3 *Cisco Unity Connection Call Handler Types*

Keep in mind the following points regarding the call handlers:

- System call handlers are used for greetings and can offer the caller different call actions per digit selection. You can build an auto-attendant with these call handlers. There are three preconfigured system call handlers:
  - **Goodbye:** The call action is set to hang up after the greeting.
  - **Opening greeting:** The greeting welcomes the caller and offers to dial by extension, dial by name, or connect to the operator. The opening greeting is the greeting that a caller hears if a user who is not a subscriber or does not transmit the calling number calls the general voice-messaging system number. The opening greeting is invoked also if a call is forwarded to Unity Connection and

the forwarding number is not a primary or alternate extension or is not accessible based on the search space.

- **Operator:** Until it is reconfigured, the call action is set to take a message after the greeting. Typically, it is configured to transfer to the designated operator extension during working hours.

- An interview handler asks a caller questions and records the answers. The recorded message can be sent to any voice-mail user.
- Directory handlers allow callers to search for users in Cisco Unity Connection or connected voice-messaging systems. A directory handler allows a caller to dial by extension or by name. By default, a caller can press 4 during the opening greeting to reach the default system directory handler and search for numbers in the company directory.

Cisco Unity Connection Call Handler Comparison

Every call handler is dedicated to a specific purpose and therefore is limited in its options but optimized for its required tasks. Table 5-2 gives you a quick overview of the call handlers and what each type of handler supports.

Table 5-2 *Cisco Unity Call Handler Comparison*

Options	System Call Handler	Directory Handler	Interview Handler
Call handler templates	X		
Transfer rules	X		
Caller input	X	Limited	
Greeting management	X	Limited	
Post Greeting Recording	X		
After message/interview action	X		X
Interview question			X
Call handler owners	X		

Call Handler Reachability

This section shows how a call handler in Cisco Unity Connection can be reached. Figure 5-4 illustrates the comparison between CUCM and Unity Connection call hander reachability. Keep in mind CUCM and Unity Connection work as a team together for external callers to reach Unity Connection call handlers.

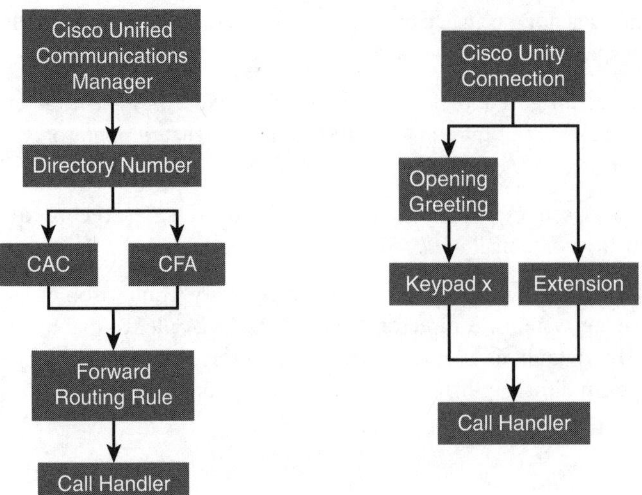

Figure 5-4 *Cisco CUCM and Unity Connection Call Handler Reachability*

If an extension is assigned to the call handler, the forwarded call can directly match the correct call handler. The preparation on CUCM to reach a call handler on Cisco Unity Connection is minimal. As when reaching a subscriber mailbox, a directory number is needed to forward the calls to Cisco Unity Connection. Call handlers need a directory number that is configured on CUCM to be directly reachable. The directory number must forward all calls to Cisco Unity Connection. On Cisco Unity Connection, configure a new forward routing rule with the call action. Then configure a rule condition for a forwarding station that matches the directory number you configured on CUCM.

A caller who already reached Cisco Unity Connection (for example, the opening greeting) can select a call handler by a menu (entering a predefined and configured digit) or simply dial the extension of the call handler.

Auto-Attendant Example

In the example shown in Figure 5-5, a system call handler answers the call. In this case, the system call handler plays a greeting and offers the caller some choices.

Note the following options as a caller dials in to the opening greeting:

- The caller can press 1 on the phone keypad to search the company directory for an employee—if that employee is listed.
- The caller can press 2 to hear another greeting that is played by another system call handler. That greeting brings the caller to an interview handler that asks for the caller name, the job for which the caller wants to apply, and so on.

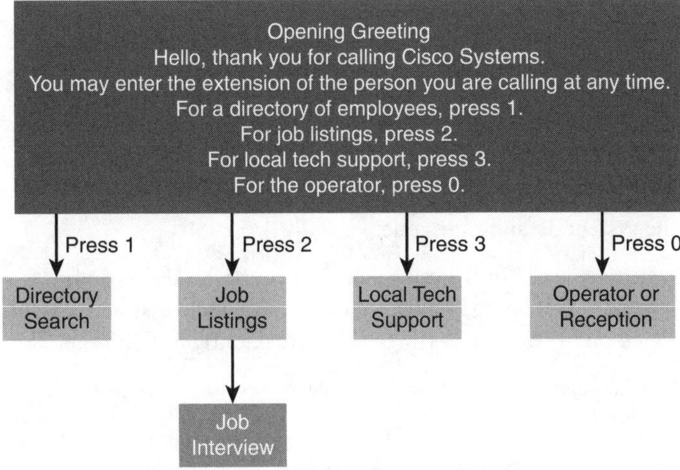

Figure 5-5 *Cisco Unity Connection Auto-Attendant Example*

- The caller can press 3 to reach local technical support with another greeting.
- The caller can press 0 to reach the operator.

A hidden menu (an option that is not announced) that requires an authentication after the caller presses a number can also be offered when building an auto-attendant. For more complex solutions, deploy Cisco Unified Contact Center Express, where you can, for example, connect databases and build modular scripts for incoming calls.

Call Handler Templates

Call handler templates are only applied when a new call handler is created. Changes in the template do not affect existing call handlers. Figure 5-6 illustrates the different call handler template options.

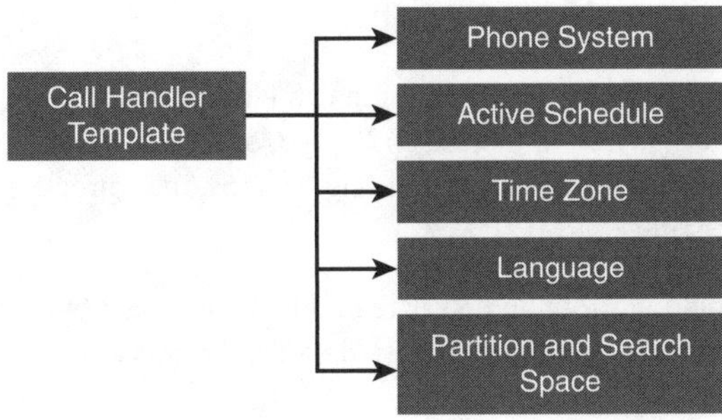

Figure 5-6 *Cisco Unity Connection Call Handler Template Options*

Configure the call handler template parameters as follows:

- **Phone System:** Choose the phone system that the template uses.
- **Active Schedule:** Choose a schedule from the list, to specify the days and times that the standard and closed greetings play. The default is All Hours.
- **Use System Default Time Zone:** Check this check box to have Cisco Unity Connection apply the system default time zone.
- **Time Zone:** Choose the time zone for the call handler, or check the Use System Default Time Zone check box to have Cisco Unity Connection use the system default time zone that is defined on the **System Settings > General Configuration** page.
- **Language:** Choose the language in which Cisco Unity Connection plays the call handler system prompts to the caller.
- **Partition:** Choose the partition to which the object belongs.
- **Search Space:** Define the search space by selecting a specific search space or inhering the search space from the call.

Call Handler Template Options

To route callers to another call handler, configure the transfer rule to transfer to the extension of the call handler. The options are illustrated in Figure 5-7.

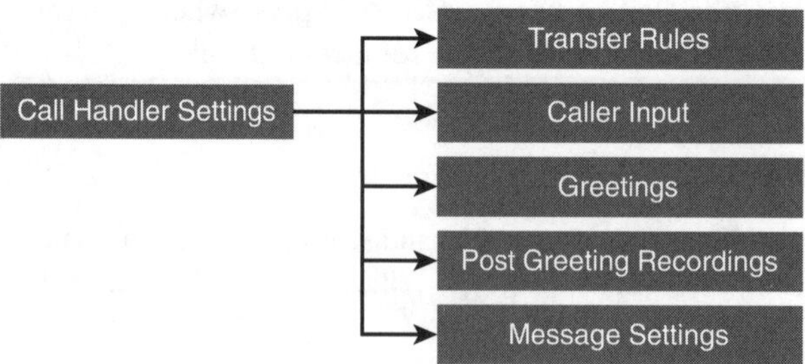

Figure 5-7 *Cisco Unity Connection Call Handler Template Options*

When transferring a call to an extension, Cisco Unity Connection can either release the call to the phone system or supervise the transfer. When Cisco Unity Connection is set to supervise transfers, it can provide call-screening and call-holding options on indirect calls. There are three predefined transfer rules:

- **Standard:** The standard rule is enabled without an end date and is always used by default. The standard transfer rule cannot be turned off. By default, the transfer action is set to Greeting.

- **Alternate:** This transfer rule when enabled, overrides the standard and closed transfer rules and is in effect at all times. For example, you can enable the alternate transfer rule, between Christmas and New Year, to transfer calls to an external phone number. By default, the alternate rule is disabled.
- **Closed:** The closed rule is disabled in the default call handler template. If the schedule for call handlers is set to weekdays only, the closed rule (if enabled) is used on the weekend and after business hours and on holidays. The default transfer action is set to Greeting. By default, no difference exists between the open and closed transfer rules.

During the greeting, the caller can be prompted with options to process the active call. The caller input can be defined for the digits 0 through 9, the asterisk or star (*), and the pound or hash sign (#). To specify the caller input options, under Caller Input settings, select a key and then define the call action. On the page with the caller input key overview, you can also define the time to wait for additional digits to be entered to reach an extension. The default is 1500 ms. If you press 2001 you reach the extension 2001, but only if there is not more than 1.5 seconds between pressing the digit 2 and the digit 0. Otherwise, you execute the call action that is defined for the key 2. You can lock a key, so extra input is ignored. This action is the default for * and #. Finally, you have the choice to prepend digits to the dialed extension to accommodate to the dial plan.

The Greetings settings offer the possibility for call handlers to be individualized with the following greetings: Standard, Alternate, Closed, Holiday, Busy, Internal, and Error. These options are the same options that are available for end users. The standard and error greetings are enabled by default. You can also play a postgreeting recording.

The following message settings are available:

- **Maximum Message Length:** Set the recording length (in seconds) that is allowed for messages left by unidentified callers. The default setting is 300 seconds.
- **Callers Can Edit Messages:** Check this check box to prompt callers to listen to, add to, rerecord, or delete their messages. The default setting is checked.
- **Message Urgency:** Indicate the action (normal, urgent, ask caller) that Cisco Unity Connection allows when a message has been left by an unidentified caller or a user who has not explicitly signed in. Messages left by unidentified callers are never marked urgent. This setting has an effect on message notification.
- **Message Sensitivity:** Indicate the action (normal, private, ask caller) that Cisco Unity Connection allows when a message has been left by an unidentified caller or by a user who has not explicitly signed in.
- **Message Security Mark Secure:** Check this check box when you want Cisco Unity Connection to mark messages as secure that are left by unidentified callers or users who have not explicitly signed in. This setting has an effect on forwarding messages. In addition, these messages can only be streamed by Cisco Unity Connection but never leave the system, for example, as an audio file.

- **Message Recipient:** Choose the user or distribution list that receives messages that are left for the call handler. When Distribution List is selected, each member of the specified list receives the call handler messages. If you check the box Mark for Dispatch Delivery, messages are sent as dispatch messages to the distribution list. When sent as a dispatch message, only one user in the group needs to act on the message.
- **Play After Message Recording:** Indicate the action (do not play recording, play recording or play system default recording) that Unity Connection performs after a message has been sent by an unidentified caller or by a user who has not explicitly signed in

Finally, set the action that Cisco Unity Connection performs after a caller leaves a message. You can choose only from the following two options: Hang Up or Route From Next Call Routing Rule. In addition, you can select any call handlers or user with a mail box. Conversations can be selected as well.

Caller Input

To define the action that Cisco Unity Connection takes in response to phone keys pressed by callers, choose from the options that are presented in Figure 5-8.

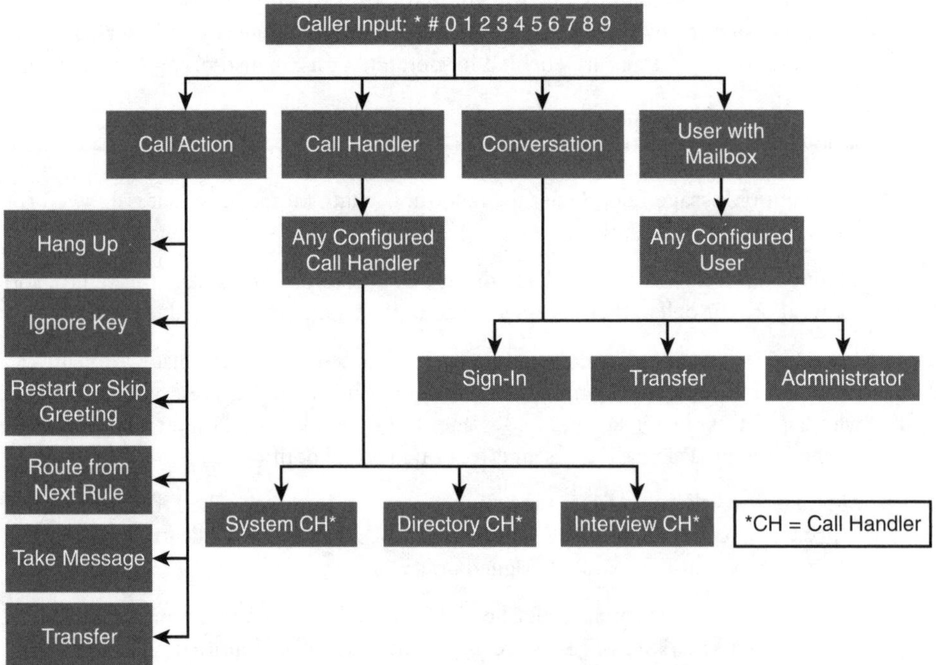

Figure 5-8 *Cisco Unity Connection Caller Input Options*

Besides selecting any configured call handler or selecting users with a mailbox, you can select the following call actions:

- **Hang Up:** Cisco Unity Connection immediately terminates the call when a caller presses the applicable phone key on the phone.
- **Ignore Key:** Cisco Unity Connection ignores the key press and continues playing the greeting. Use this option when only certain key presses should be defined.
- **Restart Greeting:** Cisco Unity Connection plays the greeting from the beginning.
- **Route from Next Call Routing Rule:** Cisco Unity Connection continues processing the call, according to the applicable call-routing table (direct or forwarded), starting at the next rule after the rule that Cisco Unity Connection previously applied to the call.
- **Skip Greeting:** Cisco Unity Connection skips the greeting and performs the after-greeting action.
- **Take Message:** Cisco Unity Connection records a message from the caller. The greeting should indicate that a message will be recorded.
- **Transfer to Alternate Contact Number:** Cisco Unity Connection transfers the call to the phone number that is specified in the Extension or URI field. You can also specify whether Unity Connection transfers the call by releasing it to the phone system or by supervising the transfer.

Default Call Handler Flow

The Cisco Unity Connection standard opening greeting is played to callers that are not configured as users with an extension or alternate extension in Cisco Unity Connection. The options in the opening greeting are illustrated in Figure 5-9.

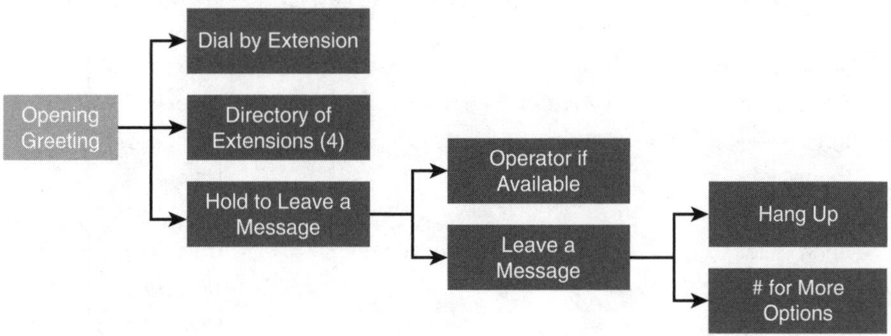

Figure 5-9 *Cisco Unity Connection Call Handler Flow*

The opening greeting call handler allows the caller to do one of the following actions:

- Dial an extension at any time.
- Press 4 for a directory of extensions.
- Be connected to the operator or leave a message.

If available, the operator is called via the preconfigured operator call handler. If the operator is not available, callers can leave a message that is sent to the mailbox of the operator.

After recording and sending a message, callers can hang up or press the pound key (#) for more options. In this example, those options are to dial an extension or to hang up.

Greeting Analysis

This section analyzes the greeting options for the opening greeting call handler.

In the opening greeting call handler, the standard and the closed greetings are configured in the same way. The greeting is played and then forwards the caller to the operator call handler.

The difference between the standard and closed greeting is that you can modify the closed greeting status but not the status of the standard greeting. You can modify the default call routing to meet your requirements, (for example, you can record a personalized company greeting).

Caller Input Analysis

Figure 5-10 shows an example of the caller input key configuration in Unity Connection.

Caller Input Keys			
Key	Action	Target	Status
*	Send caller to	Sign-In	Locked
#	Send caller to	Operator	Locked
0	Send caller to	Operator	Unlocked
1	Ignore key		Unlocked
2	Ignore key		Unlocked
3	Ignore key		Unlocked
4	Send caller to	System Directory Handler	Unlocked
5	Ignore key		Unlocked
6	Ignore key		Unlocked
7	Ignore key		Unlocked
8	Ignore key		Unlocked
9	Ignore key		Unlocked

Figure 5-10 *Cisco Unity Connection Caller Input Example*

The caller can dial an extension at any time, press 4 for the directory call handler, or wait to be transferred to the operator if available. In addition, the caller can press the asterisk or star (*) key to log in to the personal mailbox, by entering the ID and PIN. By pressing the pound (#) key or 0, the caller can reach the operator without waiting.

How does Cisco Unity Connection distinguish between, for example, the directory selection (4) and the directory number 4001? The Wait for Additional Digits 1500-ms setting gives the caller exactly 1.5 seconds to press 0 after pressing 4. If the caller waits 2 seconds, the call reaches the directory call handler, because Cisco Unity Connection will recognize only the entry 4. If the caller presses 5 only, nothing happens; this key is ignored because call action Ignore is specified.

Note Only extensions configured in Cisco Unity Connection are recognized as valid.

Note the configuration example for caller input, as shown in Figure 5-11.

Edit Caller Input
Key 4
Ignore Additional Input (Locked)
Action
Call Action Hang Up
Extension or URI Description
Transfer Type Release to Switch
Rings to Wait For 4
Call Handler Goodbye
Attempt Transfer
Go Directly to Greetings
Interview Handler
Directory Handler System Directory Handler
Conversation Broadcast Message Administrator
User with Mailbox operator
Attempt Transfer
Go Directly to Greetings

Figure 5-11 *Cisco Unity Connection Call Handler Input Configuration Example*

When a caller presses 4, the call action forwards the call to the default directory handler after 1500 ms. Because the Ignore Additional Input (Locked) check box is not checked, you are also able to reach extensions that start with 4. If you check this box, you prevent callers from dialing extensions starting with 4 because the action is initiated immediately as soon as the caller enters 4.

Operator Call Handler

This section describes the default operator call handler functionality.

Note the configuration example in Figure 5-12 to transfer callers based on their input.

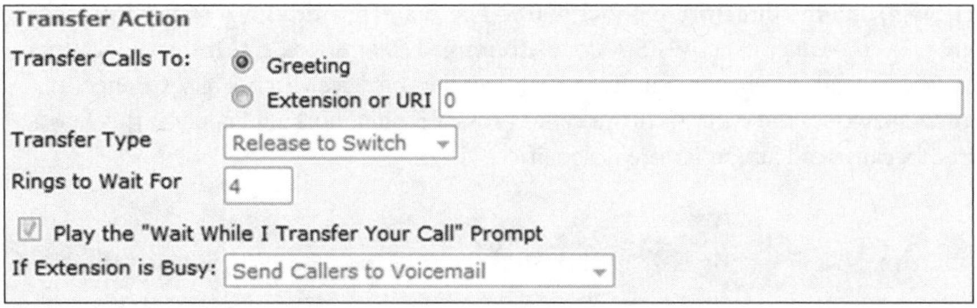

Transfer Action
Transfer Calls To: Greeting
Extension or URI 0
Transfer Type Release to Switch
Rings to Wait For 4
Play the "Wait While I Transfer Your Call" Prompt
If Extension is Busy: Send Callers to Voicemail

Figure 5-12 *Cisco Unity Connection Operator Call Handler*

The standard transfer rule is enabled without an end date. The calls are transferred to extension 0 by default. Change this setting value to the operator directory number (for example, extension 2001).

Note The operator extension in the basic configuration must remain as (0), otherwise the opening greeting call handler will not work. The extension 0 should ideally be changed to 2001 in the transfer rule settings.

When the Release to Switch transfer type is specified, the call is transferred directly to the phone system. The "Wait While I Transfer Your Call" prompt is played; this prompt can be disabled.

When you choose Supervisor Transfer instead of Release to Switch for Transfer Type, call-screening options can be used.

Operator Not Available

If the operator is unavailable, the caller can leave a message. The message recipient is the operator that is a preconfigured user with a mailbox and for an example the assigned extension of 99990. After the message is taken, the goodbye call handler is selected. To listen to the operator messages, call Cisco Unity Connection from any phone and press the Messages button or dial the voice-mail pilot number. Press the asterisk or star key (*) to reach the sign-in menu, enter the ID 99990 and the PIN.

Goodbye Call Handler

The goodbye call handler allows the caller to do the following:

- Sign in (*).
- Restart the opening greeting (#).
- Reach the operator (0).
- Dial an extension.

The after message action of the goodbye call handler is set to terminate the call after the greeting is played.

The goodbye call handler allows the caller to sign in, restart the opening greeting, reach the operator, or dial an extension.

However, the goodbye call handler greeting only announces the option to dial an extension. By default, the other three options are not announced during the greeting. If the caller does not select any option during that greeting (which is 5 seconds long), the call is terminated.

Directory Handler

The main task of the directory handler is to allow callers to search for users in Cisco Unity Connection or on connected voice-messaging systems. Figure 5-13 illustrates the options of the directory handler.

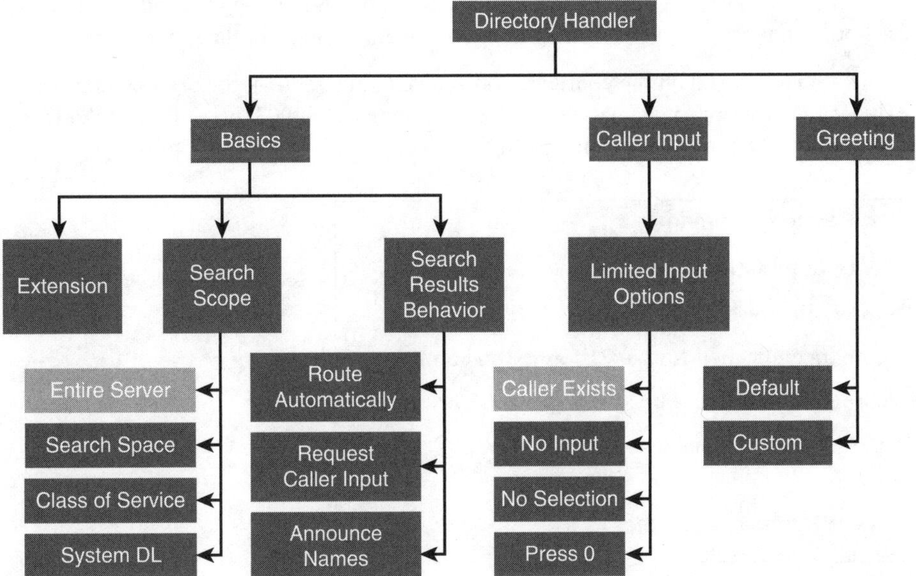

Figure 5-13 *Cisco Unity Connection Directory Handler Overview*

The user access can be restricted with the dial plan configuration. Set the basic directory-handler parameters and define the caller input and greeting:

- Play the names of users in the directory for caller selection, rather than requiring the caller to search by spelled name. This option requires voice recognition.
- Choose the method that callers use to spell a username: first name, last name, or the default method of last name, first name.
- Choose how the results are presented to the caller: Route Automatically on a Unique Match, Always Request Caller Input, Announce Matched Names Using Extension Format, or Menu Format.

The caller input allows only the following options, in combination with call actions:

- If the caller exits, the caller is sent to the opening greeting.
- If there is no input or if no selection is made, the caller is sent to the goodbye call handler.
- If the caller presses zero, the caller is sent to the operator call handler.

Note There is no definition for the selection of a single key, except the 0 key.

The greeting settings are limited to the selection of a default or custom greeting. There is no schedule to configure for the directory handler.

The default search result behavior is to always request input from the caller when selecting a user. When a caller enters 363 (for Doe), the users John Doe and Jane Doe are both announced, together with their extension numbers and calling options.

In this example based on the configuration shown in Figure 5-14, the prompt announces, "There are two matching names. For Jane Doe at extension 2003, press 1. For John Doe at extension 2001, press 2. No more matching names; for a new search, press star."

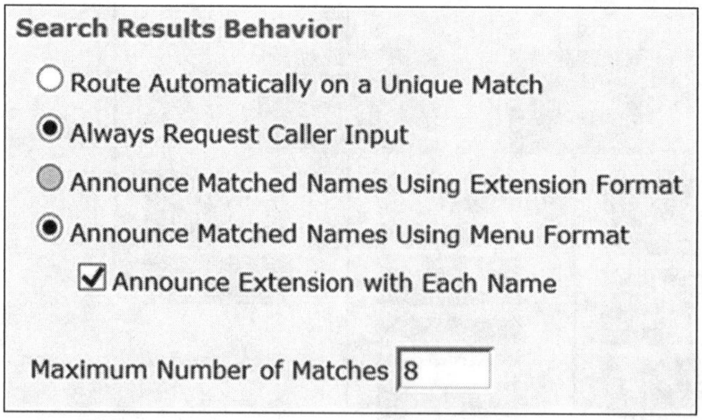

Search Results Behavior

- ○ Route Automatically on a Unique Match
- ◉ Always Request Caller Input
- ○ Announce Matched Names Using Extension Format
- ◉ Announce Matched Names Using Menu Format
  - ☑ Announce Extension with Each Name

Maximum Number of Matches 8

Figure 5-14 *Cisco Unity Connection Search Results Configuration Example*

The extension announcement can be disabled, and the maximum number of matches is limited to eight.

The user can decide whether to be listed in the directory of extensions or not. The selection is made during self-enrollment or via a user interface. In the CoS settings, you can prevent the users from delisting themselves by disallowing that option.

Interview Handler

The interview handler asks the caller for a response to as many as 99 questions. The answers are recorded and sent to a configured recipient; the questions are not recorded. Figure 5-15 gives an example of an interview handler configuration.

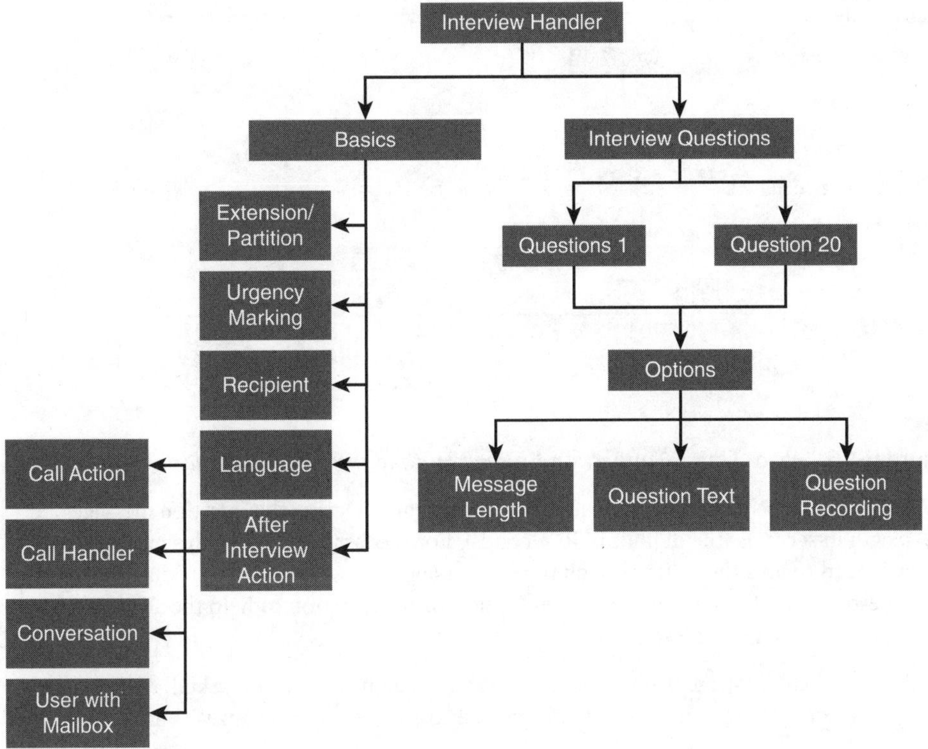

Figure 5-15 *Cisco Unity Connection Interview Handler Example*

Specify the basic settings and the interview questions:

- Define as many as 20 questions.
- Enter the recording length in seconds that is allowed for caller responses to each interview-handler question.
- Enter the text of each interview-handler question.

- Record the call handler questions.
- Activate the questions.

The example configuration shown in Figure 5-16 is for a product hotline interview handler. The first two questions ask the caller for their name and phone number. The interview handler then asks for the product name and for information about the caller's issue with the product. You may group your questions differently.

Question 1

Interview Handler Question	
Question Number	1
Maximum Reply Message Length	10 seconds
Question Text*	Name
Question Recording	Play/Record
☑ Active	

Questions 2 to 20

Interview Handler Question	
Question Number	2
Maximum Reply Message Length	15 seconds
Question Text*	Phone Number
Question Recording	Play/Record
☑ Active	

Figure 5-16 *Cisco Unity Connection Product Hotline Interview Handler Example*

Begin by choosing the question number to configure. Define the question message length in seconds (the default is 30 seconds). For the last question in this example, you will need to give the caller enough time to explain the issue with the product. In the Question Text field, enter a short description of the question to help the administrator remember what the question is about.

Record each question. If no question is recorded, a question is not asked. All answers in this example are consolidated into one message. The question answers are divided by a tone.

Summary

This section summarizes the key points that were discussed in this chapter:

- The dial plan in Cisco Unity Connection is similar to the calling privileges in CUCM. The existing objects should be placed logically in partitions

- There are three kinds of call handlers: system call handler, directory handler, and interview handler. The standard opening greeting is an example of a predefined system call handler.
- By using call handlers, administrators can minimize the required effort by predefining the correct settings for call handlers. One call handler template can be used for all three types of call handlers.
- The system call handler is a powerful call handler and offers the most configuration options: transfer rules, caller input, greetings, message settings, and so on. The default opening greeting call handler lets callers dial an extension, connect to the extension directory, or reach the operator via the operator call handler.
- The directory handler allows callers to search Cisco Unity Connection for configured extensions and to be redirected to the user. The dial plan component search space can limit searches within the directory. Users can list or delist themselves in the directory depending on the CoS settings.
- The interview handler allows callers to leave answers to specific questions. The recording is then sent as a bundled message to the message recipient.

Review Questions

Answer the following questions, and then see Appendix A, "Answers to Review Questions," for the answers.

1. **Which two parameters cannot be configured in the call handler template for search scopes? (Choose two.)**
   a. Search space
   b. Calling search space
   c. Inherit search space from call
   d. Partition

2. **Which call handler is not a preconfigured system call handler in Cisco Unity Connection?**
   a. Opening greeting
   b. Operator
   c. Closing greeting
   d. Goodbye

3. What is the default time that Cisco Unity Connection waits for further digits when analyzing the caller input to dial an extension?

a. 1000 ms

b. 1500 ms

c. 2000 ms

d. 2500 ms

e. None of the above

4. When entering a name using a directory handler, what is the default number of maximum name matches?

a. 1

b. 3

c. 5

d. 8

e. 10

f. 12

5. Which two options can be selected as the message recipient for an interview handler? (Choose two.)

a. Call handler

b. User with mailbox

c. Distribution list

d. Operator

e. Administrator mailbox

Chapter 6

Configuring Unified Messaging

Upon completing this chapter, you will be able to do the following:

- Introduce the terminology that is used in unified messaging
- Describe the Cisco Unity Connection architecture that is used to implement single inbox using a dual-store architecture.
- Describe the single inbox functionality with Exchange integration and voice message synchronization
- Describe the benefits of using unified messaging in Cisco Unity Connection
- Describe the mail systems that are supported for single inbox
- Describe the different Cisco Unity Connection deployment options
- Describe the security and compliance considerations
- Describe the dual-store message architecture in more detail
- Describe how to configure integrated messaging in Cisco Unity Connection
- Describe how to configure unified messaging in Cisco Unity Connection and gives an overview of the configuration requirements in Exchange
- Describe what happens if the Exchange administrator moves a mailbox in the Exchange environment
- List some instances that require restoration of an individual mailbox or a server

This chapter explains the single inbox feature of unified messaging. Single Inbox allows users to receive their voice messages in the company mail inbox with the proper message waiting indicator (MWI) synchronization when users are reading the e-mail on a PC or listening to the messages on the phone.

Unified Messaging Terminology

In Cisco Unity Connection, Cisco gathered several existing features under the rubric of *unified messaging*. These features include the following:

- The single inbox feature synchronizes voice messages in Cisco Unity Connection and Microsoft Exchange mailboxes. In most cases, Unified Messaging refers to the single inbox feature where the end users receive their voice messages in the company mailbox.
- Text-to-speech (TTS) access provides access to Exchange e-mail.
- Access to Exchange calendars allows users to do meeting-related tasks by phone. For example, users can hear a list of upcoming meetings, or accept or decline meeting invitations.
- Access to Exchange contacts allows users to import Exchange contacts and use the contact information in personal call transfer rules and when placing outgoing calls by using voice commands.
- Users can be notified of upcoming Cisco Unified MeetingPlace meetings on the phone, or can schedule and join MeetingPlace meetings.
- Transcription of Cisco Unity Connection voice messages using Cisco SpeechView.

Single Inbox High-Level Architecture

Figure 6-1 presents the unified messaging architecture. Unified messaging in Cisco Unity Connection provides message synchronization and a dual-store message architecture. Cisco Unity Connection does not use Microsoft Exchange as the message store, and instead includes its own authoritative message store.

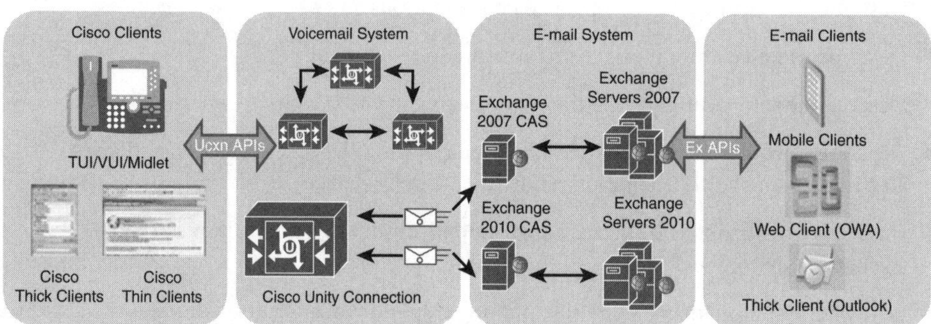

Figure 6-1 *Cisco Unity Connection Single Inbox High-Level Architecture*

Messages that are left on Cisco Unity Connection are synchronized to the Exchange servers. This approach allows the different Cisco clients to use Cisco Unity Connection via their application programming interfaces (APIs) and allows the Exchange clients to use the Exchange via their APIs. If Exchange goes down, Cisco Unity Connection is still operating and voice messages can be left and received. Users still have full access to voice mail from Cisco clients to Cisco Unity Connection.

Single Inbox Functionality

This section describes the single inbox functionality with Exchange integration and voice-message synchronization.

Unified messaging provides single inbox access to your voice mails. With single inbox, the MWI is synchronized on both systems. When an unread voice message is opened in the e-mail client—for example, the company Microsoft Outlook inbox folder—MWI is turned off on the phone.

The status for messages is also synchronized. If a user reads a message in Exchange, it is marked as read in Cisco Unity Connection. The new, deleted, or priority status is also synchronized, as well as the subject line. Secure and private messages are supported. Mobile clients like iPhone and BlackBerry work automatically because the voice mail comes into the Microsoft Exchange box and the message is picked up by the mobile phone client.

The personal call transfer rules can be based on the calendar information concerning the user's free or busy status.

Unified Messaging Benefits

This section describes the benefits of using unified messaging in Cisco Unity Connection. With Cisco Unity Connection unified messaging, a schema extension is not required.

Cisco Unity Connection does not rely on the hub transport (the edge transport servers in Exchange) to deliver voice mails from Cisco Unity Connection. Cisco Unity Connection does not depend on the mailbox server rules because Cisco Unity Connection is just synchronizing the messages into Exchange.

Cisco Unity Connection unified messaging reduces the dependencies on Exchange and Active Directory. If the message synchronization is not working because the Exchange infrastructure is not available, callers can still leave messages and users can still receive their messages. The communication between Cisco Unity Connection and Exchange is a two-way synchronization.

Cisco Unity Connection is the authoritative message store, but if a message is deleted in Exchange via Microsoft Outlook, for example, the message is also deleted in Cisco Unity Connection and vice versa.

If a user sends a message to an Exchange distribution list (or example, a voice mail using ViewMail for Outlook), the message is received in a Cisco Unity Connection inbox and in Exchange. The message will be synchronized between both systems.

When using secure messages in Cisco Unity Connection, the messages are not synchronized into Exchange. Cisco Unity Connection synchronizes a pointer instead, so that the message can be streamed from Cisco Unity Connection. Secure messaging does not allow audio files to leave the system (for example, as an attachment to an e-mail).

Exchange E-mail Integration Options

This section describes the mail systems that are supported for a single inbox comprising both e-mail and voice mail.

Cisco Unity Connection supports Exchange 2003 or later and also supports different versions running at the same time, as illustrated in Figure 6-2. If you are migrating from Exchange 2003 to 2010, and you are moving mailboxes over to the migrated Exchange Server, Cisco Unity Connection must track these moves. Cisco Unity Connection can autodetect mailbox moves in the Exchange infrastructure. Cisco Unity Connection can be local or placed across geographical boundaries from the Exchange Servers with which it is synchronizing.

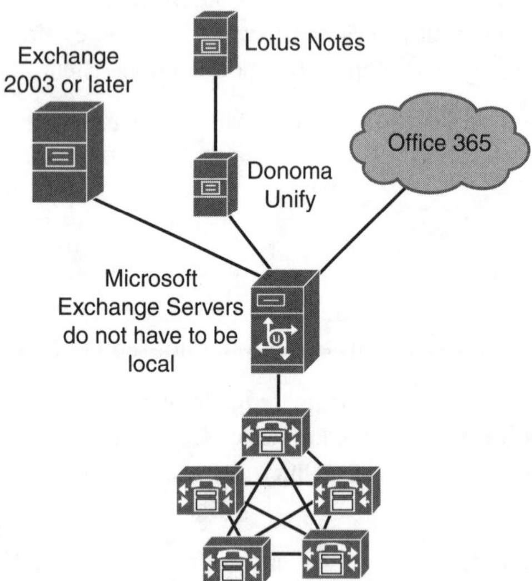

Figure 6-2 *Cisco Unity Connection Microsoft Exchange Integration Options*

Office 365 and Lotus Notes are supported as well. However, additional third-party software is required for Lotus Notes. Go to http://donomasoftware.com/donoma-unify-for-lotus-notes / for more information.

Cisco Unity Connection Deployment Options

This section describes the different Cisco Unity Connection deployment options.

Cisco Unity Connection can be deployed as a voice-mail-only solution where the users receive their messages only via the phone. The message is indicated with MWI lights on the phone.

With Integrated Messaging, the voice messages are sent to a mail client such as Microsoft Outlook via Internet Message Access Protocol (IMAP), but the voice messages appear in a separate inbox folder in the mail client when using it for company mail as well.

Cisco Unity Connection unified messaging brings many functions together: Users can still use the phone but also get voice messages in their company mail account. With unified messaging, the MWI is synchronized on the phone when messages are read or listened to in the mail client. Active Directory schema extensions are not required for any of these solutions.

Security, Compliance, and Discoverability

This section describes the security and compliance considerations.

The Cisco Unity Connection Unified Messaging architecture supports secure messages and private messages. The unencrypted messages are kept on the Cisco Unity Connection server, and Cisco Unity Connection sends the messages securely to the client. Cisco Unity Connection does not synchronize a secure message into the Microsoft Exchange message store, but instead provides only a pointer to the message in Cisco Unity Connection. To stream these messages from the mail client, use the Cisco Unity ViewMail for Outlook (VMO) plug-in.

Organizations that are worried about compliance and discoverability of voicemail in their e-mail systems might not want to use unified messaging. For those customers, you can still offer integrated messaging from a client perspective, in which voice mails are not synchronized in the Microsoft Exchange store.

Message Synchronization Architecture

This section describes the dual-store message architecture in more detail, as illustrated in Figure 6-3.

Cisco Unity Connection does not use Exchange as the only message store. When Exchange is not available, Cisco Unity Connection uses Cisco Unity Message Repository, which allows callers to leave messages for users when their primary Exchange Server is offline. New messages are logged and synchronized after the connection to Exchange is reestablished.

Note Cisco Unity is end of life and is the prior product from Cisco Unity Connection. Cisco Unity was built on the Microsoft operating system and did utilize Microsoft Exchange directly.

Cisco Unity Connection uses APIs to move messages into the Exchange store. The web-based APIs that are used by Cisco Unity Connection are Exchange Web Services (EWS) for Exchange 2007 or later and WebDAV for Exchange 2003.

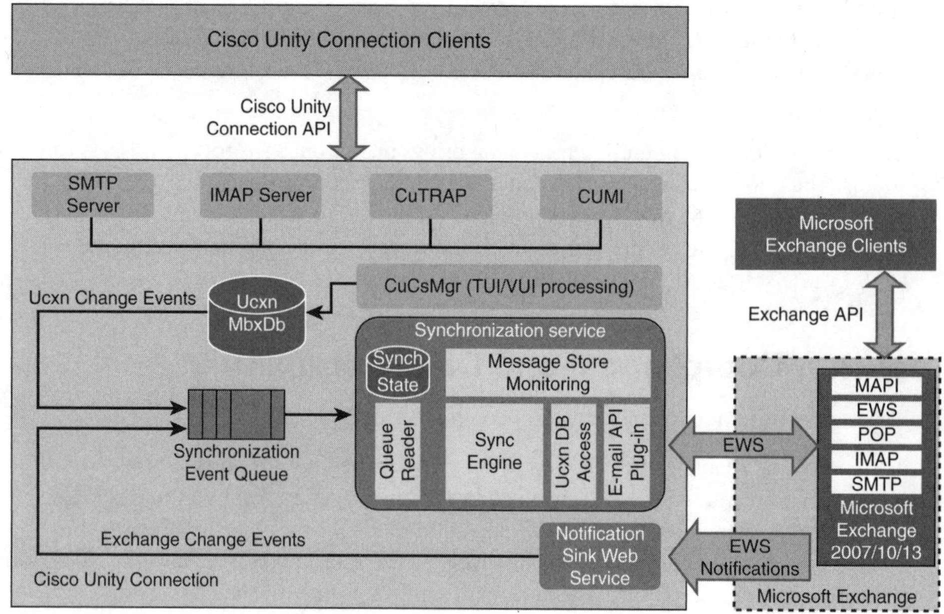

Figure 6-3 *Cisco Unity Connection Message Synchronization Architecture*

In summary, the message synchronization architecture is based on the following:

- Message synchronization is used instead of moving the messages off-box.
- Web APIs are used instead of management APIs (MAPIs).
- Microsoft EWS are used for Microsoft Exchange 2007 and later.
- WebDAV is used for Microsoft Exchange 2003.

The figure also shows what the unified messaging architecture looks like from the perspective of a developer. The synchronization service in Cisco Unity Connection interfaces with Exchange. Cisco Unity Connection clients continue to access Cisco Unity Connection via their commonly used interfaces.

Synchronization Behavior

A voice message that is received in Cisco Unity Connection is synchronized to Exchange. If a voice message is deleted in Exchange by using a Microsoft Outlook client, or in Cisco Unity ViewMail for Outlook, the voice message is also deleted in Cisco Unity Connection. If the voice message is marked as read on the phone, it is marked as read in Microsoft Outlook. The message state is also synchronized.

If a user moves a voice message from the inbox into an Outlook (.pst) file or folder, the voice message is deleted in Cisco Unity Connection. If the user moves that message from the .pst file back into the inbox, the voice message is resynchronized with Cisco

Unity Connection and appears as a new message or indicates the state of the voice message. Users can move voicemails in and out of personal folders. Once the user moves the voice message out of the inbox, the voice message is not synchronized with Cisco Unity Connection, and the voice message is deleted.

Note The message properties are synchronized and the status of the voice message as read, deleted, or new is synchronized. Therefore, the MWI is synchronized.

What happens when a voicemail is set to expire—for example, in 20 days—but the user drops the message into an Outlook folder before the expiration? The voice message will expire on Cisco Unity Connection and the message is deleted, but the message will not expire in Microsoft Exchange. If a customer is worried about that message still being in Exchange, the administrator must turn on secure voice mail for voice messages to keep the voicemails out of the Exchange store. In that case, the subject line is synchronized. If a user changes the subject on the voice message, this change is synchronized, and the priority is also synchronized. The message sensitivity and security are only initially synchronized, but if these parameters are changed in Microsoft Outlook later, that change is not synchronized.

Configure Integrated Messaging

This section describes how to configure Integrated Messaging in Cisco Unity Connection.

Integrated messaging does not require many configuration steps compared to unified messaging. In Cisco Unity Connection Administration, configure the Simple Mail Transfer Protocol (SMTP) server to allow incoming connections from untrusted IP addresses, which is not the default setting. Otherwise, the mail client will answer with an error message "550 5.5.0 Connection Refused," indicating that the connection is refused by the server.

Go to the Class of Service template and allow the users to access their voice messages via IMAP by checking the Allow Users to Access Voice Mail Using an IMAP Client and/or Single Inbox check box. This parameter has three subparameters:

- **Allow IMAP Users to Access Message Bodies:** Users have access to the entire voice mail.
- **Allow IMAP Users to Access Message Bodies Except on Private Messages:** Users have access to the entire voicemail, unless the message is marked private, in which case they have access only to the message header.
- **Allow IMAP Users to Access Message Headers Only:** Users have access only to message headers.

The parameter to allow IMAP access to messages must also be enabled for unified messaging or if you want to allow Cisco Jabber users to access voice messages.

Set up the mail client. Assuming that the user exists in Cisco Unity Connection with the minimum requirements of a configured alias and an extension, you can start setting up the mail client.

Depending on the mail client, the setup might be slightly different. When using, for example, Outlook Express, enter the name and the mail address. Then configure the IMAP protocol and the incoming and outgoing mail server IP address or hostname. Finally, enter the account name (Cisco Unity Connection alias) and the password. Finish the Account Setup Wizard and synchronize the folders from the mail server.

Account Verification

To test integrated messaging, leave a voice message for the user. After leaving the message, the mail client should instantly show a new message. As shown in Figure 6-4, John received a voice message from Jane. The audio file is attached. You can double-click the attached audio file and play the message with a media player. MWI is synchronized as well, when setting the voicemail status to Read.

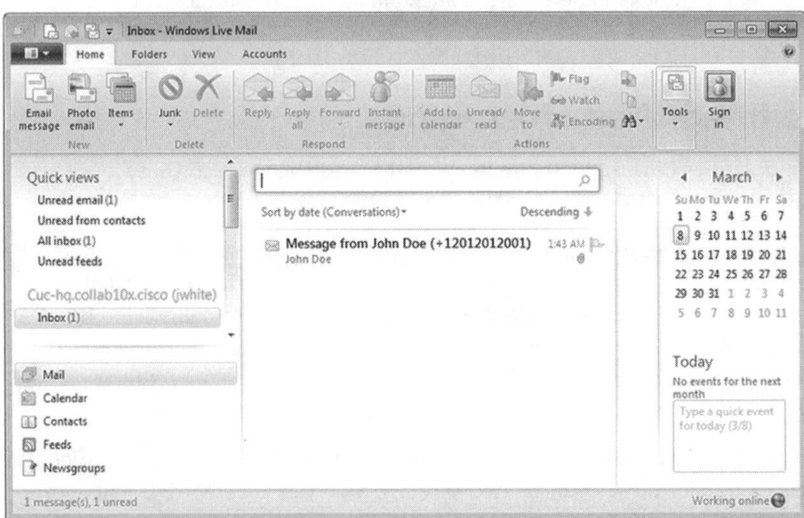

Figure 6-4 *Account Verification*

The SMTP domain that you see in the figure can be changed in the SMTP server configuration as well. The name is generated by the hostname that you entered during the Cisco Unity Connection installation.

Task List to Set Up Unified Messaging Single Inbox

This section describes how to configure unified messaging in Cisco Unity Connection and gives an overview of the configuration requirements in Exchange.

Besides checking that you have the correct software version in place for unified messaging, follow these steps to set up single inbox:

- Add a smart host and modify the SMTP domain.
- When integrating with LDAP, make sure that the Cisco Unified Communications Manager Mail ID field is synchronized with the LDAP Mail field. During the integration process, this synchronization causes values in the LDAP Mail field to appear in the Corporate E-mail Address field in Cisco Unity Connection. Unified messaging requires that you enter the Exchange e-mail address for each Unity Connection user. On the Unified Messaging Account page, each user can be configured to use either of the following values:
  - The Corporate e-mail address that is specified on the User Basics page
  - The e-mail address that is specified on the Unified Messaging Account page
- Update class of service settings as required and enable single inbox.
- Decide whether you want Cisco Unity Connection to communicate with a specific Exchange 2013, Exchange 2010, or Exchange 2007 client access server or Exchange 2003 server, or if you want Unity Connection to be able to search for and communicate with different Exchange servers as required. Unity Connection determines whether to use the HTTP or HTTPS and whether to validate certificates based on settings in the applicable unified messaging service.
- Confirm that all of the Exchange servers that Unity Connection will access are configured to use the desired authentication mode (basic, digest, or Microsoft Windows NT LAN Manager [NTLM]) and web-based protocol (HTTPS or HTTP). If you want to configure Secure Sockets Layer (SSL) to encrypt the communication between Unity Connection and Exchange, configure Exchange to use HTTPS for the web-based protocol.
- Create an Active Directory account for Unity Connection unified messaging services, and grant the applicable permissions to the account.
- Add proxy addresses to Unity Connection user accounts.
- Configure one or more Unity Connection unified messaging services and assign them to the users. Then test the unified messaging services.
- For security, upload certificates to the servers.

Exchange Mailbox Moves

This section describes what happens if the Exchange administrator moves a mailbox in the Exchange environment.

The option to specify an Exchange Server or allow Cisco Unity Connection to search for an Exchange server depends on whether Cisco Unity Connection supports the detection of moved mailboxes.

Note If you want to support Exchange 2003, 2007, 2010, or 2013 mailboxes, you may have to create multiple unified messaging services to support the various versions at the same time.

Exchange administrators often move mailboxes, especially when migrating to a new software version. If Cisco Unity Connection is set up to search for the Exchange servers automatically, it will automatically detect mailbox moves.

However, if you specify an Exchange server, the move may or may not be detected. The Cisco Unity Connection administrator may have to manually update the user mailbox settings for the unified messaging servers.

Back Up and Restore of Mailboxes

This section lists some instances that require restoration of an individual mailbox or a server.

During a restore process on the Exchange infrastructure, disable the unified messaging account for a certain user or disable the unified messaging service itself if a complete Exchange server is down.

After restoring the Exchange server or a mailbox, enable the Cisco Unity Connection unified messaging service again for all or a single user.

In the event of a complete loss of an Exchange server, stop all unified messaging services and once the Exchange servers and mailboxes have been restored, enable the Cisco Unity Connection Unified Messaging service again.

For more information, see *Restoring Microsoft Exchange Mailboxes in Cisco Unity Connection 10.x When Single Inbox Is Enabled* at http://www.cisco.com/en/US/docs/voice_ip_comm/connection/10x/unified_messaging/guide/10xcucumg040.html.

Summary

This section summarizes the key points that were discussed in this chapter:

- Unified messaging synchronizes voice messages from Cisco Unity Connection to Exchange. Microsoft clients access the Exchange Server and Cisco clients access the Cisco Unity Connection server. A change on any system is synchronized instantly by the synchronization service.
- When using integrated messaging, the mail clients connect via IMAP to the Cisco Unity Connection server. The client shows an additional mail folder in the mail client, which is only used for voice messaging with Cisco Unity Connection.
- Create a unified messaging service and enable the capabilities for that service. Assign the unified messaging service to the end users and verify that the corporate mail address is configured correctly. When configured successfully, the voice message appears in the company mailbox.

Review Questions

Answer the following questions, and then see Appendix A, "Answers to Review Questions," for the answers.

1. **A single store message architecture allows users to access their voice messages with a Microsoft Outlook client in one single inbox.**

   a. True

   b. False

2. **When the SMTP server is not configured to allow an incoming connection from untrusted IP addresses, which error message do you see?**

   a. 550 5.5.0 Address rejected

   b. 550 5.5.0 Connection Refused

   c. 550 5.5.0 Invalid EHLO/HELO

   d. 550 5.5.0 SMTP Error

   e. 550 5.5.0 User unknown

3. **WebDAV is the API that is used between Cisco Unity Connection and Microsoft Exchange 2007 or later for unified messaging.**

   a. True

   b. False

Chapter 7

Troubleshooting Cisco Unity Connection

Upon completing this chapter, you will be able to do the following:

- Describe how to approach the most common issues with Cisco Unity Connection integrations and operations
- Describe the sources of error when a user presses the **Messages** button or dials the voice-mail pilot number and gets a reorder tone rather than a Cisco Unity Connection greeting
- Describe how route patterns can affect the use of the CFwdAll softkey when entering Call Forward numbers on a phone
- Describe why a user may not be recognized and therefore cannot log in to the mailbox
- Describe various issues that can prevent a PIN from being accepted
- Describe MWI issues with a SCCP integration
- Describe how to verify the status of the MWI in Cisco Unity Connection and how to run a synchronization
- Describe how a change or new call-routing rule might interrupt the correct call routing functionality
- Describe how the schedule can be used in rule conditions for time-based call routing in Cisco Unity Connection
- Describe the TUI prompts that are played to callers if voice-messaging issues arise
- Describe how callers can be transferred via caller input, transfer rules, greetings, and message settings
- Describe issues with directory and interview call handlers
- Describe voice messaging issues together with WAN backup technologies

- Describe the general monitoring capabilities of Cisco Unified RTMT in Cisco Unity Connection
- Describe the available performance counters in Cisco Unity Connection
- Describe how to receive notifications for defined thresholds in certain performance counters
- List the reports that are available in Cisco Unity Connection Serviceability, under **Tools > Reports**
- Describe how to troubleshoot MWI issues
- Describe how to enable macro traces to troubleshoot MWI issues

This chapter explains how to resolve common issues with Cisco Unity Connection integrations and operations. In addition, the chapter presents the Cisco Unified Real Time Monitoring Tool (RTMT) to monitor Cisco Unity Connection and explains micro and macro traces for Cisco Unity Connection.

Troubleshooting Cisco Unity Connection

This section describes how to approach the most common issues with Cisco Unity Connection integrations and operations.

The following is an overview of the most common errors found with Unity Connection:

- Reorder tone plays when users call Cisco Unity Connection.
- Callers are not forwarded to Cisco Unity Connection.
- Login to mailbox is not working.
- MWI is not working.
- Callers receive the wrong greeting:
  - Standard opening greeting
  - Standard greeting instead of alternate greeting
- Callers cannot leave a voice message.
- Call handler issues exist.
- Call routing errors exist.
- The wrong greeting plays in Cisco Unified Survivable Remote Site Telephony (SRST) and Automated Attendant Routing (AAR) mode.

Some of these errors appear during configuration; some appear after weeks, and from one day to the next. This chapter gives you an overview of how to manage these issues.

Reorder Tone

This section describes the sources of error when a user presses the **Messages** button or dials the voice-mail pilot number and gets a reorder tone rather than a Cisco Unity Connection greeting.

IP phones need a calling search space (CSS) that is set to reach Cisco Unity Connection when the user manually dials the voice-mail pilot number. In this example shown in Figure 7-1, the public switched telephone network (PSTN) CSS includes the partitions to reach PSTN route patterns and devices, but the CSS is missing from the voice-mail pilot. The CSS allows calling, without restriction, to PSTN phone numbers and to all devices that are registered with Cisco Unified Communications Manager (CUCM). This will give a reorder tone when users try to access their voice mail.

Note The CSS in the voice-mail pilot needs to be selected to fit the dial plan of your environment.

Voice Mail Pilot Information

Voice Mail Pilot Number	2500
Calling Search Space	< None >
Description	Default

Figure 7-1 *Cisco Unity Connection CSS Missing in the Voice-Mail Hunt Pilot*

The Messages softkey also requires the CSS to be set on the IP phone, to reach Cisco Unity Connection. Otherwise, calls are not routed to Cisco Unity Connection. Verify that CSSs are set correctly in the voice-mail pilot and on the IP phone or line, depending on the class of service (CoS) implementation approach.

Call Forward to Cisco Unity Connection

This section describes issues with call forwarding to voice mail.

Internal and external differentiation is made for Call Forward Busy (CFB), Call Forward No Answer (CFNA), Call Forward No Coverage (CFNC), and Call Forward UnRegistered (CFUR). When configuring the Call Forward options, enable Call Forward, if available, for internal and external callers. Otherwise, only internal or external callers are forwarded to Cisco Unity Connection. The internal option is used when the call leg being forwarded ins on-net. The external option is used when the call leg being forwarded is off-net.

When users want to forward all calls via softkey or user options pages, a CSS is necessary. By default, CSSs are set to <None>. However, the CSS activation policy determines which numbers can be entered when activating Call Forward All (CFA). CSS activation policies are not used for the other Call Forward options, such as CFB. The following three choices are available for the CSS activation policy:

- Use System Default
- With Configured CSS
- With Activating Device/Line CSS

When the With Configured CSS option is chosen, the Forward All CSS that is explicitly configured in the Directory Number Configuration window controls the forward all activation and call forwarding. If the Forward All CSS is set to <None>, no CSS is configured for Forward All. A forward all activation attempt to any directory number with an assigned partition will fail.

If you prefer to combine the Directory Number CSS and Device CSS, without explicitly configuring a Forward All CSS, choose the **With Activating Device/Line CSS** option. With this option, when Forward All is activated from the phone, the Forward All CSS and Secondary CSS for Forward All are automatically populated with the Directory Number CSS and Device CSS for the activating device.

If Use System Default is configured, the CFA CSS activation policy clusterwide service parameter determines which Forward All CSS will be used. The default is With Configured CSS.

Route Pattern Affecting Call Forward

This section describes how route patterns can affect the use of the CFwdAll softkey when entering Call Forward numbers on a phone.

When configuring route patterns with overlap sending enabled, CUCM collects only a part of the number for the setup message to the PSTN. For example, a route pattern 0.x marked urgent will collect only the 0, which is a typical European PSTN access code, and one other digit. After this digit is collected, the call is routed. When using Call Forward via softkey, the user enters the number 0.x and CUCM does not collect further digits. An extra route pattern must be configured for Call Forward, which does not support overlap sending to collect the complete phone number.

Another issue can occur when Forced Authorization Codes (FAC) or Client Matter Codes (CMC) are used:

- **FAC:** Forced Authorization Code is used to authorize calls that are based on a code that is entered after the target number is dialed. If the code is provided with the code for the correct level, the call is authorized; otherwise, the caller hears a reorder tone.
- **CMC:** Client Matter Code is adding a flag to the call detail records (CDRs) (so call billing can be done based on a customer or project, for example). Mostly, the duration of the calls is used for billing (for example, when lawyers call clients).

When a user calls via a FAC-enabled route pattern, the user must enter a code after the phone number, as indicated by a beep tone. When using this route pattern for call forwarding, the calls cannot be routed. The call forwarding process cannot append a code after the digit analysis.

Login Not Working

This section describes why a user may not be recognized and therefore cannot log in to the mailbox.

If the user is calling from an external source, the reason for the user not being recognized might be that the alternate number is not configured or is incorrect. If a user gets a new mobile device or a new home office phone number (for example, because of a move), these phone number changes must be administered in Cisco Unity Connection. In addition, the phone numbers of the notification devices can be updated.

Note When using Cisco Mobile Connect, the phone and mobile numbers are recognized as remote destinations in CUCM. For these calls, the desk phone's extension is used and signaled to Cisco Unity Connection. In this case, it is not required to configure alternate extensions in Cisco Unity Connection.

Number normalization and globalization can also modify the calling numbers of incoming calls. Before these features were in use, most phones displayed a 10-digit number using the North American Numbering Plan (NANP). But when normalization and globalization are enabled, the number that is presented to the phone and to Cisco Unity Connection is +1, followed by the phone number. If the calling number is, for example, the alternate extension 408 555-1000, number modification on the gateway will add +1. Because the number +1 408 555-1000 is not configured in Cisco Unity Connection as an extension or alternate extension, the caller is not recognized. This kind of issue can be detected easily by using the Cisco Unity Connection Port Monitor in the RTMT. The Port Monitor shows the calling, called, and redirected numbers in real time.

Another issue might occur if the voice-mail mask on CUCM modifies the calling number that is sent to Cisco Unity Connection. Again, Cisco Unity Connection Port Monitor will show the calling number. The mask does not need to be set if all directory numbers in CUCM have the same length (for example, four digits). An example of using the voice-mail mask is when an assistant manages the voice messages for a manager. In this case, the proxy line (CUCM Assistant functionality) uses the voice-mail mask to send the number of the manager as the calling number, instead of using the proxy line directory number.

PIN Not Accepted

This section describes various issues that can prevent a PIN from being accepted.

After a vacation, a user might forget the PIN and simply enter the wrong PIN. In such cases, an administrator can change the PIN for the user. This change is made in the user account configuration, under **Edit > Change Password.**

Another issue might be that the dual-tone multifrequency (DTMF) tones are not transmitted. This issue typically happens with Session Initiation Protocol (SIP) phones on CUCM Express. Verify the directory number configuration on CUCM Express for the following commands:

- `voice register pool 1`
- `id mac 0024.C445.5561`
- `type 7965`
- `number 1 dn 1`
- `dtmf-relay rtp-nte`

Without the **dtmf-relay rtp-nte** command, no DTMF tones are sent when using SIP phones. For Skinny Client Control Protocol (SCCP) phones, the DTMF tones are sent correctly by default. In CUCM environment, SCCP and SIP phones also send DTMF tones by default.

If users try to log in with an incorrect PIN, Cisco Unity Connection might lock the account.

Note Prevent brute-force attacks on mailboxes by locking the mailbox when the PIN is incorrectly entered several times.

To force the lockout, verify and modify the authentication rules for voice-mail users and set the following parameters under **System Settings > Authentication Rules:**

- Set **Failed Sign-In** to **3 Attempts** (for example).
- Check the **Administrator Must Unlock** check box.

With these two parameters set, the user will be locked out after entering the wrong PIN three times. You can view the lockout status in the user configuration under **Edit > Password Settings.**

MWI Issues

This section describes message waiting indicator (MWI) issues with an SCCP integration.

An MWI that does not work in a Cisco Unity Connection and CUCM integration is typically the result of a CoS issue or MWI number mismatch.

MWI numbers are configured in CUCM. In the example shown in Figure 7-2, 2510 is configured for MWI on and 2511 is configured for MWI off. Verify that these numbers are also configured for MWI on and off in Cisco Unity Connection. Sometimes customers switch (or simply mistype) the MWI numbers.

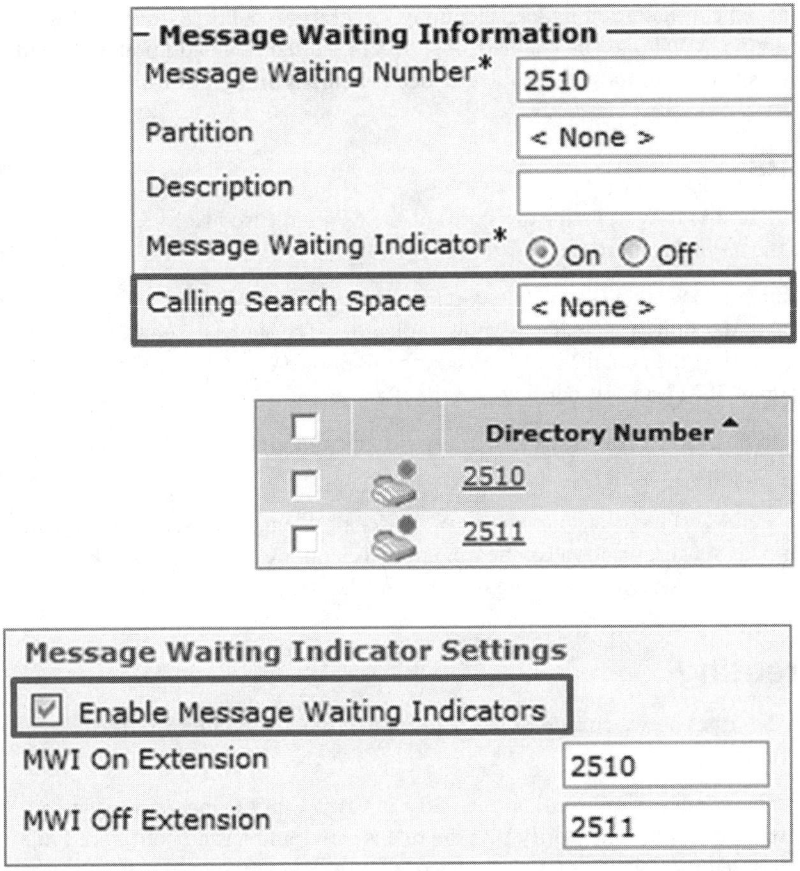

Figure 7-2 *Cisco Unity Connection Incorrect MWI Configuration*

The MWI numbers in CUCM need a CSS. This CSS must be able to call the IP phone, to turn the MWI on or off. Try to dial the MWI on number from the IP phone. If the MWI is turned on, the problem is on Cisco Unity Connection. Dialing the MWI off number turns MWI off again.

> **Note** This quick test works only if the IP phone has access rights to call the MWI on number. However, after testing is done, it would be wise to prevent a user from dialing the MWI numbers by modifying the CSSs.

If new partitions are introduced—for example, when implementing the CUCM Assistant feature—managers might lose MWI functionality. If so, the CSS for the MWI on and off numbers must be extended to include the new partition.

In the port-group configuration under **Telephony Integrations > Port Group** on Cisco Unity Connection, MWI must be enabled, as shown in the figure. In addition, the **Send MWI Requests** parameter must be enabled under **Telephony Integrations > Port.**

MWI Status

The section describes how to verify the status of the MWI in Cisco Unity Connection and how to run a synchronization.

The target state of MWIs on Cisco Unity Connection can be verified in the user account configuration under **Edit > Message Waiting Indicators.** The status in the Current Status field does not reflect the actual MWI status on the IP phone. Cisco Unity Connection cannot determine if MWI is set correctly on the IP phone.

MWI needs to be enabled for each Cisco Unity Connection user; this setting is the default when creating new users.

When you fix an MWI issue, such as a class of service problem, run a synchronization of all MWIs. This synchronization can be run under **Telephony Integrations > Phone System** for the phone system that is integrated with CUCM.

Wrong Greeting

This section describes how a change or new call-routing rule might interrupt the correct call routing functionality.

By default, only two direct call-routing rules exist in Cisco Unity Connection. The first rule is the Attempt Sign In rule. Verify that the rule is active and has no configured rule conditions, and that the caller is sent via Conversation to Attempt Sign In. Attempt Sign In sends the call to the user sign-in conversation, if the calling number belongs to a user. The calling number is compared with the extensions or alternate extensions. If the call is from an unidentified caller, the next rule in the routing table is applied. The second and by default the last rule is the standard opening greeting.

When adding a new routing rule, the new routing rule has no rule conditions and is set to Active. Therefore, all incoming calls will use the new call routing rule and the callers are sent to the system directory call handler by default and may search for a number. To prevent this behavior, set the status to Inactive immediately after creating the new routing rule. Then add the rule conditions and set the call action. When these tasks are done, activate the new routing rule again and test for correct functionality.

Rules and Conditions

If the calling number is correct and the extension exists in Cisco Unity Connection, check for a misconfiguration of the conditions and rules.

Call-routing rules are like access control lists. The search begins with the first rule and, within it, the first condition. If there is no match, the next condition is used. If no more conditions exist, the next rule is used and the same process starts again. At the end, the standard opening greeting is played for any remaining calls.

The wildcard X that is used in CUCM for one character can also be configured in Cisco Unity Connection. However, in Cisco Unity Connection, the X has a different meaning. A condition to check for a calling number 2XXX does not match calls from 2001 or 2138. Instead, the standard opening greeting is played.

Here is some additional information about writing conditions for calling numbers:

- Choose an operator (In, Equals, Greater Than, Less Than, Less Than or Equal, and Greater Than or Equal) and enter a phone number or number pattern, to apply the rule to a phone number from which calls originate. To apply the rule to all originating phone numbers, choose the **Equals** operator and enter an asterisk (*) or leave the field blank.
- When choosing the **Equals** operator, enter an asterisk (*) or question mark (?) as wildcards. The asterisk matches zero or more digits and can be used alone or with other numbers. For example, enter **212*** to control routing of all calls from the 212 area code. The question mark matches any single digit. For example, enter **555????** to control routing of all calls from seven-digit numbers that begin with 555.
- When choosing the **In** operator, enter a range of numbers (for example, 2000–2599), a comma-separated list of numbers (for example, 4001, 54001, 5554001), or a combination of both (for example, 2000–2199, 3001–3199, 5554001).
- Add multiple calling number conditions to a single routing rule to create more-complex patterns (for example, all numbers in the range 2000–3999 plus all numbers that are greater than 5000). When a call matches all conditions for the rule, the call is routed as specified in Send Call To.

Time Schedule

This section describes how the schedule can be used in rule conditions for time-based call routing in Cisco Unity Connection.

Call-routing rules are, by default, always active. The default schedules All Hours and Weekdays are used by call handlers and users. By default, call handlers use All Hours, and users use Weekdays. Because the closed greeting is not enabled by default, users in practice have an All Hours schedule. If no closed greeting is enabled, the standard greeting is used.

Voice Messages

This section describes the telephony user interface (TUI) prompts that are played to callers if voice-messaging issues arise.

To enable complete Cisco Unity Connection functionality, check the **Mounted** check box under **Message Storage > Mailbox Stores** for the Unity Messaging Database – 1.

If the Mounted check box is unchecked, Cisco Unity Connection users cannot retrieve messages, and mailbox store settings cannot be changed in Cisco Unity Connection Administration. However, callers can still leave messages, which are queued for delivery when the mailbox store is available again.

If the mailbox quota for send and receive is reached, callers cannot leave messages. The mailbox quotas can be set under **Edit > Mailbox** in the user account settings or on a system level. If the caller speaks the message and hangs up, the caller has no way of knowing that the user will not receive the message. Even if the caller presses the pound key (**#**) and **1** to send the message instead of simply hanging up the call, Cisco Unity Connection announces that the message has been sent.

Call Handler Transfer Issues

This section describes how callers can be transferred via caller input, transfer rules, greetings, and message settings.

When a call is transferred via the Call Handler option, Cisco Unity Connection sends the call to the specified system call handler. Specify whether the call should transfer to the call handler extension or go directly to the call handler greeting.

When you use the **Transfer to Alternate Contact Number** option for **Call Action**, Cisco Unity Connection transfers the call to the phone number or URI that is specified in the Extension or URI field. Specify whether Cisco Unity Connection should transfer the call by releasing it to the phone system or by supervising the transfer. If **Supervise Transfer** is selected as the transfer type, specify the number of rings to wait before Cisco Unity Connection ends the attempt to transfer.

If the call flows to CUCM, the voice-mail ports or SIP trunk is the originator of the transfer. If a proper CSS is not set on the voice-mail port or SIP trunk, no extension or directory number (DN) is reachable. For example, if all devices are in a device partition but the CSSs on the voice-mail ports or SIP trunk are set to <None>, no device is reachable.

Call Handler Issues

This section describes issues with directory and interview call handlers.

For directory handlers, most issues occur in the search scope settings. If users cannot be found when a caller uses the directory handler, the search scope might be incorrect. Verify that users and call handlers are correctly placed in partitions and that the partitions are listed in the Search Space option that is set in the directory handler. Users can choose to delist their entries from the directory of an extension, in which case there is no actual issue.

Interview handlers need defined questions. These questions must be active and recorded. Without a recorded question, the call handler will not play anything. The Interview call handler executes the After Interview Action after the questions are played. The Goodbye call handler is selected by default.

AAR and Cisco Unified SRST Issues

This section describes voice-messaging issues together with WAN backup technologies.

When AAR or Cisco Unified SRST is active, calls are routed over the PSTN instead over the WAN. Four-digit numbers are no longer used because the PSTN expects the complete phone number or at least the subscriber number depending on the PSTN provider.

For example, when a user presses the **Messages** button, the calling number is recognized as 408 555-1000 instead of 1000, which is the configured extension in Cisco Unity Connection. The user ID does not match, so the standard opening greeting is played. The solution is to configure alternate extensions that contain the complete phone number.

During a call forward, AAR might be unsuccessful. This issue happens if no AAR CSS is configured on the phones. Set the AAR CSS to a value that contains a partition with route patterns to the PSTN.

Not sending a redirected number can be caused by missing configuration parameters in various places.

When troubleshooting, start with the outgoing gateway. Use the **debug isdn q931** command to determine which information the originating gateway sends. An example of this debug output is as follows:

```
Calling Party Number i = 0x0081, '442288224001'
        Plan:ISDN, Type:International
Called Party Number i = 0xA1, '12012012100'
        Plan:ISDN, Type:National
Redirecting Number i = 0x000081, '4002'
        Plan:Unknown, Type:Unknown
```

If the redirected number is not shown at the originating gateway, verify that the router is configured to pass the information:

```
interface Serial0/0/0:23
 isdn outgoing ie redirecting-number
```

For AAR calls, verify that the **Redirecting Number IE Delivery—Outbound** parameter is set on CUCM in the gateway configuration.

If the originating gateway sends the redirecting number, use the **debug isdn q931** command at the terminating gateway to verify that the redirected number is received. Typically, the PSTN provider does not strip redirected numbers.

If the redirected number is shown on the terminating gateway, the Redirecting Number IE Delivery—Inbound parameter is not set for the gateway in CUCM.

To correct the issues, check the Display IE Delivery, Redirecting Number IE Delivery—Outbound, and Redirecting Number IE Delivery—Inbound parameters. The Display IE Delivery configuration is necessary only if calls to the PSTN must send the complete phone number as well as the calling name. The Redirecting Number IE Delivery parameters are required for voice-mail integration.

Cisco Unified RTMT

This section describes the general monitoring capabilities of Cisco Unified RTMT in Cisco Unity Connection.

Cisco Unified RTMT can be downloaded as a plug-in from any Unified Communications application. The plug-in can be installed on an administrator PC. When starting the tool, enter the Cisco Unity Connection IP address, username, and password. In addition, enter a port number and enable a secure connection to Cisco Unity Connection.

When the tool opens, choose the Default configuration. On the left side, two tabs appear, as shown in Figure 7-3. The System tab includes the System Summary, Server, Performance, and Tools submenus. The Cisco Unity Connection tab includes the Port Monitor.

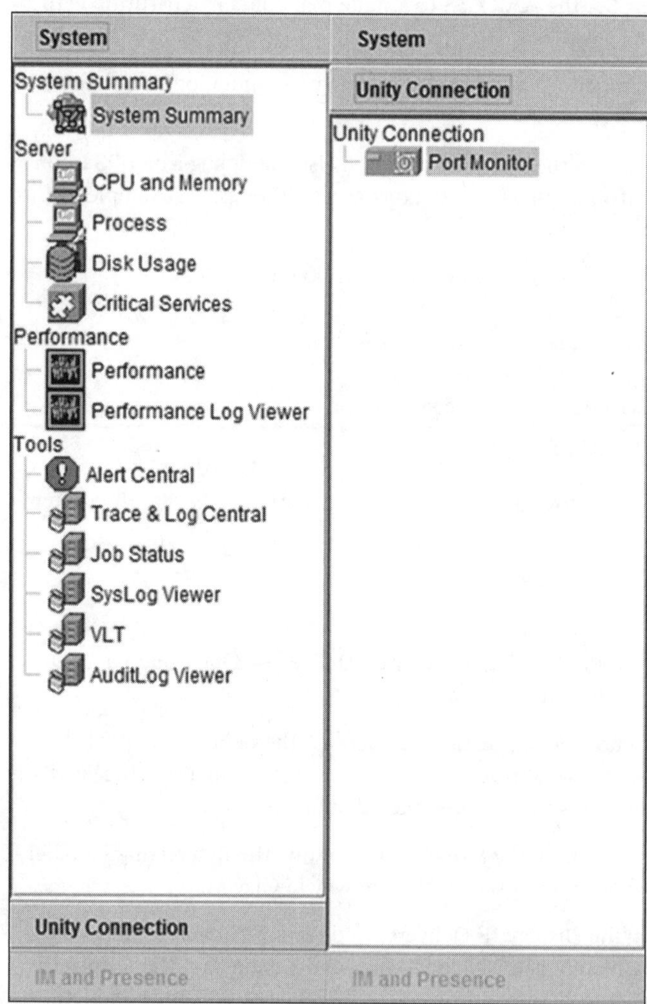

Figure 7-3 *Cisco RTMT Tool*

Cisco Unity Connection Performance Counters

This section describes the available performance counters in Cisco Unity Connection.

In Cisco Unified RTMT, performance counters are grouped in menus that are specific to Cisco Unity Connection and Cisco Unity Connection sessions. In addition, standard performance-counter groups exist for database, enterprise replication, network, partitions, processor, system, TCP, and so on. These performance counters are like those used in CUCM.

Figure 7-4 shows part of the list with the available Cisco Unity Connection performance-counter groups. Each performance-counter group includes a subset of settings that can be monitored. The figure shows a performance counter from **CUC Phone System > Incoming Calls Total.** In this example, more than 115 calls have been delivered while Cisco Unity Connection has been running.

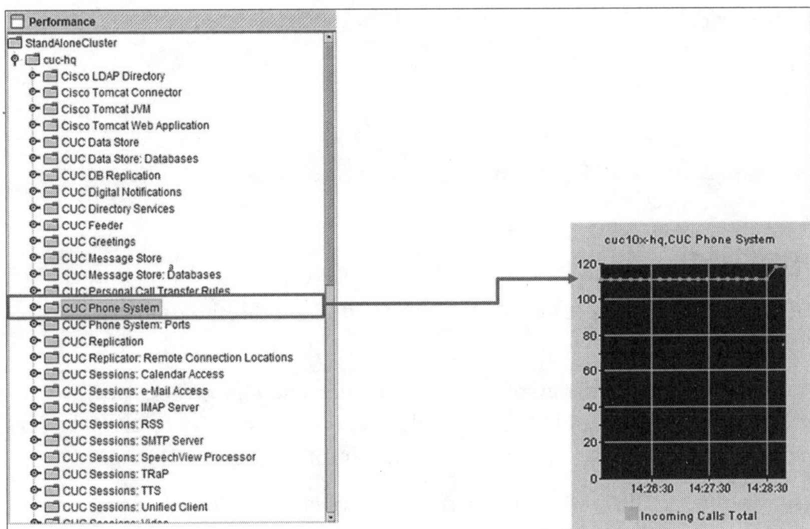

Figure 7-4 *Cisco Unity Connection RTMT Incoming Calls*

Cisco Unity Connection Session Performance Counters

As Figure 7-5 shows, you can use the Cisco Unity Connection Sessions performance counters to monitor groups and items in the groups in real time.

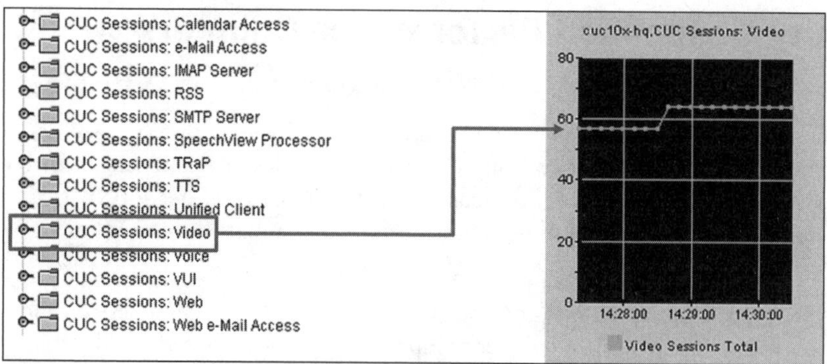

Figure 7-5 *Cisco Unity Connection RTMT Video Sessions Total*

These example items can be monitored for Cisco Unity Connection video sessions:

- Downgraded video calls
- Video records
- Video sessions

For video sessions, more than 30 performance counters are available.

Alert Properties

This section describes how to receive notifications for defined thresholds in certain performance counters.

Right-click a performance counter graphical representation and choose **Set/Alert Properties.** Enter a description and a recommended action. The severity level can be set to Emergency, Alert, Critical, Error, Warning, Notice, Informational, or Debug.

Figure 7-6 shows an example in which the current call count is monitored. If the threshold is reached (in other words, if more than ten ports are used at the same time), a warning should be sent to the administrator. If this warning is being sent too often, the current call count options may need to be redesigned (enable or disable port functionality) or additional ports may need to be activated to increase reachability.

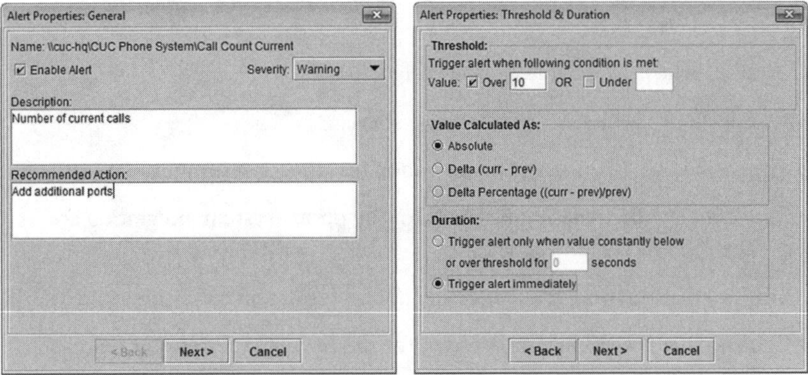

Figure 7-6 *Cisco Unity Connection RTMT Alert Properties*

In the Frequency section of the Frequency & Schedule window, choose whether the alert should be sent every time the threshold is reached, or only if the threshold is reached a certain number of times in a specified period (for example, two times in 5 minutes). In the Schedule section, specify nonstop monitoring or a time frame for monitoring the selected performance counter.

When you click **Next**, the Email Notification window opens. You can enable e-mail alerts or configure an alert action. The default is to log the alerts.

Reporting in Cisco Unity Connection

This section lists the reports that are available in Cisco Unity Connection Serviceability, under **Tools > Report**.

In Figure 7-7, the Mailbox Store Report is selected. The report can be generated as a web page, a comma-delimited file, or a PDF file. When you click Generate Report, the Mailbox Store Report appears, as shown in the figure.

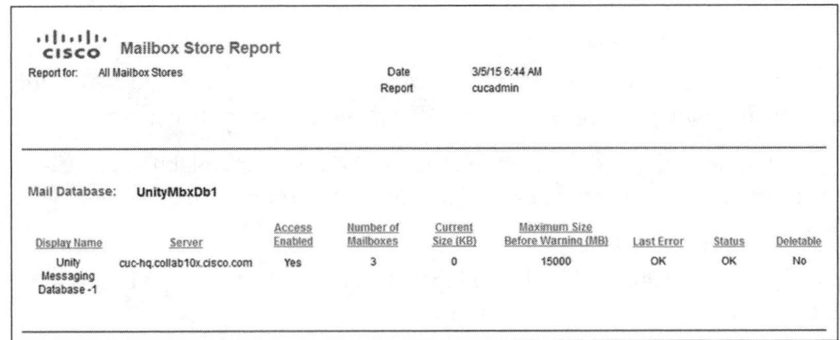

CISCO Mailbox Store Report

Report for: All Mailbox Stores Date 3/5/15 6:44 AM

Report cucadmin

Mail Database: UnityMbxDb1

Display Name	Server	Access Enabled	Number of Mailboxes	Current Size (KB)	Maximum Size Before Warning (MB)	Last Error	Status	Deletable
Unity Messaging Database -1	cuc-hq.collab10x.cisco.com	Yes	3	0	15000	OK	OK	No

Figure 7-7 *Cisco Unity Connection RTMT Reporting*

MWI Troubleshooting

This section describes how to troubleshoot MWI issues.

When troubleshooting MWI issues, follow these steps:

Step 1. Run the Check Telephony Configuration test for the relevant phone system.

Step 2. Confirm that voice-messaging ports for the phone-system integration are assigned to send MWI requests.

Step 3. Confirm that the port groups for the phone-system integration enable MWIs.

Step 4. Confirm that the settings are correct for the MWI On Extension field and the MWI Off Extension field for SCCP phones.

Step 5. Confirm that MWIs for the phone system are not forced off.

Step 6. Confirm that the MWI is enabled for the user.

Step 7. Confirm that the correct phone system is assigned to the MWI for the user.

Step 8. Confirm that the extensions that turn MWIs on and off are in the same CSS that contains the phones and voice-mail ports.

Step 9. Verify whether the Cisco Unity Connection server was upgraded, restored by using the Disaster Recovery System, or experienced an event that disrupted MWI synchronization.

Step 10. If the preceding tasks did not resolve the MWI problem, enable macro traces for MWIs.

Resynchronize MWIs for the system after a server is restored by using the Disaster Recovery System, after upgrading a system, or after a WAN outage in a system that has distributed voice-messaging through Cisco Unified SRST routers or CUCM Express routers in Cisco Unified SRST mode.

Use the following troubleshooting information if a delay occurs in turning MWIs on or off:

- If MWIs are being synchronized for a phone system integration, delayed MWIs for messages might result from the additional MWI requests that are being processed.
- The number of ports that are assigned to process MWI requests might be insufficient. For systems that process a large volume of calls, extra ports might need to be installed.
- If two or more port groups are in the phone system integration, make sure that all the port groups are correctly configured for MWIs.

Macro Traces

This section describes how to enable macro traces to troubleshoot MWI issues.

In Cisco Unity Connection Serviceability, under **Trace > Macro Traces**, choose the trace that might help you to analyze issues in Cisco Unity Connection. For MWI traces, check the **Traces for MWI Problems** check box.

Summary

This section summarizes the key points that were discussed in this chapter:

- Most Cisco Unity Connection issues can be solved by verifying the configuration. In most customer scenarios, misconfiguration is the source of the error, especially for call handlers and calls.
- Some issues involve the verification of CUCM configuration (for example, a missing or wrong CoS when call transfer or the MWI is not working).
- When you understand how Cisco Unity Connection features are working, you can resolve most issues by verifying the configuration. If the configuration seems to be correct, enable micro or macro traces to resolve the issue. The trace files can be viewed via Cisco Unified RTMT.

Review Questions

Answer the following questions, and then see Appendix A, "Answers to Review Questions," for the answers.

1. **You can use route patterns that are enabled for overlap send for Call Forward All.**

   a. True

   b. False

2. **You can use Mobile Connect with remote destinations (for example, the mobile number) in Cisco Unified Communications Manager instead of configuring alternate extensions in Cisco Unity Connection for number recognition.**

   a. True

   b. False

3. **When configuring rule conditions, which of the following matches 555–1234?**

   a. 555XXXX

   b. 555xxxx

   c. 555####

   d. 555????

4. Which command must be configured on a PSTN router to send the redirected number out to the PSTN?

    a. isdn outgoing redirected-number

    b. isdn outgoing send-ie

    c. isdn outgoing ie redirecting-number

    d. isdn outgoing display-outbound

Chapter 8

Deploying Voice-Mail Redundancy in Branch Offices

Upon completing this chapter, you will be able to do the following:

- Describe the integration and deployment model for Cisco Unity Connection SRSV
- List the supported hardware platforms and the minimum Cisco IOS Software release that is required to support the hardware platform for Cisco Unity Connection SRSV
- Explain how Cisco Unity Connection SRSV bridges the gap between centralized managed systems and distributed redundant branch systems
- Describe the licensing of Cisco Unity Connection SRSV
- Describe how certain features are supposed to work in Cisco Unity Connection SRSV mode
- Describe the configuration process for Cisco Unity Connection SRSV in a branch office
- Activate Cisco Unity Connection SRSV
- Describe how to configure Cisco Unity Connection to use self-signed certificates in SRSV mode
- Show the menu of Cisco Unity Connection SRSV including the branch site setup
- Describe the configuration of Cisco Unity Connection in the headquarters site to register the branch SRSV server
- Configure the headquarters Cisco Unity Connection site as a central site for the SRSV branch sites
- Describe how to configure automatic provisioning and voicemail polling of the branch locations
- Describe how to enable replication of system distribution lists
- Describe how to resolve SRSV deployment issues

This chapter describes the deployment of Cisco Unity Connection SRSV and its features and limitations. This chapter also describes the configuration process of the branch and the headquarters, or central, sites.

Introduction to Cisco Unity Connection SRSV

Cisco Unity Connection SRSV is a backup voice-mail solution that allows you to receive voice messages during WAN outages. It works in conjunction with Cisco Unified SRST to provide voice-mail service to a branch when the connectivity with the central Cisco Unity Connection voice-mail service is lost, as illustrated in Figure 8-1.

Cisco Unity Connection SRSV is used in a centralized Cisco Unified Communications Manager (CUCM) and Cisco Unity Connection environment with multiple branch offices or small sites. It provides limited voice-mail and auto-attendant features that remain in synchronization with the central Unity Connection voice-mail service so that when the WAN outage or failure occurs, the Unity Connection SRSV solution can provide voice-mail service to subscribers at the branch. However, as soon as the network is restored, all the voice mails that were received by the branch subscribers are automatically uploaded to the central Unity Connection voice-mail server.

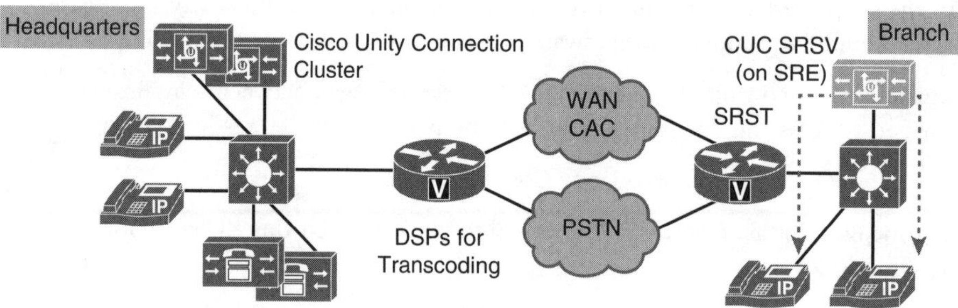

Figure 8-1 *Cisco Unity Connection SRSV*

> **Note** Cisco Unity Connection SRSV replaces Cisco Unity Express SRSV.

The Unity Connection SRSV solution requires the following two components:

- **Cisco Unity Connection:** Cisco Unity Connection is deployed at the central site along with CUCM to deliver powerful integrated messaging and voice-mail services.
- **Cisco Unity Connection SRSV:** The SRSV component is natively a part of Unity Connection and is deployed at the branch site along with CUCM Express or Cisco Unified SRST. Cisco Unity Connection SRSV is hosted on the Cisco ISR G2 platform by using Cisco Services Ready Engine Virtualization (Cisco SRE-V).

Specifications for Virtual Platform Overlay

Table 8-1 specifies the virtual platform overlays supported by Cisco Unity Connection SRSV. Any supported Cisco Unity Connection hardware that conforms to these requirements is suitable for Cisco Unity Connection SRSV.

Table 8-1 *Cisco Unity Connection Virtual Platform Overlay Options*

Product Options	Virtual Platform Overlay
CPU cores and speed per core	1 CPU with a minimum of 1.8 GHz
vRAM	4 GB
vDisk	1x160 GB
Total number of available voice ports	12
Total number of user with mailboxes	500
Approximate message storage, G-711 codec, minutes	72,944
Number of public distribution lists	500
Number of call handlers	200
Number of languages supported	2

The Cisco 2900 series ISR require IOS version 15.2(4)M4 and 3900 series ISR require IOS version 15.4(1)T for Cisco Unity Connection SRSV. However, a different Cisco IOS Software release may be required depending on the version of CUCM Express or Cisco Unified SRST that is used.

The number of ports for Cisco Unity Connection SRSV depends on the codec:

- Eight ports are required for the G.711 or G.729a codec.
- Two ports are required for iLBC or G.722 codec.

Each Cisco Unity Connection SRSV branch will support 500 users, with a maximum of 35 branches per centralized Unity Connection server. The synchronization process does not have any bandwidth requirements because it is not a real-time process.

Cisco Unity Connection SRSV Solution

Table 8-2 describes the features that customers require and the issues to overcome with a centralized voice-mail solution.

Table 8-2 *Cisco Unity Connection SRSV Problems and Solutions*

Problems	Solutions
■ Centralization lowers total cost of ownership (TCO).	■ New Cisco Unity Connection mode runs standby at branch.
■ Centralization creates a WAN.	■ Centrally managed.
Customer Requirements	■ WAN survivable voice mail and auto-attendant.
■ No lost messages	■ Greetings and call handlers auto-sync.
■ Centralized administration	■ Auto failover to SRSV as phones enter SRST.
■ Leverage existing hardware	■ Messages auto-sync with Cisco Unity Connection upon recovery.
■ Easy to manage and deploy	

Cisco Unified SRSV provides a cost-effective solution for supporting redundant voice-mail service for remote sites such as branch offices or small sites. When a remote site does not have access to the central voicemail system—for example, during a network service interruption—Cisco Unified SRSV provides voice-mail backup services to help ensure that the remote site continues to have voice-mail service.

Cisco Unity Connection SRSV Licensing

Cisco Unity Connection Basic user license that you can use for voice mail, unified messaging, or integrated messaging does not include the SRSV capability for branch office users. An Enhanced user license provides all the user and interoperability functions available with the Basic license plus the SRSV capability for branch office users. Both Basic and Enhanced capabilities are provided with Cisco Unified Workspace Licensing (Cisco UWL):

- Enhanced messaging user:
  - All basic user features and SRSV
  - Included in Cisco UWL Standard and Professional
- New opportunity to leverage existing hardware:
  - Existing Cisco Unified Communication Manager and Cisco Unity Connection customers
  - SRST customers
  - Cisco Unity Express SRSV customers

Limitations in Cisco Unity Connection SRSV Mode

Access to certain interfaces—such as Internet Message Access Protocol (IMAP), voice user interface (VUI), and web-based voice mail—is not available in SRSV mode. Messages to the system distribution list are sent only after the central Cisco Unity Connection is back online and reachable.

For the full list of limitations and restrictions, refer to *Cisco Unity Connection SRSV Limitations and Restrictions chapter of the Complete Reference Guide for Cisco Unity Connection Survivable Remote Site Voicemail (SRSV) for Release 10.x*, available at http://www.cisco.com/c/en/us/td/docs/voice_ip_comm/connection/10x/srsv/guide/10xcucsrsvx/10xcucsrsv170.html#53796.

- Other voice-mail interfaces that are supported on the central Cisco Unity Connection (such as IMAP, VUI, and web-based voicemail) are not supported.
- Compose, forward, and reply to voice message options are not supported.
- Message waiting indicator (MWI) in SRST is not supported on versions earlier than 10.5.
- Interview handlers are not supported.
- IPv6 is not supported.
- Distribution lists:
    - Voice messages that are sent to distribution lists in survivable mode are sent to the members only after the WAN recovers.
    - Private distribution lists are not supported.

SRSV Configuration Checklist for Branch Sites

The following is a configuration checklist for Cisco Unity Connection SRSV in a branch site:

- Install Cisco Unity Connection on any Cisco Unity Connection-supported server.
- Convert Cisco Unity Connection to SRSV mode.
- Set up telephony integration on Cisco Unity Connection SRSV with SRST.
- Point the SRSV branch to the central Cisco Unity Connection node.

Install and convert Cisco Unity Connection in the branch to SRSV. Configure SRST in the branch (including the phone system integration) and point SRSV to the centralized voice-messaging system.

Activate Cisco Unity Connection SRSV

For Cisco Unity Connection installation, choose the smallest OVA template for 100 users. The template actually supports more than 100 users. A total of 200 users with mailboxes are supported with Cisco Unity Connection SRSV Version 10.0.

The command **utils cuc activate CUSRSV** converts the standalone Cisco Unity Connection server to Cisco Unity Connection SRSV, as shown in Example 8-1. Converting back to normal Cisco Unity Connection mode requires a reinstallation.

Example 8-1 *Cisco Unity Connection SRSV Conversion from Standalone Cisco Unity Connection*

```
admin:utils cuc activate CUSRSV

After enabling CUSRSV mode CiscoUnityConnection will serve as
CiscoUnityConnectionSRSV
Re-Installation of CiscoUnityConnection will be required so as to convert
CiscoUnityConnectionSRSV back to CiscoUnityConnection
Now CiscoUnityConnection will be converted to CiscoUnityConnectionSRSV
Do you want to continue ?
Enter (yes/no) ? yes

Are you sure for CiscoUnityConnection to CiscoUnityConnectionSRSV conversion ?
Enter (yes/no) ? yes

 Processing [-##################################-]

The system is going down for reboot NOW!
 Processing [|####|]
Mode Switch Action Completed System Will Restart
```

DNS, Domains, and Self-Signed Certificates

When using SRSV, you must set up a DNS server and add the new branch site where you deploy SRSV. You must also add a domain name on the Cisco Unity Connection SRSV server. The central (headquarters) Cisco Unity Connection server name must also be configured in the DNS server and requires a configured domain name.

You can use self-signed certificate-based access for communication between the central Cisco Unity Connection server and Cisco Unity Connection SRSV. By default, the central Cisco Unity Connection server and Cisco Unity Connection SRSV do not accept self-signed certificates. To accept self-signed certificates on the central Cisco Unity Connection server and Cisco Unity Connection SRSV, you must enter the first command shown in Example 8-2.

Example 8-2 *Cisco Unity Connection SRSV Self Signed Certificates*

```
admin:run cuc dbquery unitydirb EXECUTE PROCEDURE
csp_ConfigurationModify (pFullName='System.SRSV.AcceptSrsvSelfSignedCertificates
',pValue='1')

Admin:run cuc dbquery unitydirb select objected,fullname,value from
  vw_configuration where fullname like '%SRSV%'
```

After changing the value of System.SRSV.AcceptSrsvSelfSignedCertificates to 1, you must restart the Connection Branch Sync Service and Tomcat Service to reflect the changes and allow the self-signed certificate access.

Cisco Unity Connection SRSV Menu Overview

Compared to Cisco Unity Connection, SRSV offers only a subset of the Cisco Unity Connection menus. If you choose **Users > Subscribers** or **Distribution Lists > System Distributions** Lists, you will not see an Add New button. Subscribers and lists can only be synchronized from the central site but not configured locally.

You must integrate SRSV with the phone system in the branch office.

Then configure the Cisco Unity Connection SRSV in the branch site to point to the central voice-messaging system. Simply enter the IP address of the centralized Cisco Unity Connection system (headquarters site). There is no further configuration necessary on Cisco Unity Connection SRSV. The testing can be done only after the central site is configured.

SRSV Configuration Checklist for Headquarters Site

In the headquarters site, create a partition for branch users and set up the synchronization based on schedules. Then activate the branch to offer voice-mail functionality during a WAN failure. Then setup provisioning and polling schedules.

Set Up Headquarters Cisco Unity Connection

This section shows how to configure the headquarters Cisco Unity Connection site as a central site for the SRSV branch sites.

To add a new branch, choose **Networking > Branch Management > Branches**, as shown in Figure 8-2.

New Branch

Branch Reset Help

New Branch

Display Name*	BR
Server Address*	10.1.5.24
Username*	cucadministrator
Password*	••••••••••
SMTP Domain Name*	cuc
PAT Port Number*	443
Partition*	BR
Operator	operator

Provisioning Synch Options

- [x] Synch voice name for users
- [x] Synch greetings for users

Save

Fields marked with an asterisk (*) are required.

Figure 8-2 *Cisco Unity Connection New Branch*

When setting up the central site, point to the server IP address of the branch Cisco Unity Connection site and enter the user credentials.

Enter a Port Address Translation (PAT) port number that the central Cisco Unity Connection server uses to communicate with the branch. This port number specifies the port on the public side of the NAT, which further maps to port 443 for communicating with the branch.

In this example, only users that are located in the partition BR are synchronized to the SRSV server in the branch site. You can also choose to synchronize the recorded voice names and greetings of the end users.

Automatic Provisioning and Polling

Enable automatic synchronization between the headquarters and the branch Cisco Unity Connection servers. You can run the synchronization after system startup, regularly after 10 or more minutes, or specify a certain day per week or month.

The provisioning flow is as follows:

- The headquarters Cisco Unity Connection sends a request for provisioning.
- The branch is ready for provisioning.
- The headquarters Cisco Unity Connection sends the provisioning data in the form of a TAR chunk.
- The branch confirms receipt of the provisioning data TAR chunk and verifies the integrity on last chunk.
- Provisioning is started at the branch.
- A notification is sent to the headquarters Cisco Unity Connection when provisioning is complete.
- The headquarters Cisco Unity Connection acknowledges branch provisioning.

The branch voice-mail polling task polls the branches that are defined in the headquarters Cisco Unity Connection and schedules those branches for voicemail upload if they have voice mails.

The voice-mail upload flow is as follows:

- The headquarters Cisco Unity Connection checks for new voicemails for the branch.
- The branch confirms that a new message is available.
- The headquarters Cisco Unity Connection requests message information from the branch.
- The branch sends the message details.
- The headquarters Cisco Unity Connection fetches the new message as a WAV file.
- The branch responds with a WAV file.
- The headquarters Cisco Unity Connection confirms the message delivery and asks the branch to delete the messages.
- The branch deletes the messages.

Monitor the Provisioning and Polling Status

At the Branch Sync Results page under **Networking > Branch Management**, you can see the result of synchronization. The result can be any of the following:

- **In Progress:** This result signifies that the synchronization activity is in progress.
- **Success:** This result signifies that the synchronization activity is completed successfully.
- **Partial Success:** This result signifies that the synchronization activity is partially completed. For example, if you initiated synchronization of four users from the headquarters Cisco Unity Connection server to the branch, it is possible that two of the four users are synchronized successfully and two are not. In such scenarios, you must check the error logs to determine the reason for the failure and take the appropriate action to resolve the problem.
- **Failed:** This result signifies that the synchronization activity has failed. To check the reason for the failure, refer to the associated logs.

Replicate System Distribution List

Check the **Replicate to SRSV Branches** check box to synchronize the distribution lists from the headquarters Cisco Unity Connection server to the branch, as shown in Figure 8-3. Verify the synchronization on the Branch Sync Results page.

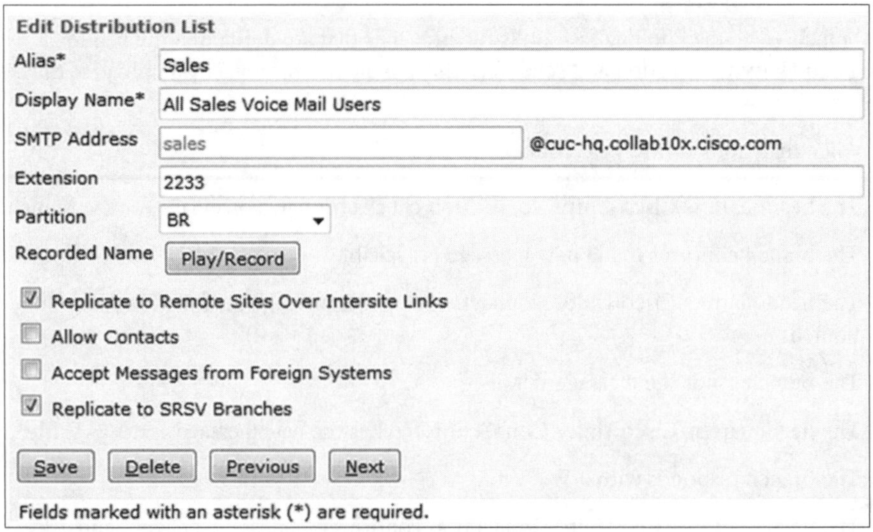

Figure 8-3 *Cisco Unity Connection SRSV Distribution Lists*

Troubleshooting Issues in Provisioning

Follow this list to resolve issues that are related to SRSV setup. If these steps do not resolve the issue, enable traces for SRSV.

Status of provisioning remains in progress or is not working:

- Check the network connectivity of the central Cisco Unity Connection and the branch.
- Ensure that the branch username and password is not expired by logging into the branch administration pane.
- Check whether the VMREST and Connection Branch Sync Service are active on both the headquarters and branch.
- Check license and certificate status.
- If automatic provisioning is not working at the scheduled time, then check whether the branch provisioning synchronization task is enabled or not.

If the previous steps do not resolve the issue, enable all micro traces for CUCESync and VMREST services for the central Cisco Unity Connection. Check for any exceptions or failures in the traces for the CUCESync service.

The VMREST micro traces provide diagnostic information on the use of the API. The VMREST micro traces are written to the Tomcat diagnostic files. Collect logs for CUCESync service and Cisco Tomcat services from Cisco Unity Connection at both the headquarters and branches. If automatic provisioning is not working at the scheduled time, then provisioning is scheduled at the next cycle.

Summary

This section summarizes the key points that were discussed in this chapter.

- Cisco Unity Connection SRSV replaces Cisco Unity Express SRSV. It can be installed on any Cisco Unity Connection-supported server in a virtualized way.
- Install Cisco Unity Connection and convert it to Cisco Unity Connection SRSV via the CLI. Set up the headquarters and branch, and enable automatic provisioning and voice message polling. The user base for each branch is selected and synchronized on a partition level.

Review Questions

Answer the following questions, and then see Appendix A, “Answers to Review Questions,” for the answers.

1. **Cisco Unity Express SRSV is the predecessor of Cisco Unity Connection SRSV.**

   a. True

   b. False

2. **Which command is used to convert Cisco Unity Connection into Cisco Unity Connection SRSV?**

    a. **set cuc activate CUSRSV**

    b. **utils cuc activate CUSRSV**

    c. **utils cuc convert CUSRSV**

    d. New installation with Cisco Unity Connection SRST media

3. **When enabling micro traces for Cisco Unity Connection SRSV troubleshooting, which one of the following can be used?**

    a. CDL

    b. CsEws

    c. CUCESync

    d. MiuReplication

4. **Users can be synchronized or added locally in Cisco Unity Connection SRSV.**

    a. True

    b. False

Chapter 9

Designing and Deploying Cisco Unity Express

Upon completing this chapter, you will be able to do the following:

- Describe the product and feature options in Cisco Unity Express
- Describe the hardware that hosts the Cisco Unity Express application
- Describe the user access to Cisco Unity Express
- Describe the Cisco Unity Express auto-attendant feature
- Describe Cisco Unity Express schedules
- Describe integrated messaging on Cisco Unity Express
- Describe Cisco Unity Express distribution lists
- Describe message notification in Cisco Unity Express
- Describe the Cisco Unity Express message notification for scheduled backups
- Describe the Cisco Unity Express integration options with different call-processing systems
- Describe the supported Cisco Unity Express deployment models
- Describe the main differences between Cisco Unity Express and Cisco Unity Connection

Cisco Unity Express provides a feature-rich messaging solution that is ideal for the requirements of branch locations or small to medium-sized businesses. This chapter describes the features and characteristics of Cisco Unity Express.

Cisco Unity Express

This section describes the product and feature options in Cisco Unity Express.

The Cisco Unity Express web-based graphical user interface (GUI) assists with configuring telephony information in Cisco Unified Communications Manager (CUCM) or CUCM Express (CUCME), and provides ubiquitous remote access for managing, configuring, and provisioning Cisco Unity Express. Figure 9-1 illustrates that Cisco Unity Express (CUE) notifies IP phones when there is one or more voice-mail messages, and the user can then retrieve the voice mails from the phone.

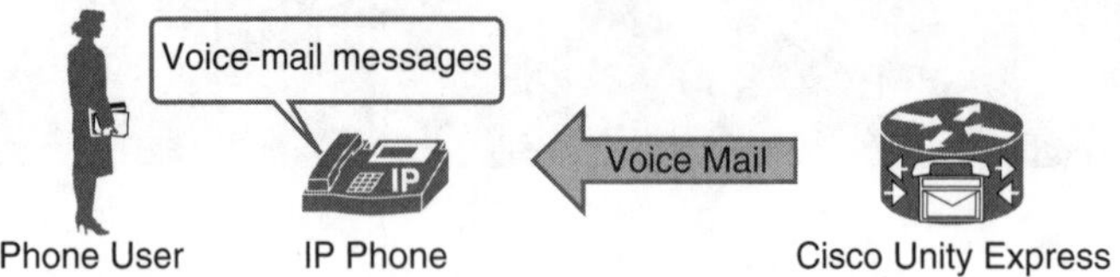

Figure 9-1 *Cisco Unity Express Voice Mail*

The GUI allows the import of information that is shared with CUCM and CUCME and eases management of end users and group affiliations.

CUE can scale up to 500 mailboxes and 32 voice-mail ports and provides commonly used voice-mail features for optimal management of messages. These voice-mail features include the following:

- Replying, forwarding, and saving messages
- Message tagging for privacy or urgency or future delivery
- Alternative greetings
- Pause, fast forward, rewind
- Envelope information
- Secure messaging

CUE provides an autoconfiguration feature, which is invoked after initial software installation. The postinstall autoconfiguration feature will allow the system to go online after a clean installation without requiring the administrator to run the postinstall script. The postinstall script prompts for system configuration parameters.

After software installation and system reboot, the CUE administrator has 2 minutes to respond to the postinstall script prompt for input. If there is no input entered by the administrator after 2 minutes, the postinstall autoconfiguration feature runs.

The postinstall autoconfiguration feature will automatically configure the following:

- The primary NTP server is set to the local host router.
- The time zone is set to GMT.

- The DNS is not configured.
- The call agent is set to the local CUCME system.

If there is no response for 120 seconds, the system boots with the default configuration if there is one. If there is no default configuration, the system will boots with a startup configuration. If there is no startup configuration, the system will boots by autoconfiguring the system. The system will go online without prompting for an administrator account. At the first access of the command-line interface (CLI), the system prompts to create an administrator account.

Cisco Services-Ready Engine

This section describes the hardware that hosts the CUE application.

Figure 9-2 shows the Cisco Internal Service Module-Services Ready Engine (Cisco ISM-SRE) and Cisco Service Module-Services Ready Engine (Cisco SM-SRE).

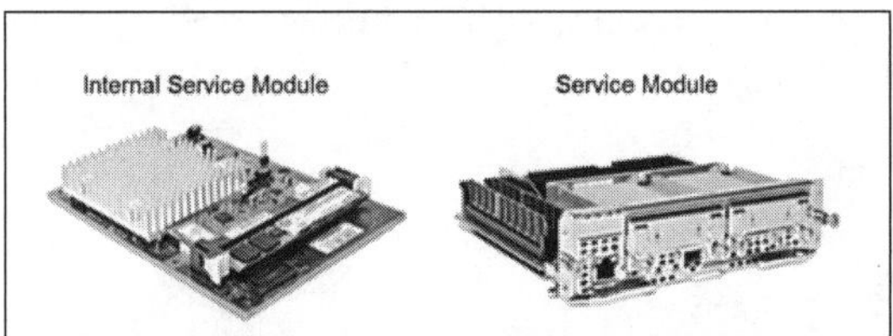

Figure 9-2 *CUE Services-Ready Engine*

The Cisco SRE modules are router blades for the Cisco Integrated Services Routers (ISR) G2 series. These modules provide the capability to host Cisco, third-party, and custom applications. The modules have their own processors, storage, network interfaces, and memory that operate independently of the host router resources, helping ensure maximum concurrent routing and application performance.

The modules come in two compact form factors that are designed to reduce the physical footprint, lower power consumption, and simplify hardware installation at the branch office. The Cisco SRE includes a software controller that enables you to install applications on the module remotely at any time. This solution can help your organization quickly deploy new branch office applications on demand, reduce operating costs, and consolidate the branch office infrastructure.

Cisco SRE offers the next-generation application hosting platform that combines networking, collaboration, compute and storage services, and centralized management into a cohesive system designed to simplify infrastructure, support evolving business needs, and reduce operating costs at the branch office. It integrates all elements necessary to optimize branch office IT infrastructure for delivery of applications from the data center and deployment of branch office applications on demand and houses them in a single chassis, the Cisco ISR G2.

The module can host Cisco Collaboration Systems applications such as CUE, Cisco Prime Network Analysis Module (NAM), Cisco Unified Computing System Express (UCS Express), and others. The Cisco SRE 910 is equipped with an Intel Core2 Duo processor with a core speed of 1.86 GHz, 4 GB DRAM, and two 500-GB SATA hard disks.

User Access

This section describes the user access to CUE.

CUE users can manage their voice messages and greetings with these features:

- Intuitive telephone prompts allow users to easily access menus.
- VoiceView Express is an easy-to-use visual voice-mail telephony user interface. VoiceView Express allows voice-mail subscribers to browse, listen, send messages, and manage their voice-mail messages from their IP phone displays using softkeys. This feature is an alternative to the normal TUI for performing common tasks.
- CUE includes a straightforward GUI for simple user administration and management of personal settings such as greetings and recordings. CUE can be accessed from the GUI or the TUI, as shown in Figure 9-3.

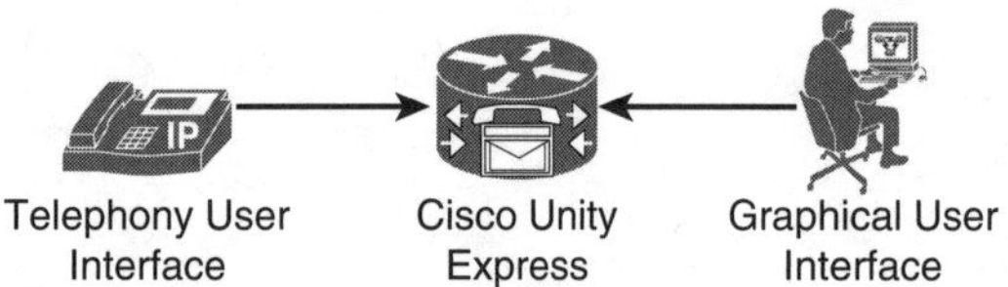

Figure 9-3 *CUE User Access*

CUE Auto-Attendant

This section describes the CUE auto-attendant feature.

CUE has a built-in auto-attendant with dial-by-name, dial-by-extension, and return-to-operator features. The standard auto-attendant services that are provided with CUE simplify self-service for callers by allowing them to quickly reach the right person, 24 hours a day, without the assistance of an operator, as illustrated in Figure 9-4. Users can return to an operator at any time if they need more assistance.

Figure 9-4 *CUE Auto-Attendant*

CUE offers two standard auto-attendant options:

- One includes dial-by-name and dial-by-extension features.
- A second allows single-digit dialing for up to nine users or groups.

A web-based auto-attendant editor allows the administrator to change the parameters of the built-in auto-attendant, which makes managing and updating the call easy enough for a nontechnical user. For more advanced functions where the auto-attendant structure needs to be modified, the administrator can use the feature-rich CUE Editor.

Administrators can create a custom auto-attendant with CUE Editor. The CUE Editor is a Microsoft Windows GUI-based visual scripting tool that gives administrators a simple way to create separate, customized auto-attendant flows in addition to the system auto-attendant.

Using the CUE Editor, system administrators can create up to 16 multilevel auto-attendant flows that provide hierarchical dual-tone multifrequency (DTMF)-based menus. At any time, only five auto-attendant applications can be active—either the built-in AA and four custom, or five custom. The multilevel auto-attendant allows callers to reach individuals, departments, or prerecorded information such as directions or business hours. It also provides customizable time-of-day or day-of-week call management.

In addition, administrators can easily record custom auto-attendant prompts through the CUE Administration by Telephone (AvT) feature. The administrator can record prompts using AvT, through the TUI, or use an offline WAV file recording. This ability allows auto-attendant administrators to modify prompts without needing GUI access to change filenames. Alternative greetings can also be used.

The AvT application is a telephony-based interface that allows CUE to offer administrators the opportunity to record new audio prompts or delete existing custom audio prompts.

Schedules

This section describes CUE schedules.

CUE supports the use of time-based schedules:

- **Holiday schedules:** CUE allows you to define holidays and set up a customized auto-attendant prompt to be played during the holidays. These prompts, which are easily updated through the AvT, can give you customized information about the operation of the business or special events.
- **Business hours:** The business-hours function allows the administrator to define up to four schedules. This function can provide different auto-attendant prompts that are played based on the time of day, without the need for manual intervention.

The AvT application is a telephony-based interface that allows CUE to offer administrators the opportunity to record new audio prompts or delete existing custom audio prompts. CUE announces the auto attendant audio to a phone, as shown in Figure 9-5.

Figure 9-5 *CUE Auto-Attendant*

Integrated Messaging

This section describes integrated messaging on CUE.

Integrated messaging on CUE allows voice-mail users to retrieve, delete, and change the state of their voice messages through Internet Message Access Protocol (IMAP), as illustrated in Figure 9-6.

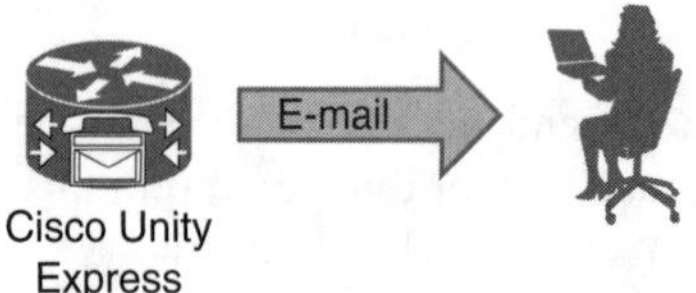

Figure 9-6 *CUE Integrated Messaging*

Taking advantage of existing messaging infrastructure and IMAP e-mail clients, CUE desktop messaging access provides simple, native access to voice mail from Microsoft Outlook, Microsoft Outlook Express, and others, providing continuous and global access to messages. CUE also supports IMAP access on the iPhone.

The Cisco ISM ISM-SRE-300-K9 supports up to 50 IMAP sessions, and the Service Module SM-SRE-910-K9 supports up to 250 IMAP sessions.

Distribution Lists

This section describes CUE distribution lists.

CUE supports the use of distribution lists as follows:

- The public and private distribution list function of CUE allows callers to simply and quickly address a voice-mail message to a list of predefined recipients, saving time and minimizing keying errors.
- CUE includes an All Users public distribution list and the capability for a privileged user to define up to 25 other public lists.

CUE administrators and end users can configure distribution lists to include nonsubscriber numbers along with subscriber numbers (such as a sales distribution list, as shown in Figure 9-7). When sending a message to a distribution list containing nonsubscriber numbers, CUE delivers the message directly to the mailboxes of subscribers and calls the nonsubscriber numbers and plays the message.

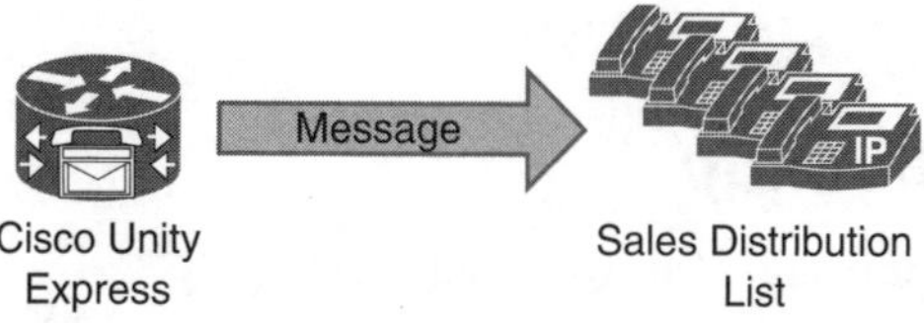

Figure 9-7 *CUE Distribution List*

Broadcast messages, like distribution lists, allow for delivery of messages to multiple recipients. Broadcast messages can also be assigned a priority. Top priority can be assigned to important communications in the voice-message queue. These special messages are played before any other messages and will remain in the mailbox until the messages are completely retrieved or expire, helping ensure that essential communications are received.

Notifications

This section describes message notification in CUE.

CUE supports remote message notification, as illustrated in Figure 9-8. The CUE system notifies the user upon the arrival of all new or urgent messages.

Figure 9-8 *CUE Notifications*

Each mailbox can be configured with notifications that are sent to multiple destinations simultaneously. Users or administrators can configure notification destinations and manage a notification schedule for each destination using the TUI, GUI, or VoiceView Express.

Message notification cascading allows notifications to be sent to a widening circle of recipients. For example, the administrator may create a hierarchy of message notifications for a technical support department as follows:

- The first message notification is sent immediately to the front-line technical support representative pager.

- After a delay of 15 minutes, the next notification is sent to the department manager pager.
- A third notification is sent to an employee in the problem-resolution group after a delay of 30 minutes.

Notifications continue to cascade according to the options selected until a recipient saves or deletes the message.

Notification for Scheduled Backup

This section describes the CUE message notification for scheduled backups.

The administrator can receive notifications of the results of scheduled backups, as illustrated in Figure 9-9. A backup schedule can be configured for voice and text notifications. The notification settings are defined for each backup, not for the user account.

Figure 9-9 *CUE Notification for Scheduled Backup*

Because a scheduled backup will generally run late at night or during nonbusiness hours when the administrator is not onsite, CUE can be configured to send notifications of the results of a scheduled backup.

Notifications of the results of a scheduled backup are sent to the administrator via e-mail, e-page, or voice message. The results notification is placed in a mailbox and indicates the success or failure of a backup.

The notification consists of a short message informing the administrator that a scheduled backup has failed or succeeded. In the case of a failure, the administrator will be able to access CUE and identify the reasons for the failure and take any necessary actions.

CUE Integration

This section describes the CUE integration options with different call-processing systems.

Cisco IP phones are controlled by a call control system, such as CUCM. CUE can provide a voice-mail solution when integrated with the call control system. CUE supports integration, as shown in Figure 9-10, with the following call control systems:

- CUCM
- CUCME
- Cisco Unified Survivable Remote Site Telephony (Cisco Unified SRST) router

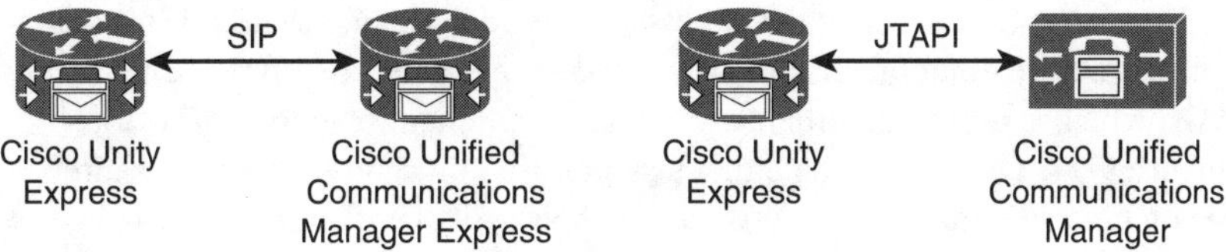

Figure 9-10 *CUE Integration Options*

Protocols that are used between CUE and CUCM are as follows:

- IP phones are controlled via SCCP or SIP through the call-processing system.
- CUE is controlled via JTAPI (via CTIQBE) from CUCM. JTAPI supports telephony call control. It is an extensible application programming interface (API) that is designed to scale for use in a range of domains, from first-party call control in a consumer device to third-party call control in large distributed call centers.
- The message waiting indicator (MWI) on the IP phone is activated when CUE communicates a change of mailbox content to CUCM via CTIQBE. CUCM sends an MWI message to the phone to change the state of the lamp.

CUCME is the most likely choice for a cost-effective small office or branch solution. With CUCME, you integrate CUE with the SIP.

MWI information is also exchanged across the SIP interface. CUE supports SIP Subscribe/Notify and Unsolicited Notify methods for generating MWI notifications, in both Unified CME and SRST modes.

Deployment Models

This section describes the supported CUE deployment models.

CUE can be deployed in a centralized or distributed call-control environment:

- Centralized CUCM
- Distributed CUCME

CUE also supports three primary messaging deployment models:

- Single-site messaging
- Multisite WAN deployment with centralized messaging
- Multisite WAN deployment with distributed messaging using Voice Profile for Internet Mail (VPIM) for networking

Although the call-processing deployment models for CUCM and CUCME are independent of the messaging deployment models in CUE, each has implications for the other that must be considered.

As shown in Figure 9-11, in the single-site messaging model, the messaging systems and messaging infrastructure components are all located at the same site, on the same highly available LAN, which is represented below the public switched telephone network (PSTN) in Figure 9-11. The site can be either a single site or a campus site that is interconnected via high-speed metro-area networks (MANs). All clients of the messaging system are also located at the single (or campus) site. The key distinguishing feature of this model is that there are no remote clients.

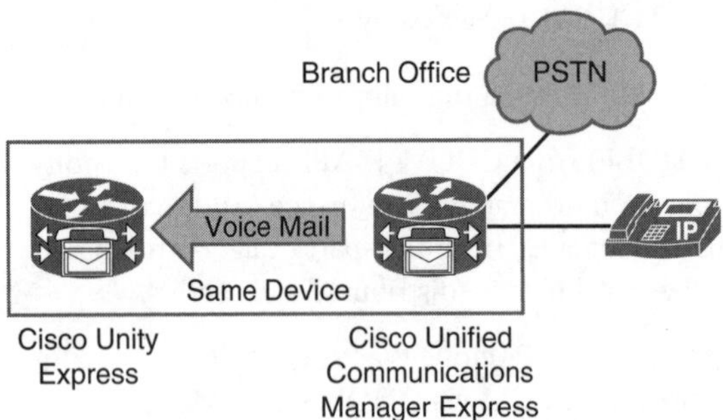

Figure 9-11 *CUE Single-Site Messaging*

A single-site CUE and CUCME deployment provides an all-in-one Cisco Collaboration Systems solution with voice-mail, auto-attendant, and Interactive Voice Response (IVR) functionalities at a lower cost. This type of deployment is ideal for small to medium-sized businesses or branch sites that require a complete voice-mail solution without depending on other sites.

This type of solution provides deployment flexibility and application integration with fewer devices to manage. The result is a cost-effective, integrated Cisco voice-mail solution for IP phones in the branch or remote office as part of the full-service branch.

The same solution could use CUCM instead of CUCME, but the cost would be significantly greater.

In the multisite centralized messaging model as shown in Figure 9-12, like the single-site model, all the messaging system and messaging infrastructure components are located at the same site. The site can be one physical site or a campus site that is interconnected via high-speed MANs. However, unlike the single-site model, centralized messaging clients can be located both locally and remotely. CUE supports multiple CUCME remote sites. This type of deployment ensures centralized voice-mail and auto-attendant features and is ideal for an environment with only a few users at each remote site.

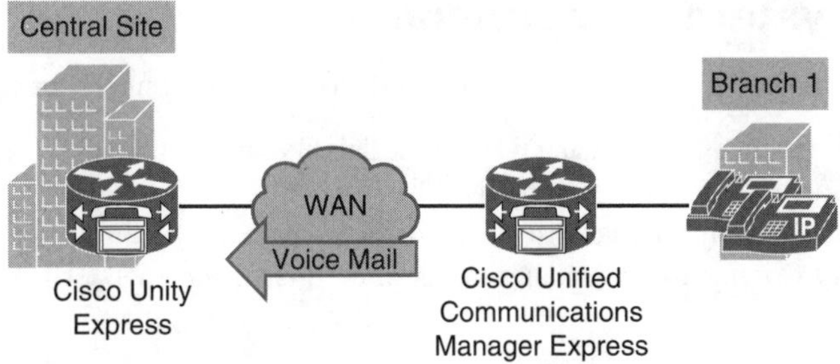

Figure 9-12 *CUE Multisite Centralized Messaging*

Because messaging clients may be either local or remote from the messaging system, special design considerations apply to the following clients: Cisco Unity ViewMail for Outlook (Cisco Unity VMO), the use of the Telephone Record And Playback (TRAP), and message streaming features. Remote clients should not use TRAP and should be configured to download messages before playback. Because different features and operations for local and remote clients can cause user confusion, TRAP should be disabled on the voice ports. GUI clients should be configured to download messages and not use TRAP, regardless of whether the client is local or remote. This procedure also applies to Cisco Unity VMO for Cisco Unity Connection IMAP clients. The CUE TUI operates the same way for both local and remote clients.

A distributed messaging model consists of multiple single-site messaging systems that are distributed with a common messaging backbone, as shown in Figure 9-13. There can be multiple locations, each with its own messaging system and messaging infrastructure components. All client access is local to each messaging system, and the messaging systems share a messaging backbone that spans all locations. Message delivery from the distributed messaging systems occurs via the messaging backbone through a full-mesh or hub-and-spoke type of message-routing infrastructure.

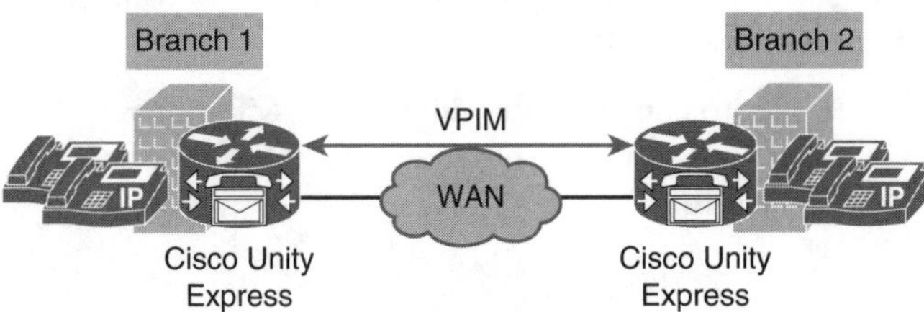

Figure 9-13 *CUE Multisite Distributed Messaging*

Distributed messaging is essentially multiple single-site messaging models with a common messaging backbone.

In the distributed messaging model, CUE provides distributed voice mail at each remote office. The result is efficient networking of CUE systems across different locations. For interbranch communications, voice-mail messages are sent between CUE systems at each site.

Voice Messaging System Comparison

This section describes the main differences between CUE and Cisco Unity Connection.

Table 9-1 shows the main differences from characteristics, scalability, and availability perspectives. If you need more than 500 users or high availability, choose Cisco Unity Connection. Features like Unified Messaging with Microsoft Exchange, for example, may also require Cisco Unity Connection. In smaller or distributed environments, CUE may be the right choice.

Table 9-1 *CUE Voice Messaging System Comparison*

	CUE	Cisco Unity Connection
Version	8.6	10.x
Platform	Router with Service Module	Server with Linux appliance
Port Capacity	32	250/500
Mailboxes	500	20,000
High Availability	No	Yes (Cluster)

For a complete overview, go to the Feature Comparison - Cisco Messaging Products at http://www.cisco.com/c/en/us/products/collateral/unified-communications/unity/product_data_sheet0900aecd806bfc37.html.

Summary

This section summarizes the key points that were discussed in this lesson:

- The built-in CUE auto-attendant provides quick and easy voice-mail access without the need for operator assistance. Callers can be prompted to use dial-by-name, dial-by-extension, and return-to-operator features.
- CUE uses an internal SIP interface to communicate with the CUCME router. Integrating voice mail and call control in a single platform offers flexibility and is ideal for branch office deployments.

Review Questions

Answer the following questions, and then see Appendix A, "Answers to Review Questions," for the answers.

1. **How many users are supported on CUE?**

   a. 150

   b. 250

   c. 300

   d. 500

   e. 600

2. **The Cisco Services-Ready Engine can only be used to host CUE.**

   a. True

   b. False

3. **CUE supports integrated and unified messaging.**

   a. True

   b. False

4. **How many public lists can be created on CUE by the administrator?**

   a. 5

   b. 15

   c. 20

   d. 25

   e. 50

5. **How does Cisco Unified Communications Manager integrate with CUE?**

   a. SCCP

   b. SIP

   c. JTAPI

   d. SMTP

   e. VPIM

Chapter 10

Integrating Cisco Unity Express with Cisco Unified Communications Manager Express

Upon completing this chapter, you will be able to do the following:

- Describe the prerequisite configuration tasks for a Cisco Unity Express integration with Cisco Unified Communications Manager Express
- Describe the Cisco Unity Express service module configuration in CUCM Manager Express
- Describe the CUCM Manager Express dial peer configuration that is required for the Cisco Unity Express integration
- Describe the voice-mail setup for SCCP phones on CUCM Manager Express
- Describe the MWI setup on CUCM Manager Express for SIP phones
- Describe the CUCM Manager Express ephone-dns that is used to configure MWI
- Describe how to configure an external SIP-based MWI server
- Describe how to subscribe an ephone-dn extension to an external SIP-based MWI server
- Explain the requirements for transcoding devices when using Cisco Unity Express and codecs other than G.711
- Describe how to access the Cisco Unity Express module and initiate the service module
- Describe how to download and install the Cisco Unity Express service module software
- Describe how to view the Cisco Unity Express related information such as installed software and version
- Describe the configuration of the trigger number in Cisco Unity Express that answers incoming calls to the voice-messaging system

- Describe how to configure Cisco Unity Express to use the outcall MWI process
- Describe how to configure Cisco Unity Express to use the SIP notify MWI process

This chapter describes how to integrate Cisco Unity Express with Cisco Unified Communications Manager (CUCM) Express using Session Initiation Protocol (SIP). Sections that are covered include the setup of the Cisco Unity Express service module and the IP routing for Cisco Unity Express access. The various message waiting indicator (MWI) and dual-tone multifrequency (DTMF) options are also discussed.

Voice Mail Integration on CUCM Manager Express

This section describes the prerequisite configuration tasks for a Cisco Unity Express integration with CUCM Manager Express.

The router that hosts the Cisco Unity Express module requires some configuration before the Cisco Unity Express integration. These tasks cannot be accomplished without the Cisco Unity Express hardware module being physically installed.

There are prerequisite configuration tasks for Cisco Unity Express integration on CUCM Manager Express. The Cisco IOS router prerequisites are as follows:

- Routing and IP addressing must be configured correctly.
- The Cisco Unity Express hardware module IP addressing must be configured. Static or dynamic routing can be used to the IP address of the Cisco Unity Express module.

CUCM Manager Express prerequisites are as follows:

- A SIP dial peer must exist with specific configuration for directing calls into Cisco Unity Express.
- MWI must be configured to turn message indicators on and off.

Service Module

This section describes the Cisco Unity Express service module configuration in CUCM Manager Express.

The first step in integrating Cisco Unity Express with CUCM Manager Express is the installation of the Cisco Unity Express service module hardware in the CUCM Manager Express router platform. The service module hardware appears as an interface in CUCM Manager Express.

After you successfully install the Cisco Unity Express module in the chassis of the router, it still requires some configuration to function properly. The interface service engine must have an IP address that is on the same subnet as the service module. These two IP addresses represent the two ends of the virtual Ethernet connection across the backplane. The administrator must configure CUCM Manager Express with IP addressing for the Cisco Unity Express service module to provide IP connectivity between the router and the Cisco Unity Express module. The module has an internal IP address and a default gateway configuration as follows:

- Service engine interface static IP address
- Service module on same subnet as host router
- IP default gateway to be the service engine address

The router has a service-engine interface with an IP address, which might be unnumbered. Using the **ip unnumbered** command for configuration allows the Cisco Unity Express module to use a network subnet IP address that is associated with a specific router egress port, such as GigabitEthernet0/0. This method requires a static route to the service-engine interface. The router interface that is associated with the Cisco Unity Express interface must be in an "up" state at all times for communication between the router and module. Example 10-1 shows an unnumbered configuration:

Note The logical Interface Loopback can also be used instead of a physical interface in the CUCME configuration.

Example 10-1 *CUCME IOS Configuration Example to CUE*

```
interface GigabitEthernet0/0.130
 description BR2 Voice
 encapsulation dot1Q 223
 ip address 10.1.130.1 255.255.255.0
 ip helper-address 10.1.5.15
!
interface ISM0/0
 ip unnumbered GigabitEthernet0/0.130
 service-module ip address 10.1.130.2 255.255.255.0
 !Application: CUE Running on ISM
 service-module ip default-gateway 10.1.130.1
!
ip route 10.1.130.2 255.255.255.255 ISM0/0
```

Use static or dynamic routing to provide network access to the Cisco Unity Express module.

Use the **service-module ISM/SM module/port session** command to connect to Cisco Unity Express command line interface to start software installation (if needed) or configuration (if newly shipped from the factory).

Dial Peer Configuration

This section describes the CUCM Manager Express dial peer configuration that is required for the Cisco Unity Express integration.

CUCM Manager Express must be configured with a dial peer that is pointing to the Cisco Unity Express IP address, as illustrated in Figure 10-1.

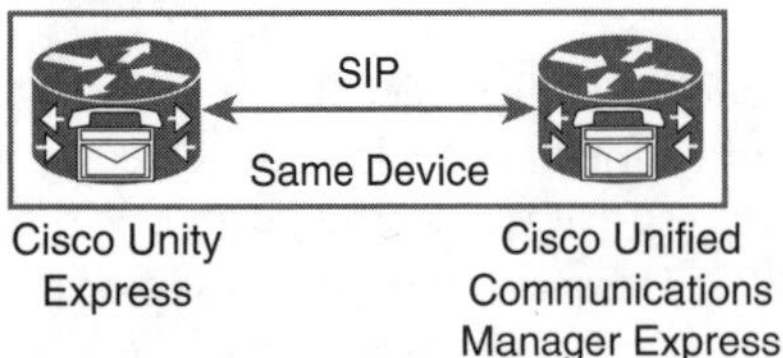

Figure 10-1 *Cisco Unity Express Dial Peer Configuration*

The dial peer must have these certain configuration settings:

- SIP Version 2 must be used.
- DTMF relay option must be set to match Cisco Unity Express.
- G.711 codec must be used.
- VAD must be disabled.

The settings on the SIP dial peer are very specific and include the **session protocol sipv2** command. This command instructs the router to use the SIP protocol for this dial-peer destination. Specify the IP address of Cisco Unity Express as the session target. When the voice-mail number, for example 4500, is dialed, the CUCM Manager Express will pass the call to the Cisco Unity Express module:

```
dial-peer voice 4500 voip
 destination-pattern 45..
 session protocol sipv2
 session target ipv4 : 10.1.130.2
 dtmf-relay sip-notify
 codec g711ulaw
 no vad
```

The **dtmf-relay** command instructs the dial peer to take all DTMF digits that are pressed and send them in-band using NTEs in the RTP stream or out-of-band as a SIP Notify message. There are other options available for DTMF relay. Ensure, that the DTMF settings on Cisco Unity Express match the parameter that is specified in CUCM Manager Express on the dial peer to Cisco Unity Express.

Because Cisco Unity Express only supports G.711, change the codec on the dial peer to G.711. Use the **no vad** command to disable voice activity detection (VAD). VAD is a mechanism that suppresses packets when no detectable voice is traversing the RTP stream. Disable VAD for communication with Cisco Unity Express.

Voice Mail Access for SCCP Phones

This section describes the voice-mail setup for Skinny Client Control Protocol (SCCP) phones on CUCM Manager Express.

Configure the telephone number that is speed-dialed when the Messages button on an IP phone is pressed. The same telephone number is configured for voice messaging for all Cisco IP phones connected to the router. To define the telephone number that is speed-dialed when the Messages button on an SCCP IP phone is pressed, use the voice-mail command in **telephony-service** configuration mode. The following configuration is performed in global configuration mode:

```
telephony-service
  voicemail 4500
ephone=dn   1
  number 4001
  call-forward busy 4500
  call-forward noan 4500 timeout 8
```

To configure call forwarding so that all incoming calls to a directory number are forwarded to another directory number, use the **call-forward** command in ephone-dn or ephone-dn-template configuration mode. Call-forwarding options are Call Forward All (CFA), Call Forward No Answer (CFNA), and Call Forward Busy (CFB). In addition, you may configure call forwarding for the following:

- The maximum number of digits that are allowed for CFA from an IP phone
- The forward call on activated night-service

MWI for SIP-Controlled IP Phones

This section describes the MWI setup on CUCM Manager Express for SIP phones.

To enable a specific Cisco IP phone extension (directory number) that is associated with a SIP phone to receive MWI notification, use the **mwi** command in voice-register-dn configuration mode.

The call-forward configuration for a SIP IP phone would look like that shown in Example 10-2.

Example 10-2 *CUCME Configuration Example for MWI on SIP-Controlled Phones*

```
Voice register global
 Voicemail 4500
voice register dn  1
 number 4002
 call-forward b2bua busy 4500
 call-forward b2bua noan 4500 timeout 10
```

```
 mwi
!
voice register pool  1
 id mac 0021.A086.E80E
 type 7965
 number 1 dn 1
 dtmf-relay rtp-nte
    codec g711ulaw
```

MWI Options

This section describes the various MWI options available.

The options for MWI messaging between Cisco Unity Express and CUCM Manager Express are the following:

- MWI outcall for local and remote SIP-controlled phones
- MWI using either the SIP subscribe notify or the SIP unsolicited notify method
- SIP MWI for SCCP ephone-dns

There are three methods available for setting the MWI: MWI outcall, subscribe notify, and unsolicited notify (as illustrated in Figure 10-2).

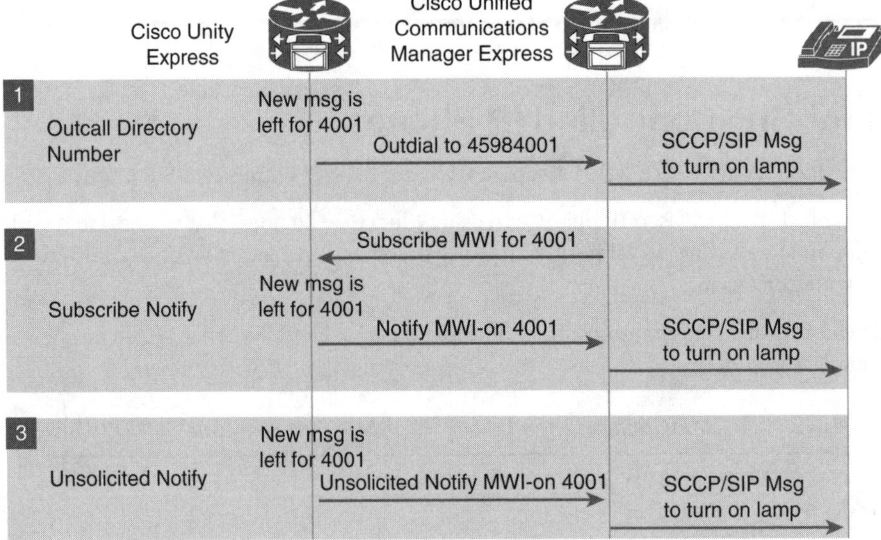

Figure 10-2 *Cisco Unity Express MWI Options*

A single MWI method is configured for the entire Cisco Unity Express system. It is not possible to mix notification methods. The following describes the features of each type of MWI:

- MWI outcall is compatible with older versions of CUCM Manager Express and Cisco Unity Express.
- All extension numbers must be the same length.
- There are potential problems with dial plans.
- IP phones can get out of sync with the true message status.
- Subscribe notify and unsolicited notify have these characteristics:
  - These methods show accurate message status.
  - The recommended method is subscribe notify.

MWI Outcall

This section describes the CUCM Manager Express ephone-dns that are used to configure MWI.

- The MWI mechanism turns on the light indicator on the phones.
- Assign ephone-dns to turn the MWI light on or off:

  ```
  CME (config-ephone-dn)#
  mwi [on | off]
  ```

- For this configuration, the directory numbers (DNs) on the phone need to have the same length (in this example, four digits):

```
ephone-dn 10
  number 4598....
  mwi on
ephone-dn 19
  number 4599....
  mwi off
```

The following describes the internal MWI mechanism of the CUCM Manager Express router:

Step 1. The IP phone with the extension 4001, for example, receives a call and the call is not answered.

Step 2. The IP phone with the extension 4001 forwards the call to voice mail.

Step 3. The greeting for extension 4001 is played and a voice-mail message is left.

Step 4. Cisco Unity Express places an MWI notification call to the MWI processing ephone-dn 4598 and appends 4001 as the calling-party ID for the notification call. The number 45984001 is dialed.

Step 5. Ephone-dn 4598 accepts the MWI notification call and switches on the message waiting light for extension 4001.

Step 6. When the phone user at extension 4001 listens to all of the voice mail, Cisco Unity Express places an MWI notification call to ephone-dn 4599 and appends 4001 as the calling-party ID. The number 45994001 is dialed.

For these events to occur, the **mwi on** and **mwi off** commands are required. MWI status notification calls are processed by system ephone-dns, which are ephone-dns that are not used for phone calls. The syntax of this command is the following: **mwi {off | on | on-off}**.

One MWI processing ephone-dn must be allocated to activate MWIs, and another must be allocated to deactivate MWIs.

The **mwi on-off** command can be used on a single ephone-dn to set the MWI to both on and off, using primary and secondary phone numbers on the ephone-dn. For example, the primary number turns on the MWI light and the secondary phone number turns off the MWI light.

To specify the type of MWI notification that a directory number can receive and process, use the **mwi-type** command in ephone-dn or ephone-dn-template configuration mode. This command enables a directory number to receive audible, visual, or both (audible and visual) MWI notification from an external voice-messaging system.
To disable this feature, use the no form of this command. By default, if MWI is enabled for a directory number, the directory number will receive visual MWI. The syntax of this command is as follows: **mwi-type** {**visual** | **audio** | **both**}.

MWI Using SIP Notification Messages

This section describes how to configure an external SIP-based MWI server, as shown in Figure 10-3.

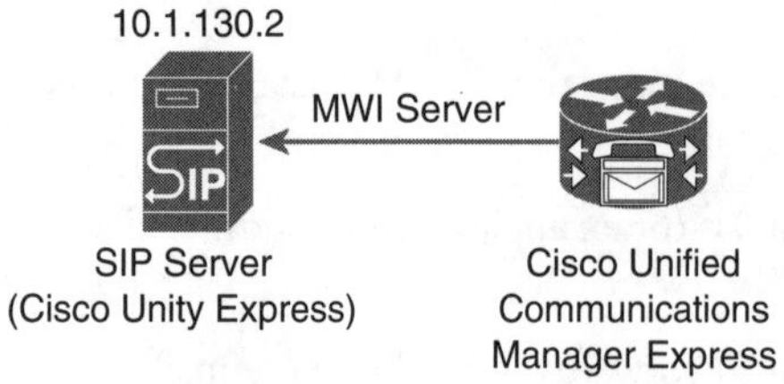

Figure 10-3 *Cisco Unity Express MWI Using SIP Notification Messages*

To configure parameters that are associated with an external SIP-based MWI server, use the **mwi sip-server** command in telephony-service configuration mode:

```
CME(config-sip-ua)
mwi sip-server ip-address [transport tcp | transport udp] [port port-number]
[reg-e164] [unsolicited [prefix-string]]
sip-ua
  mwi-server ipv4:10.1.130.2
```

The SIP notification message process sends an IP-to-IP SIP message that does not use a voice-mail port. Oversubscribed voice-mail ports can lead to missed MWI indicators. Subscription SIP MWI messaging is considered best practice. This setting must match the setting in the **ccn sip subsystem** in Cisco Unity Express.

The parameters of the **mwi sip-server** command are the following:

- Configure the IP address of an external SIP MWI server. This IP address is an argument in the **mwi sip** (ephone-dn) command, which is used to subscribe individual ephone-dn extension numbers to the notification list of the MWI SIP server.
- The **transport tcp** keyword is the default setting. The **transport udp** keyword allows for integration with a SIP MWI client.
- The optional **port** keyword is used to specify a port number other than 5060, the default.
- The default registration is with an extension number, so the **reg-e164** keyword allows the administrator to register with an E.164 10-digit number.
- The administrator can specify that the CUCM Manager Express system should accept unsolicited SIP Notify messages for MWI that include a prefix string as a site identifier. The Optional **unsolicited** parameter allows Cisco Unity Express to send SIP Notify messages for MWI without any need to send a Subscribe message from the CUCM Manager Express.
- **Prefix:** Central voice-messaging servers that provide mailboxes for several CUCM Manager Express sites may use site codes or prefixes to distinguish among similarly numbered ranges of extensions at different sites.

MWI SIP for Ephone-dns

This section describes how to subscribe an ephone-dn extension to an external SIP-based MWI server. Figure 10-4 illustrates the MWI from the SIP Server in CUE to an IP phone.

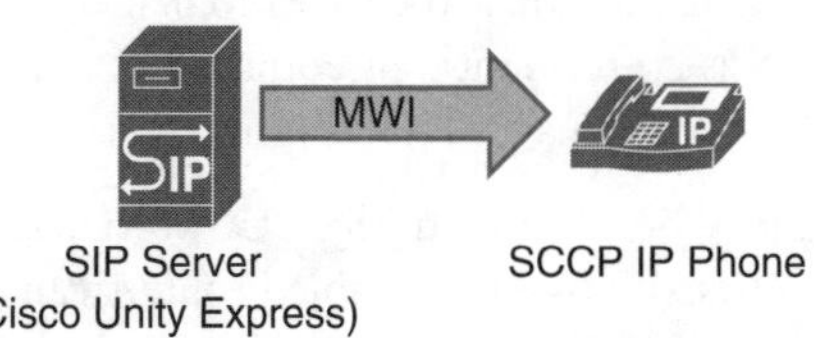

Figure 10-4 *Cisco Unity Express MWI*

To subscribe an ephone-dn extension in a CUCM Manager Express system to receive message waiting indications from a SIP-based MWI server, use the **mwi sip** command in ephone-dn or ephone-dn-template configuration mode:

```
telephony-service

mwi sip-server 10.1.130.2

ephone-dn 1
  number 4001
  mwi sip
```

The CUCM Manager Express system is configured with an external SIP-based MWI server.

Transcoding

This section explains the requirements for transcoding devices when using Cisco Unity Express and codecs other than G.711.

Cisco Unity Express supports G.711 calls only. When callers use a different codec, calls to voice mail will fail. Transcoding is required to convert codecs when CUCM Manager Express uses a different codec than Cisco Unity Express. For example, transcoding will convert a G.729 call to G.711 or vice versa, as shown in Figure 10-5.

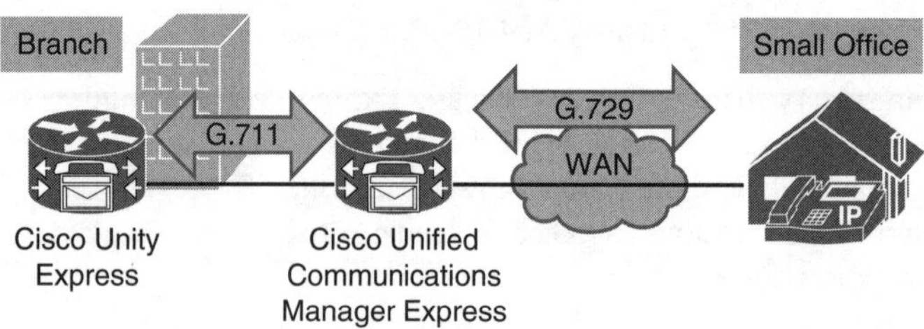

Figure 10-5 *Cisco Unity Express with Transcoding*

External hardware transcoders are required to perform transcoding. These transcoding resources can be located locally at each messaging system site. CUCM Manager Express routers can be configured with digital signal processors (DSPs) that support transcoding. Hardware DSPs reside directly on a voice network module, or on a packet voice DSP module generation 2 or 3 (PVDM2/3) card.

The DSP resources that are used for transcoding can be internal to CUCM Manager Express. In this case, the transcoding is referred to as co-resident transcoding. The control of coresident DSP resources is local to the CUCM Manager Express router.

The DSP resources that are used for transcoding may be external to the CUCM Manager Express system. DSP farms that are supported on Cisco IOS voice-enabled routers can be controlled by CUCM Manager Express using SCCP. Using external transcoding resources allows for expansion by adding additional DSPs. External transcoding resources also allow distribution of the resources across the network to best suit the implementation. The DSP farm must be reachable within the IP network.

The following example shows how to configure a transcoder on CUCM Manager Express:

```
voice-card 0
 dspfarm
 dsp services dspfarm

sccp local Vlan130
sccp ccm 10.1.130.1 identifier 1 priority 1 version 7.0+
```

Note The version parameter used with the **sccp ccm** command is 7.0+, which works well with CUCM Manager or CUCM Manager Express 10.0. There is no option to select version 8, 9, or 10, because the integration is the same from a protocol perspective. Transcoding can be configured in CUCME to allow different incoming codecs to be transcoded to G.711 to meet the CUE G.711 codec requirement, as illustrated in Example 10-3.

Example 10-3 *CUCME Transcoding Example*

```
Sccp

sccp ccm group 1
 associate ccm 1 priority 1
 associate profile 1 register BR-XCODE

dspfarm profile 1 transcode
 codec g711ulaw
 codec g711alaw
 codec g729ar8
 codec g729abr8
 codec g729br8
 codec g729r8
 maximum sessions 6
 associate application SCCP

telephony-service
 sdspfarm units 1
 sdspfarm transcode sessions 6
 sdspfarm tag 1 BR-XCODE
```

Connecting and Initiating Cisco Unity Express Module

This section describes how to access the Cisco Unity Express module and initiate the service module.

To access the Cisco Unity Express command-line interface (CLI), establish a Telnet session to the CUCM Manager Express router, and use the **service-module** command:

```
CME#
Service-module SM mod/slot [reload | session | shutdown | status]
```

The command offers the following options:

- **default-boot:** Set or clear default boot for the next reboot.
- **heartbeat-reset:** Enable or disable heartbeat failure to reset the service module.
- **install:** Install an application.
- **log:** History of logs.
- **password-reset:** Password reset of the service module.
- **reload:** Reload the service module.
- **reset:** Hardware reset of the service module.
- **session:** Connect to the service module.
- **shutdown:** Shutdown the service module.
- **statistics:** Generate service module statistics.
- **status:** Show service module information.
- **uninstall:** Uninstall an application.
- **upgrade:** Upgrade a currently installed application.

The CUCM Manager Express router **service-module** command is mainly used to reset, reload, view the service module status, or shut down the Cisco Unity Express service module using the **reset**, **reload**, **status**, or **shutdown** keywords. The **service-module** command allows these functions without the need to log in to Cisco Unity Express.

To disconnect from the Cisco Unity Express module and return to the CLI of the host router, enter **exit** from the Cisco Unity Express module.

Sometimes it is necessary to wipe the Cisco Unity Express service module configuration clean and restore the factory default settings. Restoring the system to the factory defaults has the following effects:

- Replaces the current database with an empty database.
- Returns the LDAP server to an empty state.
- Replaces the startup configuration with the template startup configuration that ships with the system.

- Erases all post-installation configuration data.
- Deletes all subscriber and custom prompts.

When the system is clean, the administrator will see a message that the system will reload, and the system begins to reload. When the reload is complete, the system prompts the administrator to go through the post installation process. When logging in to the graphical user interface (GUI), the administrator can run the initialization wizard.

Note All configurations and voice mail are lost when entering the command **restore factory default.** First, enter the command **offline** to go into offline mode. Then enter the **restore factory default** command, as shown in Example 10-4.

Example 10-4 *CUE CLI Example to Restore to Factory Defaults*

```
CUE# offline
!!!WARNING!!!: If you are going offline to do a backup, it is recommended that you
  save the current running configuration using the 'write' command,prior to going to
  the offline state.

Putting the system offline will disable management interfaces.

Are you sure you want to go offline?[confirm]
CUE(offline)# restore factory default
!!!WARNING!!!: This operation will cause all configuration and data on the system to
  be erased. This operation is not reversible.
Do you wish to continue?[confirm]
```

When you log in for the first time after the post-installation process, Cisco Unity Express prompts you with the following: se-10-1-130-2#. The abbreviation of service engine and the IP address of the Cisco Unity Express module generate the hostname. You can specify a different hostname during the post installation process or at any time using the command **hostname** *<hostname>*.

Software Installation

This section describes how to download and install the Cisco Unity Express service module software.

- Download software from an FTP server to install later.
  - **Clean:** For a new installation
  - **Upgrade:** To upgrade an existing installation

```
CUE#
software download [abort | clean | status | upgrade]
```

- Install previously downloaded software on Cisco Unity Express.
- Option to install directly from FTP without previous download:

```
CUE#
software install [add | clean | downgrade | upgrade]
```

Administrators can download the Cisco Unity Express software files and add additional language packages. Once downloaded to a PC, the administrator extracts the core files from the zip file and copies the extracted files and the language package files to the FTP server.

Install the Cisco Unity Express software from the FTP server. Enter the **software download clean** command to download the software from the FTP server for a new installation:

```
CUE#
software download [abort | clean | status | upgrade]
```

To upgrade an existing configuration, enter the **software download upgrade** command to download the software from the FTP server. The **status** option can be used to the check the download status.

Enter the **software install download** command to install previously downloaded software.

Alternatively, the **software install** command can be used to install directly from an FTP server without downloading first:

```
CUE#
software install [add | clean | downgrade | upgrade]
```

Software Versions and Licenses

This section describes how to view the Cisco Unity Express related information such as installed software and version.

To display characteristics of the installed software, use the **show software** command in Cisco Unity Express EXEC mode:

```
CUE#
Show software {directory | download | install | packages | versions}
```

The following main options are available:

- **directory:** This option displays the software directory.
- **download:** This option displays the IP address of the FTP server.
- **install:** This option displays installed software.
- **packages:** This option displays the configured Cisco Unity Express application packages.
- **versions:** This option displays the current versions of the configured software and applications.

Example 10-5 shows an example of **show software** command output.

Example 10-5 *show software Command Output*

```
CUE# show software packages

Installed Packages:

 - Installed Packages:

 - Installer (Installer application) (8.6.9.0)
 - Thirdparty (Service Engine Thirdparty Code) (8.6.9)
 - Infrastructure (Service Engine Infrastructure) (8.6.9)
 - Global (Global manifest) (8.6.9)
 - GPL Infrastructure (Service Engine GPL Infrastructure) (8.6.9)
 - Voice Mail (Voicemail application) (8.6.9)
 - Bootloader (Secondary) (Service Engine Bootloader) (2.1.36)
 - Core (Service Engine OS Core) (8.6.9)
 - Auto Attendant (Service Engine Telephony Infrastructure) (8.6.9)

Installed Plug-ins:

 - CUE Voicemail Language Support (Languages global pack) (8.6.9)
 - CUE Voicemail US English (English language pack) (8.6.9)



CUE# show software  versions
Cisco Unity Express version (8.6.9)
Technical Support: http://www.cisco.com/techsupport Copyright (c) 1986-2014 by Cisco
   Systems, Inc.

Components:

 - CUE Voicemail Language Support version  8.6.9
```

Customers must purchase licenses to use Cisco Unity Express features. These licenses must be downloaded and installed on the Cisco Unity Express system. It is possible to upgrade and downgrade licenses.

Cisco Unity Express 8.x licenses are based on the Cisco Software Licensing system. With Cisco software licenses, the mailbox license count includes both personal mailboxes and GDMs. The type of the mailbox is determined when it is configured. Also, the call agent is no longer specified using licenses and can be configured either as part of the post installation process or during boot. Cisco Unity Express software activation enables the various feature sets on a device using license keys. There are several types of licenses available.

Once permanent licenses are installed, they provide all the permissions that are needed to access features in the software image. All permanent licenses are node-locked and validated by the licensing infrastructure during software installation and once a permanent license is installed, it is not necessary to upgrade for subsequent releases.

Cisco manufacturing preinstalls the appropriate permanent license on the ordered device for the purchased feature set. No customer interaction with the Cisco software activation processes is required to enable a license on new hardware.

Temporary licenses are limited to a specific usage period (for example, 60 days) and an end user license agreement must be accepted before they can be activated.

If device failure occurs, and if the replaced device does not have the same licenses as the failed device, to avoid network downtime, customers can use an emergency license (evaluation license) embedded in their software image, which ensures that needed features can be configured without requiring a license key. However, the customer must still accept an end user license agreement and must acknowledge that there is a 60-day usage limit for this type of license.

The Cisco Unity Express license system limits the available resources, such as the maximum number of mailboxes allowed or the number of ports to reach the voice-messaging system. To install the licenses, use the **license install** command in Cisco Unity Express EXEC mode.

Use the **show license** command to display Cisco Unity Express license information:

```
CUE#
license install URL
CUE#
Show license {agent | all | detail evaluation | expiring | feature | file | in-use
| permanent | statistics | status | udi}
```

License information includes the following:

- **Feature:** Displays the feature name.
- **License Type:** Evaluation, Emergency, Extension, Permanent, or Temporary.
- **License State:** Active, Expired, or In Use, and the license period and remaining time is displayed.
- **License Count:** Maximum allowed license count and number of licenses used.

Configure SIP Triggers for Default Applications: Voice Mail

This section describes the configuration of the trigger number in Cisco Unity Express that answers incoming calls to the voice-messaging system.

The administrator must define the SIP triggers that will invoke Cisco Unity Express applications such as voice mail or auto-attendant. The configuration shows the Cisco Unity Express CLI commands to configure a trigger number that activates the voice-mail application when the SIP connection called party equals 4500:

```
CUE(config)#
ccn trigger sip phonenumber 4500
  application "voicemail"
  enabled
  maxsessions 6
  end trigger
```

The following parameters are configured for the SIP trigger:

- Telephone number that triggers the application
- Application name
- Maximum number of sessions that are allowed for the application

Note The maximum sessions cannot exceed the system limit.

Configure MWI Outcall Directory Numbers

This section describes how to configure Cisco Unity Express to use the outcall MWI process.

The outcall MWI process requires two ephone-dns to be defined in CUCM Manager Express:

```
CUE(config)#
ccn application ciscomwiapplication aa
  enabled
  maxsessions 10
  script "setmwi.aef"
  parameter "CallControlGroupID" "0"
  parameter "strMWI_OFF_DN" "4599"
  parameter "strMWI_ON_DN" "4598"
  end application
```

To activate this feature, modify the MWI On and MWI Off parameters, under the ciscomwiapplication application in Cisco Unity Express, to reflect the configured directory numbers. For example:

- parameter “strMWI_OFF_DN” “4599”
- parameter “strMWI_ON_DN” “4598”

To set the MWI notification mechanism, use the **mwi sip outcall** command in Cisco Unity Express SIP configuration mode:

```
mwi sip {outcall | sub-notify | unsolicited}
```

Only CUCM Manager Express can use the SIP **outcall** mechanism to generate MWI notifications. The **outcall** option will not work between Cisco Unity Express and a CUCM Manager system. The **outcall** option is available for backward compatibility. It is recommended that you use either **sub-notify** or **unsolicited** for the MWI notification option.

To use the **outcall** option, configure ephone-dns on CUCM Manager Express to receive MWI notifications as follows:

```
ephone-dn 9
  number 4598....
  mwi on
ephone-dn 10
  number 4599....
  mwi off
```

Configure MWI Using SIP Notify

This section describes how to configure Cisco Unity Express to use the SIP notify MWI process.

To set the MWI notification mechanism, use the **mwi sip** command in Cisco Unity Express SIP configuration mode: **mwi sip** {**outcall** | **sub-notify** | **unsolicited**}:

```
CUE(config)#
ccn subsystem sip
  gateway address "10.1.130.1"
  mwi sip unsolicited dtmf-relay sip-notify
end subsystem
```

Both CUCM Manager Express and CUCM Manager in Cisco Unified Survivable Remote Site Telephony (Cisco Unified SRST) mode can use the **sub-notify** and **unsolicited** mechanisms for generating MWI notifications. With these mechanisms, the MWI notifications will reflect the accurate status of messages in a subscriber voice mailbox.

After an ephone-dn is configured with the **sub-notify** option, CUCM Manager Express sends a Subscribe message to Cisco Unity Express to register the phone for MWI notifications. When a new voice message arrives in the voice mailbox for the ephone-dn, Cisco Unity Express updates the MWI status. If Cisco Unity Express does not receive the Subscribe message for the ephone-dn, Cisco Unity Express will not update the MWI status when a new message arrives.

To use the **sub-notify** option, CUCM Manager Express must configure each ephone-dn that is registered to receive MWI notifications as follows:

```
sip-ua
   mwi-server ipv4:10.1.130.2
!
ephone-dn 1
  mwi sip
```

To set the SIP DTMF relay mechanism, use the **dtmf-relay** command in Cisco Unity Express SIP configuration mode. Administrators may configure more than one option for transferring DTMF signals. The order in which you configure the options determines their order of preference. To configure more than one signal option, specify them using a single **dtmf-relay** command:

```
dtmf-relay {cisco-rtp | h245-alphanumeric | h245-signal | rtp-nte | sip-info |
sip-kpml | sip-notify}
```

- **rtp-nte:** This option uses the media path to relay incoming and outgoing dual-tone multifrequency (DTMF) signals to Cisco Unity Express.
- **sip-info:** This option uses the Info message to relay outgoing DTMF signals from Cisco Unity Express to the Cisco IOS SIP gateway.
- **sip-kpml:** This option uses Keypad Markup Language, or KPML, with SIP Subscribe and Notify messages to relay DTMF signals.
- **sip-notify:** This option uses Unsolicited SIP Notify messages to relay incoming and outgoing DTMF signals.

To use the **sip-notify** option, verify that CUCM Manager Express (or Cisco IOS SIP gateway) is configured to use Unsolicited Notify for SIP calls, as shown in the following example:

```
dial-peer voice 4500 voip
 destination-pattern 45..
 session protocol sipv2
 session target ipv4:10.1.130.2
 dtmf-relay sip-notify
 codec g711ulaw
 no vad
```

Summary

This section summarizes the key points that were discussed in this chapter:

This chapter described the initial voice-mail integration configuration on Cisco Unity Express and CUCM Manager Express.

- The Cisco Unity Express service module is a hardware module installed in the CUCM Manager Express router. CUCM Manager Express uses a SIP dial peer to communicate with Cisco Unity Express.
- Each extension might be configured to forward calls to voice mail (for example, Call Forward No Answer or Call Forward Busy).
- The SIP subscribe mechanism and DTMF relay method must match between Cisco Unity Express and the SIP MWI notification server.

Review Questions

Answer the following questions, and then see Appendix A, "Answers to Review Questions," for the answers.

1. **Which command is used to assign an IP address to the Cisco Unity Express service module?**

   a. **ip address 10.1.130.2 255.255.255.0**

   b. **ip address service-module 10.1.130.2 255.255.255.0**

   c. **service-module ip address 10.1.130.2 255.255.255.0**

   d. None of the above

2. **Which command is used to access the Cisco Unity Express module via the CLI when using an ISM?**

   a. **service-module ISM module/port session**

   b. **service-module service-engine module/port session**

   c. **service-module SM module/port session**

   d. **service-module module/port session**

3. **Cisco Unity Express supports the G.711 and G.729 codecs.**

   a. True

   b. False

4. **Which option is not a valid MWI option when integrating Cisco Unity Express with CUCM Manager Express?**

   a. MWI Outcall

   b. Subscribe Notify

   c. Solicited Notify

   d. Unsolicited Notify

5. **Which command wipes out an existing Cisco Unity Express module configuration?**

   a. **configure factory default**

   b. **factory default**

   c. **initialize factory default**

   d. **restore factory default**

Chapter 11

Configuring Cisco Unity Express User Accounts and Features

Upon completing this chapter, you will be able to do the following:

- Describe the Cisco Unity Express system settings that are required to set up the system after the initialization and integration
- Describe the Cisco Unity Express user default configuration for the authentication rules
- Describe the subscribers, or users, in Cisco Unity Express
- Describe how to import users from Cisco Unified Communications Manager Express into the Cisco Unity Express database
- Describe the Cisco Unity Express mailbox types
- Describe the Cisco Unity Express mailbox defaults
- Describe the mailbox parameters you may set when adding a mailbox in Cisco Unity Express
- Describe the distribution lists in Cisco Unity Express
- Describe the Cisco Unity Express time-based schedules
- Describe how the Cisco Unity Express Web Inbox can be used to manage the user's voice messages and personal mailbox settings
- Describe the Cisco Unity Express Message Notification feature
- Describe the user privileges in Cisco Unity Express controlling the access rights
- Describe Cisco Unity Express VoiceView Express
- Describe the Cisco Unity Express Integrated messaging feature using the IMAP

This chapter describes the Cisco Unity Express system settings. The configuration of mailboxes and distribution lists will be covered. Cisco Unity Express time-based schedules and other features such as integrated messaging will also be discussed.

System Settings

This section describes the Cisco Unity Express (CUE) system settings that are required to set up the system after the initialization and integration. After you log in to the web interface of CUE, Figure 11-1 shows the menus in the system settings within Cisco Unity Express.

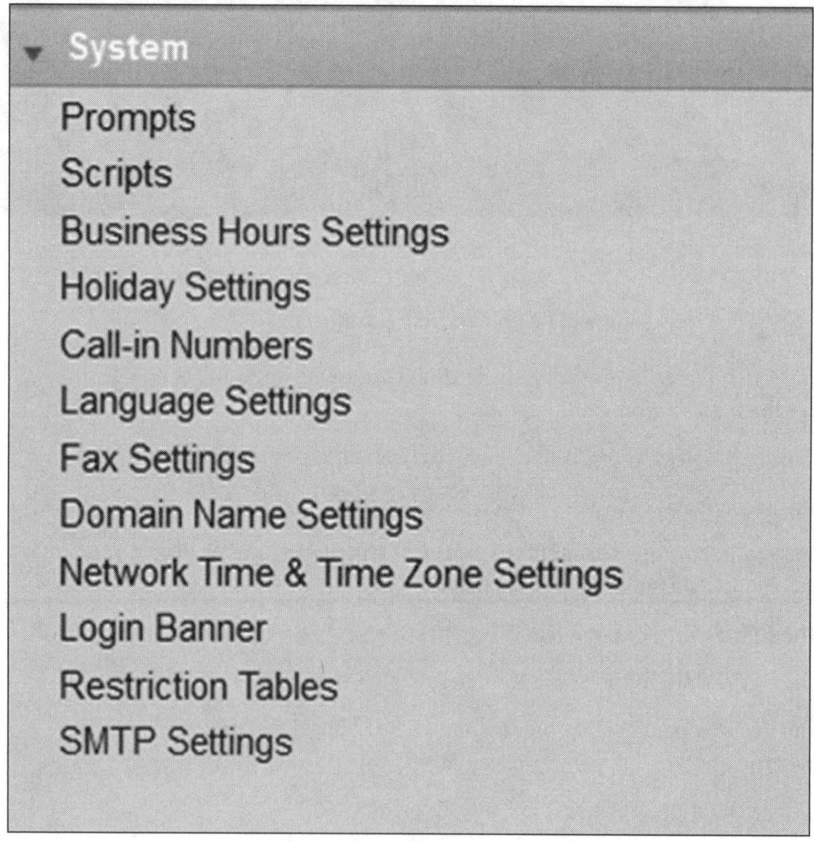

Figure 11-1 *Cisco Unity Express System Settings*

In the Call-In Numbers menu, you will find the trigger number that is configured to accept calls to the Cisco Unity Express system. In the Domain Name Settings menu, you can specify the hostname and domain or add DNS servers. In the Network Time & Time Zone Settings menu, you can modify the Network Time Protocol (NTP) servers, country, and time zone.

Authentication Rules

This section describes the Cisco Unity Express user default configuration for the authentication rules.

Figure 11-2 shows the settings that are set in the **Configure > User Defaults** menu for the user authentication take effect when you create a new user.

Password & PIN options	**Password**		**PIN**	
Auto-generation policy:	(•) Random ( ) Blank		(•) Random ( ) Blank	
Enable expiry (days):	[ ] 90	(3 - 365)	[ ] 90	(3 - 365)
History depth:	1	(1 - 10)	1	(1 - 10)
Minimum length:	3	(3 - 32)	3	(3 - 16)
Account lockout policy for consecutive failed login attempts				
Account lockout policy:	Disable lockout		Disable lockout	
Number of attempts for temporary lock:	3	(1 - 200)	3	(1 - 200)
Temporary lockout duration (mins):	5		5	
Maximum number of failed attempts:	24	(1 - 200)	24	(1 - 200)

Figure 11-2 *Cisco Unity Express Authentication Rules*

Specify the password or PIN policy for end users. This default set of parameters is only applied when a new user is created. After configuring defaults in this window, you can still change the password policy for an individual user when adding a new user.

Subscribers

This section describes the subscribers, or users, in Cisco Unity Express.

Each user is associated with a mailbox in a one to one relationship as shown in Figure 11-3.

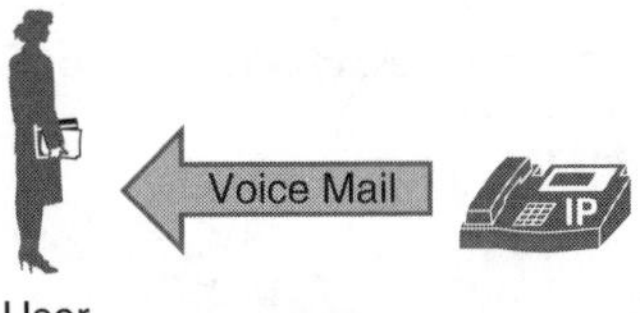

Figure 11-3 *Cisco Unity Express Subscribers*

The mailbox is optional, but it is required if the user wants to receive voice messages. An example of a user without a mailbox could be an administrator, although it may be very useful for the administrator to also have a mailbox.

Note The scalability limitation in Cisco Unity Express is based on the number of mailboxes.

When adding a user with the mandatory parameters, preset a password and PIN for the user to log in. A random password and PIN is more secure than a general (same) password sent to every new user.

Note If you selected a random password or PIN in the authentication rules, a message appears with the new system-generated password and PIN. This information must be manually distributed to each user.

User Import

This section describes how to import users from Cisco Unified Communications Manager (CUCM) Express into the Cisco Unity Express database.

Users, or subscribers, that are configured in CUCM Express can be imported into the Cisco Unity Express database, as shown in Figure 11-4.

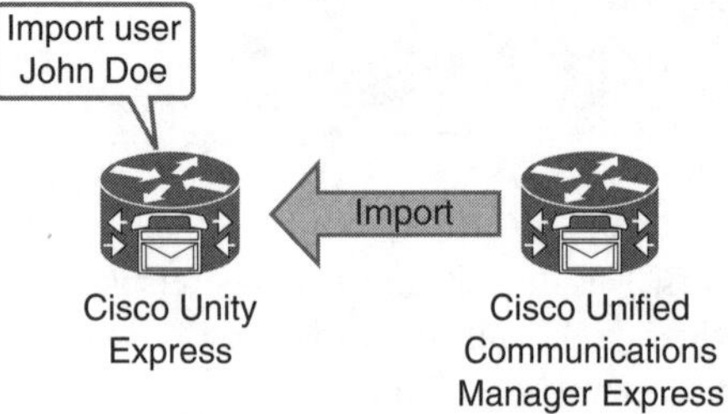

Figure 11-4 *Cisco Unity Express User Import*

To import users into Cisco Unity Express, the administrator must first configure the host system (CUCM Express) with the usernames and passwords and then import users from the host system. Cisco Unity Express does not automatically synchronize its database with the call-processing database.

To synchronize the Cisco Unity Express and CUCM Express databases, choose **Administration > Synchronize Information.**

Note When changing a CUCM Express user password on Cisco Unity Express with Configure > Users, the password for that user is also updated on CUCM Express. However, the reverse is not true. A user password that is changed on CUCM Express is not updated to Cisco Unity Express.

Mailboxes

This section describes the Cisco Unity Express mailbox types.

Two types of mailboxes are available in Cisco Unity Express:

- **Personal (user) mailbox:** An individual user may be assigned to a telephone that is connected to your telephone network. The administrator can assign a mailbox to an individual user, which is linked to a primary extension.

- **General delivery mailbox (GDM):** One or more people in the company can access a general delivery mailbox, for example, you may create a GDM for a team (hunt group). A caller can leave a message for the group by logging in to their personal mailbox and then select the option that allows them to check the associated GDM. Then members of the group can log in to the mailbox and retrieve the message. Any member can delete a message from the general delivery mailbox. The caller does not know anything about the people who can access the general delivery mailbox. For example, a caller may leave a message for the sales team but does not know who is a member of the sales team. Before configuring a general delivery mailbox, you must create a group.

Mailbox Defaults

This section describes the Cisco Unity Express mailbox defaults.

Figure 11-5 shows the VM Defaults configuration window.

Mailbox Size:	10800	seconds
Maximum Caller Message Size:	240	seconds
Message Expiry Time:	30	days

Figure 11-5 *Cisco Unity Express Mailbox Defaults*

The default values that are used depend on the hardware and software (license) that is used and vary based on the Cisco Unity Express module.

When creating a mailbox, the defaults that are set in the VM Defaults window take effect. Use this procedure to specify the default maximum mailbox size, the maximum caller message size, and the message expiry time. This default set of parameters is applied only when a new mailbox is created. Choose **Voice Mail > VM Defaults** to modify the settings.

Adding Mailboxes

This section describes the mailbox parameters you may set when adding a mailbox in Cisco Unity Express.

When adding a new mailbox in Cisco Unity Express, you must associate each mailbox with a user during the creation. When you select an Announcement Only mailbox, the following settings are applied to this mailbox:

- **Mailbox Size:** 300 seconds
- **Maximum Caller Message Size:** 0 seconds
- **Message Expiry Time:** 0 days

You may allow pinless login. However, this feature can only be enabled for personal mailboxes and not for a GDM. Pinless login can also be configured when accessing mailbox from any number, which is a significant security threat, or it can be set only for access from the subscriber number. If the user calls in with the associated phone (subscriber number), no PIN is required. This option is a significant security risk, because anyone with physical access to the phone can press the messages button and listen to the messages.

Occasionally, a mailbox becomes locked (if configured), and the owner cannot access the stored messages. A "Mailbox Is Currently in Use" message is played when a user tries to access a mailbox that is locked. Mailboxes can be unlocked from the mailbox overview window, available under **Voice Mail > Mailboxes.**

Members of a group can retrieve voice messages that are left in the GDM. Members of the GDM can be individual users or other groups:

- Individual users also have their individual mailboxes.
- Groups that are members of another group have their own mailboxes.

You can also configure voice-mail application settings and behavior, such as enabling the message waiting indicator (MWI) for broadcast messages. Choose **Voice Mail > VM Configuration** to modify the settings.

Distribution Lists

This section describes the distribution lists in Cisco Unity Express.

Distribution lists allow subscribers to send a voice-mail message to multiple recipients at the same time, as shown in Figure 11-6.

Figure 11-6 *Cisco Unity Express Mailbox Defaults*

The sender can send voice messages to distribution lists only on the local system. The sender cannot address a voice message to a distribution list on a remote system. Cisco Unity Express supports the following two types of distributions lists:

- Public distribution lists
- Private distribution lists

Members can be added to the distribution list. Each member is a voice-mail message recipient. Distribution list members can be any combination of the following:

- Users
- Groups
- GDMs
- Other public or private lists

When a subscriber addresses a voice message to a public or private distribution list, the system verifies that the list has members. If the list is empty, the system plays a prompt indicating that the list contains no members and does not allow the list to be used as a recipient of the message.

Recursive distribution lists are permitted. For example, list A can be a member of list B, and list B can be a member of list A.

Cisco Unity Express supports up to a maximum of 25 public distribution lists and a total of 1000 members or owners across all of these public distribution lists. You must be a member of the administrators group or a member of a group with public list manager capability to add a distribution list. Distribution lists can be added in the menu **Voice Mail > Distribution Lists > Public Lists.** It is not possible to modify the default public distribution list named everyone, which contains all users in the system.

Distribution lists owners are responsible for maintaining the membership of the list and can add and delete new members. A list owner can be either an individual local user, or a group. If a list is owned by a group, all members of that group are owners of the list. Members of the administrators group are implicit owners of all public distribution lists. A list owner does not have to be a member of that list.

Users can only add members to their own private distribution lists or to public distribution lists that they own. Any local subscriber can create private distribution lists that are accessible only to that subscriber. The following limits apply to private distribution lists:

- The maximum number of lists a local subscriber can create is five.
- The sum of all members in all private lists that are owned by a subscriber is 50.
- The owner of a private distribution list is the local subscriber who created it.
- The owner of a private list cannot be changed.

Schedules and Holidays

This section describes the Cisco Unity Express time-based schedules.

Cisco Unity Express supports business hours and holiday schedules. Business hours schedules are based on the days and times of the week when the company is open for business. Holiday schedules are based on the days when the company is closed for holidays. Cisco Unity Express applications, such as Cisco Unity Express auto-attendant, can be configured to use holiday and business hours schedules.

The auto-attendant is configured with the name of the business schedule that the system uses to determine the open and closed hours for the business. Callers receive different prompts during defined schedules. For example, the following prompts can be received:

- The welcomePrompt is the message that the caller hears when the auto-attendant begins to play during normal working hours.
- The holidayPrompt is the name of the .wav file that contains the message that the caller hears after the welcome prompt if the current day is a holiday.

Cisco Unity Express administrators can add, modify, or delete business hours schedules containing the days and times of the week when the company is open for business. The configuration is done under **System > Business Hours Settings**.

Administrators must enter a unique name for each new business hours schedule. Business hours schedule names cannot contain spaces. A new business hours schedule can be created as a new schedule or it can be based on an existing schedule.

Cisco Unity Express administrators can add or delete schedules when the company is closed for holidays under **System > Holiday Settings**.

Web Inbox

This section describes how the Cisco Unity Express Web Inbox can be used to manage the user's voice messages and personal mailbox settings.

Individual users can access the Cisco Unity Express database to manage personal mailbox settings. The graphical user interface (GUI) provides user access to mailbox settings, as shown in Figure 11-7.

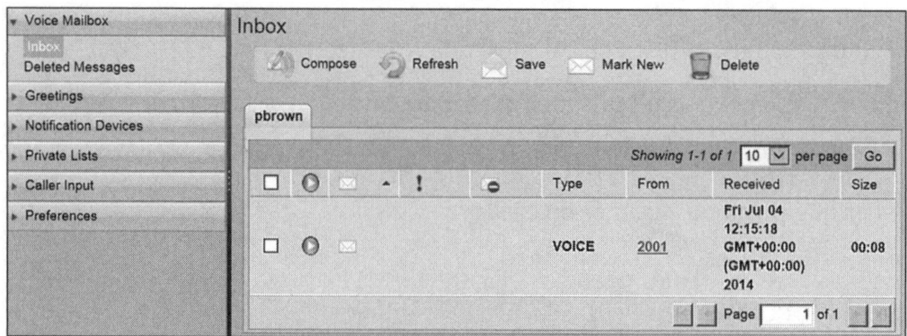

Figure 11-7 *Cisco Unity Express Mailbox Defaults*

Cisco Unity Express users can access the user GUI using the following URL: http://<CUE-IPaddress>/user.

The user GUI Greetings window allows users to record and manage their mailbox greetings. Users can activate greetings or specify greeting start and stop times. The following greetings can be managed by each user:

- Standard
- Closed
- Internal
- Busy

Additionally, any of the following greetings can be used:

- Alternate
- Meeting
- Vacation
- Extended Absence

For each mailbox, the mailbox owner or system administrator can assign actions to the telephone keys for caller input. This feature allows actions to be defined on a per-user basis.

Each subscriber in Cisco Unity Express can manage the Caller Input actions for their associated extensions. Caller Input actions include the following:

- Ignore Caller Input
- Skip Greeting
- Repeat Greeting
- Transfer To
- Transfer to Operator
- Play Good-bye
- Subscriber Sign-in

The User Preferences window allows each subscriber to configure preferences for their own mailboxes. These preferences are the following:

- Record, play, or upload the spoken name sound file
- Change password
- Change PIN
- Modify the display name
- Specify the mailbox language

Message Notification

This section describes the Cisco Unity Express Message Notification feature.

Cisco Unity Express provides several options for notifying subscribers of new messages in their voice mailboxes, as shown in Figure 11-8.

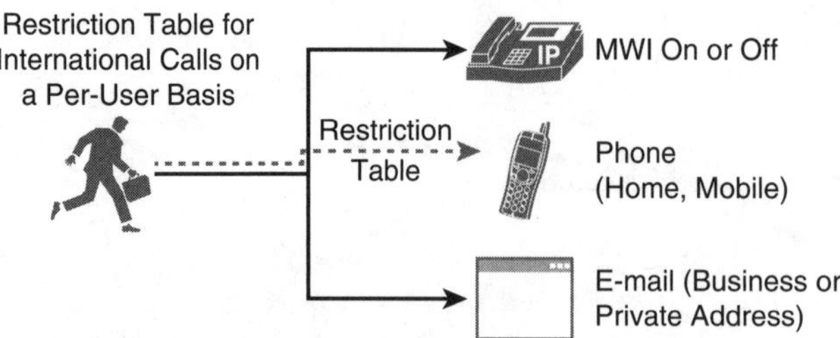

Figure 11-8 *Cisco Unity Express Message Notification*

The system generates a notification when a new voice-mail message arrives in a mailbox of a subscriber. Existing messages that are marked as new do not generate notifications.

The administrator can set the type of messages for which notifications will be sent: all messages or urgent messages. Urgent is the default. The administrator can change the preference for specific subscribers or groups to a value other than the systemwide setting.

Message notifications can be sent to the following devices: cell phone, home phone, work phone, numeric pager, text pager, and e-mail.

Each device has a configurable schedule during which notifications can be received. The subscriber can disable notification or prevent login to the mailbox during the notification period for phone devices (work phone, home phone, and cell phone).

Cisco Unity Express provides a default notification profile for each subscriber and group that has a voice mailbox. Each subscriber or group can have one or more of the supported devices that are configured in the notification profile. After the profile information is configured, the subscriber or group will receive message notifications. A notification profile contains the configuration settings for each subscriber or group such as device types, phone numbers, e-mail address, notification schedule, and others.

For Cisco Unity Express to send message notifications to external telephony devices, such as a cell phone or home office telephone, the integrated CUCM Express voice-mail solution must be configured for public switched telephone network (PSTN) access.

The Cascading Settings allow additional message notifications to be sent after a configured time delay to a widening circle of recipients. For example, notify jdoe, after 5 minutes notify jwhite, after 10 minutes notify the sales group. Notifications for e-mail and text pager devices are sent using the SMTP. For e-mail and text pager notifications, configure the External SMTP Server in the **System > SMTP** Settings window.

A separate message notification schedule can be configured for each notification device for each user. The administrator can set a schedule that activates the notification feature for a specific device. Time slots are available 24 hours a day for any day of the week in half-hour increments. The default schedule is Monday through Friday, 8:00 a.m. (0800) to 5:00 p.m. (1700).

When a subscriber or GDM receives a new voice message, the system checks whether message notification is enabled for that mailbox. If notification is enabled, the system checks for an enabled device and the notification schedule for that device. If the system finds an enabled device with permission to receive the notification at the time the message is received, the system sends the notification to the device.

These restrictions are available only for phone devices and numeric pagers. The system checks the restriction table when the subscriber is assigning phone numbers to phone devices or before making an outcall. If restricted, notification calls will not be made to that number. The table applies to all subscribers and groups on the system. A typical use of this table is to prevent the use of long distance or international numbers for a message notification.

Privilege Levels

This section describes the user privileges in Cisco Unity Express controlling the access rights.

Cisco Unity Express privilege levels provide different access rights to user groups. The CUE manager logs into CUE, as illustrated in Figure 11-9.

Figure 11-9 *Cisco Unity Express Privilege Levels*

Default privilege levels are provided by the system, or new privilege levels can be created. Privilege levels are assigned to user groups. This assignment provides different access rights to user groups. To modify these settings, choose **Configure > Privileges**.

Privilege levels are assigned to a group, and any member of the group is granted the privilege level rights. The software initialization process creates an Administrator group from the imported subscribers that are designated as administrators. Other groups can be created with these privileges.

Cisco Unity Express software recognizes these main privileges for subscribers:

- **superuser:** The superuser privilege permits subscribers to log in to the Cisco Unity Express GUI as an administrator. Additionally, it permits subscribers to record spoken names for remote subscribers and locations through Administration via Telephone (AvT).
- **managePrompts:** The prompt management subscriber has access to the AvT but not to any other administrative functions.
- **broadcast:** The broadcast privilege permits the subscriber to send broadcast messages across the network.
- **managePublicList:** The ManagePublicList privilege permits the subscriber to create and modify public distribution lists.
- **viewRealTimeReports:** The ViewRealTimeReports privilege permits the subscriber to view real-time reports.

In addition to adding operations to a privilege, administrators can also configure a privilege to have another privilege nested within it. A privilege that is configured with a nested privilege includes all operations that are configured for the nested privilege. It is not possible to modify the superuser privilege.

Cisco Unity Express VoiceView Express

This section describes Cisco Unity Express VoiceView Express.

The VoiceView Express feature allows voice-mail subscribers to browse, listen to, send, and manage their voice-mail messages from their IP phone. This feature is an alternative to the telephone user interface (TUI) for performing common tasks.

The number of simultaneous VoiceView Express sessions that are supported depends on the Cisco Unity Express hardware module and the version where the maximum is 32 sessions. The system counts VoiceView Express sessions separately from GUI sessions. When a subscriber is listening to or recording a voice message or greeting with VoiceView Express, the system counts the session as a VoiceView Express session and a TUI session. If the subscriber is browsing through voice messages on the VoiceView Express phone screen, the system counts the session as a VoiceView Express session.

The administrator can configure the maximum number of minutes that a VoiceView Express session can remain idle. The timeout is a systemwide parameter and cannot be configured for individual subscribers or groups. The default limit per session is 5 minutes (range 5–30 minutes).

The Cisco Unity Express system starts an authentication server that acts as the primary authentication server for VoiceView Express. The Authentication Manager is a network server that processes authentication requests for IP phone tasks as illustrated in Figure 11-10.

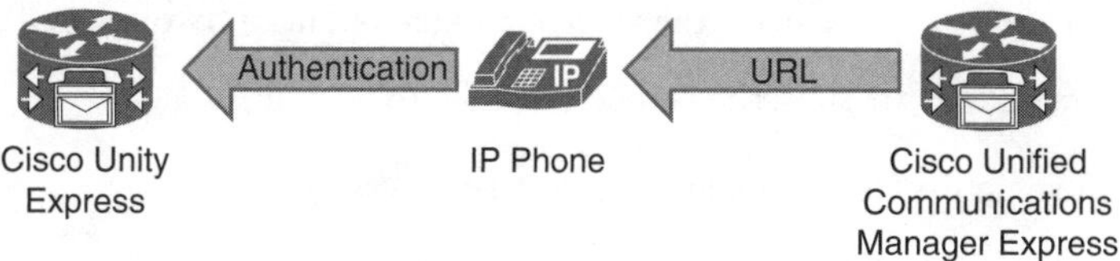

Figure 11-10 *Cisco Unity Express Authentication Manager*

The IP phones learn the authentication server URL during the phone registration process. The CUCM Express authentication server IRL points to the Cisco Unity Express authentication server:

```
CME (config-telephony)#
url authentication http://<cue-ip>/voiceview/authentication/authenticate.do
```

The CUCM Express administrator must ensure that the CUCM Express authentication server URL points to the Cisco Unity Express authentication server.

The administrator must enable the VoiceView Express service on IP phones. Configure the CUCM Express service URL to point to the Cisco Unity Express server VoiceView Express login:

```
CME (config-telephony)#
url services http://<cue-ip>/voiceview/common/login.do
```

The IP Phone Services button is used to access the Cisco Unity Express VoiceView Express service login. Figure 11-11 illustrates a phone screen with a VoiceView display for mbrown.

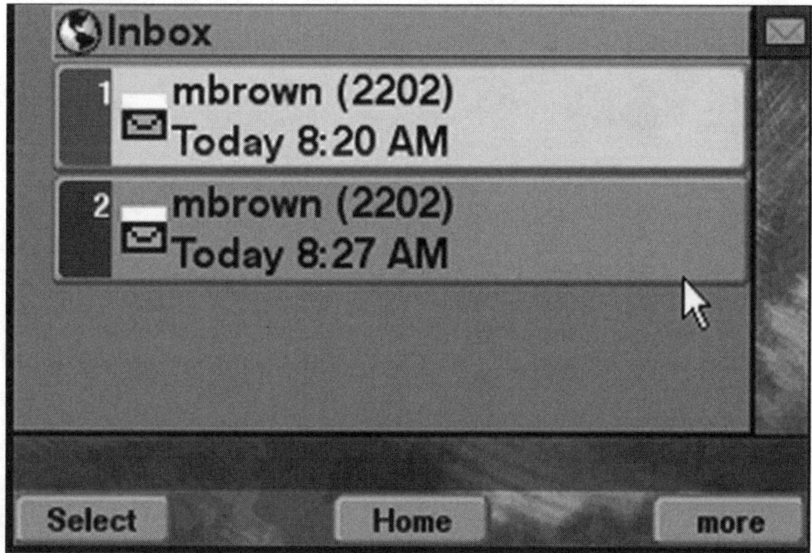

Figure 11-11 *Cisco Unity Express Phone Service Access on an IP Phone*

Log in with the extension and PIN to manage the voice messages and mailbox options.

VoiceView Express menus allow the subscriber to perform the following:

- Manage the voice-mail inbox (for example, read or delete messages).
- Send messages.
- Configure options such as greetings, message settings, and personal settings.
- Additional options may be available depending on the user privileges (for example, administer broadcast messages).

Note If your voice mailbox was not initialized and you do not have a PIN, you cannot log in to Cisco VoiceView Express. To enable access, first call your voice mailbox from your extension. Set up your voice mailbox using the voice-mail system TUI.

Choose **Voice Mail > VoiceView Express > Sessions** to view or terminate VoiceView Express sessions. You can select individual sessions to terminate or terminate all sessions.

Integrated Messaging

This section describes the Cisco Unity Express Integrated messaging feature using the Internet Mail Access Protocol (IMAP).

Integrated messaging is a feature of Cisco Unity Express that allows users to manage voice-mail messages by using an IMAP-compatible e-mail client, as shown in Figure 11-12.

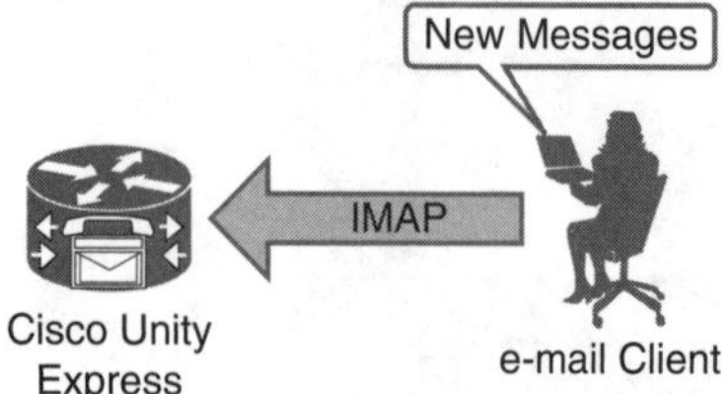

Figure 11-12 *Cisco Unity Express Integrated Messaging*

Integrated messaging on Cisco Unity Express is the convergence feature for voice-mail and e-mail systems. It allows subscribers to have an integrated view of their e-mails and voice-mail messages from a single e-mail client using IMAP. Subscribers can delete voice-mail messages or mark them as read or unread as they would for e-mail messages. Cisco Unity Express does not support the ability to create, send, or reply to voice mails from the e-mail client.

The e-mail client is configured with the user ID and password of the Cisco Unity Express subscriber. The subscriber must have network access to the Cisco Unity Express system. The voice-mail messages are downloaded as attachments to e-mail messages. Subscribers can access the voice-mail messages over the network or can download them selectively. If the messages are downloaded, subscribers can play them locally using standard media players without requiring a connection to Cisco Unity Express. Accessing voice-mail messages from GDMs is not supported. To access this feature, subscribers must be configured with the vm-imap privilege.

Subscribers cannot retrieve the following types of messages from their personal mailboxes:

- Broadcast messages
- Private messages

Summary

This section summarizes the key points that were discussed in this chapter:

- Cisco Unity Express distribution lists can be used to send messages to users or groups of users. Voice-mail messages are delivered to personal mailboxes. GDM members must log in to the mailbox to retrieve messages.
- By defining holiday or business hours schedules, Cisco Unity Express administrators can ensure that callers receive the appropriate prompts based on the working environment and opening hours. An NTP server is recommended to ensure that Cisco Unity Express uses the correct date and time.
- The Message Notification feature allows users to receive messages on devices such as cell phones or home office phones. Privilege levels provide restricted GUI access to user accounts.
- Users can browse their messages on their IP phone using VoiceView Express. IMAP supports receiving messages on e-mail clients.

The chapter described how to configure Cisco Unity Express general settings such as mailboxes and time-based greeting schedules and other features like VoiceView Express and Integrated Messaging.

Review Questions

Answer the following questions, and then see Appendix A, "Answers to Review Questions," for the answers.

1. **Which greeting is not a valid entry in the Cisco Unity Express Web Inbox?**

   a. Standard

   b. Closed

   c. Internal

   d. Busy

   e. Holiday

2. Message notifications can be cascaded in Cisco Unity Express.

a. True

b. False

3. The default mailbox size is derived from the hardware capacity and is automatically calculated.

a. True

b. False

4. Which two commands are required to set up VoiceView Express? (Choose two.)

a. url authentication http://<cue-ip>/voiceview/authentication/authenticate.do

b. url authentication http://<cue-ip>/voiceview/authenticate.do

c. service url http://<cue-ip>/voiceview/common/login.do

d. url service http://<cue-ip>/voiceview/common/login.do

5. How many IMAP sessions are supported at maximum in Cisco Unity Express?

a. 25

b. 50

c. 100

d. 250

e. 500

Chapter 12

Configuring Call Routing with Cisco Unity Express Auto-Attendant

Upon completing this chapter, you will be able to do the following:

- Describe the Cisco Unity Express auto-attendant application
- Describe the Cisco Unity Express auto-attendant operation by using an example with three auto-attendants
- Compare the Cisco Unity Express script editing options
- Describe a comparison of the Cisco Unity Express script editing options
- Describe the steps to configure a new Cisco Unity Express auto-attendant
- Describe Cisco Unity Express prompts and custom prompts
- Describe AvT
- Describe the default system scripts
- Describe the call flow of an auto-attendant
- Describe how to manage the Cisco Unity Express application ports
- Describe the Editor Express and the possible options for scripting
- Describe the Cisco Unity Express Script Editor

This chapter describes the Cisco Unity Express auto-attendant applications and options. Many businesses require an automated system for processing inbound calls. For example, when customers call the business number, they hear a welcome message and are prompted to press telephone buttons for different services. This type of service is referred to as an automatic attendant or auto-attendant.

Cisco Unity Express Auto-Attendant Overview

This section describes the Cisco Unity Express auto-attendant application.

The Cisco Unity Express auto-attendant functionality plays messages that callers hear when they dial the auto-attendant trigger number and provides prompts to guide callers to specific extensions or employees, as shown in Figure 12-1.

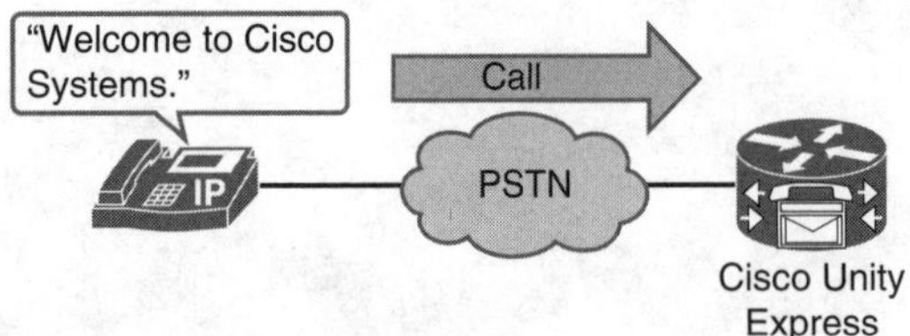

Figure 12-1 *Cisco Unity Express Auto-Attendant*

Cisco Unity Express can have more than one auto-attendant application per system at the same time. This configuration allows callers to dial different numbers to reach different departments or locations with their own sets of prompts and menus. If the default system auto-attendant is not usable, customize your own auto-attendant. This option allows you to use custom prompts and custom call flows in the auto-attendant.

Within the auto-attendant, it is often desirable to have a message that is set up to play at the front of the auto-attendant script during an emergency. This feature allows the administrator to toggle the Emergency Alternate Greeting (EAG) on and off through the telephony user interface (TUI) by using a phone and dialing the Administration via Telephone (AvT) number. The EAG is recorded through the TUI or recorded offline and uploaded into the system. If uploaded, it must have the filename AltGreeting.wav.

If active, the EAG is played before the welcome greeting of the system auto-attendant. If the EAG is included in custom auto-attendant scripts, a call to a subflow to checkaltgreet.aef must be inserted in the script. If the EAG is deactivated through the TUI, the current prompt (AltGreeting.wav) is deleted. If the EAG is activated through the TUI, the recorded prompt is stored as AltGreeting.wav.

Cisco Unity Express Auto-Attendant Operation Example

This section describes the Cisco Unity Express auto-attendant operation by using an example with three auto-attendants.

Enterprises commonly have multiple phone numbers and want a different auto-attendant for each department or location. Figure 12-2 gives a simple example of an auto-attendant call flow.

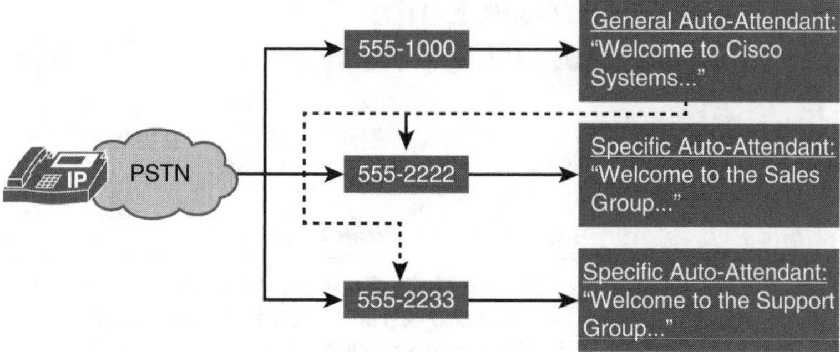

Figure 12-2 *Cisco Unity Express Auto-Attendant Operation Example*

This setup allows an enterprise to customize the interaction with the caller based on the dialed number. You can also associate multiple phone numbers to run the same auto-attendant. If additional customization is required, a custom script can be constructed and associated with a phone number.

The figure shows an example with a general auto-attendant and two groups. Each group requires a different auto-attendant. A separate call-in number is used to direct the call to the correct auto-attendant script for each group:

- Call-in number 555-1000 is associated with the general auto-attendant with a greeting such as, "Welcome to Cisco Systems."
- Call-in number 555-2222 is associated with a specific auto-attendant with a greeting such as "Welcome to the sales group."
- Call-in number 555-2233 is associated with a specific auto-attendant with a greeting such as "Welcome to the support group."

You may link the general auto-attendant to other groups.

Cisco Unity Express Auto-Attendant Features

This section describes the Cisco Unity Express auto-attendant features.

Administrators can create an auto-attendant script file using either of the following methods:

- Offline, using the Cisco Unity Express Script Editor PC software and uploading the script to the Cisco Unity Express system. Cisco Unity Express Script Editor is a full-featured script editor that runs on Microsoft Windows PCs.
- Online, using Cisco Unity Express GUI (Editor Express), which allows simple script editing on the Cisco Unity Express system.

In addition to the default system auto-attendant, Cisco Unity Express supports a maximum of 16 custom auto-attendant applications residing on Cisco Unity Express. Remember that only four (plus the built-in AA) or five of these can be active at any time.

Cisco Unity Express Windows Editor for Auto-Attendant Interactive Voice Response Script Comparison

Table 12-1 shows a comparison of the Cisco Unity Express script editing options.

Table 12-1 *Cisco Unity Express Auto-Attendant Operation Example*

Editor Express GUI	Cisco Unity Express Windows Editor for Auto-Attendant Interactive Voice Response Script
Directly configures Cisco Unity Express in real time.	Configured offline on a PC and uploaded to Cisco Unity Express.
Provides only basic script features such as modifying prompts, dial-by-name, dial-by-extension, and transfer.	Feature rich and advanced script creation. Includes adding new variables for complex scripts
Simple, easy to use, and intuitive menu.	More complex. Very powerful step-by-step creation of scripts.
No debug. Not required due to simple menu interface.	Script validation and detailed online or offline debugging.

Editor Express is a simplified web-based GUI editor with fewer options compared to the full-featured Cisco Unity Express Windows Editor for Auto-Attendant Interactive Voice Response Script Editor, which is based on Microsoft Windows.

Editor Express provides high-level steps that enable administrators to create or modify auto-attendant scripts that can be opened and viewed using the full-featured Cisco Unity Express Editor. These high-level steps are the equivalent of a set of steps in the full-featured script editor. For example, features such as dial-by-name are represented as one option using drop-down menus.

The PC-based Cisco Unity Express Windows Editor for Auto-Attendant Interactive Voice Response Scripts provides feature-rich, advanced script creation and troubleshooting. Administrators can add new script variables to store and use (for example, the calling number during the call). Scripts can be tested and verified offline before uploading them to Cisco Unity Express.

Editor Express provides only basic script features such as modifying prompt, dial-by-name, dial-by-extension, and transfer. Script changes are applied directly to Cisco Unity Express in real time when the script is saved. Troubleshooting script issues is difficult because Editor Express does not provide any script debugging; however, the script editing is easy and standardized with basic steps.

When creating a new script, Editor Express also provides a basic script template that can be customized. It is possible to save incomplete scripts and return to them later. In a few situations in which an incomplete script is saved, it might not be usable with the Cisco Unity Express auto-attendant application. For example, if a script requests a transfer without providing the number, Cisco Unity Express Editor Express sends an error message and does not allow the user to save the script.

Editor Express uses the same *.aef file format as the full-featured Cisco Unity Express Windows Editor for Auto-Attendant Interactive Voice Response Script. Therefore, administrators can use the full-featured script editor to open and modify a script that is generated by Editor Express. However, the reverse is not true. Administrators cannot use Editor Express to open and modify a script that is generated by the full-featured Cisco Unity Express Windows Editor for Auto-Attendant Interactive Voice Response Scripts.

Cisco Unity Express Auto-Attendant Configuration Checklist

Perform the steps as follows to configure a new Cisco Unity Express auto-attendant:

- Configure Cisco Unified Communications Manager Express with a dial peer for the auto-attendant.
- Prepare the script via the Script Editor or via Editor Express.
- Create and upload required prompts:
- Upload offline scripts to Cisco Unity Express.
- Add an application on Cisco Unity Express:
  - Associate the script with the application.
  - Set the number of ports and the pilot number for the application.
- Test the application by calling the pilot number.

Prompts

Figure 12-3 shows the Cisco Unity Express five default prompts.

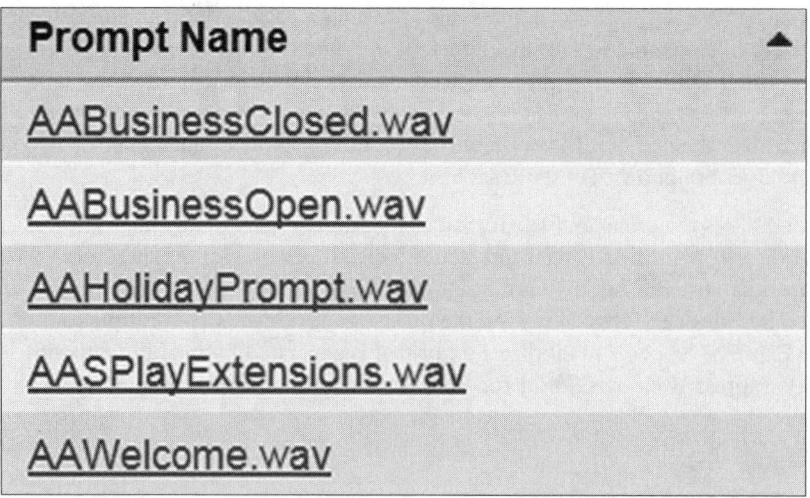

Figure 12-3 *Cisco Unity Express Default Prompts*

A prompt is simply an audio file. To view a list of voice-mail prompts, choose **System > Prompts.** Five system prompts are available and shown in the figure.

The administrator can also create a WAV file with the following properties:

- G.711 mu-law, 8 kHz, 8 bit, mono.
- The file cannot be larger than 1 MB (about 2 minutes).

After recording new WAV files, upload the prompt files to the Cisco Unity Express module. Error checking is performed on the file format when it is uploaded from the graphical user interface (GUI). Cisco Unity Express provides a built-in application AvT that lets administrators record customized prompt files directly to the module using a phone.

Administration via Telephone

The Administration via Telephone (AvT) has the following characteristics.

- Cisco Unity Express Administrator GUI:
  - View the list of prompts on the system.
  - Upload or download prompts.
  - Assign prompts to auto-attendant script parameters.
- TUI access:
  - Extension and PIN required; privileges required.
  - Entry point phone number defined for TUI.

- System script menu associated with TUI.
- Call into the TUI number; script walks caller through managing and recording prompts.
- Prompts saved with a unique filename: UserPrompt_DateTime.wav; (for example: UserPrompt_08182014132334.wav).

Administrators can use AvT to record a greeting or prompt. AvT features include deleting, recording, rerecording, and listening to prompts. Dial the AvT telephone number and select the option to record a greeting. A script walks the caller through managing and recording prompts.

Save the file when recording is complete. AvT automatically saves the file in Cisco Unity Express. The AvT prompt filename has the format UserPrompt_DateTime.wav (for example, UserPrompt_11152014144055.wav). CLI commands or GUI options can be used to rename the file with a meaningful name.

The Cisco Unity Express Administrator GUI can be used to view the list of prompts on the system, and to upload or download prompts and assign prompts to auto-attendant script parameters.

Cisco recommends using AvT to record greetings and prompts because AvT provides higher sound quality as compared to WAV files that are recorded using other methods.

Default System Scripts

The following system default scripts are present after the installation of Cisco Unity Express:

- **aa.aef:** The system auto-attendant
- **checkaltgreet.aef:** The script that plays the EAG before the system auto-attendant
- **msgnotify.aef:** The script that is used for SIP endpoint MWI notification
- **promptmgmt.aef:** The script that controls the prompt management system
- **setmwi.aef:** The script that controls the MWI light (on or off)
- **voicebrowser.aef:** The script that controls voice-mail interaction
- **xfermailbox.aef:** The script that is used to transfer a caller to a mailbox

The system uses the seven default scripts that are presented in the figure to perform system functions such as MWI notifications.

To view or modify scripts, choose **System > Scripts**. A button is available to view or hide the system scripts. System scripts are indicated with an asterisk next to their name and cannot be modified or deleted. Scripts that the administrator creates do not have an asterisk next to their name and can be edited.

Call Flow

Cisco Unity Express can be configured to use multiple scripts. For example, you may want to create separate scripts for the sales and support departments of an organization, as illustrated in Figure 12-4. Each script will be activated by a separate trigger number or call-in number.

Figure 12-4 *Cisco Unity Express Call Flow*

Calls to a Cisco Unity Express call-in number trigger the associated application; for example, the sales auto-attendant. Once triggered, the application script runs. The script performs actions and plays prompts based on the user input. The caller is prompted to choose menu options such as dial-by-extension or return-to-operator.

Calls to the auto-attendant extension 2500, for example, trigger the auto-attendant script called AAScript. The AAScript plays a welcome prompt informing the caller about the available input choices.

Application Ports

Figure 12-5 illustrates the Cisco Unity Express application ports.

Example: Module maximum 8 ports, 3 applications each with maximum 4, 3, and 3 ports. Worst-case scenario comes if any two applications reach maximum sessions; 4 + 3 = 7 ports used.

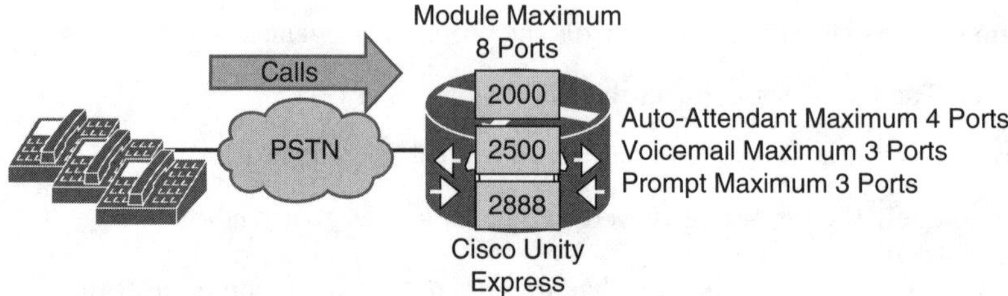

Figure 12-5 *Cisco Unity Express Application Ports*

One of the parameters that administrators can configure for the voice-mail and auto-attendant applications is the maximum number of callers who can concurrently access the application at any specific time. This parameter, called maxsessions, is limited by the number of ports on the Cisco Unity Express module.

Consider the expected call traffic when assigning the number of ports to an application. One application might need more ports than another, but each application must have at least one port available for incoming calls.

For example, the Cisco Unity Express module has four ports and the administrator assigns four ports to the voice-mail application and four ports to the auto-attendant. If four callers access voice mail simultaneously, no ports will be available for auto-attendant callers.

Suppose, instead, that the administrator assigns three ports to the voice-mail application and three to the auto-attendant. At no time will one application use all four ports. If voice mail has three active calls, one caller can still access the auto-attendant. A second call to the auto-attendant will not go through at that moment.

Similarly, the administrator must assign the maxsessions parameter to each application trigger, which activates the script of the application. The value of the maxsessions of the trigger cannot exceed the maxsessions value of the system.

As shown in the figure, the Cisco Unity Express module has a maximum of eight ports available. Three applications (called Auto-Attendant, Voice Mail, and Prompt Management) are each configured with 4, 3, and 3 ports maximum, respectively. In the worst-case scenario, if any two applications reach maximum sessions, there will always be at least one port available for the remaining application. That is, if the application called Auto-Attendant and another application are out of free capacity, the total ports in use is 7 (4 + 3), therefore leaving one port free for the remaining application.

Editor Express

Figure 12-6 shows the Editor Express and the possible options for scripting by navigating to **System > Scripts**.

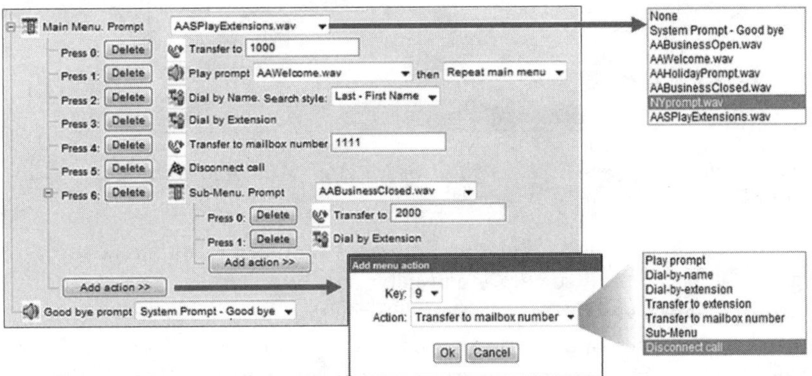

Figure 12-6 *Cisco Unity Express Editor Express*

The administrator can use Editor Express to configure scripts on the Cisco Unity Express system. Click **Add Action** to add an option and choose the key and corresponding action from the drop-down lists. In the example shown in the figure, pressing 1 will connect you to the extension 1000, pressing 2 plays a welcome prompt, and so forth. You may select one of the default prompts or upload department or location-based prompts.

Cisco Unity Express Windows Editor for Auto-Attendant Interactive Voice Response Scripts

Figure 12-7 gives an example of a populated script within the Cisco Unified Communications Express Editor.

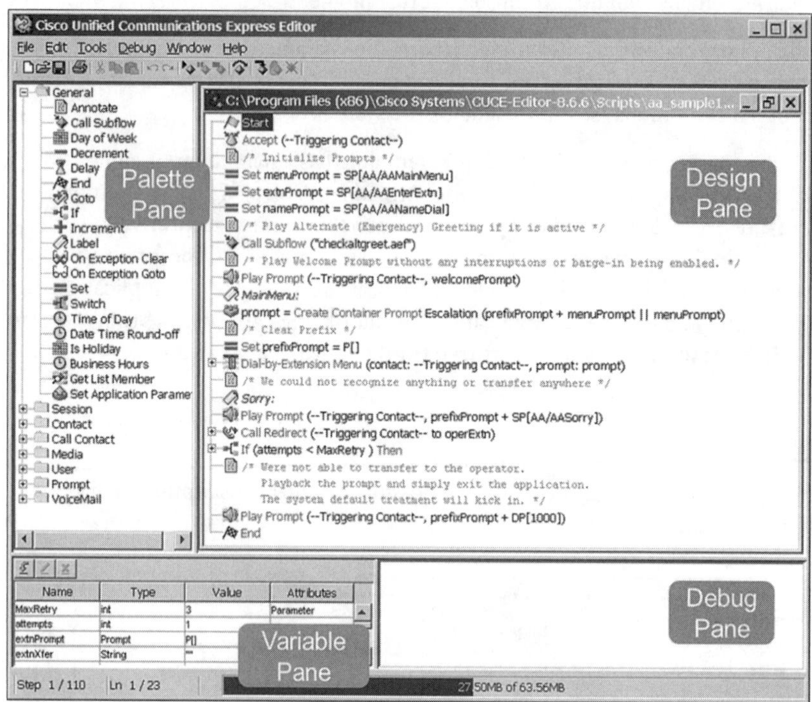

Figure 12-7 *Cisco Unity Express Windows Editor for Auto-Attendant Interactive Voice Response Scripts*

Download the Cisco Unity Express Windows Editor for Auto-Attendant Interactive Voice Response Scripts from Cisco.com and install it on a Windows PC. You may also download script examples you can reuse and modify for your purposes. This editor allows for the easy construction of scripts by using prebuilt modules, called steps. Place the logic-block steps in a specific order to provide the required service. You can then save these steps to a script that you can upload to the Cisco Unity Express module.

Figure 12-7 shows the script editor with an opened auto-attendant script. On the top left, you see the navigation pane with steps you can use. A script always requires a start and an end step. In between, you can configure the available steps to meet your requirements.

The top section on the right shows the script with all its used steps. Use annotations to describe what the script is doing. The programming is like other programming languages but simplified by dragging and dropping the steps into the correct script flow.

In the bottom left pane, you see the variables you can add, for example, string, integer, Boolean, or other. You can preset the variable values in the script or initialize the variables when the script is triggered.

The lower-right window shows debugging information when using reactive debugging on Cisco Unity Express.

Scripts

Cisco Unity Express uses scripts to control call processing for applications such as the Cisco Unity Express auto-attendant or Interactive Voice Response (IVR). Figure 12-8 shows the flow.

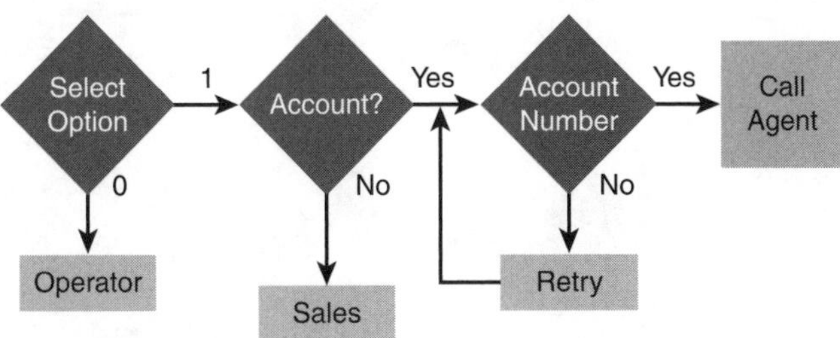

Figure 12-8 *Cisco Unity Express Script Flow*

A script that is stored in Cisco Unity Express runs in response to a request from a user or a predetermined condition. The scripts allow callers to receive recorded audio messages and prompts for further action.

If, for example, a caller calls a business during nonbusiness hours, the caller can hear either a recorded message stating the business hours of operation or hear a prompt to leave a message. The message and prompt are the result of the Cisco Unity Express software running a script.

Note Cisco Unity Express scripts do not support database integration on skill-based routing.

Summary

This section summarizes the key points that were discussed in this chapter:

- The default system auto-attendant can be modified to allow callers to self-direct by entering an extension or name.
- Administrators can use default scripts and prompts or upload new scripts and prompts to Cisco Unity Express.

- The directory number that triggers the auto-attendant script is configured as a call-in number.
- Business hours schedules allow for different prompts to be played to callers at different times of day.

This chapter described the Cisco Unity Express auto-attendant application, how to use the default system auto-attendant, and provided examples on configuring custom prompts and scripts.

Review Questions

Answer the following questions, and then see Appendix A, "Answers to Review Questions," for the answers.

1. **What is the maximum number of custom auto-attendant scripts supported in Cisco Unity Express?**

   a. 5

   b. 8

   c. 16

   d. 20

   e. 25

2. **Which option is not a valid call action when using Editor Express in Cisco Unity Express?**

   a. Dial-by-name

   b. Transfer to mailbox number

   c. Submenu

   d. Disconnect call

   e. Select agent

3. **Reactive debugging is debugging a call on Cisco Unity Express in real time.**

   a. True

   b. False

Chapter 13

Troubleshooting Cisco Unity Express

Upon completing this chapter, you will be able to do the following:

- Describe the areas where you can start troubleshooting, depending on the issue classification
- Describe how to follow a voice-mail call logically through the system
- Describe the Cisco Unity Express troubleshooting tools
- Describe logging in Cisco Unity Express
- Describe the Cisco Unity Express trace tool
- Describe the Cisco Unity Express **trace** command
- Describe how to enable Cisco Unity Express trace options using the GUI
- Describe how to troubleshoot the SIP integration of Cisco Unity Express and Cisco Unified Communications Manager Express
- Describe a SIP call flow between Cisco Unified Communications Manager Express and Cisco Unity Express
- Describe a SIP troubleshooting issue
- Describe an MWI troubleshooting scenario
- Describe an example mailbox troubleshooting scenario
- Describe how to troubleshoot TUI scripts and subscriber input

This chapter describes how to troubleshoot issues within a Cisco Unity Express voice-mail solution using Cisco Unified Communications Manager (CUCM) Express as the call-processing system.

Call Processing to Messaging System Call Flow

This section shows the areas where you can start troubleshooting, depending on the issue classification.

When troubleshooting, it is a good idea to identify the main areas and to focus on the key components. Figure 13-1 illustrates a high-level flow of Unity Express call processing.

Figure 13-1 *Cisco Unity Express Call Processing*

A detailed understanding of the sequence of events is also useful. Looking in depth at a specific area may not be helpful. For example, consider a situation where voice-mail calls do not arrive at Cisco Unity Express. Detailed Cisco Unity Express troubleshooting is not necessary because the problem area must be located somewhere earlier in the sequence of events—perhaps in CUCM Express. To troubleshoot calls that are forwarded to voice mail, the key areas are as follows:

- CUCM Express
  - **IP phone configuration:** Is the phone configuration correct and are the phones correctly registered? Changes for Session Initiation Protocol (SIP) phones require creating new configuration profiles and a reset of the phones.
  - **Voice-mail dial peer:** The dial peer to voice mail has certain requirements, for example, SIP, DTMF settings, and the codec G.711.
- Cisco Unity Express
  - **Voice-mail application:** The trigger number must be set up and match the destination pattern on the dial peer to be able to accept the calls. There must be enough sessions available to the application to prevent call blocking.
  - **Subscriber configuration:** The user must be configured with a mailbox. The mailbox must be enabled and unlocked.

CUCM Express

This section describes how to follow a voice-mail call logically through the system.

Always verify the CUCM Express configuration and the phone setup. Note the call flow to voice mail, as shown in Figure 13-2.

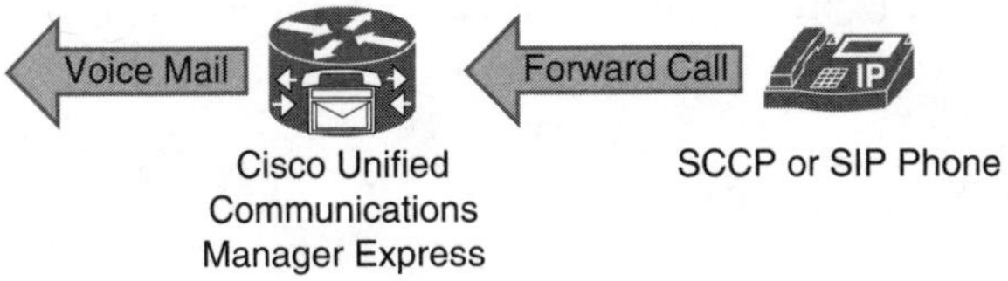

Figure 13-2 *Cisco Unified Communication Manager Express Call Flow to Voice Mail*

As an example, note the following key configuration commands required to route to voice mail shown in Example 13-1.

The troubleshooting sequence could begin from the ephone-dn call forwarding configuration and go to the voice-mail dial peer, or a direct call where the user presses the Messages button on the phone.

Example 13-1 *CUCME Dial Peers to CUE*

```
dial-peer voice 4500 voip
  description voicemail CUE
  destination-pattern 45..
  session protocol sipv2
  session target ipv4:10.1.130.2
  dtmf-relay sip-notify
  codec g711ulaw
  no vad

telephony-service
  voicemail 4500
ephone-dn  1
  number 4001
call-forward noan 4500 timeout 10
```

Troubleshooting can be simplified by following the voice-mail sequence of events and the associated CUCM Express configuration. For example, calls are forwarded from an individual phone to the voice-mail extension. The voice-mail extension is defined as a destination pattern in the voice-mail dial peer, which specifies the Cisco Unity Express IP address as the session target.

The most likely reasons for a reorder tone are the following:

- Cisco Unity Express not set up and initialized.
- The trigger number for the voice-mail application not set or is incorrect.
- No ports are available for the voice-mail application.
- The wrong codec is used or transcoders are not working properly.

Use **show** commands to verify CUCM Express configuration and operation:

- **show telephony-service ephone-dn**
- **show dial-peer voice summary**
- **show call history voice**
- **show call active voice**

The CUCM Express **debug** commands can be turned on and off independently for specific modules. Each module has several options that can be turned on individually. For example, the **debug voip** module has many options, including the **dialpeer** option.

By default, the debug output is sent to the CUCM Express router console. No debug output will be displayed if the administrator uses Telnet or Secure Shell (SSH) to access the router. Use the **terminal monitor** command to direct debug output to Telnet or SSH. Debug settings return to their default if the router is rebooted. By default, all debugging options are off.

The following are some useful **debug** commands for troubleshooting CUCM Express voice-mail integration issues:

- The **debug ephone** command is useful for troubleshooting IP phones.
- The **debug voice** command is useful for troubleshooting voice problems.
- The **debug voip** command is useful for troubleshooting VoIP.

To debug the voice call control API, use the **debug voip ccapi** privileged EXEC command. To trace the execution path through the call control API, use the **debug voip ccapi inout** command. The call control application programming interface (API) serves as the interface between the call session application and the underlying network-specific software. This command shows how a call flows through the system.

Use the **debug** ccsip command to troubleshoot problems with SIP. The **calls** option traces the SIP call details as they are updated in the SIP call control block. The **all** option displays all SIP-related debug information. Use the **messages** option to view SIP messages.

Cisco Unity Express Troubleshooting

The GUI, although effective for day-to-day additions, moves, and changes, is not an effective tool for troubleshooting the Cisco Unity Express system. You can use the GUI for reporting, to reload Cisco Unity Express, view system configuration, refresh MWI lights if they are out of synchronization, and turn on the tracing function. To effectively troubleshoot, you must use the CLI tools and functions.

There are three categories of tools that can be used from the Cisco Unity Express CLI. The first category is the **show** commands. Use the many available **show** commands to view the configuration, settings, and status of the Cisco Unity Express system.

Logging messages is another troubleshooting tool that you can use to diagnose a problem. The unsolicited messages that come out of the system have a severity level that is associated with them. These messages usually go to an internal login memory or to an external syslog server, if configured.

Tracing is the equivalent of debugging in Cisco IOS Software. Summary information to detailed information is displayed on the screen, sent to a syslog server, or stored in memory. Use the trace tools to focus on a specific aspect of the system.

To start troubleshooting Cisco Unity Express, use the **show errors** command to see which components of the system have errors. Invoke the problem that is occurring, if it is repeatable, and try to identify which modules are increasing the error counters.

Then, use the **show logs** command to view the logs and the **show log name** *log-name* command to view the contents of the log files. This information may further define the problem or component that is causing the errors.

Logging

This section describes logging in Cisco Unity Express.

There are four levels of output within the logging functions of Cisco Unity Express. These levels are listed here in order, from least significant to most significant:

- **Info:** Informational messages and notices
- **Warning:** Events that may require attention
- **Error:** Significant events that can affect functions
- **Fatal:** Critical alerts and emergencies that can affect the stability of the system

By default, a Cisco Unity Express Network Module system sends all four categories of logging messages to a messages.log file on the hard disk or flash. The message.log text file is limited to a 100-MB maximum size. A history of two message log files is kept as follows:

- When the message.log file reaches a set size, the system renames it messages.log.prev and starts a new messages.log file.
- When the messages.log file once again reaches a predetermined size, the old messages.log.prev is deleted. The current messages.log file is renamed messages.log.prev, and another new messages.log file is created. This loop continues indefinitely.

The logging output can be directed to the following three destinations:

- **Messages.log:** The logging messages can be sent to this text file, which resides on the storage of the Cisco Unity Express module. This action is the default.
- **Console:** Real-time messages or historical logs that can be displayed on the Cisco Unity Express console.
- **Syslog:** The logging messages can be sent to an external syslog server.

Cisco Unity Trace Tool

This section describes the Cisco Unity Express trace tool.

- Equivalent of Cisco IOS Software **debug** command
- Composed of modules
  - Modules are composed of one or more entities.
  - Entity may have one or more activities under it.
- Output to trace buffer or stored in atrace.log file
- Used as temporary troubleshooting tool

Although logging consists of unsolicited messages, tracing is configured by the administrator. Tracing in Cisco Unity Express is the equivalent of using **debug** commands in Cisco IOS Software.

Knowledge of the system architecture is useful for understanding the structures within the trace settings. Within trace, there are modules. Within the modules, there are entities. Entities are composed of one or more activities. When configuring tracing, the administrator can enable all of these entities or any combination of these entities.

The trace output is stored in the atrace.log, which is stored on the storage of the Cisco Unity Express module.

Use the **log trace local enable** command to allow the trace buffer to be written to flash:

```
CUE (config)# log trace local enable
CUE# show trace
MODULE          ENTITY          SETTING
config-ccn      sip-subsystem   00000001
config-ccn      jtapi-subsystem 00000001
config-ccn      sip-trigger     00000001
...
LOG NAME                        STATUS
atrace.log                      enabled
```

Note Turning on excessive tracing can cause performance issues in the Cisco Unity Express system. Use tracing only as a temporary troubleshooting tool. Turn off tracing when the relevant output has been gathered.

Using trace Commands via CLI

To enable tracing from the CLI, use the **trace** command. The **trace** command can be used to turn on a specific trace entity, a whole trace module, or all tracing. Turning on tracing for a higher-level object overrides tracing of lower-level objects.

Much like debugging in Cisco IOS Software on a router, tracing does not survive the reboot of Cisco Unity Express. The trace setting returns to its defaults on a reboot. The **no trace all** command turns tracing off.

Example 13-2 shows how to view the **trace** command options.

Example 13-2 *CUE Trace Options*

```
CUE# trace ?
  vmclient          Module
  aaa               Module
  voiceview-ccn     Module

  management        Module
  um2               Module
  sysdb             Module
  operation         Module
  editorexpress     Module
  BackupRestore     Module
  configapi         Module
  gateway           Module
  dbclient          Module
  ccn               Module
  config-ccn        Module
  snmp              Module
  voicemail         Module
  all               Every module, entity and activity
  rest              Module
  ums               Module
  security          Module
  imap              Module
  udppacer          Module
  caff-sip          Module
  voiceview         Module
  capi              Module
  entityManager     Module
  smtpclient        Module
  webInterface      Module
  limitsManager     Module
  webapp            Module
  license           Module
  eecompiler        Module
  superthread       Module
  networking        Module
  sitemanager       Module
```

```
csta              Module
ntp               Module
dns               Module
```

The **copy log** *logname* **url** *url* command is used to copy the logging files to a server, such as an FTP server. Once copied, the text-based log files can be viewed using a text editor.

Because the amount of information in the file can be significant, the search features of text editors can be useful for finding specific information or time stamps.

The trace.log trace output file is not text-based and cannot be viewed using a text editor. It may be necessary to send the trace.log file to Cisco when requested by technical support.

The **log server address** {*ip-address* | *hostname*} command is used to configure an external server for saving log messages.

If no syslog server is present in the network, the logging messages that are stored in the log file can be viewed by sending the messages.log file to an FTP server. After the file is on the server, you can view the file by using any text editor. Using a text editor is much easier than trying to view the messages.log file on the console of the Cisco Unity Express system. To save the trace configuration upon rebooting, use the **log trace boot** command.

To display a list of events in memory, use the **show trace buffer** command in Cisco Unity Express EXEC mode. Stop the output by pressing **Ctrl+C**. The trace buffer in memory can be up to 10 MB in size. To display a list of events from the atrace.log file, use the **show trace store** command in Cisco Unity Express EXEC mode.

To trace large amounts of data, send the information directly to the FTP server. Offline traces have the least performance impact. This activity is accomplished from configuration mode as follows:

- Use the **log trace server url** command to define the FTP server.
- Use the **log trace server enable** command to enable trace output to the FTP server.

Note Issue the **show trace buffer tail** command to view trace information in real time.

GUI Macro Feature

Figure 13-3 illustrates how to enable Cisco Unity Express trace options using the GUI.

To enable Cisco Unity Express trace options using the GUI, choose **Administration > Traces.** The window displays a hierarchical listing of the system components.

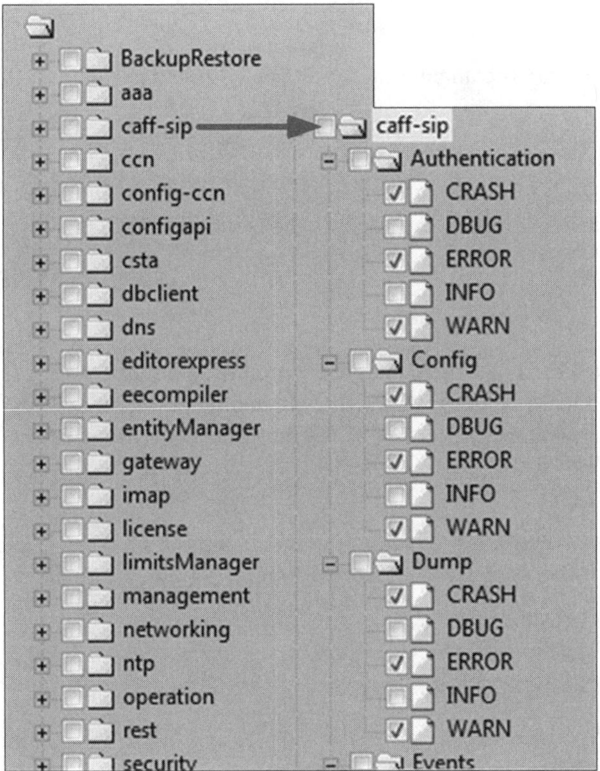

Figure 13-3 *Cisco Unity Express GUI Macro Feature*

To enable a trace on a system component, check the check box next to the name of the component. To expand the listing of components, click the plus (+) sign next to the upper-level components. Check the box next to an upper-level component (a module or entity) to enable the traces for all of the components under that component. Uncheck the box next to an upper-level component to disable the traces for all of the components under that component.

Note The GUI and CLI have the same trace options. However, traces cannot be viewed from the GUI.

The Cisco Unity Express GUI macro feature speeds up the process of selecting trace options. When selecting a trace module, the macro automatically selects the individual suboptions. For example, after selecting the voice-mail check box, all nested boxes are also checked. Individual options can be checked or unchecked at the micro level.

SIP Troubleshooting

CUCM Express and Cisco Unity Express communicate via SIP, as illustrated in Figure 13-4.

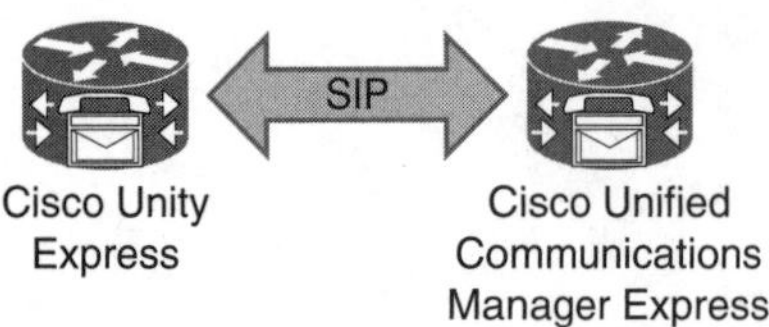

Figure 13-4 *Cisco Unity Express SIP*

This method of communication means that voice-mail integration issues require troubleshooting of SIP between these systems. Verify that SIP configuration parameters, such as IP address and protocol version (SIP Version 2), are the same for both systems.

SIP Call Flow

Figure 13-5 shows a SIP call flow between CUCM Express and Cisco Unity Express.

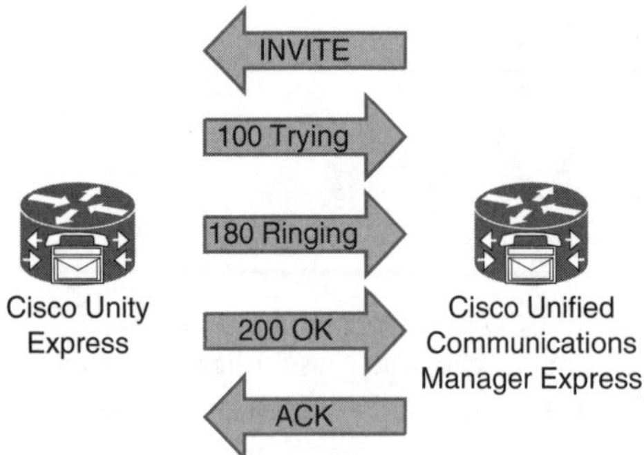

Figure 13-5 *Cisco Unity Express SIP Call Flow*

SIP uses different message types to initiate and control voice calls. The SIP request messages are as follows:

- **INVITE:** This message indicates that a user or service is being invited to participate in a call session.
- **ACK:** This message confirms that a client has received a final response to an INVITE request.
- **BYE:** This message terminates an existing call, and can be sent by either user agent (UA).

- **CANCEL:** This message cancels pending searches, but does not terminate calls that have been accepted.
- **OPTIONS:** This message queries the capabilities of servers.
- **REGISTER:** This message registers the UA with the registrar server of a domain.

The SIP response messages are numbered and grouped in the following ranges:

- **1xx:** Information
- **2xx:** Successful responses
- **3xx:** Redirection responses
- **4xx:** Request failure responses
- **5xx:** Server failure responses
- **6xx:** Global responses

The SIP INVITE message initiates the call setup between CUCM Express and Cisco Unity Express. The INVITE message direction depends on which side originates the call. The SIP 200 OK message is sent when the call is answered.

The following summarizes a successful SIP call setup:

- Send INVITE message.
- Receive 100 Trying.
- Receive 180 Ringing.
- Send 200 OK.
- Receive ACK.

The following summarizes a successful SIP call clearing:

- Send BYE message.
- Receive 200 OK.
- Receive ACK.

Note Refer to RFC 3261 for more information about the SIP message types.

Common SIP configuration problems are the following:

- Incorrect IP address for Cisco Unity Express.
- Incorrect codec configuration.

- Wrong destination pattern is configured, so the dial peer is not triggered for voice-mail calls.
- Misconfigured dual-tone multifrequency (DTMF) relay.
- Incorrect SIP version.
- Voice activity detection (VAD) is enabled by default. It must be disabled.

To enable Cisco Unity Express SIP trace options using the GUI, navigate to the Cisco Unity Express GUI, choose **Administration > Traces**, and check the **caff-sip** macro check box.

SIP messages are the same as messages that are viewed using the Cisco IOS Software **debug** command. Additional internal Cisco Unity Express messages may also be displayed in trace output.

> **Note** Trace output is viewed via the CLI. For example, use the **show trace buffer tail** command to view trace output in real time.

Troubleshooting SIP Issues

In the SIP troubleshooting scenario in Figure 13-6, a company is using a Cisco Unity Express voice-mail solution with CUCM Express.

Figure 13-6 *Cisco Unity Express Call Processing*

Currently, all users are experiencing problems accessing their voice mail. What may be the reason?

The problem is experienced by all voice-mail users, so the administrator suspects a problem with the voice-mail system or an integration issue. The first action is to verify the CUCM Express and Cisco Unity Express configurations. In this example, no issues are found during the initial verification of the configurations and integration between CUCM Express and Cisco Unity Express.

The next step is to look at the connection between Cisco Unity Express and CUCM Express. Use Cisco Unity Express SIP tracing to view traffic between CUCM Express and Cisco Unity Express. Alternatively, use the CUCM Express debug command to view the SIP traffic.

In this example, the codec was configured incorrectly. When debugging or tracing, take a look at the SIP INVITE message. The INVITE will contain SDP parameters for the call setup. In the trace, the INVITE and 200 OK SIP messages will have different codec types as follows:

- INVITE requests G.729: a = rtpmap:18 G729/8000 0
- 200 OK requests G.711ulaw: a = rtpmap: 0 PCMU/8000

In a trace, the BYE message will contain a reason code for the call disconnection (cause = 65). Cause 65 indicates "bearer capability not implemented," which indicates the wrong codec.

Additional and commonly seen cause codes include the following:

- Unallocated (unassigned) number = 1
- Normal call clearing = 16

Note See the ITU Q.850 Recommendation for a complete list of cause codes.

In this example, the dial peer is not configured to use the G.711 mu-law codec, so the default G.729 will be used. The voice-mail dial peer must be configured for G.711 mu-law using the **codec** dial peer configuration command to resolve the issue.

Troubleshooting MWI Issues

In this message waiting indicator (MWI) troubleshooting scenario, a company is using a Cisco Unity Express voice-mail solution with CUCM Express. Currently, voice mail is working normally. All users are able to access their voice mail. Messages can be recorded and retrieved.

The problem is that the MWI is not working, as shown in Figure 13-7.

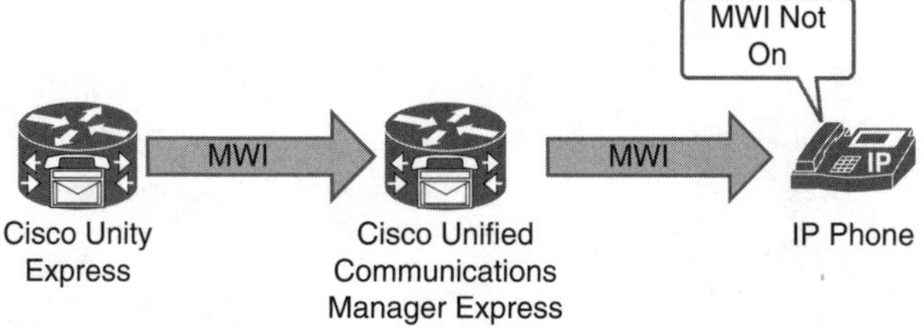

Figure 13-7 *Cisco Unity Express MWI Troubleshooting*

On IP phones, the MWI light does not change to indicate that there are new messages. What may cause this issue?

Occasionally, the MWI setting for a telephone can be out of synchronization with the user's message status in the voice-mail database. For example, a user could have pending messages, but the MWI does not turn on. The administrator can refresh the MWI light so that the light reflects the current message status in the voice-mail database. Use the following procedure to refresh the MWI for a single mailbox or for all mailboxes:

- Choose **Voice Mail > Message Waiting Indicators > Refresh.**
- To refresh one mailbox, check the box next to the user or group ID of the mailbox owner and click **Refresh Selected.** To refresh all mailboxes, click **Refresh All.**

> **Note** Cisco Unity Express will send MWI messages to refresh the MWI state. These messages are useful when troubleshooting or debugging MWI problems.

Enable Cisco Unity Express MWI tracing. Place a call, leave a voice-mail message, and view the trace output. Use trace **voicemail mwi all** command.

You may also use the CUCM Express **debug ccsip message** command to verify the MWI notification.

In this example, the DTMF method was not set on the dial peer in Cisco Unity Express. So, there was no match in the DTMF method configuration on CUCM Express and Cisco Unity Express.

Troubleshooting Mailbox Issues

In this mailbox troubleshooting scenario, a company is using a Cisco Unity Express voice-mail solution with CUCM Express in a medium-sized office environment. Currently, voice mail appears to be working for most users. However, few subscribers cannot access their voice mail, as shown in Figure 13-8.

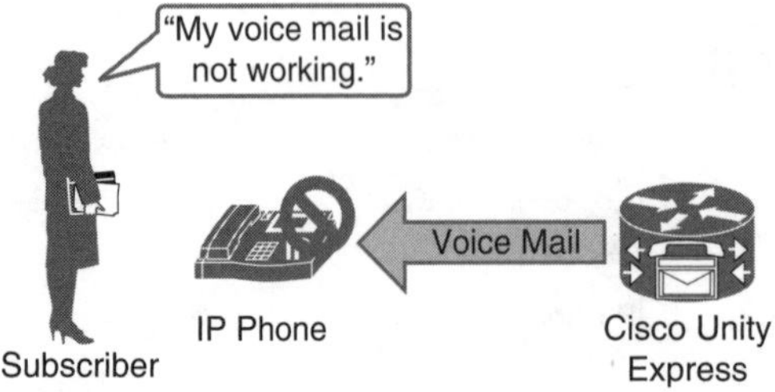

Figure 13-8 *Cisco Unity Express Troubleshooting Mailbox Issues*

Most subscribers can use their mailbox, so it seems that voice-mail integration between CUCM Express and Cisco Unity Express is working. The first step is to verify that individual IP phones are configured correctly in CUCM Express.

Check that the IP phones that are associated with the users who are reporting problems are configured to forward calls to the correct voice-mail extension. Compare the phones that are having problems with IP phones that work.

Verify the Cisco Unity Express mailbox configuration as follows:

- Check that the subscriber has a mailbox associated.
- Verify that the mailbox is enabled.
- Verify that the extension of the subscriber is designated as a primary extension. Cisco Unity Express does not send an MWI to an E.164 number.

Occasionally, a mailbox becomes locked, and the owner cannot access the stored messages. A "mailbox is currently in use" message is typically played when a user tries to access a mailbox that is locked.

To unlock the mailbox, choose **Voice Mail > Mailboxes**. Check the box next to the mailbox that you want to unlock and click **Unlock**.

If these steps do not resolve the issue, enable Cisco Unity Express Mailbox trace options using the graphical user interface (GUI). Attempt to access a mailbox and view trace output via the CLI.

Interpreting TUI Sessions

Always verify scripts and subscriber input. The script voicebrowser.aef provides the functionality of the Cisco Unity Express voice-mail application. This script uses Voice Extensible Markup Language (VXML) to implement its functionality. These functions can be viewed by using the **trace voicemail vxml all** command, which provides the following information:

- Displays received DTMF and prompts played in response to them
- Uses caller ID for differentiating different calls into voice mail
- Displays voice-mail telephone user interface (TUI) position
- Various levels of prompts and menus within the TUI

The caller ID of users calling into voice mail is checked. If there is a mailbox that is associated with that phone number, users are prompted for the PIN. If there is no matching mailbox, users are prompted to enter the extension with which their mailboxes are associated.

To view a call arriving in voice mail and a message being left for a subscriber in the form of **trace** command output, enter the **trace voicemail vxml all** command. The output can include the prompts that are played and any corresponding .wav files that are mapped to those prompts. The input of the caller can also be displayed in the output of the **trace** command.

Summary

This section summarizes the key points that were discussed in this chapter:

- A problem-solving methodology should be used when troubleshooting voice-mail issues in Cisco Unity Express.
- CUCM Express **debug** commands can be used to troubleshoot SIP connectivity issues with Cisco Unity Express.
- The Cisco Unity Express MWI Refresh feature generates messages to synchronize the MWI state of IP phones. These messages are helpful for troubleshooting.
- The **trace voicemail vxml** command output shows TUI input as well as menus and prompts.

This chapter covered troubleshooting Cisco Unity Express in a CUCM Express environment.

Review Questions

Answer the following questions, and then see Appendix A, "Answers to Review Questions," for the answers.

1. How many levels are available for logging in Cisco Unity Express?

a. 1

b. 2

c. 4

d. 5

e. 7

2. Cisco Unity Express trace files can be viewed in a text editor.

a. True

b. False

3. Which command is used to allow the trace buffer to be written to flash?

a. log trace enable

b. log trace local enable

c. log trace enable local

d. log local enable flash

4. **Enabling tracing in the Cisco Unity Express GUI provides you with less trace information than using the CLI.**

    a. True

    b. False

5. **Which order is correct for a SIP call flow?**

    a. Invite, 100 Trying, 200 OK, ACK

    b. Invite, 100 Trying, 180 Ringing, 200 OK

    c. Invite, 180 Ringing, 200 OK, ACK

    d. Invite, 100 Trying, 180 Ringing, 200 OK, ACK

Chapter 14

Designing and Deploying Cisco Unified IM and Presence

Upon completing this chapter, you will be able to do the following:

- Describe native presence in Cisco Unified Communications Manager without Cisco Unified Communications IM and Presence (IM&P) servers
- Describe how the subscribe CSS controls presence watchers
- Describe how presence groups add more granularity to the presence functionality
- Describe the requirements when using Cisco Jabber for presence functionality
- Describe how to integrate a Cisco presence solution within a Microsoft environment in an enterprise
- Describe the characteristics of the Cisco Unified Communications IM&P OVA templates and the required physical resources
- Describe the Cisco Unified Communications IM&P cluster architecture
- Describe how to deploy Cisco Unified Communications IM&P in different scenarios
- Describe how Cisco Jabber discovers services to register
- Describe the Cisco Jabber quality of service issues with trust boundaries
- Describe the different ports that Cisco Jabber uses to communicate
- Describe how to connect Cisco Unified Communications IM&P clusters within the same domain
- Describe how to connect Cisco Unified Communications IM&P clusters that are in different domains
- Describe SIP federations with Microsoft domains

- Describe the state mappings between Cisco Unified Communications IM&P and Microsoft Skype for Business
- Describe the preparation that is necessary to implement a federated presence network

This chapter describes the Cisco Unified Communications IM and Presence (IM&P) architecture and design. Native presence in Cisco Unified Communications Manager (CUCM) is presented and the different Cisco Unified Communications IM&P approaches are described. Cisco Unified Communications IM&P can be configured to peer with another Cisco Unified Communications IM&P cluster in the same domain or can be federated with Cisco Unified Communications IM&P clusters in a different domain.

Note The previous name of IM&P was Cisco Unified Presence Server (CUPS) in prior versions of Cisco UC.

CUCM Presence Introduction

This section describes native presence in CUCM without Cisco Unified Communications IM&P servers, as shown in Figure 14-1.

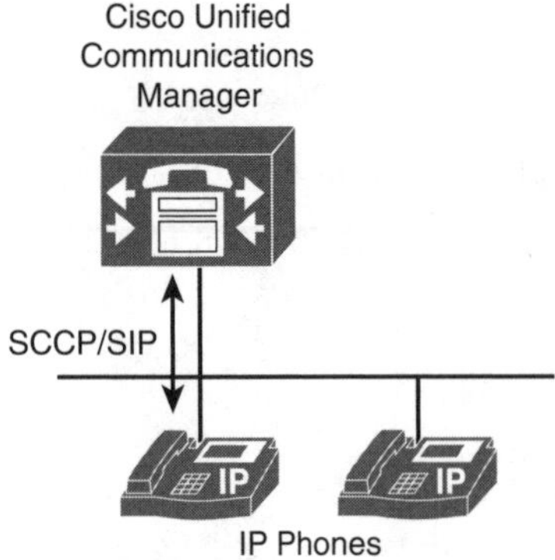

Figure 14-1 *CUCM Presence*

CUCM offers very limited native presence functionality on IP phones. Although a Cisco Unified Communications IM&P server is not required in this simple example, only these native presence features of the CUCM are available:

- **CUCM speed-dial presence:** CUCM administratively supports the ability for a speed dial to have presence capabilities via a BLF speed dial. BLF speed dials work as both a speed dial and a presence indicator.
- **CUCM call history presence:** CUCM administratively supports presence capabilities for call lists and directories on the phone.
- **CUCM presence policy:** CUCM provides the capability to set policy for users who request presence status.

CUCM Presence

This section describes the integration of external presence entities into the native presence solution.

All presence requests for users, whether inside or outside a cluster, are processed by CUCM, as shown in Figure 14-2.

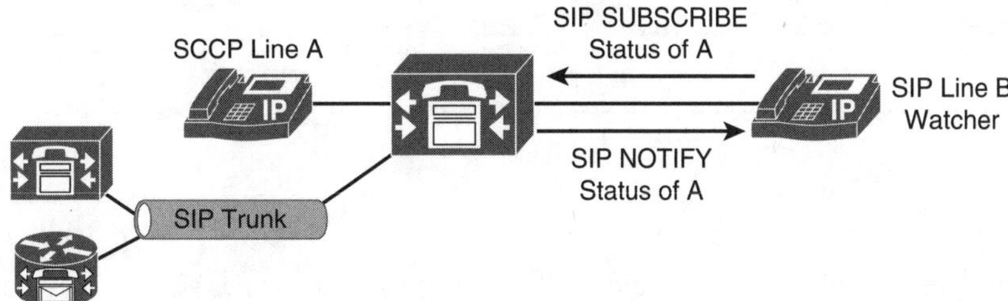

Figure 14-2 *CUCM Native Presence*

A CUCM watcher that sends a presence request will receive a direct response, including the presence status, if the watcher and presence entity are both located within the cluster.

If the presence entity exists outside the cluster, CUCM will query the external presence entity through the Session Initiation Protocol (SIP) trunk. For A watcher that is not in a CUCM cluster, the CUCM can send a presence request off cluster entity by way of a SIP trunk. If the off-cluster entity supports presence, it will respond with the current presence status. If the off-cluster entity does not support presence, it will reject the presence request with a SIP error response.

Skinny Client Control Protocol (SCCP) endpoints can request the presence status of the indicated presence entity by sending SCCP messages to CUCM. If the presence entity resides within the CUCM cluster, CUCM responds to the SCCP line-side presence request by sending SCCP messages to the presence watcher that indicate the status of the presence entity.

CUCM uses the term *SIP line* to represent endpoints supporting SIP that are directly connected and registered to CUCM, and the term *SIP trunk* to represent trunks supporting SIP. SIP line-side endpoints acting as presence watchers can send a SIP SUBSCRIBE message to CUCM requesting the presence status of the indicated presence entity.

If the presence entity resides outside the CUCM cluster, CUCM routes a SUBSCRIBE request out on the appropriate SIP trunk, based on the SUBSCRIBE CSS and presence groups. When CUCM receives a SIP NOTIFY response on the trunk that indicates the presence entity status, it responds to the SCCP line-side presence request by sending SCCP messages to the presence watcher indicating the status of the presence entity.

Indicators for Speed-Dial Presence

Table 14-1 describes the native presence indicators on IP phones.

Table 14-1 *Cisco Unified Communications Speed-Dial Presence*

State	Icon	LED
Idle		
Busy		
Unknown		

CUCM supports the ability for a speed dial to have presence capabilities via a Busy Lamp Field (BLF) speed dial. BLF speed dials work as both a speed dial and a presence indicator. Only the system administrator can configure a BLF speed dial. A system user is not allowed to configure or modify a BLF speed dial.

The administrator must configure the BLF speed dial with a target directory number that is resolvable to a directory number within the CUCM cluster or an entity accessed by a route pattern at accessed by a SIP trunk destination. The BLF speed-dial indicator is a line-level indicator and not a device-level indicator.

The BLF speed-dial indicators show the real-time state of the monitored phone:

- **Idle:** The user phone is on hook and the user is available.
- **Busy:** The user phone is off hook and the user is not available.
- **Unknown:** The real-time state cannot be determined. The phone might be disconnected, the users are not in the same presence group, or the users are not allowed to see the presence status.

CUCM Call Presence

Call list presence capabilities are controlled via the BLF for the Call Lists enterprise parameter within CUCM Administration. The BLF for the Call Lists enterprise parameter impacts all pages that use the phone Directories button and it is set on a global basis, as shown in Figure 14-3.

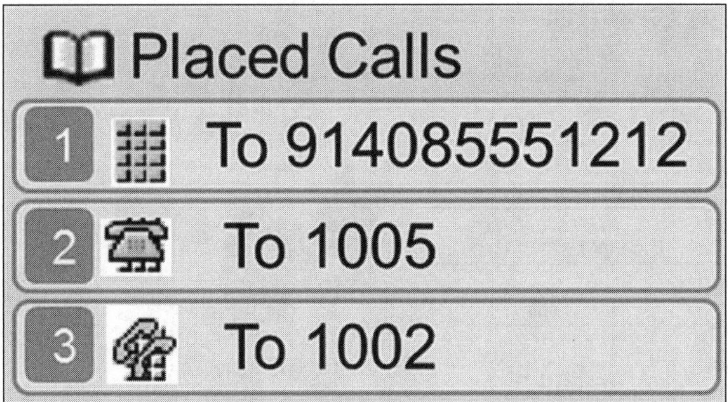

Figure 14-3 *CUCM Presence Call History on an IP Phone*

CUCM Subscribe CSS

Figure 14-4 describes how the subscribe CSS controls presence watchers.

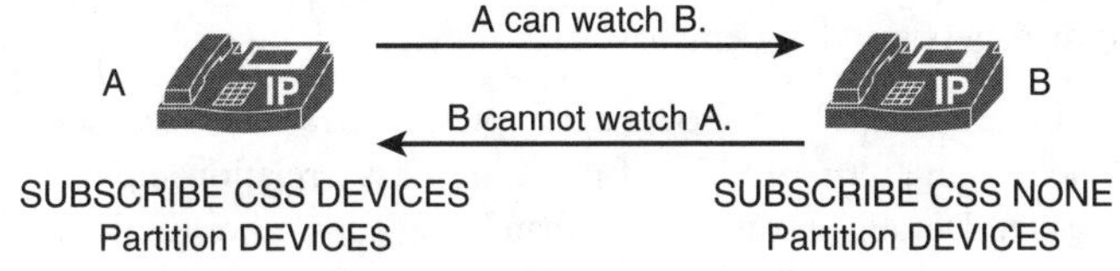

Figure 14-4 *CUCM Subscribe CSS*

CUCM provides the capability to set policy for users who request presence status:

- Configure a CSS to route SIP SUBSCRIBE messages for presence status.
- Configure presence groups with which watchers can be associated, that specify rules for viewing the presence status of presence entities that are associated with another group.

The first aspect of presence policies for CUCM is the subscribe CSS. CUCM uses the subscribe CSS to determine how to route presence requests. Presence requests are SUBSCRIBE messages with the Event field set to Presence. These messages are sent from the watcher, which can be a phone or a trunk. The subscribe CSS is associated with the watcher and lists the partitions that the watcher is allowed to see. This mechanism provides an additional level of granularity for the presence SUBSCRIBE requests to be routed independently from the normal call-processing CSS.

With the subscribe CSS set to <None>, BLF speed dial and call list presence status does not work (if no directory number or route pattern is associated with the <None> partition) and the subscription message is rejected as "user unknown." When a valid subscribe CSS is specified, the indicators work and the SUBSCRIBE messages are accepted and routed properly.

CUCM Presence Groups

Figure 14-5 illustrates how presence groups add more granularity to the presence functionality.

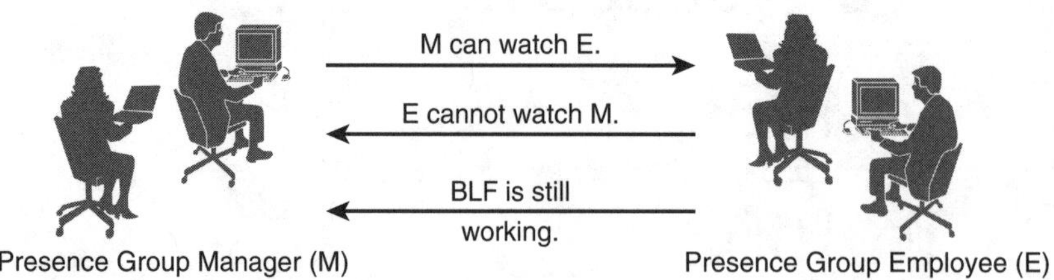
M can watch E.
E cannot watch M.
BLF is still working.
Presence Group Manager (M)
Presence Group Employee (E)

Figure 14-5 *CUCM Presence Groups*

Devices, directory numbers, and users can be assigned to a presence group, and by default, all users are assigned to the same standard presence group. By default, if the subscribe calling search space (CSS) permits, all watchers can watch all other entities.

A presence group controls the destinations that a watcher can monitor, based on the association of a user with a defined presence group; for example, employees watching managers is disallowed, but managers watching employees is allowed.

When multiple presence groups are defined, as shown in the picture, the Inter-Presence Group Subscribe Policy service parameter is applied. If one group has a relationship to another group via the Use System Default setting, rather than being allowed or disallowed, the value of this service parameter will take effect. If the Inter-Presence Group Subscribe Policy service parameter is set to Disallowed, CUCM will block the request even if the subscribe CSS allows it.

Note The Inter-Presence Group Subscribe Policy service parameter applies only for presence status with call lists and is not used for BLF speed dials.

Observe the following guidelines when configuring presence within CUCM:

- Define a presence policy for presence users.
- Use subscribe CSSs to control the routing of a watcher presence-based SIP SUBSCRIBE message to the correct destinations.
- Use presence groups to define sets of similar users and to define whether presence status updates of other user groups are allowed or disallowed.
- Call list presence capabilities are enabled on a global basis. The user status can be secured by using a presence policy.
- BLF speed dials are administratively controlled and are not impacted by the presence policy configuration.

Cisco Unified Communications IM&P Introduction

Figure 14-6 illustrates the components when using Cisco Jabber for presence functionality.

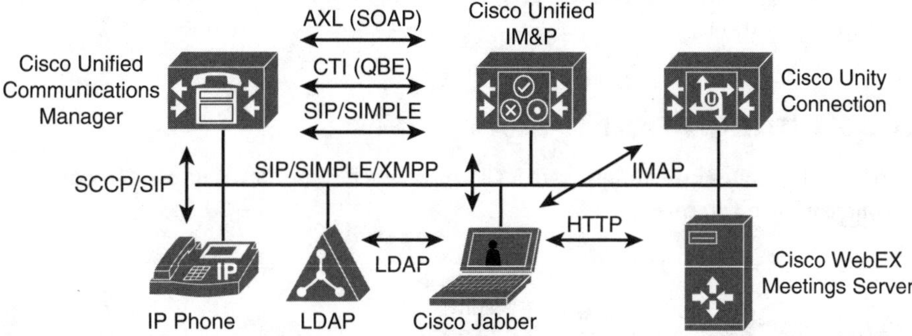

Figure 14-6 *CUCM IM&P*

Integrating Cisco WebEx Meetings Server, Cisco Unity Connection, and other applications into the presence network offers a feature-rich communications environment with the Cisco Jabber client application as the single interface for voice and video calls, voice-mail playback, web conferencing, and integrated directories.

The following are available features in this deployment:

- **Real-time availability:** This feature provides real-time availability of other Cisco Jabber users.
- **Contact list:** This feature allows users to search the corporate directory from one easy-to-use interface to locate contacts quickly. Simply click to call.
- **Media escalation:** This feature provides the ability to add communication methods during a session; for example, add video to an existing audio session, or add web conferencing to an existing audio or video session.
- **Click-to-call:** This feature provides the ability to dial from the contact list by using the integrated softphone or an associated IP phone.
- **Integrated voice and video calling:** This feature provides the ability to exchange ideas face to face with a coordinated video display on the PC screen and audio conversation with the softphone. Users can place video calls to other users.
- **IP phone association:** This feature allows users to use Cisco Jabber to control an IP phone and make or receive calls.
- **Conferencing:** This feature allows users to create multiparty voice or video conferencing sessions by simply merging conversation sessions by using the Cisco Jabber intuitive interface.

- **Web conferencing:** This feature allows users to launch a web conferencing session immediately to share content, such as a presentation, with others.
- **Voice messages:** This feature allows users to access Cisco Unity Connection voicemail messages—view, play back, sort, and delete messages—all from the same client application.

Microsoft Integration

Figure 14-7 illustrates how to integrate a Cisco presence solution within a Microsoft environment in an enterprise.

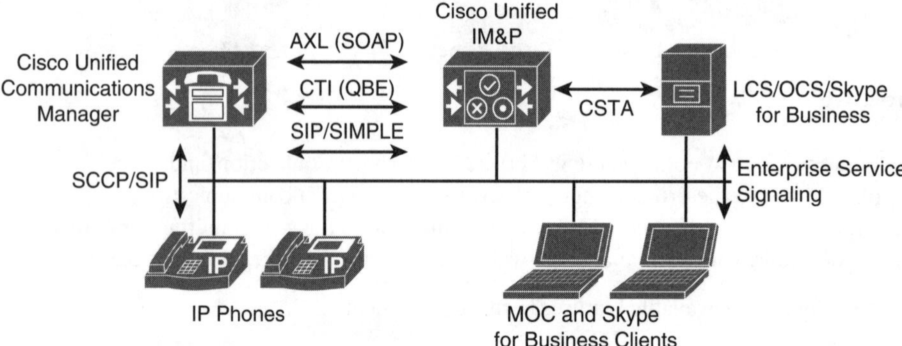

Figure 14-7 *Cisco to Microsoft Integration*

Cisco Unified Communications IM&P implements a Computer-Supported Telephony Application to Computer Telephony Integration (CSTA-to-CTI) bridge to integrate with Microsoft Office Communications Server (OCS) and Skype for Business interfaces. Cisco Unified Communications IM&P includes the following CTI gateway functionalities:

- CSTA over SIP interface to Microsoft Skype for Business and OCS server is available.
- A CTI interface to CUCM is available.
- A linkage of the older Microsoft Office Communicator (MOC) and the current Microsoft Skype for Business client and CUCM endpoints for a specific user is realized, which supports monitoring of CUCM endpoint activity via Microsoft clients. Support for call establishment and call modification for CUCM endpoints via Microsoft clients is also included.
- The functionality provides click to dial, phone hook status reporting, and general phone control directly from the Microsoft client.

OVA Template for Cisco Unified Communications IM&P

Table 14-2 presents the available VM overlays for Cisco Unified Communications IM&P installations.

Table 14-2 *OVA Template for Cisco Unified Communications IM&P*

User Capacity	vCPUs	Memory (GB)	vDisk	vNIC
500	1	2	1 x 80 GB	1
1000	1	2	1 x 80 GB	1
2000	1	4	1 x 80 GB	1
5000	2	4	2 x 80 GB	1
15,000	4	8	2 x 80 GB	1

The 500-user OVA template is the minimum VM configuration for use with the Cisco Hosted Collaboration Solution. The 1000-user OVA template is only supported for Cisco Business Edition 6000.

Another important factor is the number of presence or IM users. When using only IM, without presence, higher user counts are supported per server and cluster:

- 500 full UC users, 1000 IM-only users, 6 single nodes, or subclusters
- 1000 full UC users, 2000 IM-only users
- 2000 full UC users per node, 2000 IM-only users, 3 single nodes, or subclusters
- 5000 full UC users, 12,500 IM-only users, 6 single nodes, or subclusters
- 15,000 full UC users, 25,000 IM-only users, 6 single nodes, or subclusters

Note These templates may be adjusted and optimized with new releases of Cisco Unified Communications applications or VMware vSphere ESXi and can be found at http://docwiki.cisco.com/wiki/Virtualization_for_Unified_CM_IM_and_Presence.

IM&P Service maximum capacities per cluster are as follows:

- **Cisco Unified Communications mode:** In this mode, IM&P service integrates into a full Cisco Collaboration Systems environment to provide an enterprise-class IM&P solution in conjunction with the full suite of Cisco Collaboration Systems services, including voice and video. In this mode, IM&P service supports Cisco Collaboration Systems clients, such as the Cisco Jabber platform, and Cisco Jabber SDK, as well as third-party Extensible Messaging and Presence Protocol (XMPP) standard-based clients. When operating in Cisco Unified Communications mode, IM&P Service scales up to a maximum of 45,000 users in a multinode CUCM cluster environment.

- **IM-only user mode:** IM&P Service provides an enterprise-class IM&P solution for enterprise users who are not using CUCM for call control. In IM-only user mode, IM&P Service supports Cisco Collaboration Systems clients such as the Cisco Jabber client, and Cisco Jabber SDK for all enterprise-class IM&P services. IM&P Service also supports the ability for third-party XMPP standard-based clients to interface with CUCM for IM&P services. When operating in Cisco IM-only user mode, IM&P Service scales up to a maximum of 75,000 users in a multinode cluster environment. Users deployed as part of the Jabber for Everyone offer without voice and video services operate in IM-only user mode.
- **Microsoft Skype for Business interoperability mode (or Microsoft Remote Call Control):** In this mode, IM&P Service allows Microsoft Skype for Business users on a PC to interoperate with Cisco Unified IP phones on CUCM by providing click-to-dial and associated phone monitoring capabilities. Interoperability is made available by activating Microsoft Skype for Business interoperability mode in IM&P Service and configuring Microsoft Skype for Business users. When operating in this mode, IM&P Service scales up to 40,000 Microsoft Office Communicator users per CUCM cluster.

Cisco Unified Communications IM&P Cluster

Figure 14-8 illustrates the Cisco Unified Communications IM&P cluster architecture maximum option of up to six servers per cluster.

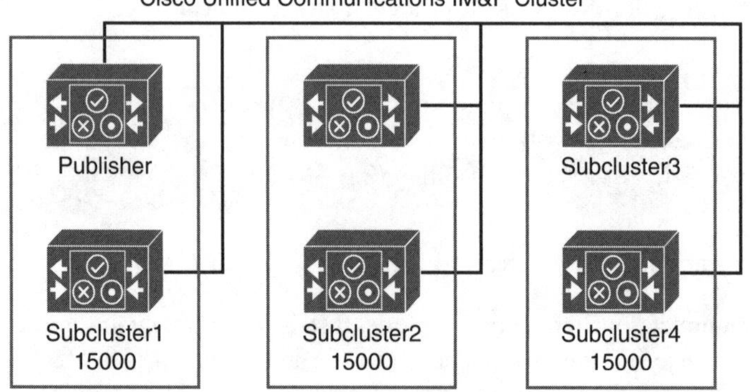

Figure 14-8 *Cisco Unified IM&P Cluster*

A cluster can be formed to scale Cisco Unified Communications IM&P to support up to 45,000 licensed presence users. The Cisco Unified Communications IM&P server uses the same virtualization approach that is used by CUCM or Cisco Unity Connection.

Cisco Unified Communications IM&P consists of up to six servers, including one server that is designated as a publisher. Cisco Unified Communications IM&P utilizes the same architectural concepts as the CUCM publisher and subscriber. Within a Cisco Unified Communications IM&P cluster, individual servers can be grouped to form a subcluster, and the subcluster can have at most two servers that are associated with it.

The figure shows the topology for a Cisco Unified Communications IM&P cluster. The Cisco Unified Communications IM&P cluster can also have mixed subclusters, where one subcluster is configured with two servers while other subclusters contain a single server. The Cisco Unified Communications IM&P servers form their own cluster even if they are integrated as subscribers in the CUCM cluster.

CUCM Deployment Options

This section describes how to deploy Cisco Unified Communications IM&P in different scenarios. Figure 14-9 illustrates CUCM and IM&P in different locations.

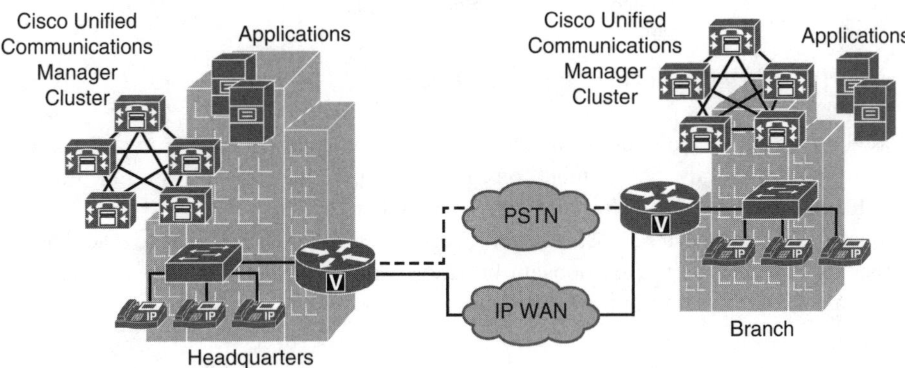

Figure 14-9 *Cisco Unified IM&P Cluster*

Cisco IM&P is supported with all CUCM deployment models. However, Cisco recommends locating the Cisco IM&P publisher in the same physical datacenter as the CUCM publisher due to the initial user database synchronization. All on-premises Cisco IM&P servers should be physically located in the same datacenter within the Cisco IM&P cluster, with the exception of geographic datacenter redundancy and clustering over the WAN.

A CUCM cluster can only connect to a single Cisco Unified Communications IM&P cluster. When you have a distributed CUCM deployment with two or more CUCM clusters, you also need two or more Cisco Unified Communications IM&P clusters per site. These Cisco Unified Communications IM&P servers can be connected using intercluster peers, when the clusters are in the same domain. If the Cisco Unified Communications IM&P clusters use different domains, a federation must be set up.

Service Discovery

When the Cisco Jabber client is opened the first time after a standard installation, you are asked to enter your e-mail address, as shown on the left of Figure 14-10.

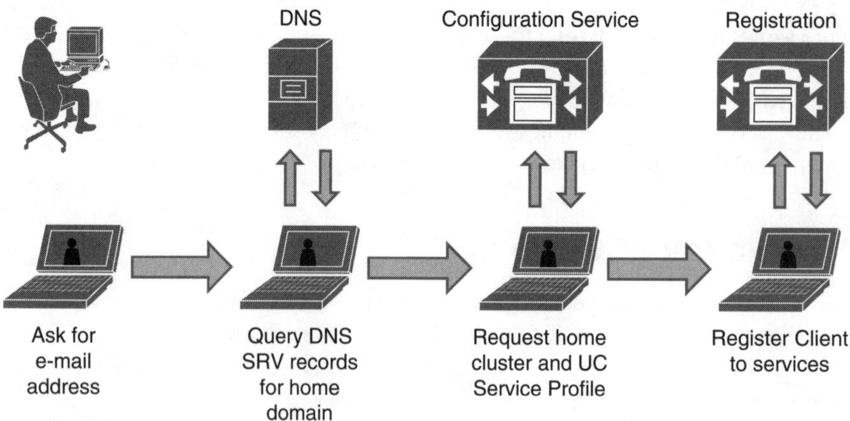

Figure 14-10 *Cisco Unified IM&P Service Discovery*

Based on the domain in your e-mail address, Cisco Jabber asks the DNS server for server records for _cisco-uds._tcp.example.com, as shown in the figure. The answer includes the IP address of a CUCM cluster server. Cisco Jabber contacts the CUCM server and requests the home cluster and service profile information that is required to reach the other application servers. Additional information is received via the jabber-config.xml file from the TFTP server in the CUCM cluster.

Quality of Service

This section describes the Cisco Jabber quality of service issues with trust boundaries.

The Cisco Jabber client marks call-signaling traffic with a differentiated services code point (DSCP) value of 24, or a PHB value of CS3, and it marks RTP media traffic with a DSCP value of 46 (PHB value of EF). Video traffic will be marked with a per-hop behavior (PHB) value of AF41 (DSCP value of 34), as illustrated in Table 14-3.

Table 14-3 *Quality of Service DSCP Markings*

Application	IP-Precedence	PHB	DSCP	CoS
Voice	5	EF	46	5
Video	4	AF41	34	4
Call signaling	3	CS3	24	3

Typically, networks are configured to strip DSCP markings from computer traffic. Therefore, if the administrator wants Cisco Jabber traffic to be marked, the administrator must configure switches and routers to preserve DSCP markings for packets originating from the Jabber client application.

Cisco Jabber Port Usage

Table 14-4 describes the different ports that Cisco Jabber uses to communicate.

Table 14-4 *Cisco Jabber Port Usage*

Port	Protocol	Description
53	UDP/TCP	DNS traffic
69/6790	UDP	TFTP/HTTP config download
80/443	TCP	HTTP/HTTPS to Cisco Unity Connection or WebEx
143	TCP	IMAP (TLS or plain TCP) to Cisco Unity Connection
389/636	TCP	LDAP/LDAPS
993	TCP	IMAP (over SSL) to retrieve and manage voice messages
2748	TCP	CTI gateway
3268/3269	TCP	Global Catalog/LDAPs
5060	UDP/TCP	SIP call signaling
5061	TCP	Secure SIP call signaling
5070	UDP	Binary Floor Control Protocol (BFCP) for video desktop sharing
5222	TCP	XMPP
7993	TCP	IMAP (over TLS) access to secure voice messages
8191	TCP	SOAP web services
8443	TCP	HTTPS for CCMCIP profiles and UDS
16384-32766	UDP	RTP media streams for audio and video

As shown in the table, Cisco Jabber uses a number of protocols for communication. In addition, these protocols may be used and are listed here for your reference:

- **Port 7080:** Protocol TCP (HTTPS); used for Cisco Unity Connection for notifications of voice messages (new message, message update, and message deletion)
- **Port 37200:** Protocol SOCKS5 Bytestreams; used for peer-to-peer file transfers. In on-premises deployments, the client also uses this port to send screen captures.

Enterprise Instant Messaging

This section describes enterprise instant messaging (EIM).

Cisco Unified Communications IM&P incorporates the supported EIM features of the Cisco Jabber Extensible Communications Platform (XCP), while allowing for modifications to enhance support for the multidevice user experience. Text conferencing, sometimes referred to as multiuser chat, is defined as ad hoc group chat. Persistent group chat is supported as part of the Jabber XCP feature set. In addition, offline IM (storing instant messages for users who are currently offline) is also supported as part of the Jabber XCP feature set. Cisco Unified Communications IM&P manages storage for each of these IM features in different locations, as shown in Table14-5.

Table 14-5 *Cisco EIM Features*

Feature	Stored in
Offline instant messaging	Cisco Unified Communications IM&P IDS database
Ad hoc group chat	Cisco Unified Communications IM&P memory
Persistent chat	External database to store rooms and conversations

Note The supported external databases are PostgreSQL (see http://www.postgresql.org/) and Oracle (see http://www.oracle.com).

If persistent chat is enabled, ad hoc rooms are stored on the external PostgreSQL database for the duration of the ad hoc chat. This procedure allows a room owner to escalate an ad hoc chat to a persistent chat; otherwise, these ad hoc chats are purged from PostgreSQL at the end of the chat. If persistent chat is disabled, ad hoc chats are stored in volatile memory for the duration of the chat.

Multicluster Deployment

Figure 14-11 illustrates how to connect Cisco Unified Communications IM&P clusters within the same domain.

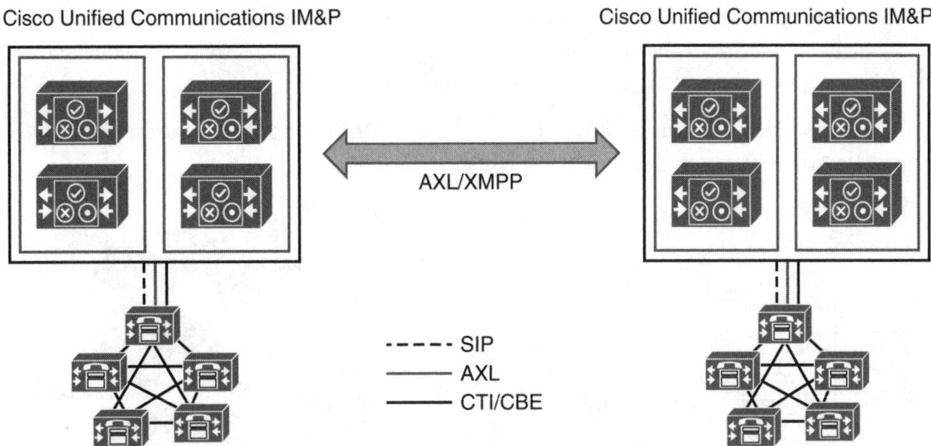

Figure 14-11 *Cisco Unified IM&P Cluster*

To extend presence and IM capability and functionality, these standalone clusters can be configured for peer relationships, thus enabling communication between clusters within the same domain. The figure represents the peer relationship between Cisco Unified Communications IM&P clusters when multiple clusters or sites are interconnected. This functionality provides the ability for users in one cluster to communicate and subscribe to the presence of users in a different cluster within the same domain.

To create a fully meshed presence topology, each Cisco Unified Communications IM&P cluster requires a separate peer relationship with each of the other Cisco Unified Communications IM&P clusters within the same domain. The address that is configured in this intercluster peer could be a DNS server FQDN that resolves to the remote Cisco Unified Communications IM&P cluster servers. The address could also simply be the IP address of the Cisco Unified Communications IM&P cluster servers.

The interface between Cisco Unified Communications IM&P clusters is twofold, an Administrative XML - Simple Object Access Protocol (AXL-SOAP) interface, and (SIP or XMPP). The AXL-SOAP interface manages the synchronization of user information for home cluster association, but it is not a complete user synchronization. The signaling protocol interface (SIP or XMPP) manages the subscription and notification traffic, and it rewrites the host portion of the URI before forwarding if the user is on a remote Cisco Unified Communications IM&P cluster within the same domain.

Federated Deployment

This section describes how to connect Cisco Unified Communications IM&P clusters that are in different domains.

Interdomain federation parameters:

- Two different DNS domains
- Cisco Adaptive Security Appliance (ASA) appliance in demilitarized zone (DMZ)

Cisco Unified Communications IM&P allows for business-to-business communications by enabling interdomain federation, which provides the ability to share presence and IM communications between different domains.

Federation is a term that describes data servers in different domains that can securely connect to one another, as shown in Figure14-12.

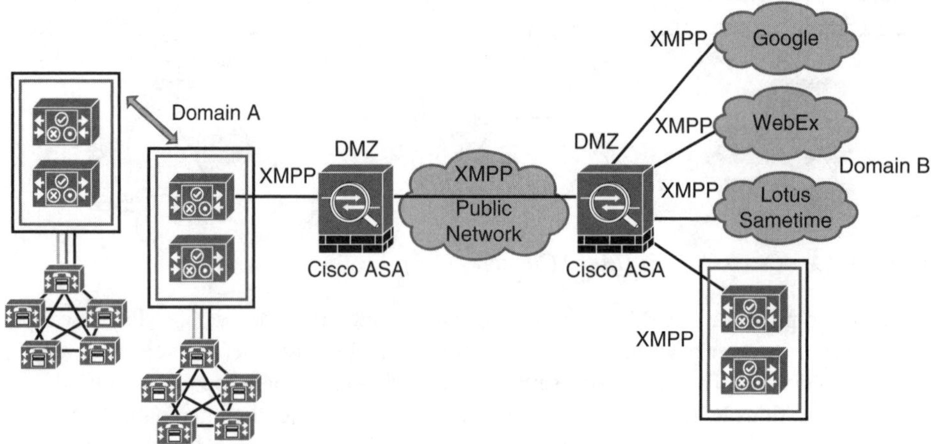

Figure 14-12 *Cisco Unified IM&P Federation Deployment*

Interdomain federation requires that two explicit DNS domains are configured, as well as a security appliance (Cisco ASA) in the DMZ to terminate federated connections with the enterprise.

Figure 14-12 shows a basic interdomain federation deployment between two different domains, indicated by Domain A and Domain B. The Cisco Adaptive Security Appliance in the DMZ is used as a point of demarcation into the enterprise. XMPP traffic is passed through, whereas SIP traffic is inspected. All federated incoming and outgoing traffic is routed through the Cisco Unified Communications IM&P server that is enabled as a federation node, and is routed internally to the appropriate server in the cluster where the user resides. For multicluster deployments, intercluster peers propagate the traffic to the appropriate home cluster within the domain. Multiple nodes can be enabled as federation nodes within large enterprise deployments, where each request is routed based on a round-robin implementation of the data that is returned from the DNS server lookup.

Microsoft Skype for Business Federation

Figure 14-13 illustrates Cisco SIP federations with one or more Microsoft domains.

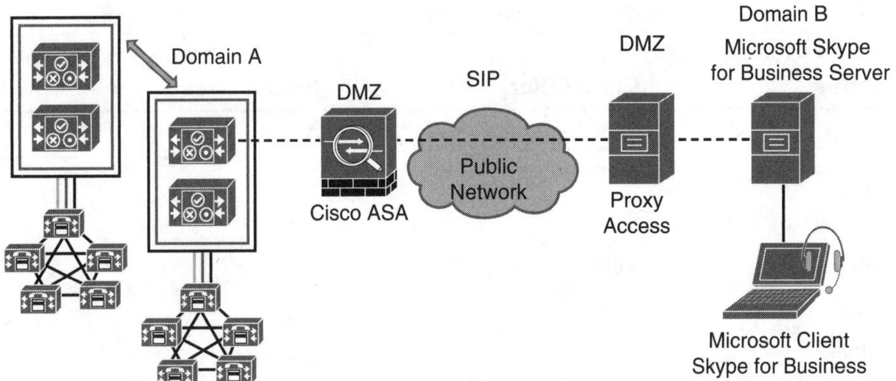

Figure 14-13 *Cisco and Microsoft Skype for Business Federation*

Cisco Unified Communications IM&P provides interdomain federation with Microsoft Skype for Business and the older Microsoft OCS, Microsoft Live Communications Server (LCS) to provide basic presence (available, away, busy, offline), and point-to-point IM.

Cisco Unified Communications IM&P must publish a DNS server record (SIP, XMPP, and each text conferencing node) for the domain to allow other domains to discover the Cisco Unified Communications IM&P servers through the DNS server records. With a Microsoft deployment, this procedure is required because Cisco Unified Communications IM&P is configured as a public IM provider on the access edge server. If the Cisco Unified Communications IM&P server cannot discover the Microsoft domain using DNS server records, the administrator must configure a static route on Cisco Unified Communications IM&P for the external domain.

The Cisco Unified Communications IM&P federation deployment can be configured with redundancy using a load balancer between the Cisco Adaptive Security Appliance and the Cisco Unified Communications IM&P server. Redundancy can also be achieved with a redundant Cisco Adaptive Security Appliance configuration.

In an intercluster and a multinode cluster Cisco Unified Communications IM&P deployment, when a foreign Microsoft domain initiates a new session, the Cisco Adaptive Security Appliance routes all messages to a Cisco Unified Communications IM&P server that is designated for routing purposes. If the Cisco Unified Communications IM&P routing server does not host the recipient user, it routes the message via intercluster communication to the appropriate Cisco Unified Communications IM&P server within the cluster. The system routes all responses that are associated with this request through the routing Cisco Unified Communications IM&P server.

Mapping of Presence Status

As Cisco's and Microsoft's products are developed separately by the different companies, in a federation between Cisco and Microsoft presence, not all presence fields have the same meaning. Table 14-6 shows a comparison between Cisco and Microsoft presence.

Table 14-6 *Cisco to Microsoft Mapping of Presence Status*

Cisco Status	Cisco Color	Status to Microsoft Skype for Business
Out of office	Red	Away
Do not disturb	Red	Busy
Busy	Red	Busy
On the phone	Yellow	Busy
In a meeting	Yellow	Busy
Idle on all clients	Yellow	Away
Available	Green	Available
Unavailable/offline	Gray	Offline

Rich presence capability (on the phone, in a meeting, on vacation, and so on), as well as advanced IM features, are not supported in an interdomain federation.

Federation Preparation

Additional preparation is required before implementing a federated deployment including routing, allocating public IP addresses, providing DNS records, and certificates. The following list gives you a quick overview of the tasks you must consider when building a federation on Cisco Unified Communications IM&P. Depending on the company, many departments may be involved when deploying presence federations.

- Routing configuration
  - Cisco Unified Communications IM&P to Cisco ASA appliance to foreign domain
  - Access lists and firewalls
- Public IP address
  - Outside interface of the Cisco ASA appliance
  - Use Network Address Translation (NAT) or Port Address Translation (PAT)
- DNS configuration
  - Cisco Unified Communications IM&P must publish a DNS server record
  - Publish the DNS server record _xmpp-server
- Certificate authority server
  - When using TLS, upload root certificate to Cisco Unified Communications IM&P server.

Summary

This section summarizes the key points that were discussed in this chapter:

- CUCM supports native presence for BLF or call history. Cisco Unified Communications IM&P is required for Cisco Jabber and presence functionality.
- Cisco Unified Communications IM&P can be federated with other domains via XMPP (for example, with Google Talk or via SIP with Microsoft Skype for Business).
- Persistent chat, message archiving, and compliance require external databases (for example, PostgreSQL).
- When designing Cisco Unified Communications IM&P, the limit is 45,000 users enabled for presence per cluster. A CUCM cluster can only connect to one Cisco Unified Communications IM&P cluster.

This chapter explained how to design and deploy a Cisco Unified Communications IM&P solution in different CUCM scenarios.

Review Questions

Answer the following questions, and then see Appendix A, "Answers to Review Questions," for the answers.

1. **Native presence in CUCM requires a Cisco Unified Communications IM&P server to function properly.**

   a. True

   b. False

2. **Which protocol is used between Cisco Unified Communications IM&P and Microsoft Skype for Business when integrating in an enterprise network?**

   a. AXL

   b. CSTA

   c. SIP

   d. XMPP

3. **Which two options identify the maximum number of presence users and the maximum number of IM-only users that are permitted in a Cisco Unified Communications IM&P cluster? (Choose two)**

   a. 40,000 presence users

   b. 45,000 presence users

   c. 75,000 presence users

d. 45,000 IM-only users

e. 75,000 IM-only users

f. 80,000 IM-only users

4. How many servers can be in a Cisco Unified Communications IM&P cluster?

a. 2

b. 4

c. 5

d. 6

e. 8

5. Which port number must be opened in a firewall to allow Cisco Jabber to discover services?

a. 53 DNS

b. 69 TFTP

c. 3268 Global Catalog

d. 5060 SIP

e. 5222 XMPP

Chapter 15

Describing Cisco Unified Communications IM and Presence Components and Communication Flows

Upon completing this chapter, you will be able to do the following:

- Describe Cisco Jabber in deskphone mode to control the desk phone to initiate and answer calls
- Describe how Cisco Jabber makes calls in softphone mode when there is no access to the deskphone device
- Describe Cisco Jabber in phone-only mode without IM and Presence (IM&P) functionality
- Describe how Cisco Jabber accesses voice mail
- Describe how conference servers allow Cisco Jabber users to start conferences
- Describe how LDAP integration enables end users to search and add contacts from the corporate directory
- Describe the integration of Microsoft Active Directory and Exchange
- Describe the architecture of Cisco Unified Communications IM&P and the protocols and interfaces that are used to connect to other applications
- Describe the communication between Cisco Unified Communications Manager and the Cisco Unified Communications IM&P cluster
- Show the login flow of Cisco Jabber registering with Cisco Unified Communications Manager
- Describe how Cisco Jabber can access corporate resources from any location

This chapter describes the Cisco Unified Communications IM&P architecture, protocols, interfaces, and call flows.

Cisco Unified Communications IM&P Architecture

Figure 15-1 illustrates the architecture of Cisco Unified Communications IM&P and the protocols and interfaces that are used to connect to other applications.

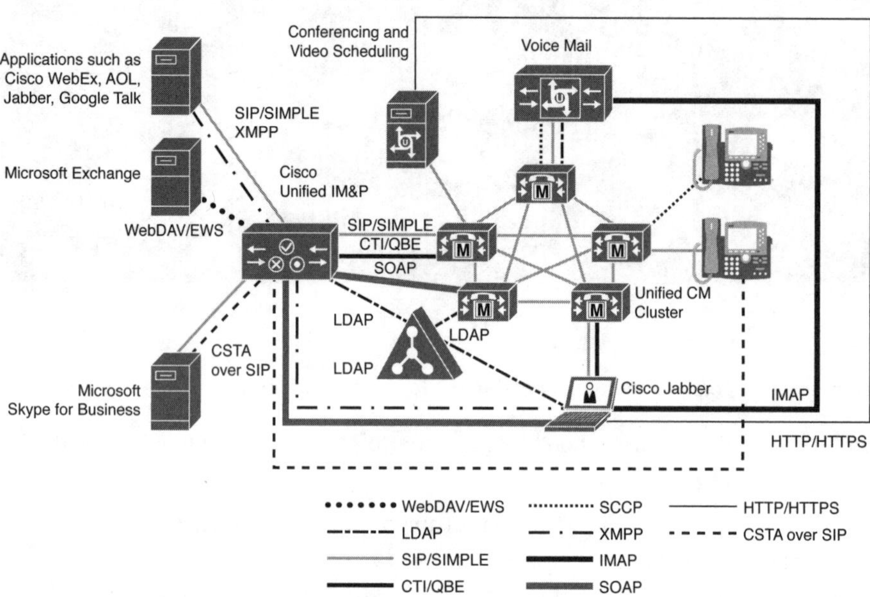

Figure 15-1 *Cisco Unified Communications IM&P Architecture*

Cisco Unified Communications IM&P consists of many components that enhance the value of a Cisco Unified Communications solution. Cisco Unified Communications IM&P incorporates the Jabber Extensible Communications Platform (Jabber XCP) and supports Session Initiation Protocol (SIP), SIP for Instant Messaging and Presence Leveraging Extensions (SIMPLE), and Extensible Messaging and Presence Protocol (XMPP) for collecting information about the availability status and the communications capabilities of the user. The availability status of the user indicates whether the user is actively using a particular communications device such as a phone. The communications capabilities indicate the types of communications that the user is capable of using, such as video conferencing, web collaboration, IM, and others.

Cisco Unified Communications IM&P encompasses the components presented in the figure. Cisco Unified Communications IM&P uses standards-based SIP, SIMPLE, and XMPP to provide a common demarcation point for integrating clients and applications into Cisco Collaboration Systems. Cisco Unified Communications IM&P also provides an HTTP interface that has a configuration interface through SOAP and a presence interface through Representation State Transfer (REST). The Cisco Unified Communications

IM&P server collects, aggregates, and distributes user capabilities and attributes using these standards-based SIP, SIMPLE, XMPP, and HTTP interfaces.

Cisco or third-party applications can integrate with presence and provide services that improve the end-user experience and efficiency. The core components of the Cisco Unified Communications IM&P server consist of the following:

- Jabber XCP, which manages presence, IM, roster, routing, policy, and federation management
- Rich Presence Service, which manages presence state gathering, network-based rich presence composition, and presence-enabled routing functionality
- Support for ad hoc group chat storage with persistent chat and message archiving that is handled by an external database

Applications (either Cisco or third party) can integrate presence and provide services that improve the end-user experience and efficiency. The Cisco Unified Communications IM&P server also contains support for interoperability with Microsoft Skype for Business Server, including the clients for any phone that is connected to a Cisco Unified Communications Manager.

Cisco Unified Communications IM&P Cluster

Figure 15-2 illustrates the communication between Cisco Unified Communications Manager (CUCM) and the Cisco Unified Communications IM&P cluster.

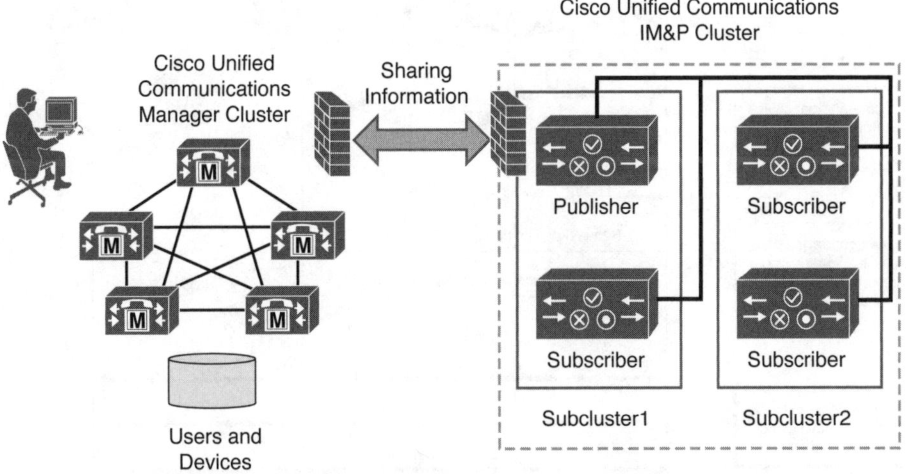

Figure 15-2 *Cisco Unified Communications IM&P Cluster*

Starting with Version 10.x, the Cisco Unified Communications IM&P server is a subscriber server in the CUCM cluster. However, the Cisco Unified Communications IM&P cluster has still its own publisher and subscriber servers within the subcluster concept for high availability. Both clusters require configuration so that Cisco Jabber can register and work properly.

The Cisco Unified Communications IM&P publisher utilizes and builds upon the database that is used by the CUCM publisher by sharing the end-user and device information. A Cisco Unified Communications IM&P cluster supports only a single CUCM cluster. Therefore, all presence users of the Cisco Unified Communications IM&P cluster must be defined within the same CUCM cluster.

Intracluster traffic participates at a very low level between Cisco Unified Communications IM&P and CUCM and between the Cisco Unified Communications IM&P publisher and subscriber servers. Both clusters share a common host file and have a strong trust relationship using IP tables.

The Cisco Unified Communications IM&P publisher communicates directly with the CUCM publisher via the AXL application programming interface (API) using the Simple Object Access Protocol (SOAP) interface.

Cisco Jabber Login Flow

Figure 15-3 shows the login flow of Cisco Jabber registering with CUCM.

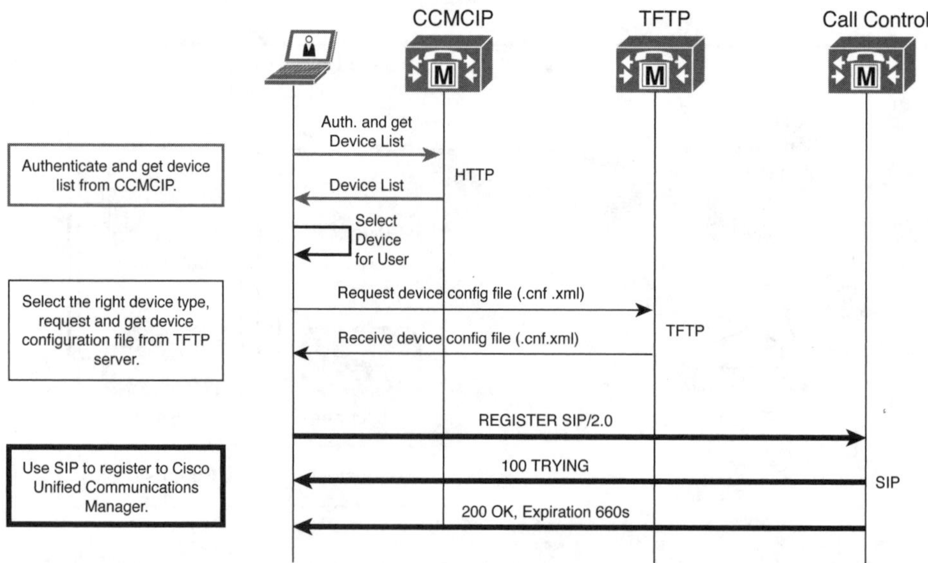

Figure 15-3 *Cisco Jabber Login Flow*

First, Cisco Jabber queries the DNS server for the SRV records, which is not shown in the figure. If Cisco Jabber is on the corporate network, the local DNS should reply with the _cisco-uds server record to provide the location of CUCM (Version 9.0 or later) or with the _cuplogin server record to provide the location of Cisco Unified Presence.

Cisco Jabber uses the CCMCIP profile to receive a list of available devices that are bound to the user that is logging in to Cisco Jabber. After receiving the device list, the user can select a device if more devices are configured.

Then, the configuration file is requested from the TFTP server. After reading out the configuration file, the device registers using SIP messages as shown in the figure.

Remote Access for Cisco Jabber Without VPN

Figure 15-4 describes how Cisco Jabber can access corporate resources from any location via the Internet.

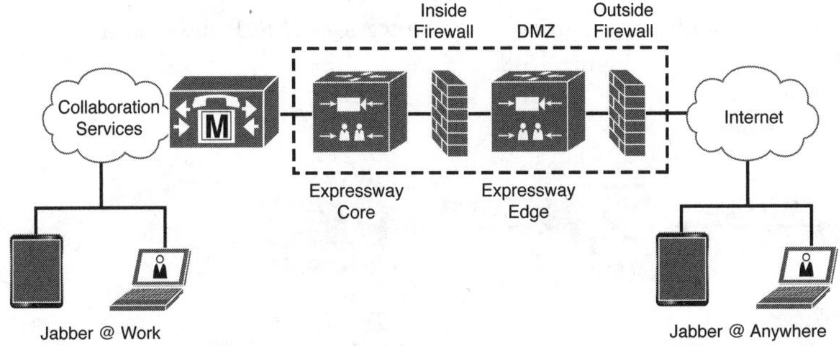

Figure 15-4 *Remote Access for Cisco Jabber Without VPN*

Cisco Collaboration Systems mobile and remote access is a core part of the Cisco Collaboration Edge architecture. It allows endpoints such as Cisco Jabber to have their registration, call control, provisioning, messaging, and presence services provided by CUCM when the endpoint is not within the enterprise network. The Cisco Expressway provides secure firewall traversal and line-side support for CUCM registrations.

After you download the ISO software from Cisco.com for Video Communications Server (VCS), adding the licensed option codes transforms the function of the VM into either Expressway Control or Expressway Edge. Both virtual machines (VMs) are required for this remote access solution.

The overall solution provides the following:

- **Off-premises access:** The Cisco Collaboration Systems solution offers a consistent experience outside the network for Cisco Jabber and Cisco EX, MX, and SX series clients.

- **Security:** The Cisco Collaboration Systems solution provides secure business-to-business communications.
- **Cloud services:** The Cisco Collaboration Systems solution provides enterprise-grade flexibility and scalable solutions providing rich WebEx integration and service provider offerings.
- **Gateway and interoperability services:** The Cisco Collaboration Systems solution provides media and signaling normalization, and support for nonstandard endpoints.

Signaling traverses the Cisco Expressway solution between the mobile endpoint and CUCM. Media traverses the Cisco Expressway solution and is relayed between endpoints directly; all media is encrypted between Cisco Expressway-C and the mobile endpoint.

Cisco Jabber Information Flow in Deskphone Mode

When using Cisco Jabber in deskphone mode, Cisco Jabber registers with both the Cisco Communications Manager and Cisco Unified Communications IM&P and downloads the configuration file, as shown in Figure 15-5.

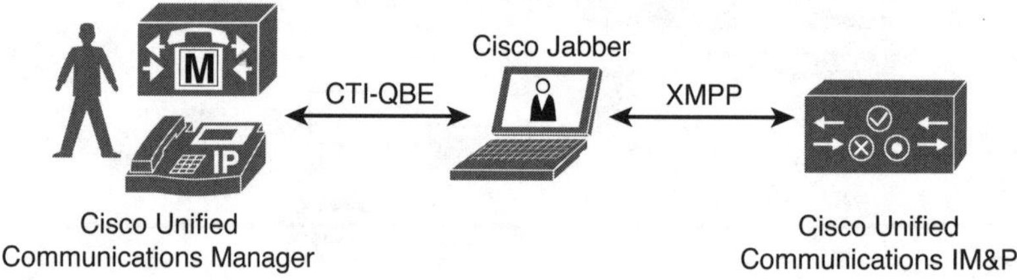

Figure 15-5 *Cisco Jabber Information Flow in Deskphone Mode*

The end user logs in with the end-user credentials that are configured in CUCM or the Lightweight Directory Access Protocol (LDAP) server, depending on the setup for authentication services.

With the Cisco CallManager Cisco IP Phone (CCMCIP) service, Cisco Jabber receives the list of controlled and user-associated devices. The end user utilizes the computer telephony integration Quick Buffer Encoding (CTIQBE) interface to control the selected phone. The end user can only select the IP phone when multiple IP phones are registered and associated with the end user.

Cisco Jabber uses XMPP for chat features and sends all instant messages to Cisco Unified Communications IM&P.

Cisco Jabber Information Flow in Softphone Mode

This section describes how Cisco Jabber makes calls in softphone mode, when there is no access to the deskphone device, as shown in Figure 15-6.

Figure 15-6 *Cisco Jabber Information Flow in Softphone Mode*

When no IP phone is available or the user is not in the office, Cisco Jabber softphone mode allows the user to place and receive calls using the Jabber desktop application.

The Cisco Unified Client Service Framework (CSF) uses SIP REGISTER messages to register with CUCM as a Cisco Unified CSF device, and uses SIP as the signaling protocol. Cisco Jabber connects to the primary TFTP server. When the connection is established, Cisco Jabber downloads the configuration file from CUCM.

The configuration file contains a list of CUCM primary and failover server addresses. This file also contains the transport protocol for Cisco Jabber to use in softphone mode to connect to CUCM.

After Cisco Jabber downloads the configuration file, the configuration parameters are made available to other Cisco Jabber subsystems. Each time Cisco Jabber tries to download the configuration file, the application attempts to contact the primary TFTP server. If the primary TFTP server does not respond, Cisco Jabber fails over to the backup TFTP server. If all TFTP server connections fail, Cisco Jabber tries to load the last valid downloaded configuration from the local hard disk.

Cisco Jabber uses XMPP to access Cisco Unified Communications IM&P for instant messages and roster updates.

Cisco Jabber in Phone-Only Mode

This section describes Cisco Jabber in phone-only mode without IM&P functionality, as shown in Figure 15-7.

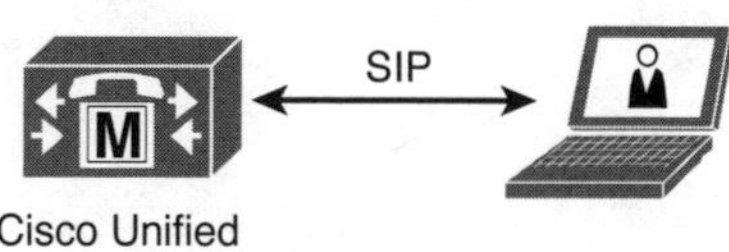

Figure 15-7 *Cisco Jabber Information Flow in Phone-Only Mode*

With Cisco Jabber for Windows, you have the ability to choose the phone-only mode, where the client authenticates directly with CUCM. In this mode, you are provisioned with audio or video capabilities without the functionality of presence or IM. Therefore, it is important to have the ability to determine when the Jabber client is deployed in phone-only mode, and to understand the features that are affected.

The phone(-only) mode can be selected when Cisco Jabber starts. Choose **Advanced Settings.** Then you can choose **Cisco Unified Communications Manager** for phone capabilities only. Other options are **Automatic, Cisco IM & Presence, WebEx Messenger**, or using a default or specified **Login Server.**

Cisco Jabber and Voice Mail

Figure 15-8 illustrates how Cisco Jabber accesses voice mail.

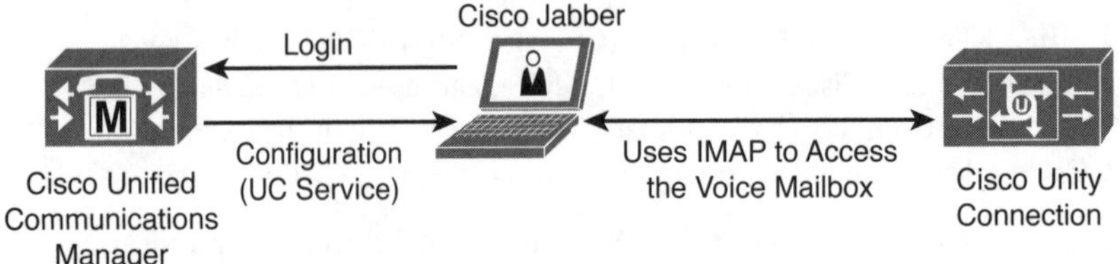

Figure 15-8 *Cisco Jabber and Unity Connection Voice Mail*

Cisco Unity Connection can be integrated with CUCM so that end users can access their voice mailbox in Cisco Jabber. Cisco Jabber voice-mail integration uses IMAP to access the voice mailbox, which provides the following features:

- Voice messages can be accessed directly from the conversation history pane in the Cisco Jabber client.
- The integrated media player can be used to play and delete messages directly from the Cisco Jabber client.
- Presence and availability information can be easily accessed for the caller in the Cisco Jabber client. The user can then click to call the person to escalate to a web chat, video, or other multimedia sessions.

Cisco Jabber and Conferencing

Figure 15-9 describes how conference servers allow Cisco Jabber users to start conferences.

Figure 15-9 *Cisco Jabber and Conferencing*

Cisco Jabber uses Cisco WebEx for its web conferencing capability. The web conferencing features of Cisco WebEx use HTTP or HTTPS as the transport protocol. You can also add the Cisco TelePresence Management Suite as a video conference scheduling portal.

Integration with LDAP for Cisco Jabber

Figure 15-10 describes how LDAP integration enables end users to search and add contacts from the corporate directory.

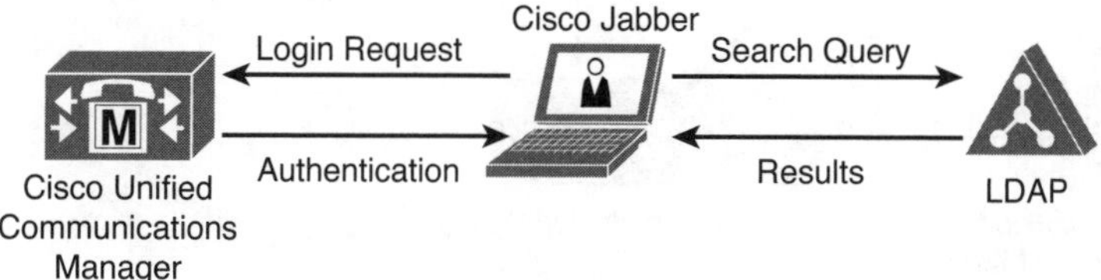

Figure 15-10 *Cisco Jabber LDAP Integration*

Administrators can provision users automatically from the LDAP directory into the CUCM database. CUCM synchronizes with the LDAP directory so the administrator does not have to add, remove, or modify user information manually each time a change occurs in the corporate directory. LDAP integration also provides authentication for Cisco Jabber client users.

To enhance the user experience, you can display user photos in Cisco Jabber. To achieve the best result with Cisco Jabber, your contact photos should have specific formats and dimensions. Cisco Jabber supports the following formats for contact photos in your directory: JPG, PNG, and BMP. Cisco Jabber does not apply any modifications to enhance rendering for contact photos in GIF format. As a result, contact photos in GIF format might render incorrectly or with less than optimal quality. To obtain the best quality, you should use the PNG format for your contact photos. The optimum dimensions for contact photos are 128 pixels by 128 pixels with an aspect ratio of 1:1.

If contact photos in your directory are smaller or larger than 128 pixels by 128 pixels, the client automatically resizes the photos. For example, if contact photos in your directory are 64 pixels by 64 pixels, Cisco Jabber resizes the photos to 128 pixels by 128 pixels when the photo is retrieved.

Cisco Unified Communications IM&P, Active Directory, and Microsoft Exchange

Figure 15-11 describes the integration of Microsoft Active Directory and Exchange with Cisco Unified Communications.

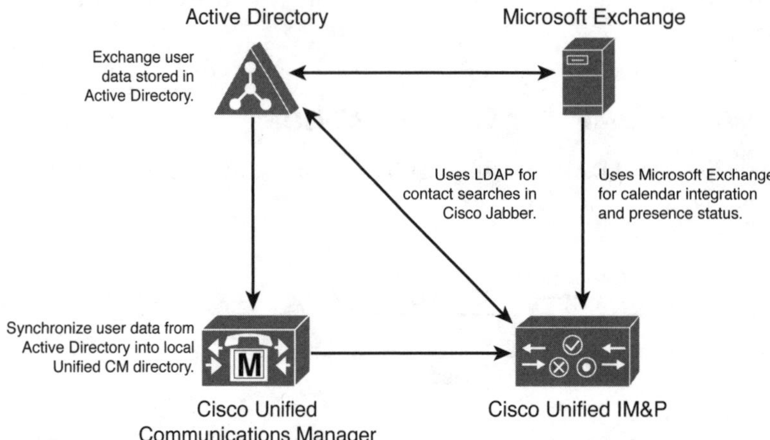

Figure 15-11 *Cisco Unified Communications IM&P, Active Directory, and Exchange*

CUCM and Cisco Unified Communications IM&P can be integrated with the enterprise LDAP directory and Microsoft Exchange. This integration allows users to sign in with their LDAP user credentials and synchronize their presence status with Microsoft Outlook calendar entries.

An LDAP directory lookup allows Cisco Jabber client users, or third-party XMPP clients, to search for and to add contacts from the LDAP directory. The search results are displayed in the search window from Cisco Jabber.

Cisco Unified Communications IM&P communicates with the Microsoft Exchange Server using OWA, a WebDAV interface that is available on the Microsoft Exchange Server 2003. For Microsoft Exchange 2007 and later, Exchange Web Services (EWS) is used.

Summary

This section summarizes the key points that were discussed in this chapter:

- Cisco Unified Communications IM&P servers are subscriber servers in a CUCM cluster.
- Through downloading a service profile comprising the different UC services, Cisco Jabber knows how to connect to Cisco Unity Connection and other applications.
- LDAP is used to authenticate users, but also to resolve numbers into names or to show photos of users.

This chapter explained how Cisco Jabber integrates with various applications.

Review Questions

Answer the following questions, and then see Appendix A, "Answers to Review Questions," for the answers.

1. **Which service is used by Cisco Jabber to request a list of assigned devices?**

   a. CCMCIP

   b. CTIQBE

   c. XMPP

   d. LDAP

2. **Which protocol is used between Cisco Jabber and Cisco Unity Connection to retrieve voice messages?**

   a. HTTP

   b. IMAP

   c. POP3

   d. SMTP

3. **What is the optimal photo size for Cisco Jabber photo retrieval?**

   a. 64 pixels by 64 pixels

   b. 128 pixels by 128 pixels

   c. 256 pixels by 256 pixels

   d. 512 pixels by 512 pixels

4. **When deploying access for Cisco Jabber without a VPN, which device is placed into the DMZ?**

   a. Expressway Core

   b. Expressway DMZ

   c. Expressway Edge

   d. CUCM

Chapter 16

Integrating Cisco Unified Communications IM and Presence

Upon completing this chapter, you will be able to do the following:

- Describe the requirements on CUCM for integration with IMP Cisco Unified Communications IM and Presence (IM&P) with Cisco Unified Communications Manager
- Describe the requirements on CUCM for integration with IM&P
- Describe the steps to configure CUCM for a presence integration
- Describe the service profile including the UC Services that are required for a user to use presence
- Describe the requirements on IM&P to integrate with CUCM
- Describe the steps to integrate IM&P with CUCM
- Describe the Cisco Unified Communications IM&P services
- Describe the benefits of Cisco Jabber service discovery
- Describe how Cisco Jabber discovers the service domain
- Describe how Cisco Jabber discovers the operating mode
- Describe the call flow when using Cisco UDS service records
- Describe the DNS SRV records for Cisco Jabber
- Describe the priorities and weights of the DNS SRV records
- Show how to verify and troubleshoot configured Cisco UDS SVR records
- Describe the installation options for the Cisco Jabber MSI installer
- Describe how to create a customized Cisco Jabber installer file

This chapter describes the integration of Cisco Unified Communications Manager (CUCM) and Cisco Unified Communications IM&P. First, CUCM is prepared for integration with Cisco Unified Communications IM&P. Cisco Unified Communications IM&P is then set up to connect with CUCM and system settings are modified. Network services are then established so that Cisco Jabber can discover its domain and services. Finally, the chapter discusses the Cisco Jabber installation options.

Set Up CUCM for Presence

The components that are presented in the Figure 16-1 must be implemented on CUCM to prepare for integration with Cisco Unified Communications IM&P. These components allow a Cisco Jabber client to register, show the presence status, and reflect changes when, for example, a line is in use.

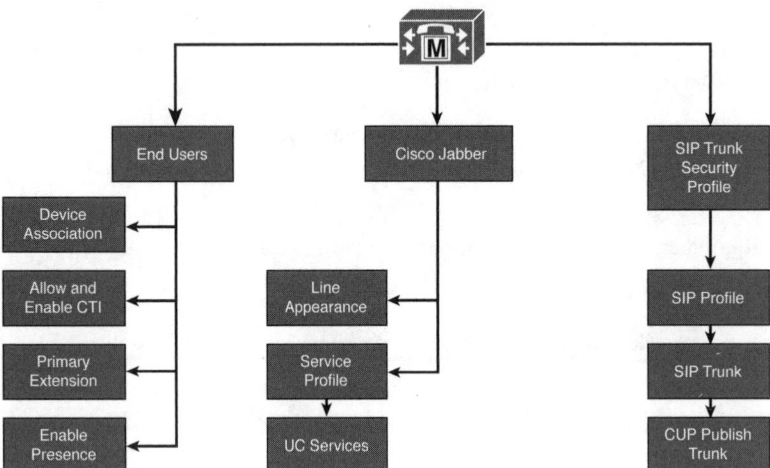

Figure 16-1 *Set Up CUCM for Presence*

Synchronize the end users from a directory and configure the associated devices. Bind the device to the user and configure the primary extension. Verify that Computer Telephony Integration (CTI) is enabled for the device and the line. Ensure that the user has the correct CTI access control groups assigned. Finally, enable presence for the end user and assign the service profile that contains the services that were selected under UC services in the CUCM menu.

For softphone mode, Cisco Jabber must be added as a Cisco Unified Client Services Framework (CSF) device to register with CUCM. Every line that is used by a presence user must be associated with the user in the line configuration page, because the presence indicator is line-based and not device-based. This setting allows contacts to see the busy status with the message "On the Phone."

Configure a Session Initiation Protocol (SIP) trunk security profile for a SIP trunk pointing to the Cisco Unified Communications IM&P server. There can be only one CUP SIP publish trunk selected on CUCM. In other words, one CUCM cluster can connect to only one Cisco Unified Communications IM&P cluster. However, additional Cisco Unified Communications IM&P clusters can be peered or federated.

Checklist for CUCM Setup

This section describes the steps to set up CUCM for presence integration.

The checklist below can be used as a guideline to set up the CUCM for integration with Cisco Unified Communications IM&P.

- Configure a SIP trunk pointing to Cisco Unified Communications IM&P:
  - Add a presence-specific SIP trunk security profile.
  - Configure the Cisco Unified Communications IM&P publish trunk. (You can also configure this trunk on Cisco Unified Communications IM&P.)
- Activate the required services on CUCM:
  - Cisco AXL service
  - CTI Manager

CUCM and Cisco Unified Communications IM&P are connected via a SIP trunk. The SIP trunk must be enabled to support presence information. To specify these presence settings, add a SIP trunk security profile and enable the following four check boxes:

- Check the **Accept Presence Subscription** check box to accept presence subscription requests that come via the SIP trunk.
- Check the **Accept Out-of-Dialog Refer** check box to accept incoming non-INVITE, Out-of-Dialog REFER requests that come via the SIP trunk.
- Check the **Accept Unsolicited Notification** check box to accept incoming non-INVITE, unsolicited notification messages that come via the SIP trunk.
- Check the **Accept Replaces Header** check box to accept new SIP dialogs that have replaced existing SIP dialogs.

The settings that are not mentioned are not required or can be left with the default settings for an integration with Cisco Unified Communications IM&P.

Configure the SIP trunk pointing to Cisco Unified Communications IM&P and select the previously configured SIP trunk security profile. In the SIP Information configuration area, set the following parameters:

- **Destination Address:** The destination address represents the remote SIP peer with which the trunk will communicate; in this case, the Cisco Unified Communications IM&P server. Use the FQDN or IP address. SIP trunks only accept incoming requests from the configured destination address and the incoming port that is specified in the SIP trunk security profile that is associated with this trunk. The default port is 5060 for SIP. Make sure that DNS servers and domains are set up in both systems when using FQDNs.
- **BLF Presence Group:** The presence group does not affect the Cisco Unified Communications IM&P integration. The same is true for the SUBSCRIBE calling search (CSS).

The settings that are not mentioned are not required for integration with Cisco Unified Communications IM&P. However, you must set standard settings such as device pools and other mandatory SIP trunk settings.

Configure the **IM&P Publish Trunk** in the Cisco CallManager service parameters. This parameter can be set on Cisco Unified Communications IM&P as well. The IM&P Publish Trunk parameter specifies the SIP trunk that CUCM uses to send PUBLISH messages that pertain to the presence activities in Cisco Unified Communications IM&P.

Cisco Unified Communications IM&P reads out information from the CUCM database via the AXL. Verify that the AXL service is activated on CUCM. For deskphone mode, you must also enable the CTI Manager service to control the desk phones with Computer Telephony Integration Quick Buffer Encoding (CTIQBE).

Cisco Jabber UC Services

Figure 16-2 illustrates the service profile including the UC Services options for a user to use presence.

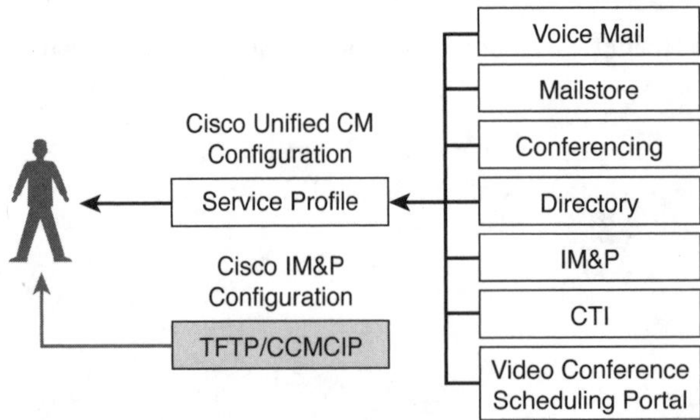

Figure 16-2 *Cisco Jabber UC Services*

UC services are configured in CUCM Administration beginning with CUCM Version 9.

Before Version 9, all user profile settings for presence were configured in the Cisco Unified Presence server.

After configuring the UC services, you can group them into service profiles that you associate with end users. After end users have a service profile, their clients can download this profile for seamless integration with the configured Unified Communications services.

The following briefly describes the Unified Communications services that are configured in CUCM:

- **Voice mail:** The voice-mail service specifies the product type. The available options are Cisco Unity and Cisco Unity Connection. The default port is 443. Cisco recommends that you use HTTPS as the voice-mail transport protocol for Cisco Unity Connection.
- **Mailstore:** Cisco Jabber clients use the mailstore service for visual voice-mail functionality. The default port number is 143. For secure voice messaging with Cisco Unity Connection, use port 7993.
- **Conferencing:** Choose a product type that applies to your network configuration. One of the available options among others is Cisco WebEx. Use port 80 for HTTP and port 443 for HTTPS communications.
- **Directory:** Choose the product type directory or enhanced directory. The default port is 389. The enhanced directory is only used when connecting to CUCM UDS.
- **IM&P:** Choose a supported IM&P product type. The available options are Unified Communications Manager (IM&P) or WebEx (IM&P).
- **CTI:** Soft clients use the CTI service for deskphone control. The default port is 2748.
- **Video Conference Scheduling Portal:** The only product supported at the time of the writing is Telepresence Management System.

Implementing Cisco Unified Communications IM&P

Figure 16-3 shows the parameters that are related to different requirements of a Cisco Unified Communications IM&P implementations.

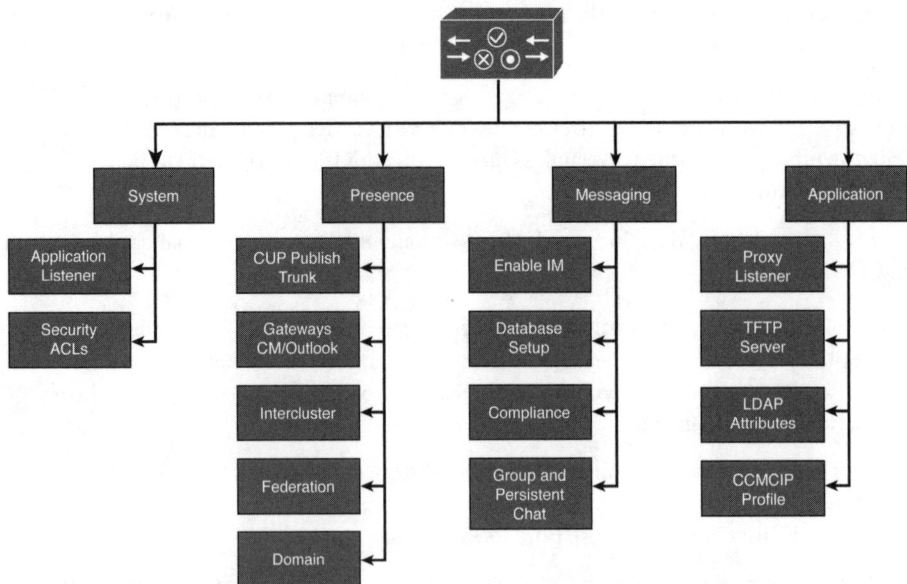

Figure 16-3 *Implementing Cisco Unified Communications IM&P*

The application listener settings must match the SIP settings (especially the port) that are configured on CUCM. In addition, you can optimize the presence behavior, enable or disable presence availability, or limit the number of contacts.

Messaging can be set up with a database to log all messages for archiving and compliance. For Cisco Jabber, the TFTP server and CUCM IP Phone (CCMCIP) profile must be set so that the client can retrieve its configuration file and the list of controlled devices.

Checklist for Cisco Unified Communications IM&P Setup

Follow this checklist to set up Cisco Unified Communications IM&P for presence integration:

- Add CUCM as a presence gateway.
- Configure and select the SIP TCP listener and enable event routing.
- Verify the domain settings.
- Activate the required services.
- Run the system troubleshooter to verify the integration.

On Cisco Unified Communications IM&P, add CUCM as the presence gateway. This action allows Cisco Unified Communications IM&P to know where to send the presence information. The IM&P service will then trigger the CUCM (or Exchange as a presence gateway for calendar integration) to publish phone presence information when the line status is changed or, on initial synchronization, when subscribing to presence information.

The SIP TCP listener is the Cisco Unified Communications IM&P component that receives SIP messages. Verify that the preconfigured Default Cisco SIP Proxy TCP Listener on Cisco Unified Communications IM&P has the same parameters that are configured in CUCM in the SIP trunk and SIP trunk security profile. Application listeners carry requests to Cisco Unified Communications IM&P services and control request routing behavior. In addition, turn on method/event routing. If this setting is turned off, users cannot share their availability.

Verify the domain settings and specify the DNS domain name. Typically, the domain name should be a top-level enterprise domain name (for example, cisco.com). Then activate the necessary services.

Cisco Unified Communications IM&P has a system troubleshooter that executes more than 60 tests to see if the integration was successful for different modules and features in Cisco Unified Communications IM&P.

Cisco Unified Communications IM&P Services

In Cisco Unified Communications IM&P Serviceability, navigate to **Tools > Service Activation** and note the services, as shown in Figure 16-4.

Database and Admin Services

	Service Name
☑	Cisco AXL Web Service
☐	Cisco Bulk Provisioning Service

Performance and Monitoring Services

	Service Name
☐	Cisco Serviceability Reporter

IM and Presence Services

	Service Name
☑	Cisco SIP Proxy
☑	Cisco Presence Engine
☑	Cisco XCP Text Conference Manager
☑	Cisco XCP Web Connection Manager
☑	Cisco XCP Connection Manager
☑	Cisco XCP SIP Federation Connection Manager
☑	Cisco XCP XMPP Federation Connection Manager
☑	Cisco XCP File Transfer Manager
☑	Cisco XCP Message Archiver
☑	Cisco XCP Directory Service
☑	Cisco XCP Authentication Service

Figure 16-4 *Cisco Unified Communications IM&P Services*

Review the service description and enable only the required services instead of simply enabling all services to optimize the resource utilization. When not configured or configured incorrectly, some services stop after a short time.

Database and administrative services are the following:

- **Cisco AXL Web Service:** Cisco AXL Web Service is enabled by default on all cluster nodes. Cisco recommends that you always leave the service activated on the IM&P database publisher node. This service communicates with CUCM to exchange database information.
- **Cisco Bulk Provisioning Service:** If you use the BAT to administer users, you must turn on this service.

Performance and monitoring services are the following:

- **Cisco Serviceability Reporter:** The service only generates reports on the publisher node even if you turn on the service on other nodes.

IM&P services are the following:

- **Cisco SIP Proxy and Cisco Presence Engine:** Activate these services on all nodes in the cluster to enable presence functionality.
- **Cisco XCP Text Conference Manager:** Turn on this service if you deploy the chat feature on Cisco Unified Communications IM&P. The permanent chat feature requires an external database. If you enable the permanent chat feature, you must also configure an external database before starting the Text Conference Manager service. The Text Conference Manager service will not start if the permanent chat feature is enabled and an external database is not configured.
- **Cisco XCP Web Connection Manager:** Turn on this service if you integrate XMPP-based application programming interface (API) web clients with IM&P (for example Cisco Jabber Messenger for the Web, which works with any web browser).
- **Cisco XCP Connection Manager:** Turn on this service if you integrate XMPP clients with Cisco Unified Communications IM&P.
- **Cisco XCP SIP Federation Connection Manager:** Turn on this service if you deploy a federation over SIP (for example, to a Microsoft Skype for Business domain).
- **Cisco XCP XMPP Federation Connection Manager:** Turn on this service only if you deploy a federation over the XMPP protocol to another Cisco Unified Communications IM&P domain or any other XMPP domain.
- **Cisco XCP Message Archiver:** Turn on this service if you deploy the compliance feature on IM&P. If you turn on the Message Archiver before you configure an external database, the service will not start.

- **Cisco XCP File Transfer Manager:** Turn
- **Cisco XCP Directory Service:** Turn on this service if you integrate XMPP clients on IM&P with an LDAP directory. If you turn on the Directory Service before you configure the Lightweight Directory Access Protocol (LDAP) contact search settings for third-party XMPP clients, the service will start and then stop again.
- **Cisco XCP Authentication Service:** Turn on this service if you integrate XMPP clients with IM and Presence.

Cisco Jabber Service Discovery

This section describes the benefits of Cisco Jabber service discovery. While optional for Jabber to register to CUCM, the benefits of Jabber service discovery are as follows:

- Enables Cisco Jabber to automatically acquire client configuration:
  - Unified Communications services domain
  - Operating mode (on-premises, cloud, or hybrid)
  - Operating location (inside or outside corporate network)
  - Home cluster in multicluster environment
- Enhances end user experience:
  - No prompt to ask for configurations
  - Reduces support calls due to misconfiguration
- Cisco Jabber cross-platform initiative:
  - Windows, Mac OS X
  - iOS and Android

To make Cisco Jabber rollouts easy to execute, Cisco Jabber discovers its services based on DNS SRV records. Depending on the DNS answer, the client knows whether it is located inside or outside of the enterprise and also if it connects to cloud or on-premises solution.

After receiving DNS information, Cisco Jabber can connect to the appropriate system (for example, CUCM) and download its configuration file including information about all controllable devices. Depending on the mode, the client registers with CUCM (phone-only and softphone mode) or with Cisco Unified Communications IM&P (deskphone mode).

Because Cisco Jabber has service discovery, there is no need to configure any device settings on the client for login.

Service Discovery: Domain

This section describes how Cisco Jabber discovers the service domain. The two options to discover the domain are as follows:

- Option 1
  - Client prompts end user to enter user ID with domain
  - Mail address or Jabber ID (JID)
  - Client uses domain portion to resolve the service type
  - This information is cached for future logins
- Option 2
  - Administrator provides client domain information
  - User is not prompted
  - Use command-line option or create customized MSI installer

Before Cisco Jabber can send a DNS request, Cisco Jabber must know the service domain. Cisco Jabber can use the default method to determine the service domain, where the user is simply prompted to enter the user ID with the domain. The domain is used to send a DNS request and discover the services.

The automated option is to use a command line option during Cisco Jabber installation. The more scalable solution is to customize the MSI installer file of Cisco Jabber and to distribute the software with a software distribution system. When the user logs in for the first time, the domain is already known by the client, and there is no prompt to enter the domain. In combination with single-sign on (SSO), you can suppress the prompt for the username and password as well.

Service Discovery: Operating Mode

This section describes how Cisco Jabber discovers the operating mode. Jabber sends the service discovery requests according to Table 16-1. Use your domain, such as acme.com, for the <domain> entry in the table.

Table 16-1 *Service Discovery: Operating Mode*

Priority	Service	HTTP Request or DNS SRV
1	WebEx Messenger	HTTP CAS lookup
2	UC Manager 9.x or newer	_cisco-uds._tcp.<domain>.com
3	Cisco Presence 8.x	_cuplogin._tcp.<domain>.com
4	Collaboration Edge	_collab-edge._tls.<domain>.com

The _cisco-uds service record provides the location of CUCM Version 9.0 and higher. The client can retrieve service profiles from CUCM to determine the authenticator. This setting enables the client to discover the home cluster of the user. As a result, the client can automatically get the user's device configuration and register the devices. This mode also supports mixed product modes. You can easily deploy users with full Unified Communications, IM only, or phone mode capabilities.

The _cuplogin service record provides the location of Cisco Unified Presence and sets Cisco Unified Presence as the authenticator. This setting supports deployments with CUCM and Cisco Unified Presence Version 8.x.

The _collab-edge service record provides the location of Cisco TelePresence Video Communication Server Expressway (Cisco VCS-E). The client can retrieve service profiles from CUCM to determine the authenticator. This mode is used for deployments in which Cisco VCS-E is configured for mobile and remote access.

The following steps describe how the client locates services with SRV records:

Step 1. The client's host computer or device establishes a network connection and receives the address of a Domain Name System (DNS) name server from the Dynamic Host Configuration Protocol (DHCP) settings.

Step 2. The client issues an HTTP query to a Connect Authentication Service (CAS) URL for the Cisco WebEx Messenger service. This query enables the client to determine if the domain is a valid Cisco WebEx domain.

Step 3. The client queries the name server for the following service (SRV) records in order of priority: _cisco-uds, _cuplogin, and _collab-edge.

Step 4. The client caches the results of the DNS query to load on subsequent launches.

In addition to querying the DNS server for SRV records to locate available services, the client sends an HTTP query to the CAS URL for the Cisco WebEx Messenger service. This request enables the client to determine cloud-based deployments and authenticate users to the Cisco WebEx Messenger service.

When the client receives a domain from the user's entry, it appends that domain to the following HTTP query:

```
http://loginp.webexconnect.com/cas/FederatedSSO?org=domain.com
```

That query returns an XML response that the client uses to determine if the domain is a valid Cisco WebEx domain. If the client determines that the domain is a valid Cisco WebEx domain, it prompts users to enter their Cisco WebEx credentials. The client then authenticates to the Cisco WebEx Messenger service and retrieves the configuration and UC Services that are configured in Cisco WebEx Org Admin. If the client determines that the domain is not a valid Cisco WebEx domain, it uses the results of the query to the DNS name server to locate an available service.

Cisco UDS SRV Record

This section describes the call flow when using Cisco UDS service records, as illustrated in Figure 16-5.

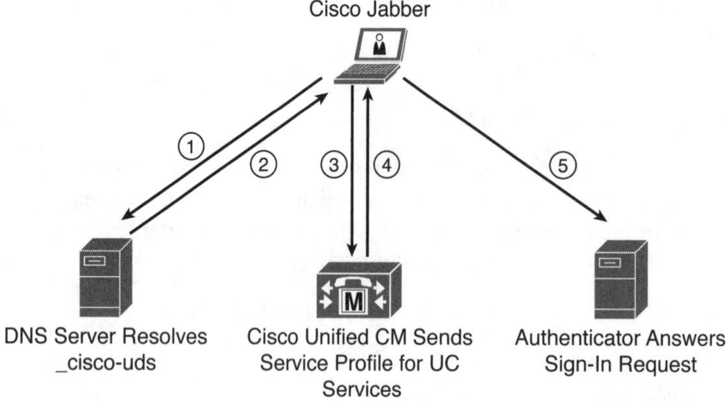

Figure 16-5 *Cisco UDS SRV Record*

In deployments with CUCM Version 9 and higher, the client can automatically discover services and configuration with the service (SRV) record _cisco-uds:

- The client queries the domain name server for SRV records.
- The name server returns the _cisco-uds SRV record.
- The client locates the user's home cluster. As a result of automatically locating the user's home cluster, the client can retrieve the device configuration for the user and automatically register telephony services.

Note In an environment with multiple CUCM clusters, you must configure the Intercluster Lookup Service (ILS). ILS enables the client to find the home cluster of the user.

- The client retrieves the user's service profile. The user's service profile contains the addresses and settings for UC services and client configuration. The client also determines the authenticator from the service profile.
- The client signs the user into the authenticator.

SRV Records

You need to deploy multiple DNS SRV records in different locations in your enterprise DNS structure.

You can provision the _cisco-uds SRV record on internal name servers so the client can discover services. This record provides the location of CUCM Version 9 and higher. In an environment with multiple CUCM clusters, you must configure the Intercluster Lookup Service (ILS). ILS enables the client to find the home cluster of the user and discover services.

Note You should use the fully qualified domain name (FQDN) as the hostname in the SRV record.

The following is an example of the _cisco-uds SRV record:

```
_cisco-uds._tcp.cisco.com      SRV service location:
          priority        = 10
          weight          = 10
          port            = 8443
          svr hostname    = pub-hq. collab10x.cisco.com
```

You must provision the _collab-edge SRV record on external name servers as part of the configuration for Cisco TelePresence Video Communication Server (Cisco VCS) Expressway mobile and remote access. You must use the FQDN as the hostname in the SRV record. The client requires the FQDN to use the cookie that the Cisco VCS Expressway server provides.

The following is an example of the _collab-edge SRV record:

```
collab-edge._tls.cisco.com    SRV service location:
          priority        = 10
          weight          = 10
          port            = 8443
          svr hostname    = vcse.cisco.com
```

DNS SRV Record Priorities and Weights

This section describes the priorities and weights of the DNS SRV records. The following in an example of DNS SRV entries configured on a DNS server:

```
_service._protocol.domain TTL   class   SRV   priority  weight  port  target
_cisco-uds._tcp.cisco.com                 3600 IN         SRV 10        60   8443
cucm1.cisco.com
_cisco-uds._tcp.cisco.com                 3600 IN         SRV 10        20   8443
cucm2.cisco.com
_cisco-uds._tcp.cisco.com                 3600 IN         SRV 10        20   8443
cucm3.cisco.com
_cisco-uds._tcp.cisco.com                 3600 IN         SRV 20        0    8443
cucm4.cisco.com
```

A DNS SRV entry contains the following parameters:

- **_service:** This parameter is the name of the service and it begins with an underscore (for example, _cisco-uds, _sip, or _ldap).
- **_protocol:** This parameter is the transport protocol of the service and must start with an underscore (for example, _tls, _tcp, or _udp).
- **Domain:** This parameter is the domain name for which this record is valid (for example, cisco.com).
- **TTL:** This parameter is the Time to Live (TTL) and defines how long the resolved record can be stored in the cache.
- **Class:** This parameter is the standard DNS class field. (This parameter is always IN.)
- **Priority:** This parameter is the priority of the target host. A lower value indicates a more preferred priority. The range is 0 to 65535.
- **Weight:** This parameter is a relative weight between 0 and 65535 for records with the same priority.
- **Port:** This parameter is the port on which the service is found.
- **Target:** This parameter is the hostname of the machine providing the service.

In the example above, for the service _cisco-uds._tcp.cisco.com, are four DNS SRV entries in the enterprise DNS server. The first three records share the same priority level 10. The last DNS SRV entry has a priority of 20. Cisco Jabber will use the first three DNS SRV entries, because the lower priority is more preferred. For entries with the same priority (value 10 in the example) the entry weight is used to determine which entry should be used. Weight values allow an administrator to configure load balancing. In the example above, cucm1.cisco.com will be used 60 percent of the time, and the servers cucm2.cisco.com and cucmm3.cisco.com will each be used 20 percent of the time.

Troubleshoot DNS SRV Entries

This section shows how to verify and troubleshoot configured Cisco User Data Services (Cisco UDS) SVR records.

To ensure that the DNS server is configured correctly and responds with the correct DNS SRV entries, use a client computer and verify that the client uses the same DNS server as the Cisco Jabber client that you are troubleshooting. As an example, on a Microsoft computer, open a command prompt and enter **nslookup**, as shown in Figure 16-6.

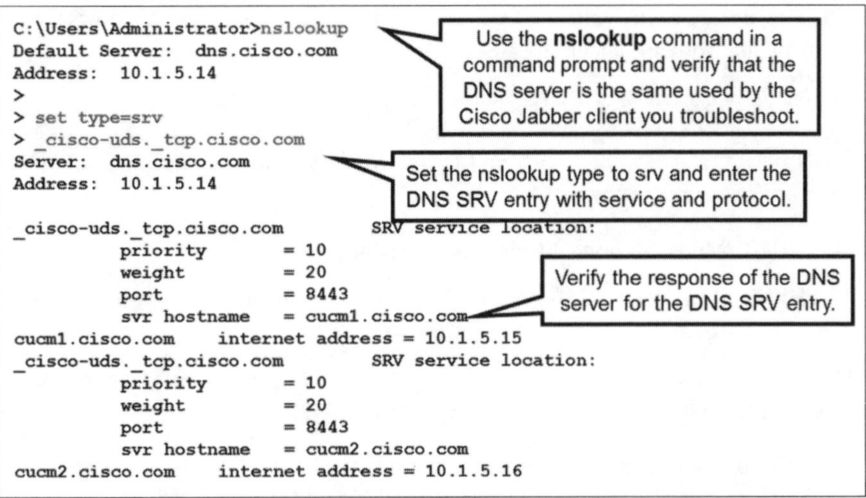

Figure 16-6 *DNS Test with nslookup*

Set the nslookup type to DNS SRV entries with the command **set type= srv**. Use the previously configured DNS entry and add the service _cisco-uds and the protocol _tcp (for example, **_cisco-uds._tcp.cisco.com**). The DNS server should now respond with all DNS SRV entries that are configured on the DNS server for this particular service. Verify the response and ensure that the priority, weight, port, and the *svr hostname* are configured correctly, and that the *svr hostname* can be resolved to the IP address of the CUCM servers.

Methods of Installation

Cisco Jabber for Windows provides an MSI installation package that can be used in the following ways:

- **Command line:** Specify arguments in a command line window to set installation properties. Choose this option if you plan to install multiple instances.
- **Run the MSI manually:** Run the MSI manually on the file system of the client workstation and then specify connection properties when you start the client. Choose this option if you plan to install a single instance for testing or evaluation purposes.
- **Create a custom installer:** Open the default installation package, specify the required installation properties, and then save a custom installation package. Choose this option if you plan to distribute an installation package with the same installation properties.
- **Deploy with group policy:** Install the client on multiple computers in the same domain.

The following describes the command syntax to install Cisco Jabber for Windows using the command line with arguments:

```
msiexec.exe /i CiscoJabberSetup.msi /quiet CLEAR=1
```

CLEAR=1 deletes any existing bootstrap file, and **/quiet** specifies a silent installation. The other options are as follows:

- **PRODUCT_MODE=Phone_Mode** sets the client to phone mode.
- **AUTHENTICATOR=CUCM** sets CUCM as the authenticator. Other options are CUP and WEBEX.
- **TFTP=1.2.3.4** sets 1.2.3.4 as the IP address of the TFTP server that hosts the client configuration. Other options are the hostname and FQDN.

To deploy Cisco Jabber with group policies, install Cisco Jabber for Windows using the Microsoft Group Policy Management Console (GPMC) on Microsoft Windows Server. To install Cisco Jabber for Windows with Group Policy, all computers or users for which you plan to deploy Cisco Jabber must be in the same domain.

For more information, refer to the *Cisco Jabber 10.6 Deployment and Installation Guide* http://www.cisco.com/c/en/us/td/docs/voice_ip_comm/jabber/10_6/CJAB_BK_C56DE1AB_00_cisco-jabber-106-deployment-and-installation-guide.html.

Create a Custom Installer with Microsoft Orca

Use Microsoft Orca to create custom installers. Microsoft Orca is available as part of the Microsoft Windows SDK for Windows 7 and .NET Framework 4. You must have the default transform file to modify the installation package with Microsoft Orca. Download the Cisco Jabber administration package from Cisco.com. Copy CiscoJabberProperties.mst from the Cisco Jabber administration package to your file system.

To create a custom installer, use a transform file. Transform files contain installation properties that you apply to the installer. The default transform file lets you specify values for properties when you transform the installer. You should use the default transform file if you are creating one custom installer. Some Microsoft Orca field examples for Jabber include the following:

- CLEAR
- SERVICES DOMAIN
- USE FT GATEWAY
- LOGIN RESOURCE
- CCMCIP
- CTI
- TFTP

- PRODUCT MODE
- AUTHENTICATOR
- CUP ADDRESS
- FORGOT PASSWORD URL
- TFTP FILE NAME
- LANGUAGE
- SSO ORG DOMAIN
- VOICE SERVICES DOMAIN
- EXCLUDED SERVICES

Summary

This section summarizes the key points that were discussed in this chapter:

- On CUCM, configure a SIP trunk and make it the CUP SIP publish trunk. This trunk is used to exchange presence information with the Cisco Unified Communications IM&P server.
- The user configuration and many other features are configured in CUCM. Over time, CUCM and Cisco Unified Communications IM&P merged from the administration perspective.
- Cisco jabber discovers the domain and services, so the user only needs to enter the username and password. The _cisco-uds SVR record is used by Cisco Jabber. This SRV record must be set up on the internal DNS server.
- You can customize the MSI installer file for Cisco Jabber to pass along information, such as the domain name, to the installation process.

This chapter explained how CUCM and Cisco Unified Communications IM&P are integrated. The service discovery and the installation of the Cisco Jabber client were discussed as well.

Review Questions

Answer the following questions, and then see Appendix A, "Answers to Review Questions," for the answers.

1. **Cisco Unified Communications IM&P uses device-based presence to show "On the Phone" in the presence status in Cisco Jabber.**

   a. True

   b. False

2. **Which option is not a valid parameter that is required in the SIP trunk security profile when integrating CUCM and Cisco Unified Communications IM&P?**
   a. Accept Presence Group Notification
   b. Accept Out-of-Dialog REFER
   c. Accept Unsolicited Notification
   d. Accept Replaces Header

3. **Which option is not a UC Service that you can specify in the service profile?**
   a. Mailstore
   b. Conferencing
   c. Directory
   d. IM&P
   e. CCMCIP

4. **What are the protocols and port used for SIP by default in the SIP trunk security profile? (Choose three.)**
   a. TCP
   b. TLS
   c. UDP
   d. 5060
   e. 5061
   f. 5070

5. **Which option is a valid DNS service request by Cisco Jabber to discover its services?**
   a. _cisco_uds._tcp.cisco.com
   b. _cisco-uds.tcp.cisco.com
   c. _cisco-uds._tls.cisco.com
   d. _cisco-uds._tcp.cisco.com

Chapter 17

Configuring Cisco Unified Communications IM and Presence Features and Implementing Cisco Jabber

Upon completing this chapter, you will be able to do the following:

- Describe how to set up Cisco Jabber for phone-only mode without a Cisco Unified Communications IM and Presence (IM&P) server
- Describe how to configure Cisco Jabber to run in softphone mode
- Describe the TFTP and CCMCIP profiles that are configured on Cisco Unified Communications IM&P
- Describe the UC service applications and protocols
- Use the Jabber Config File Generator to generate the correct XML file
- Describe how Cisco Jabber can access voice messages and present them in Cisco Jabber in a visual interface
- Describe Cisco Jabber in softphone mode
- Describe the phone account options that Cisco Jabber presents if the service profile is configured
- Present the Cisco Jabber connection status tool
- Describe how to test the LDAP server and add contacts in Cisco Jabber
- Describe how to test the voice-mail profile in Cisco Jabber using the visual interface to access voice messages
- Describe how to configure desk phone control for Cisco Jabber
- Explain how Cisco Jabber functions in deskphone mode

This chapter describes how Cisco Jabber can be used in phone-only mode as compared to Cisco Jabber in softphone mode. The chapter explains the profiles that must be used (for example, the profiles for voice messaging) and how deskphone mode is implemented to control desk phones.

Configure Cisco Jabber in Softphone Mode

In Cisco Unified Communications Manager Administration, create a Cisco Unified Client Services Framework (CSF) device. This device is used by Cisco Jabber in softphone and deskphone mode. For deskphone mode, additional Computer Telephony Integration (CTI) configuration is required. The main difference is the registration. In softphone mode, Cisco Jabber registers with Cisco Unified Communications Manager using Session Initiation Protocol (SIP). In deskphone mode, Cisco Jabber registers with Cisco Unified Communications IM&P using Extensible Messaging and Presence Protocol (XMPP) and controls the desk phone via CTIQBE.

Follow the list to set up a Cisco Unified CSF device for Cisco Jabber in softphone mode:

- Configure the end user:
  - Create and associate the new CSF device.
  - Set the primary extension.
  - Enable User for Unified CM IM&P.
- Add a new device:
  - Add a Cisco Unified CSF device.
  - Although prior versions of the Cisco Unified Communications Manager mandated a naming convention, current versions have no restrictions
  - Add the user as owner of the device and set the primary phone.
  - Add the DN and associate a user with the line:
  - Device will register with Cisco Unified Communications Manager using SIP.
- Add legacy client configuration (TFTP and CCMCIP profile).
- Configure UC profiles and service profile for presence functionality.

When the Cisco Unified CSF device is created, add the directory number (DN) of the phone or device profile of the user to the new device. The DN is a shared line and the devices sharing this number are listed under associated devices. After saving, associate the end user with the line by clicking the **Associate End Users** button. This action is important, because the presence status is shown per line, not per device status.

Then associate the Cisco Unified CSF device with the end user. When the Cisco Unified CSF device is successfully created, associate the device to the end user configuration. Choose **User Management > End User** and select the user. Click **Device Association**, search for the previously created Cisco Unified CSF device, and click **Add Selected.** The device is now displayed in the Controlled Devices list. After the association is done, the primary line can be selected.

Legacy Client Settings

This section describes the TFTP and Cisco Unified Communications Manager IP Phone (CCMCIP) profiles that are configured on Cisco Unified Communications IM&P.

In Cisco Unified Communications IM&P, choose **Applications > Legacy Client > Settings** and set the primary TFTP server to the IP address of the Cisco Unified Communications Manager (CUCM) that is hosting the TFTP server. If available, configure a backup TFTP server address. Cisco Jabber connects to the primary TFTP server. When the connection is established, Cisco Jabber downloads the configuration file from CUCM.

The configuration file contains the list of CUCM primary and failover server addresses. The configuration file also contains the transport protocol for Cisco Jabber to use in softphone mode to connect to CUCM. After Cisco Jabber downloads the file successfully, the configuration information is made available to other Cisco Jabber subsystems.

Each time Cisco Jabber tries to download the configuration file, the application attempts to contact the primary TFTP server. If the primary TFTP server does not respond, Cisco Jabber fails over to the backup TFTP servers, if any exist. Cisco Jabber fails over to the backup TFTP servers in the order that is specified in Cisco Unified Communications IM&P Administration. If all TFTP server connections fail, Cisco Jabber tries to load the last valid downloaded configuration from the local hard disk.

Choose **Application > CCMCIP Profile** and add a new profile. Enter a name for the CCMCIP profile and define the primary CCMCIP and backup CCMCIP hosts. Both fields are mandatory. This profile offers a list of associated devices to Cisco Jabber when it is used in the deskphone mode. However, this profile must be created, even if you only use softphone mode in Cisco Jabber, otherwise the client does not successfully register.

Cisco Jabber UC Services

Presence is enabled per user in the user configuration. In addition, you must specify a service profile with options as shown in Table 17-1.

Table 17-1 *Cisco Jabber UC Services*

UC Service	Application	Protocol
Mailstore	Exchange	TCP, SSL, TLS, or UDP
Voice mail	Unity or Unity Connection	HTTP, HTTPS
Conferencing	WebEx	HTTP, HTTPS
Directory	Directory, Enhanced Directory	TCP, UDP, TLS

Table 17-1 *Continued*

UC Service	Application	Protocol
IM&P	Unified CM (IM&P), WebEx (IM&P)	XMPP
CTI	N/A	TCP
Video Conference Scheduling Portal	TelePresence Management System	HTTP, HTTPS

Via this service profile and the UC services selected in the profile, you can add feature access to Cisco Jabber.

To allow Cisco Jabber to present voice messages in a graphical form, you must configure the voice-mail service for Cisco Unity Connection using HTTP or HTTPS. In addition, you need to specify the mailstore, which enables visual access to voice messages. Cisco Unity creates subscriber mailboxes for message storage on the Microsoft Exchange server. Cisco Unity Connection provides a mailstore service, and hosts the mailstore service on the same server.

When integrating Cisco MeetingPlace Express, Cisco MeetingPlace Classic, or Cisco WebEx, create a conferencing service using HTTP or HTTPS. In addition, you can add a conference scheduling portal as a service.

When adding a directory service, Cisco Jabber can connect to the Active Directory server for contact search and number-to-name resolution. However, not all clients can use this service. For Cisco Jabber for Windows, you need to deploy an additional jabber-config.xml file. If you select UDS–Enhanced Directory for directory integration, you can use UDS for directory searches without selecting any primary, secondary, or tertiary servers. Clients connect to UDS using DNS SRVs.

The IM&P service specifies the Cisco Unified Communications IM&P server addresses (using XMPP) and the CTI service specifies CUCM with CTI Manager service activated.

Visual Voice-Mail Interface for Cisco Jabber

In Cisco Unity Connection, choose **Class of Service > Class of Service**. Select, for example, the default class of service **Voice Mail User CoS**, which is used by all end users. Scroll down and note the entries as shown in Figure 17-1.

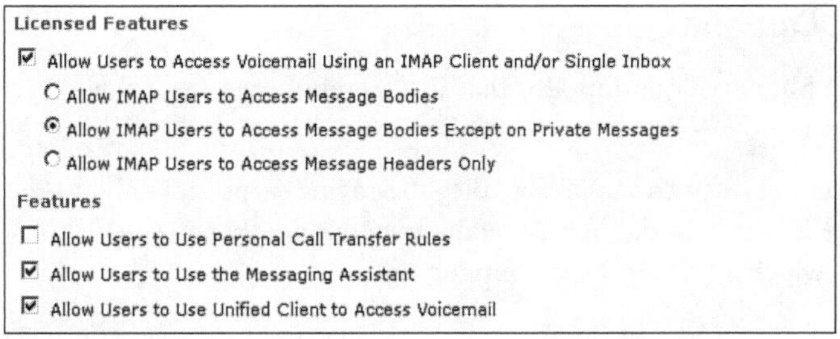

Licensed Features

☑ Allow Users to Access Voicemail Using an IMAP Client and/or Single Inbox

○ Allow IMAP Users to Access Message Bodies

◉ Allow IMAP Users to Access Message Bodies Except on Private Messages

○ Allow IMAP Users to Access Message Headers Only

Features

☐ Allow Users to Use Personal Call Transfer Rules

☑ Allow Users to Use the Messaging Assistant

☑ Allow Users to Use Unified Client to Access Voicemail

Figure 17-1 *Cisco Unity Licensed Features for Jabber*

Enable Cisco Jabber to access voice messages and check the following boxes:

- **Allow Users to Access Voice Mail Using an IMAP Client:** Check this check box to give users who are assigned to this CoS access to voice messages by using an IMAP client. The check box not checked by default. When this check box is checked, you must also check one of the following options:
  - **Allow Users to Access Message Bodies:** Users have access to the entire voice mail.
  - **Allow Users to Access Message Bodies Except on Private Messages:** Users have access to the entire voice mail, unless the message is marked private, in which case they have access only to the message header.
  - **Allow Users to Access Message Headers Only:** Users have access only to message headers.

Note Encrypted message bodies cannot be accessed from an IMAP client.

- **Allow Users to Use Unified Client to Access Voice Mail:** Check this check box to give users who are assigned to this CoS access to voice messages via Cisco Jabber.

Cisco Jabber in Softphone Mode

Start Cisco Jabber, enter the username, and set the account type to **Automatic**. The service domain is discovered first, followed by the network services. Enter your mail address to receive the IP address of the CUCM. When Cisco Jabber tries to connect to CUCM, you must authenticate with user credentials, which in most cases are the domain username and password when LDAP integration and authentication is set up.

You can simply enter a phone number in the search field. However, CoS applies here as well. If you did not configure a CSS for the Client Services Framework device, you cannot make any calls. Starting a video might not be shown as an option if the client workstation does not have a camera.

Cisco Jabber Account Options

This section describes the phone account options that Cisco Jabber presents if the service profile is configured.

A Cisco Jabber option account—for example, for voice messaging—appears only if the corresponding UC service is configured. The Cisco Jabber menus are dynamic and show only account options for which a UC service is configured.

End users must provide the credentials in Cisco Jabber for the account they are configuring (for example, voice mail or conferencing). In the example in Figure 17-2, a Microsoft Outlook service is selected.

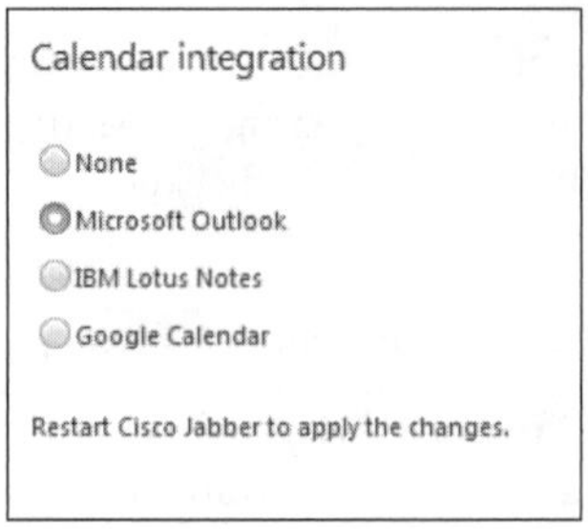

Calendar integration

None
Microsoft Outlook
IBM Lotus Notes
Google Calendar

Restart Cisco Jabber to apply the changes.

Figure 17-2 *Cisco Jabber Client Options*

The user must enter the Cisco Unity Connection local password if the voice-mail service is imported from CUCM and the Lightweight Directory Access Protocol (LDAP) credentials if the voice-mail service is imported from the LDAP server.

For voice mail and conferencing, you can set the Credentials Source parameter so that the voice-mail service can share user credentials with other services. If you want to share the voice-mail service user credentials with another service, select the appropriate service from the Credentials Source list. The user credentials are automatically synchronized with the services that you select. The credentials can be entered for voice mail, conferencing, and LDAP. Other profiles are transparent to end users. In addition, the user can configure calendar integration.

Connection Status

In Cisco Jabber, you can use the Connection Status tool to see a status overview of the configured and assigned UC services. As shown in Figure 17-3, you can easily spot issues, where an incorrect hostname, IP, or port is configured. If there is an error, an error code describes the issue that is occurring with that specific UC service.

Choose **Help > Show Connection Status** in Cisco Jabber as shown in Figure 17-3.

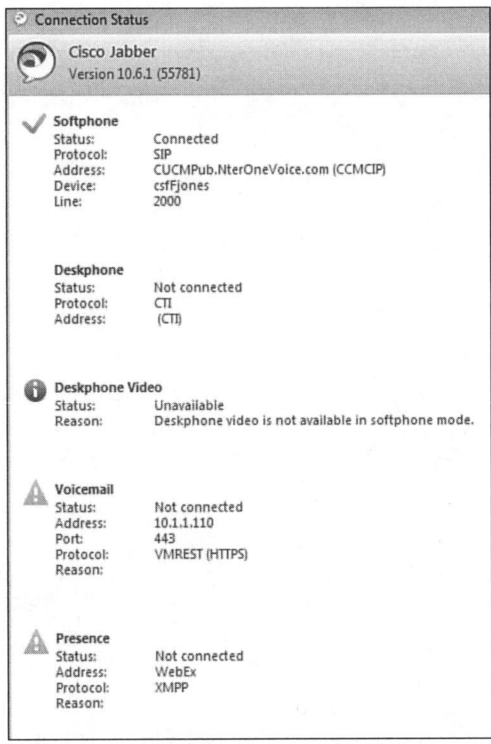

Figure 17-3 *Cisco Jabber Connection Status*

The tool shows the status for LDAP, presence, deskphone, and others. The green check marks indicate that the modules are correctly set up. A blue circle with an exclamation mark is informational, describing, for example, that deskphone video is not available in softphone mode. An orange triangle with an exclamation mark shows an error. The Reason field provides additional information when an error occurs. In the example in the figure, the reason is "Deskphone video is not available in softphone mode."

LDAP Profile Test

In Cisco Jabber, you can search for a user that is located on the LDAP server, but may or may not be located in CUCM, to test the LDAP profile. In this example shown in Figure 17-4, the search string is only one character, j. The search result displays one user Joe Miller.

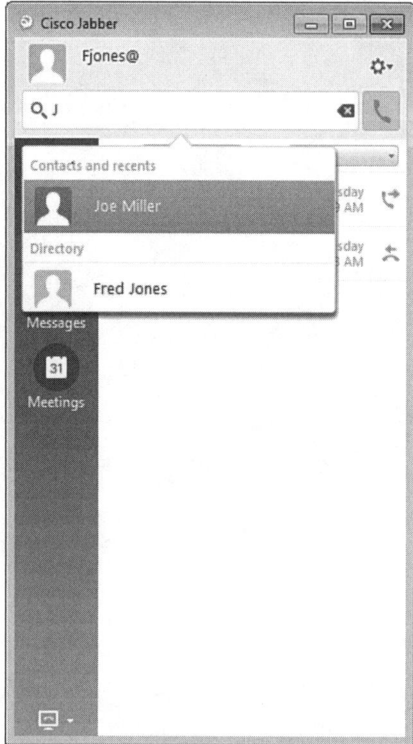

Figure 17-4 *Cisco Jabber User Search Example*

> **Note** The search tool of the Jabber client searches for contacts in the locally entered repository (Jabber) or in the repository of the directory service configured. The results indicate in which repository the user was found (for instance Contact and Recents or Directory).

> **Note** When you enter the search string, be aware that for the new LDAP queries at least three characters are required. This means that the results to search strings one character long, can include only locally defined contacts or results from previously performed queries. This can be easily verified by adding new users either locally or at the directory. Check what the search results indicate as the source of information when entering less than three and subsequently when entering at least three characters.

Displaying these results shows you that the LDAP profile is correctly applied. Mouse over the search results and click the plus sign (+) to add the user to the contact list. When adding the first user, you must create a group (for example, Cisco). Then you can add the user to the contact list for that group. When you add the first user, make sure that offline users are also shown in the contact list to avoid having to troubleshoot a situation where the issue does not really exist.

Note Cisco Jabber for Windows requires a jabber-config.xml file that includes the information necessary to reach the LDAP server. If you configure only the UC service in the service profile without the jabber-config.xml file, you will not be able to search for contacts in the Active Directory server.

Upload Jabber-Config File to TFTP Server

Use the Jabber Config File Generator to generate the correct XML file. The generator can be found at https://supportforums.cisco.com/docs/DOC-25778.

The generator renders the proper jabber-config.xml file for you after you answer a few questions in an easy-to-use form. Then you can simply copy and paste the result into an XML file. Example 17-1 shows an XML file example for Jabber.

The generator has built-in logic that verifies that you are entering the correct information for the deployment selected, as well as valid XML characters.

Example 17-1 *XML File Example for Jabber*

```
<?xml version="1.0" encoding="utf-8"?>
<config version="1.0">
 <Options>
  <Set_Status_Away_On_Inactive>false</Set_Status_Away_On_Inactive>
 </Options>
 <Directory>
  <ConnectionType>1</ConnectionType>
  <PrimaryServerName>10.1.5.14</PrimaryServerName>
  <BDIPrimaryServerName>10.1.5.14</BDIPrimaryServerName>
  <ServerPort1>389</ServerPort1>
  <UseWindowsCredentials>0</UseWindowsCredentials>
  <ConnectionUsername>Administrator@collab10x.cisco.com</ConnectionUsername>

<BDIConnectionUsername>Administrator@collab10x.cisco.com</BDIConnectionUsername>
  <ConnectionPassword>Cisco1234</ConnectionPassword>
  <BDIConnectionPassword>Cisco1234</BDIConnectionPassword>
</Directory>
</config>
```

This example XML file constrains the Jabber Config File Generator-generated content. The example XML file connects to a Microsoft Active Directory server with the IP address 10.1.5.14 and the port 389. The username is Administrator@collab10x.cisco.com, and the password is Cisco1234. Because the network services are discovered, you do no need to specify a CUCM IP address. In previous Cisco Unified Communications IM&P versions, the Cisco Unified Communications IM&P server was contacted first.

With Cisco Unified Communications IM&P Release 10.x, the Cisco Jabber client contacts CUCM first and receives the necessary information from the device-specific configuration file and the jabber-config.xml file.

The XML file structure is rendered in JavaScript, so you still need to paste the contents into a text file (saved as an XML file) and upload the file to the CUCM TFTP server using exactly the same name jabber-config.xml. Without this XML file, the Cisco Jabber for Windows client will not support the directory search for end users. Other features, such as URI dialing, are also enabled in the Jabber Config File Generator.

Voice-Mail Profile Test

In Cisco Jabber, the Voice Mail button indicates new voice messages. In this example in Figure 17-5, there is one new voice message. Click the **Voicemail** button to use visual voice mail. The voice message list is shown. One new message from John Doe (2001) is shown in the figure. Note how Jane can call John Doe back at number 2001.

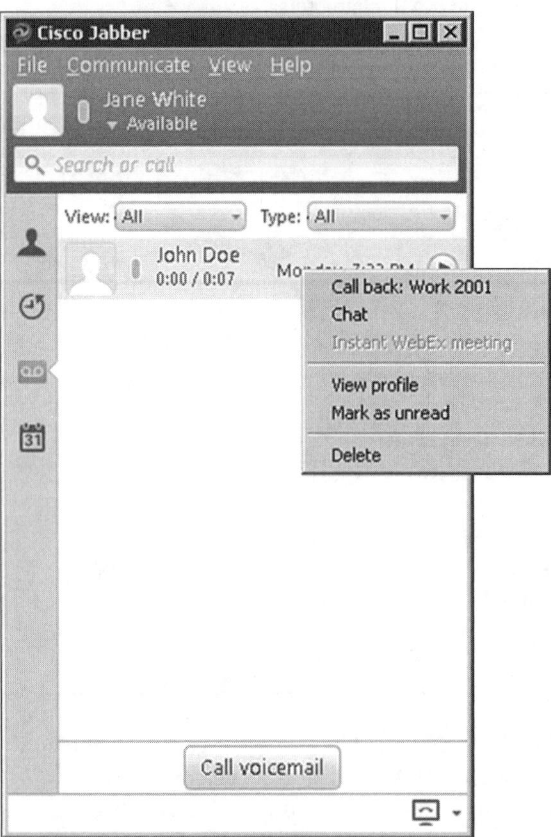

Figure 17-5 *Cisco Jabber Voice-Mail Profile Test*

Click the play message icon to listen to the voice message. If you right-click the voice message entry as shown in the figure, you can choose to perform the following actions:

- Place a call to 2001.
- Chat with John.
- Mark as read or unread (this action synchronizes the MWI).
- Delete the message.

Configure Cisco Jabber in Deskphone Mode

This section describes how to configure desk phone control for Cisco Jabber.

CTI must be enabled for end users to use Cisco Jabber to control the desk phone. In the end-user configuration window, go to the Permissions Information configuration. To allow CTI control in deskphone mode, add the user to the appropriate groups:

- For all IP phone types, add the user to the Standard CTI Enabled group.
- For Cisco Unified IP Phones 6900 series, also add the user to the Standard CTI Allow Control of Phones Supporting Rollover Mode group.
- For Cisco Unified IP Phones 8900 and 9900 series, add the user to the Standard CTI Allow Control of Phones Supporting Connected Xfer and Conf group.

Verify that the box **Allow Control of Device from CTI** is checked on the user configuration page. This setting is the default. The device and directory number must be enabled for CTI as well. In CUCM Administration, go to the phone of the end user. Verify that the **Allow Control of Device from CTI** check box is checked. Then go to the directory number configuration and verify that the same box is checked.

A UC service for CTI is required. Add a new UC service for CTI and enter the IP address of the CUCM where you enabled the Cisco CTIManager service. The port is set to 2748 by default. Then go to the service profile, where you can set a maximum of three servers for CTI service.

Cisco Jabber in Deskphone Mode

After setting up the CTI configuration, switch Cisco Jabber from softphone mode to deskphone mode. This mode can also be used with virtualized desktops because Cisco Jabber uses the phone to initiate the call and the call is done using the phone as shown in Figure 17-6.

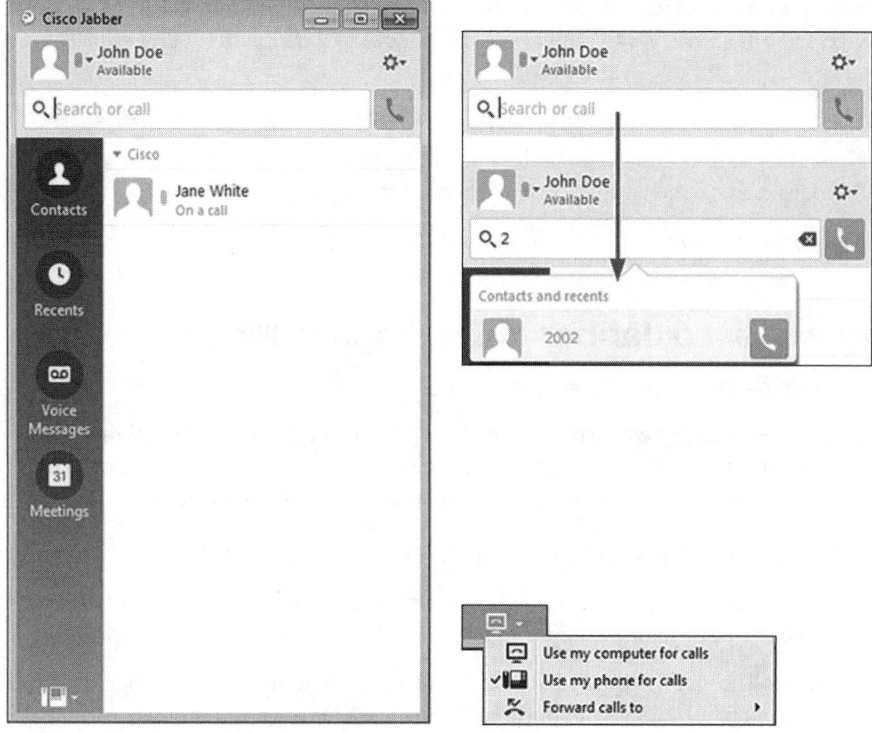

Figure 17-6 *Cisco Jabber in Deskphone Mode*

The CUCM IP Phone (CCMCIP) profile acquires the associated device list information from CUCM when going into deskphone mode (choose the option **Use My Phone for Calls**). When a phone can be controlled with Cisco Jabber, the CTI gateway profile is used. To dial a number, type the digits into the Search or call field. The phone of Jane White will start the call and go into loudspeaker mode.

Cisco Jabber in Phone-Only Mode

The following list describes how to set up Cisco Jabber for phone-only mode without a Cisco Unified Communications IM&P server.

- Configure Cisco Jabber in phone-only mode:
    - Cisco Unified Communications IM&P server is not required.
    - Presence and IM features are not available.

- Checklist for phone-only mode configuration:
  - Add a new end user and do not enable presence.
  - Add a new Cisco Unified CSF device; set the mandatory parameters and the owner ID.
  - Add the directory number (DN), the route partition, and other mandatory settings.
- Install Cisco Jabber:
  - Set the account type to **Automatic**.
  - Log in with the **UserName** to discover the service domain.
- The following are not available in phone-only mode:
  - Desk phone control is not available.
  - There is no LDAP server connection available for contact search.

Cisco Jabber registers with CUCM using SIP. In phone-only mode, features like IM, presence, and directory access are not available.

Follow the configuration checklist to set up Cisco Jabber in phone-only mode.

Note Do not enable presence for users or devices in phone-only mode.

Summary

This section summarizes the key points that were discussed in this chapter.

- Cisco Jabber can be configured in softphone mode. This option requires the configuration of a Cisco Unified CSF device in CUCM.
- In Cisco Jabber, configure the account settings for the LDAP, voice mail, and conferencing profiles. Use the connection status tool to troubleshoot client issues.
- In CUCM, enable CTI for the user, device, and directory number. In Cisco Unified Communications IM&P, configure the presence gateway and enable the desk phone control application.

This chapter explained how to set up Cisco Jabber in phone-only, softphone, and deskphone mode. In addition, the UC services are described and grouped into a service profile for presence that is assigned to the end user.

Review Questions

Answer the following questions, and then see Appendix A, "Answers to Review Questions," for the answers.

1. **Cisco Jabber in phone-only mode supports IM but not presence functionality.**
   a. True
   b. False

2. **Which option is not a valid Cisco Jabber client mode?**
   a. Deskphone mode
   b. Phone-only mode
   c. Presence mode
   d. Softphone mode

3. **What is the name of the file that you must upload to the TFTP server for additional features in Cisco Jabber?**
   a. jabberconfig.xml
   b. jabber-config.xml
   c. configjabber.xml
   d. config-jabber.xml

4. **When enabling voice messaging in Cisco Jabber, users that are imported from CUCM and LDAP can log in with the LDAP user credentials in the Account Option page for voice mail.**
   a. True
   b. False

5. **Which port is used when enabling CTI control in a UC service?**
   a. 2000
   b. 2002
   c. 2748
   d. 5060
   e. 5222

Chapter 18

Configuring Cisco Jabber Mobile and Integrating Directory Servers

Upon completing this chapter, you will be able to do the following:

- Describe how the Cisco Jabber codebase is aligned among the different kinds of Cisco Jabber clients
- Describe how configuration URLs can simplify the user's first login process
- Describe how Cisco Jabber behaves when the network status is changed
- Describe the Cisco Jabber video features, codecs, and resolution
- Explain the DVO-R calling feature
- Describe how Cisco Jabber adjusts the bandwidth consumption and path depending on the network status
- Describe how Cisco Jabber can be cross-launched by other applications
- Describe how Cisco Jabber can be secured on mobile devices
- Describe how different mobile devices are added in Cisco Unified Communications Manager
- Describe how to create the Cisco Jabber XML configuration file
- Describe how Cisco Jabber builds its operating configuration files.
- Describe how Cisco Jabber accesses different resources for contacts
- Describe how Cisco Jabber searches the directory according to the request
- Describe how Cisco Jabber uses Cisco UDS as a contact source
- Describe how Cisco Jabber receives contact photos

This chapter describes how to configure and deploy Cisco Jabber Mobile and how the client accesses the directory for contact search and number resolution.

Cisco Jabber Framework Alignment

Jabber for Everyone is a new offering that makes Cisco Jabber IM and Presence (IM&P) available at zero cost for an end-user license to all employees of Cisco customers who have deployed Cisco Unified Communications Manager (CUCM) for all or even part of their organization.

The Jabber for Everyone solution provides the complete flexibility of Jabber's bring your own device (BYOD) capabilities for presence and IM, as illustrated in Figure 18-1. The full range of Cisco Jabber clients that are deployable on Windows, OS X, iPad, iPhone, BlackBerry, and Android are supported. Customers can also build and deploy presence and IM-enabled applications using the Jabber Web SDK.

As part of the offer, employees who are existing Cisco IP telephony users can leverage Cisco Jabber clients to control their IP desk phone to initiate and manage calls. In addition, employees who are existing Cisco Unity Connection users can leverage Cisco Jabber clients for visual voice mail. Customers who are fully licensed for Cisco Collaboration Systems can easily expand beyond the Jabber for Everyone IM&P offer to leverage the complete Cisco Jabber Unified Communications capabilities, including WebEx Meetings, and standards-based voice and high-definition (HD) video across desktop and mobile devices.

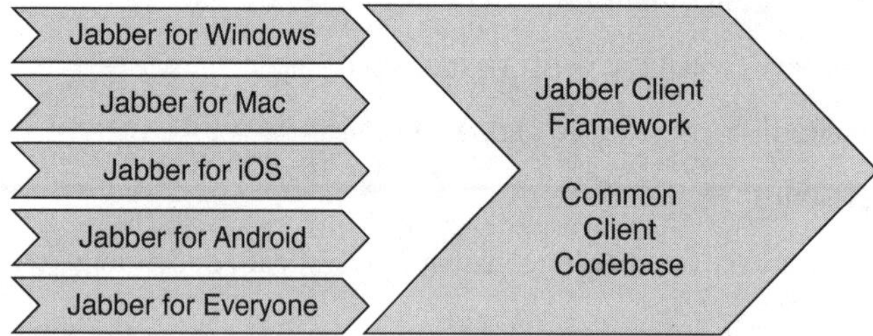

Figure 18-1 *Cisco Jabber Framework Alignment*

The following features are not included in Jabber for Everyone:

- Audio
- Video (softphone and softphone control)
- Desktop sharing
- Options for phone configuration

Jabber for Everyone comprises the following server components:

- **CUCM:** This component provides user configuration, device configuration, licensing and directory integration services.

- **IM&P Service:** This component provides instant messaging and presence capabilities.
- **External directory source:** This component provides contact search and retrieval services.

Configuration URL

You can create a configuration URL to make it easier for users to set up the client for the first time. Users can click this link to cross-launch Cisco Jabber without having to manually enter service discovery information.

The configuration URL can include the following information:

- **ServicesDomain (Required):** Every configuration URL must include the domain of the IM&P server that Cisco Jabber needs for service discovery.
- **VoiceServiceDomain:** This information is required only if you deploy a hybrid cloud-based architecture where the domain of the IM&P server differs from the domain of the voice server. You must set this parameter to ensure that Cisco Jabber can discover voice services.
- **ServiceDiscoveryExcludedServices (Optional):** You can exclude any of the following services from the service discovery process: WebEx, CUCM (Cisco Unified CM), and Cisco Unified Communications IM&P. When excluding WebEx, no CAS lookup is performed. When excluding Cisco Unified CM, _cisco_uds is not looked up and when excluding Cisco Unified Communications IM and Presence _cuplogin is not looked up. You can specify multiple, comma-separated values to exclude multiple services. If you exclude all three services, the client does not perform service discovery and prompts the user to manually enter connection settings.
- The following is an example of the Jabber configuration URL:
  - Syntax:

    ```
    ciscojabber://provision?ServicesDomain=<domain_for_service_discover>
    &VoiceServicesDomain=<domain_for_voice_services>
    &ServiceDiscoveryExcludedServices=<services_to_exclude_from_serice_discover>
    ```

  - Example:

    ```
    ciscojabber://provision?ServicesDomain=cisco.com&VoiceServicesDomain=
    voice.cisco.com&ServiceDiscoveryExcludedServices=WEBEX
    ```

Note The parameters are case sensitive. When you create the configuration URL, you must use the following capitalization: ServicesDomain, VoiceServicesDomain, and ServiceDiscoveryExcludedServices.

Legacy Client Settings

A temporary network outage may occur when, for example, you walk inside a building during a call. When the device comes back with the same IP address, the active call is transitioned into call preservation mode, where the media path is preserved but the signaling path is not preserved. In this case, you can continue the call, but all the midcall functions are lost. Cisco Jabber runs edge detection by querying the SRVs to check whether Cisco TelePresence Video Communication Server Expressway (Cisco VCS Expressway) needs to be engaged. Cisco Jabber reconnects to IM&P services.

The network might be completely lost, for example, when you leave a building and connect to the mobile network. When the device comes back with a different IP address, Cisco Jabber ends all active calls and runs Cisco VCS Expressway detection. Cisco Jabber reconnects to IM&P and voice and video services using Cisco Expressway mobile and remote access.

If the network is lost and the device never comes back, the active call is put into call preservation mode. You cannot continue the call and must end the call manually.

There are two types of XMPP reconnection:

- **Resuming:** This type of reconnection is lightweight and transparent to the user. The former stream is quickly resumed rather than completing the process of stream establishment, roster retrieval, and presence broadcast.
- **Reconnecting:** This type of reconnection is heavier and involves stream re-establishment, roster retrieval, and presence broadcast, but is better than logging in again, which adds the overhead of downloading configuration files.

When Jabber detects network transition, it tries to resume four times. The first retry happens immediately. The other three attempts occur after a random interval of between 5 to 12 seconds. Reconnecting is involved if the session cannot be resumed. Cisco Jabber reconnects up to 1024 times with a random interval between 120 and 180 seconds.

Video Features

The following are the video features that are supported on the different mobile devices.

- Point-to-point video calling
- Ad hoc and rendezvous multiparty video calling
- Video call over Wi-Fi or 3G/4G
- Viewing shared desktop as composite video on video conference bridge
- Native interoperability with other Cisco video endpoints from video-enabled IP phones to Cisco TelePresence units
- H.264 AVC-standard based
- Audio codecs are G.711a/u, G.722.1, and G.729a

The functionality and video resolution depends on the mobile device, operating system and version, and the version of Cisco Jabber. Video over mobile data network is disabled by default and can be enabled in the client settings.

> **Note** Video calls may consume lots of bandwidth and generate costs for data transmission in the mobile network.

The following examples show the bandwidth of different devices using Cisco Jabber:

- **iPhone 5S and iPad Air:** 640x480 @ 30 fps, 768 kbps
- **iPhone 5, iPhone 5C, iPad 4, and iPad Mini 2:** 640x360 @ 30 fps, 521 kbps
- **Note II, S4, S3(quad core), Nexus 5, Xperia Z1, ZR:** 640x360 @ 30 fps, 384 kbps

Factors that influence video quality are as follows:

- Network conditions
- CPU load
- Light conditions
- CUCM configuration

Dial-via-Office Reverse Calling

Figure 18-2 illustrates the Dial-via-Office Reverse (DVO-R) calling feature.

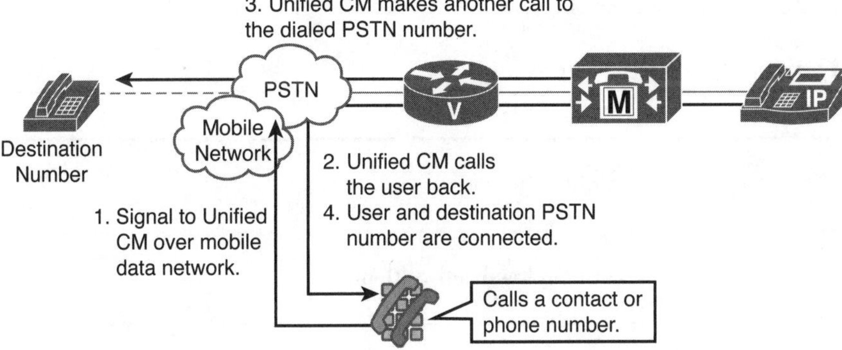

Figure 18-2 *Dial-via-Office Reverse Calling*

The following describes what happens when a user selects a contact to call or dials the destination public switched telephone network (PSTN) number:

- Cisco Jabber signals the information to CUCM over the IP connection (Wi-Fi or mobile data network).

- CUCM calls the user back at their configured mobility identity number (usually configured as their mobile phone number) or the user-defined alternate number.
- After the user answers the call, CUCM makes another call to the dialed PSTN number. The user then begins to hear ringback.
- Once the call is answered at the destination PSTN number, the user and the destination PSTN number are connected.

The signaling path is via the Wi-Fi or mobile data network. The media flow uses the PSTN or mobile network.

DVO-R has the following calling options:

- DVO-R is preset to Voice over IP by default.
- Choose Mobile Voice Network to always use DVO-R.
- Choose Autoselect to use VoIP when connecting to Wi-Fi and DVO-R when connecting to 3G or 4G.

A second variant of DVO is Dial-via-Office Forward (DVO-F). When a user makes a DVO-F call, the mobile phone dials a number that accesses the DVO-F feature, not the number that the user is trying to reach. This dialed access number is either the DVO-F service access number (if you configure one using this procedure) or the Enterprise Feature Access directory number in CUCM. Then CUCM establishes the call to the called number and extends the call.

Low-Bandwidth Mode

Table 18-1 illustrates how Cisco Jabber adjusts the bandwidth consumption and path depending on the network status.

Table 18-1 *Jabber Low-Bandwidth Mode*

Network Status	Calling Method
	VoIP
	VoIP in low-bandwidth mode
	DVO-R

The low-bandwidth mode disables video and forces Cisco Jabber to use only G.729 (low-bit-rate audio codec) for calls. This setting is disabled by default and can be enabled in the audio and video settings.

When Cisco Jabber mobile is in the background, the client suppresses the continuous presence notification, which is not necessary, causes battery drain, and only receives IM messages.

When the network connection is excellent (for example, via a corporate network or home Wi-Fi), Cisco Jabber runs in VoIP mode.

If the IP network connection is acceptable (for example, via public Wi-Fi in a coffee shop, airport, or a 3G or 4G mobile data network), Cisco Jabber runs in VoIP mode using low-bandwidth mode.

In other cases, where the IP connection is poor (for example, via a 2G mobile data network), DVO-R is used.

URL Handlers

These URL handlers enable Cisco Jabber to be cross-launched from third-party applications:

- For chat, use one of the following:
  - im:<instant_message_id>
  - xmpp:<instant_message_id>
  - ciscoim:<instant_message_id>
- For calls, use one of the following:
  - ciscotel:<phone_number>
  - tel:<phone_number>

The tel:<phone_number> is supported only by the Cisco Jabber Android client. On an iPhone, tel: :<phone_number> is reserved for the native phone application, so use ciscotel:<phone_number> instead.

Secure Cisco Jabber on Mobile

Security can be enforced for Cisco Jabber on mobile devices with the following:

- **Certificate validation:** Cisco Jabber validates all the server certificates to which it connects.
- **Secure phone:** Enable end-to-end security from call signaling (Session Initiation Protocol [SIP] over Transport Layer Security [TLS]) to real-time media (Secure Real-time Transport Protocol [SRTP]).

- **Application sandbox mechanism (provided by the operating system):** Cisco Jabber only allows an application to run in its own constrained environment so that one application cannot access the resources of other applications.
- **Cisco Jabber device footprint:** Only necessary information is stored locally on the device. All user credentials are encrypted.
- **Administrative control of saving passwords:** The administrator can configure Cisco Jabber to prohibit retention of login credentials.

Add Cisco Jabber in CUCM

To add Cisco Jabber for Mobile in CUCM you must select the correct device depending on the hardware you want to support, as shown in Table 18-2.

Table 18-2 *Add Cisco Jabber in CUCM*

Device Hosting Cisco Jabber	Device to Add in Unified CM	Naming Convention
iPhone	Cisco Dual Mode for iPhone	TCT+NAME
iPad	Cisco Jabber for Tablet	TAB+NAME
Android	Cisco Dual Mode for Android	BOT+NAME

If you want to add, for example, an iPad, you must add the device Cisco Jabber for Tablet. The name of the device has to start with TAB plus the name in all capital characters (for example, TABJDOE). The table shows the other devices and naming conventions for the iPhone and Android devices.

Cisco Jabber User Configuration XML File

Figure 18-3 illustrates the three top-level steps to create and implement the Cisco Jabber XML configuration file.

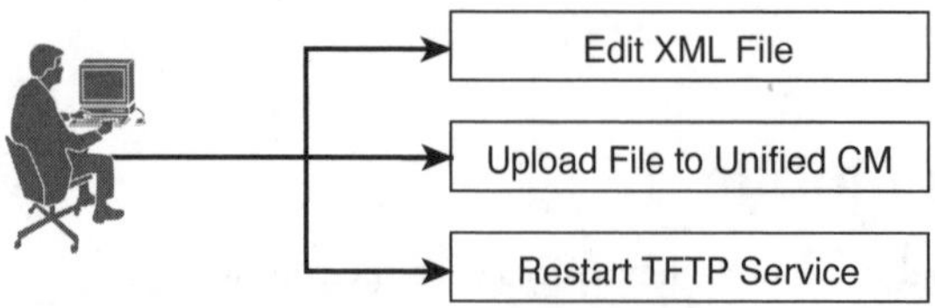

Figure 18-3 *Cisco Jabber User Configuration XML File*

> **Note** Download the Jabber Config File Generator at https://supportforums.cisco.com/docs/DOC-25778 to create a new XML configuration file.

If the service profile does not provide access to the settings, the client will download the jabberconfig.xml file. You can view the current jabberconfig.xml file at http://<*CUCM-IPaddress*>:6970/jabber-config.xml.

The Jabber configuration file provides an increasing number of customization settings including the following:

- Enable persistent chat
- Enable URI dialing
- Load on operating system start
- Docked window
- Enable screen capture
- File transfer controls
- Enable video
- Enable chat history

Cisco Jabber Configuration Sources

Figure 18-4 illustrates how Cisco Jabber builds its operating configuration files.

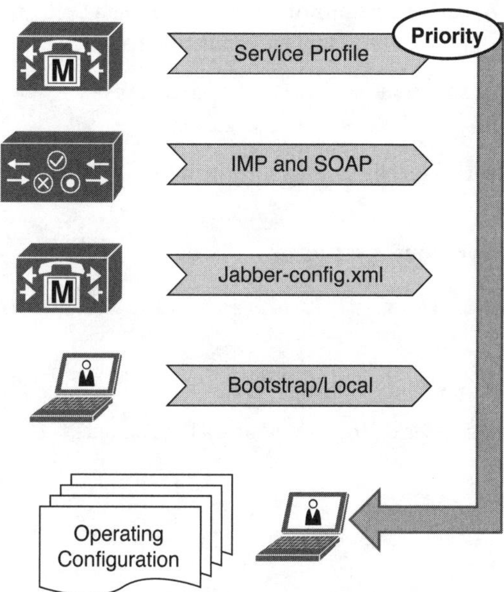

Figure 18-4 *Cisco Jabber Configuration Sources*

The Cisco Jabber operating configuration is built from different configuration sources. The configuration can also be created at the parameter level:

- LDAP host from jabber-config.xml
- LDAP user ID from the service profile
- LDAP password from the service profile

Consider the following when deploying Cisco Jabber:

- Clients running service discovery currently check for the CUCM IP Phone (CCMCIP) profile on the Cisco Unified Communications IM&P server. If the profile does not exist, telephony is disabled in the client. Create a CCMCIP profile or CTI profile for softphone and deskphone mode users. The CTI profile is the only option if the client is running in phone-only mode.
- All Cisco Jabber clients use Voicemail Representational State Transfer (VMREST) for access to Cisco Unity Connection. VMREST does not use a mailstore. However, Cisco Jabber will enable voice mail only if both the mailstore and voice-mail profiles are defined.
- Service profiles have higher priority than the Jabber XML file.

As of Cisco Jabber Version 10.6 you can delete all locally cached information using the client menu option **File > Reset Cisco Jabber**.

To delete all local cached information for earlier versions of Cisco Jabber, on a Microsoft Windows system, go to the following Cisco Jabber installation folders:

```
C:\Users\<username>\AppData\Local\Cisco\Unified Communications\Jabber\CSF
C:\Users\<username>\AppData\Roaming\Cisco\Unified Communications\Jabber\CSF
```

If there is a Jabber folder, delete it to clear all locally cached information.

> **Note** For different operating systems and versions, the folders to cache configuration information may be found in other locations.

Cisco Jabber Contact Sources

Figure 18-5 describes how Cisco Jabber accesses different resources for contacts.

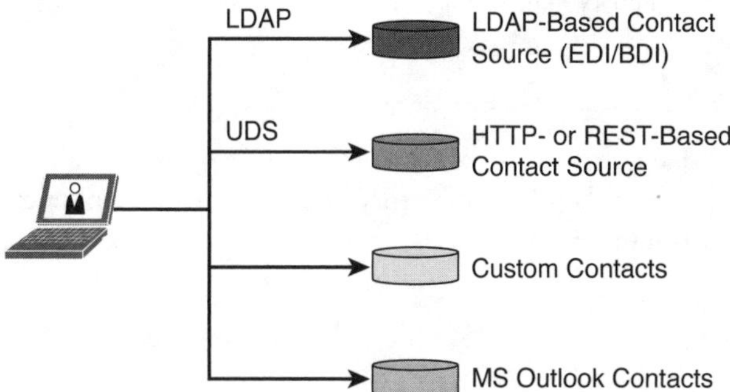

Figure 18-5 *Cisco Jabber Contact Sources*

Cisco Jabber must always be deployed with a contact source. Cisco Jabber clients reference contacts using the Jabber ID (JID). Cisco Jabber looks up contacts by using this process:

- An LDAP-based contact source (Enhanced Directory Integration [EDI] or Basic Directory Integration [BDI]) must be used for on-premises deployments. For more information about the differences between BDI and EDI, go to the *Configuring Active Directory for Cisco Unified Personal Communicator* document and review the Table 17-1 feature comparison of enhanced and basic directory integration at http://www.cisco.com/c/en/us/td/docs/voice_ip_comm/cups/8_6/english/install_upgrade/deployment/guide/dgactivedirconfig.html.
- CUCM UDS is used as an HTTP-based or REST-based contact source.
- Custom contacts are non-directory-based contacts and are stored on the Cisco Unified Communications IM&P server.
- When using Microsoft Outlook, Cisco Jabber can search for local contacts as well.

Contact Lookup

In this example, a user searched for the last name Holland and the search scope focuses on the sAMAccountname:

```
(&(objectCategory=person)(objectClass=user)
(sAMAccountName=cholland))
```

After finding a contact, Cisco Jabber presents the result and the contact attributes for the person.

Ambiguous Name Resolution (ANR) is an efficient search algorithm in Active Directory that enables you to specify complex filters involving multiple naming-related attributes in a single clause. It can be used to locate objects in Active Directory when you know something about the name of the object, but not necessarily which naming attribute has the information. Although ANR is usually used to locate user objects, it can be used to find any class of object in Active Directory. This is an example of using ANR to locate user objects:

```
(&(objectCategory=person)(objectCLass=user)(ANR=smith*))
```

For the contact lookup by telephone number, the calling number of an incoming call is used to search for a matching contact in the LDAP directory based on the home phone, telephone, and mobile number attributes:

```
(&(objectCategory=person)(objectClass=user)
(telephoneNumber=+1 (408) 555 6666))
(&(objectcategory=person)(objectClass=user)
(|(|(|(mobile=+14085555555))(homePhone=14085555555))
(otherTelephone=14085555555)))
```

Cisco UDS Directory Access

All nodes in a CUCM cluster run Cisco UDS, as illustrated in Figure 18-6.

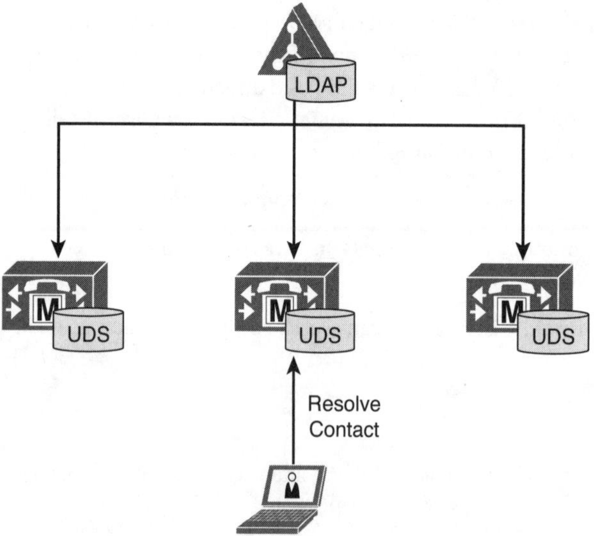

Figure 18-6 *Cisco UDS Directory Access*

Cisco Jabber will request a list of UDS nodes in its home cluster, randomize the returned list, and connect to a node in the cluster.

A CUCM node can support connections for 50 percent of the total Open Virtualization Archive (OVA) size for the server. For example, the 2500-user CUCM OVA template supports up to 1250 UDS users per server and 5000 in a cluster.

It is not recommended to use service profiles with UDS. UDS settings are not required for mobile and remote access. Cisco TelePresence Video Communication Server

Expressway edge detection will automatically switch the client to UDS as the contact source. Note that UDS does not provide the full attribute list that LDAP provides.

Photo Support

Figure 18-7 illustrates how Cisco Jabber receives contact photos.

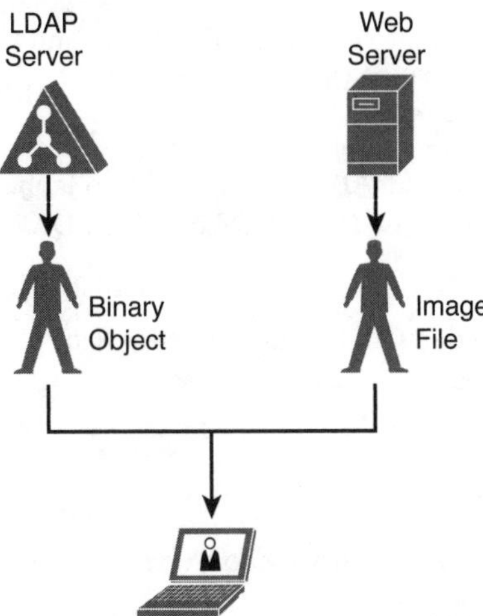

Figure 18-7 *Photo Support for Cisco Jabber*

Cisco Jabber retrieves and displays contact photos with the following methods:

- **URI substitution:** Cisco Jabber dynamically builds a URL to connect photos with a directory attribute and a URL template.
- **Binary objects:** Cisco Jabber retrieves the binary data for the photo from your database. If using binary objects from Active Directory, PhotoUriWithToken should not be set in the jabber-config.xml file.

Cisco Jabber supports the following formats for contact photos in your directory: JPG, PNG, BMP, and GIF. Cisco Jabber does not apply any modifications to enhance rendering for contact photos in GIF format. As a result, contact photos in GIF format might render incorrectly or with less-than-optimal quality. To obtain the best quality, you should use PNG format for your contact photos. The optimum dimensions for contact photos are 128 pixels by 128 pixels with an aspect ratio of 1:1.

The HTTP method can only be configured in the jabber-config.xml file. Remote users using Cisco TelePresence Video Communication Server Expressway must use the HTTP method to present contact photos.

Summary

This section summarizes the key points that were discussed in this chapter:

- Cisco Jabber runs on many different phones and tablets. To simplify the first login for end users, you can use URL configuration. In this link, you specify the domain and the product type to which you will connect when starting Cisco Jabber for the first time.
- To add Cisco Jabber for Mobile in CUCM, you need to add a specific device and to follow the naming convention; for example, use BOT+NAME (BOTJDOE) for Cisco Jabber in Android.
- For directory search and number resolution, use the LDAP server when Cisco Jabber is used within the enterprise. Outside the enterprise, use Cisco UDS because LDAP traversal is not supported.

This chapter explained how Cisco Jabber is configured in CUCM and how the client accesses the directory for contact searches and number resolution.

Review Questions

Answer the following questions, and then see Appendix A, "Answers to Review Questions," for the answers.

1. **How many times does Cisco Jabber try to resume the network connection if there is a network transition happening?**

   a. 1

   b. 4

   c. 12

   d. 128

   e. 1024

2. **What is the video bandwidth that is used for an iPhone 5S or an iPad Air when using Cisco Jabber with video?**

   a. 384 kbps

   b. 512 kbps

   c. 768 kbps

   d. 1024 kbps

   e. 2048 kbps

3. **Which option is not a URL handler for chat?**
   a. chatim://<instant_message_id>
   b. ciscoim://<instant_message_id>
   c. im://<instant_message_id>
   d. xmpp://<instant_message_id>
4. **When adding Cisco Jabber for Android, what device name format must you use?**
   a. AND+NAME
   b. BOT+NAME
   c. SAM+NAME
   d. TCT+NAME

Chapter 19

Verifying and Troubleshooting Tools for Cisco Unified IM and Presence Components

Upon completing this chapter, you will be able to do the following:

- Describe the Cisco Unified Communications IM and Presence (IM&P) system dashboard
- Describe the Cisco Unified IM&P Reporting tool
- Describe how to use the presence viewer to troubleshoot single-user-related issues
- Describe the system troubleshooter, which is a helpful tool that facilitates troubleshooting the integration of Cisco Unified Communications IM&P with other applications
- Describe the connection status report that the Cisco Jabber client generates to view the system and integrated applications information
- Describe common end-user-related issues when using Cisco Jabber
- Describe an issue in which end users cannot select their Cisco Unified IP phone
- Describe an issue in which the end user cannot receive or place a call with Cisco Jabber
- Describe an issue in which a user reports that the presence status does not change to On a Call
- Describe an issue in which end users cannot log in to Cisco Jabber
- Describe an issue in which the end user reports that adding new contacts from the directory is not possible
- Describe an issue in which the end user cannot control the Cisco Unified IP Phone 9971
- Describe the trace options in Cisco Unified Communications IM&P
- Show the most common mistakes when integrating Cisco Unified IM&P with Cisco Unified Communications Manager

This chapter covers the Cisco Unified Communications IM&P system troubleshooter and the Cisco Jabber Connection Status tool, which help the administrator resolve presence issues quickly. Some common issues for Cisco Jabber are presented and resolved. Finally, tracing is introduced.

System Dashboard

Figure 19-1 illustrates the Cisco Unified Communications IM&P system dashboard, which provides good troubleshooting information.

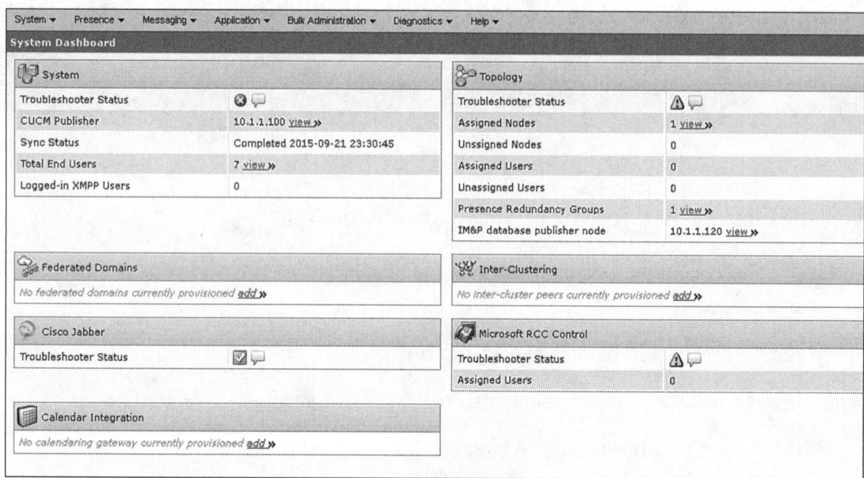

Figure 19-1 *Cisco IM&P System Dashboard*

Use the system dashboard to acquire a snapshot of the state of your IM&P Service system, including a summary data view of these system components: the number of devices, number of users, per-user data such as contacts, and primary extension. Intercluster peer and federation information will also be shown if configured. The result in the dashboard is a compressed output of the system troubleshooter.

Cisco Unified IM&P Reporting

Figure 19-2 shows the Cisco Unified IM&P Reporting tool, which is valuable for presence troubleshooting.

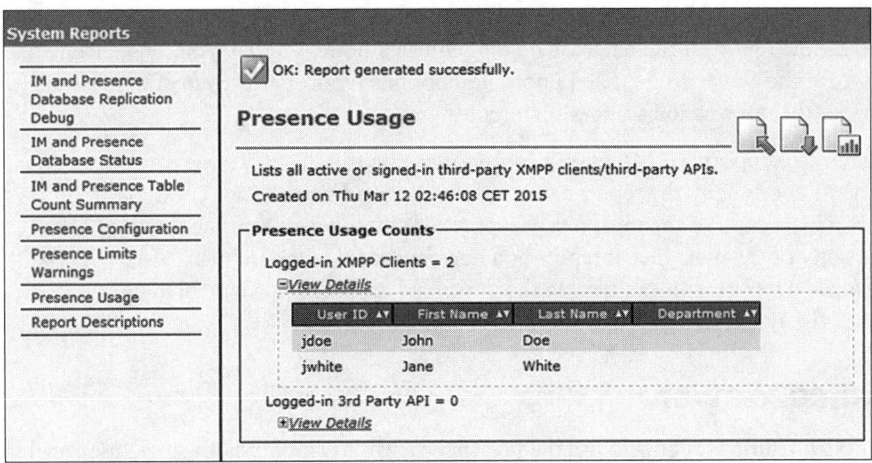

Figure 19-2 *Cisco Unified IM&P Reporting Tool*

The Cisco Unified Reporting web application, which is accessed from the Cisco Unified Communications Manager (CUCM) and Cisco Unified Communications Manager IM&P Service consoles, generates consolidated reports for troubleshooting or inspecting cluster data.

This tool provides an easy way to take a snapshot of cluster data. The tool gathers data from existing sources, compares the data, and reports irregularities. When you generate a report in Cisco Unified Reporting, the report combines data from one or more sources on one or more servers into one output view. For example, you can view a report that shows the hosts file for all servers in the cluster.

The application captures information such as the following sources on the publisher node and each subscriber node:

- Cisco Unified Real-Time Monitoring Tool (RTMT) counters
- Call Details Record-CDR Analysis and Reporting (CDR-CAR) (Unified Communications Manager only)
- Unified Communications Manager database (Unified Communications Manager only)
- Cisco Unified IM&P database (IM&P Service only)
- Disk files
- Operating system application programming interface (API) calls
- Network API calls
- Command-line interface (CLI)
- Real-Time Information Server (RIS)

The report includes data for all active clusters that are accessible at the time that you generate the report. If the database on the publisher node is down, you can generate a report for the active nodes. The Report Descriptions report in the System Reports list provides the information sources for a report.

This release supports HTML output for reports. You can identify a report in Cisco Unified Reporting by the report name and the date and time stamp. The application stores a local copy of the most recent report for you to view. You can download the local copy of the most recent report or a new report to your hard disk. After you download a report, you can rename the downloaded files or store them in different folders for identification purposes.

Presence Viewer

Figure 19-3 illustrates how to use the presence viewer to troubleshoot single-user-related issues.

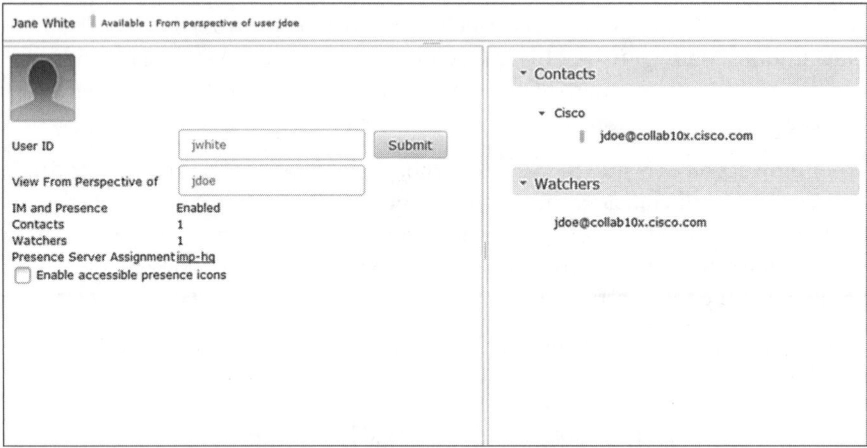

Figure 19-3 *Cisco Unified IM&P Viewer*

In CUCM, under the user configuration, click the **Presence Viewer for User** link to open the End User Presence viewer in the end user configuration page. This example shows the presence view from the perspective of John Doe when watching the contact Jane White. The contact and watchers are presented as well.

Note This tool can only be accessed by CUCM administrators.

System Troubleshooter

Figure 19-4 describes the system troubleshooter, which is a helpful tool that supports you in troubleshooting the integration of Cisco Unified Communications IM&P with other applications.

User Troubleshooter			
Test Description	Outcome	Problem	Solution
Verify all users have a unique User ID configured.	☑		
Verify all users have a Directory URI configured.	☑		
Verify all users have a unique Directory URI configured.	☑		
Verify all users have a valid Directory URI configured.	☑		
Verify all users have a unique Mail ID configured.	☑		
Verify Sync Agent service is running on the IM and Presence publisher node	☑		

Figure 19-4 *Cisco Unified IM&P System Troubleshooter*

The system troubleshooter can check the following Cisco Unified Communications IM&P modules:

- System
- Sync Agent (AXL)
- Presence Engine
- SIP Proxy
- Microsoft RCC
- Calendaring
- Interclustering
- Topology
- Cisco Jabber
- External Database
- Third-Party Compliance Server
- Third-Party LDAP Connection
- XCP
- User

Use the System Configuration Troubleshooter in the Cisco Unified Communications IM&P administration pages to diagnose IM&P Service configuration issues after your initial configuration or whenever you make configuration changes. The troubleshooter performs a set of tests on both the IM&P Service cluster and on the CUCM cluster to validate the IM&P Service configuration. After the troubleshooter finishes testing, it reports one of three possible states for each test:

- Test passed
- Test failed
- Test warning, which indicates a possible configuration issue

For each test that fails or that results in a warning, the troubleshooter provides a description of the problem and a possible solution. For any test failures or test warnings, click the fix link in the solution column to go to the CUCM IM&P Administration window where the troubleshooter found the problem. Correct any configuration errors that you find and rerun the troubleshooter.

Cisco Jabber Connection Status

Figure 19-5 illustrates the connection status report that the Cisco Jabber client generates to view the system and integrated applications information.

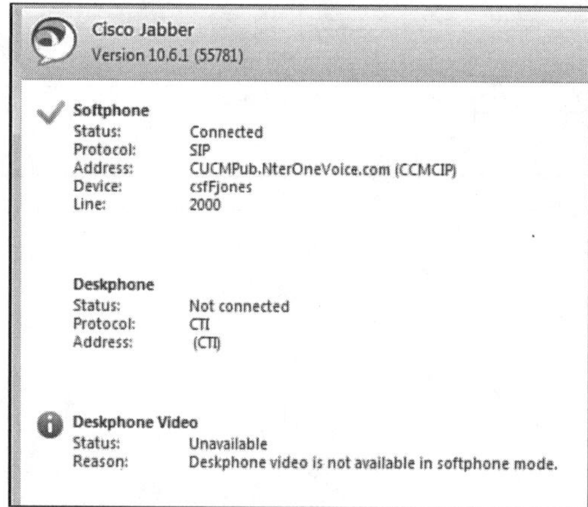

Figure 19-5 *Cisco Jabber Connection Status*

The connection status tool in Cisco Jabber offers an error notification report:

- Integration mode
  - Softphone (CCMCIP)
  - Deskphone (CTI)
- Video
- Voice mail (HTTPs)

- Presence (XMPP)
- Conferencing (HTTPS)
- Directory (LDAP)
- In addition you can generate a problem report, gather system information, and save it to a dump file.

Cisco Jabber includes a connection status tool to view and check the Cisco Unified Communications service parameters.

Note The connection status tool was called the server health tool in previous Cisco Jabber versions.

The information for a specific application is only shown when the logged-in user has a UC service that is configured for that application (for example, for the voice-mail service). If the user does not have a voice-mail service applied via the configured service profile, you will not see any voice-mail-related information. The error notification tool shows errors with a description, error code, date, and time.

Troubleshoot Common Cisco Jabber Issues

The following are some examples of common issues that are reported by end users when end users are enabled for Cisco Jabber and presence functionality:

- The Cisco Unified IP phone of the end user cannot be selected.
- In softphone mode, telephony is not possible.
- Users are not shown as On a Call in the contact list during a call.
- End users cannot log in to Cisco Jabber.
- Search for contacts in Cisco Jabber returns no results.
- The end user cannot control the Cisco Unified IP Phone 9971.

Cisco Unified IP Phone Cannot Be Selected

The following are steps to resolve issues in which end users cannot select their Cisco Unified IP phone from the Jabber client:

- Verify that the associated user devices are registered with the CUCM.
- Verify that the end user is associated with Cisco Unified IP phones in the end-user configuration.
- Ensure that the CCMCIP profile in Cisco Unified Communications IM&P is applied to the end user.

- Verify in CUCM that the device and directory number can be controlled by Computer Telephony Integration (CTI).
- Verify that the user has the correct CTI access control groups assigned.

In the example in Figure 19-6, an end user reports that after logging in to Cisco Jabber, the client responds with the error message that the selected device is not available. Typically, each end user has only one IP phone. Therefore, the selection of another phone may not be possible. Cisco Jabber will fall back and use softphone functionality.

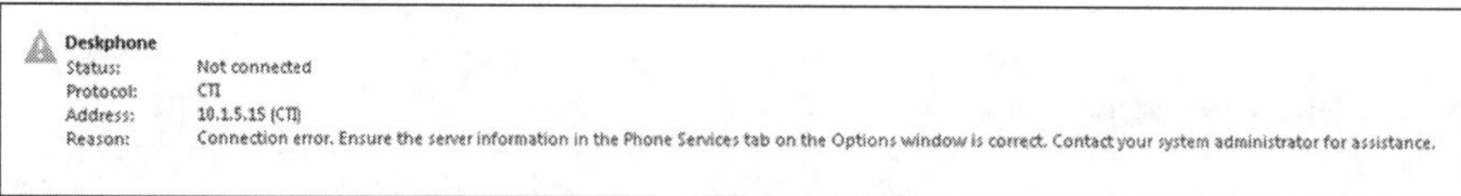

Figure 19-6 *Cisco Jabber Device Not Available*

Common reasons for this problem are the following:

- The associated IP phone is not registered with CUCM, which occurs due to a network, cabling, or phone issue.
- The IP phone is not associated in the end-user configuration in CUCM.
- The end user has no CUCM IP Phone (CCMCIP) profile that is assigned in Cisco Unified Communications IM&P.
- The IP phone or directory number cannot be controlled by CTI. This situation occurs when the Allow Control of Device from CTI check box is unchecked on the device or line.
- The user does not have the CTI Enabled and CTI Control of All Devices access control groups assigned.

In Softphone Mode, Telephony Is Not Possible

The softphone mode is typically used when an end user is not in the office. For example, an end user is currently at the airport or hotel and uses Cisco Jabber with a virtual private network (VPN) connection or mobile and remote access. When the user reports that placing a call or receiving calls is not possible, verify the following configurations:

- Verify that the end user is associated with the Cisco Unified CSF device in the end-user configuration in CUCM.
- Ensure that the Cisco Unified Client Services Framework (CSF) device is registered with CUCM. If the device is not registered, the problem may occur due to an error in the services on CUCM or the connectivity between the client and the call-processing system.
- Check the configuration of the Cisco Unified CSF device. Ensure that the correct directory number, partition, and CSS are applied.

To verify that Cisco Jabber is registered with CUCM, search for the Cisco Unified CSF device in CUCM under the menu **Device > Phone**.

In softphone mode, the Cisco Unified CSF device should show that it is registered with CUCM. When using hostnames or fully qualified domain names (FQDNs) for the TFTP server and CUCM, the issue might be that the CSF device cannot resolve the server name.

Users Are Not Shown as on the Phone During an Active Call

This section describes an issue in which a user reports that the presence status does not change to On a Call.

If everything is configured correctly, a user is automatically shown as On a Call during an active call. When the end user reports that the presence status is not displayed correctly, perform the following tasks:

- Typically, this error occurs if the line association is not configured for any of the associated directory numbers (DNs). In CUCM, check the IP phone, device profile, or Cisco Unified CSF device directory number and associate the end user with the line.
- Verify that the Session Initiation Protocol (SIP) trunk for presence subscription is configured correctly. Check the CUCM and Cisco Unified Communications IM&P site of the SIP trunk for connectivity.
- Ensure that the SIP trunk security profile in CUCM is configured correctly.

End User Cannot Log In to Cisco Jabber

An end user tries logging in to Cisco Jabber and the client responds with a Login Failed message. Verify the following settings:

- Ensure that the end-user account is not locked due to password policies in CUCM or Lightweight Directory Access Protocol (LDAP); for example, when there were too many wrong login attempts and the account was locked by the LDAP server security policy.
- Sometimes users change the server IP address or hostname by accident. Check that the user is trying to log in to the correct server. Setup of service discovery is recommended. Make sure the login credentials are the same as the mail address, so that users know what to enter; especially when subdomains are used for logins, end users may be confused.
- When using the hostname of CUCM in DNS SRVs, ensure that the DNS server is reachable and resolves the hostname to the correct IP address in the client device.
- On CUCM, verify that the user is enabled for presence and that the correct service profile is selected.

Note Before starting troubleshooting and tracing, perform basic connectivity tests. Connectivity tests include the following: check the network cable or Wi-Fi settings, try to ping CUCM and Cisco Unified Communications IM&P servers, and ensure that the user does not use Caps Lock when typing the password for the user account.

Search for Contacts Returns No Results

As an example, if the end user reports that adding new contacts to the Cisco Jabber contact list is not possible because the directory search returns no results, then perform the following steps to troubleshoot the problem:

- Ensure that the end user is associated with the correct LDAP profile. A missing LDAP profile can also be indicated when the user ID in Cisco Jabber (at the top) cannot be resolved by the LDAP directory.
- Verify that the Search Context parameter in the LDAP profile configuration is correct.
- Cisco Jabber connecting from outside the network must use the Cisco User Data Services (UDS) directory because LDAP traversal is not supported in Cisco Jabber. Within the enterprise, however, LDAP is the preferred directory for contact searches.

End User Cannot Control the Cisco Unified IP Phone 9971

As another example, the user reports that since the new Cisco Unified IP Phone 9971 was installed, CTI desk phone control of the device is not possible. With the previously used Cisco Unified IP Phone 7970, the user had no issues. Verify the following:

- On CUCM, ensure that the new Cisco Unified IP phone was associated with the end user in the end-user configuration window.
- Verify that the **Allow Control of Device from CTI** check box on the device and the line configuration on CUCM is enabled.
- Check the user groups in CUCM. The Cisco Unified IP Phone 89xx and 99xx series need an additional group. Add the end user to the Standard CTI Allow Control of Phones Supporting Connected Xfer and Conf group.

Trace Filter Settings

Figure 19-7 describes the trace options in Cisco Unified Communications IM&P.

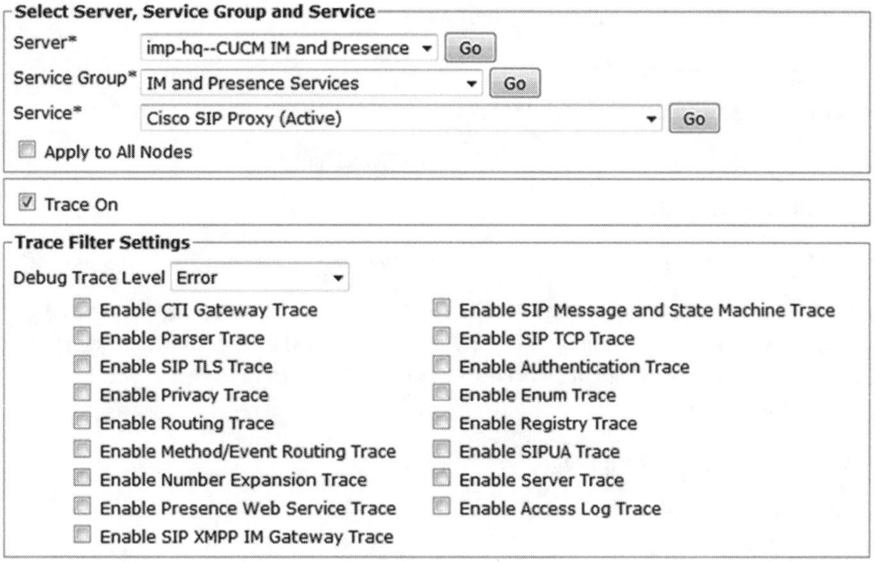

Select Server, Service Group and Service
Server* imp-hq--CUCM IM and Presence Go
Service Group* IM and Presence Services Go
Service* Cisco SIP Proxy (Active) Go
Apply to All Nodes

Trace On

Trace Filter Settings
Debug Trace Level Error
Enable CTI Gateway Trace
Enable Parser Trace
Enable SIP TLS Trace
Enable Privacy Trace
Enable Routing Trace
Enable Method/Event Routing Trace
Enable Number Expansion Trace
Enable Presence Web Service Trace
Enable SIP XMPP IM Gateway Trace
Enable SIP Message and State Machine Trace
Enable SIP TCP Trace
Enable Authentication Trace
Enable Enum Trace
Enable Registry Trace
Enable SIPUA Trace
Enable Server Trace
Enable Access Log Trace

Figure 19-7 *Cisco Trace Filter Settings*

In the Cisco Unified Communications IM&P Serviceability pages, choose the server for which you want to modify the trace settings. Choose the Service Group and Service. In addition, set the filter for the debug level.

Troubleshoot SIP Integration

If no communication is possible between CUCM and Cisco Unified Communications IM&P, but a ping is possible, check the configuration for the IP tables. The IP tables configuration is done when adding the Cisco Unified IM&P server as a server to the CUCM cluster. When changing from IP addresses to FQDNs, make sure that all cluster servers can reach the DNS server, have the domain configured, and can resolve the FQDN names.

If the SIP Cisco Unified Presence (CUP) Publish Trunk is not displayed, Cisco Unified Communications IM&P might not be able to read that information because of administrative XML (AXL) issues. Also, a misconfigured IP address or a name that cannot be resolved on the SIP trunk could be the issue.

Troubleshoot the SIP integration as follows:

- Presence status is not exchanged when the user goes off hook on the IP phone:
  - Check the SIP trunk security profile setting to determine whether relevant boxes need to be checked.
  - No line appearances are associated with the user.

  - Check access lists for incoming and outgoing traffic.
  - Check the application listener.
- Cisco Unified Communications IM&P does not work:
  - After first setup, restart the Cisco Unified IM&P server.
  - Check method/event routing status.
- If the issue still cannot be resolved, start tracing.

If the presence status is not updated for all clients, there can be several reasons for this issue. The most common reason is an incorrect configuration of the SIP trunk security profile setting. The following check boxes must be checked to receive and accept presence information:

- Accept Presence Subscription
- Accept Out-of-Dialog Refer
- Accept Unsolicited Notification
- Accept Replaces Header

The directory numbers must be associated with an end user for presence that is based on line appearances on every device. This situation would be the reason when only single users complain about missing or wrong presence indications.

Verify that the access lists are configured for incoming and outgoing traffic and allow communication between CUCM and Cisco Unified IM&P. Check whether the application listener is set up and if the default application listener is selected correctly. Method/event routing must be enabled. Method/event routing is disabled by default.

Note After the first setup of Cisco Unified IM&P, restart the server.

Some changes on Cisco Unified IM&P require a restart of a specific service. In Cisco Unified IM&P, choose **Systems > Notifications** to check whether any service needs to be restarted.

Summary

This section summarizes the key points that were discussed in this chapter:

- The system troubleshooter tests lots of different modules in Cisco Unified Communications IM&P for correct functionality. If an error is found, a solution is suggested.
- The Cisco Jabber Connection Status tool can be used to troubleshoot single-user presence issues. The profiles and associated applications can be verified easily by checking the correct IP addresses or names and port numbers.

- If the system troubleshooter and the connection status tool cannot indicate or locate the error and reviewing the configuration does not help, tracing needs to be activated. View the traces from Cisco Unified RTMT.

The chapter covered the Cisco Unified Communications IM&P system troubleshooter and the Cisco Jabber Connection Status tool. The most common Cisco Jabber issues were explained and Cisco Unified Communications IM&P tracing was introduced.

Review Questions

Answer the following questions, and then see Appendix A, "Answers to Review Questions," for the answers.

1. **The End User Presence viewer can be accessed via the Cisco Unified Communications IM&P administration GUI.**

   a. True

   b. False

2. **The Allow Control of Device from CTI check box can be set on the device and on the line.**

   a. True

   b. False

3. **When controlling a Cisco Unified IP Phone 9971 with Cisco Jabber, which access control group must be assigned to the end user?**

   a. Standard CTI Allow Control of Phones Supporting Connected Conf

   b. Standard CTI Allow Control of Phones Supporting Connected Xfer

   c. Standard CTI Allow Control of Phones Supporting Connected Xfer and Conf

   d. Standard CTI Allow Control of all Devices

4. **When using Cisco Jabber with mobile and remote access, the user can use the LDAP server for contact search and photo retrieval.**

   a. True

   b. False

5. **Which of these parameters is not set in the SIP trunk security profile for Cisco Unified Communications IM&P integration?**

   a. Accept CTI Refer

   b. Accept Unsolicited Notification

   c. Accept Replaces Header

Chapter 20

Deploying Cisco Collaboration Systems Applications with Cisco Prime™ Collaboration

Upon completing this chapter, you will be able to do the following:

- Describe Cisco Prime™ Collaboration and its modules and architecture
- Describe how the lifecycle management is done with Cisco Prime™ Collaboration
- Describe the features that are available in Cisco Prime™ Collaboration Provisioning Standard and Advanced
- Describe the automated system provisioning with Cisco Prime™ Collaboration
- Describe how you can combine domains, service areas, and different subscriber types for automated provisioning
- Describe how different administrators can be set up to manage different domains
- Describe the benefits of information synchronization from the LDAP server to the Cisco Prime™ Collaboration server
- Describe the subscriber roles in Cisco Prime™ Collaboration
- Describe the Day 1 and Day 2 activities, where Cisco Prime™ Collaboration helps you manage and automate these tasks
- Describe the Day 1 deployment option allowing you to quickly integrate and set up the Cisco Collaboration Systems applications
- Describe the Day 2 services such as managing daily moves, adds, and changes
- Describe how Cisco Prime™ Collaboration offers on single interface to set up phones with lines, user, mailboxes, and features in one step
- Describe the Cisco Prime™ Collaboration dashboard
- Explain the Cisco Prime Telephone Self-Care portal and the options that a user can select and configure

This chapter introduces the Cisco Prime™ Collaboration modules and focuses on provisioning. Day 1 and Day 2 activities are described. The use of the design and deployment options in Cisco Prime™ Collaboration are discussed, and the Cisco Prime Telephone self-care portal is covered.

Cisco Prime™ Collaboration Overview

Figure 20-1 illustrates Cisco Prime™ Collaboration and its modules and architecture.

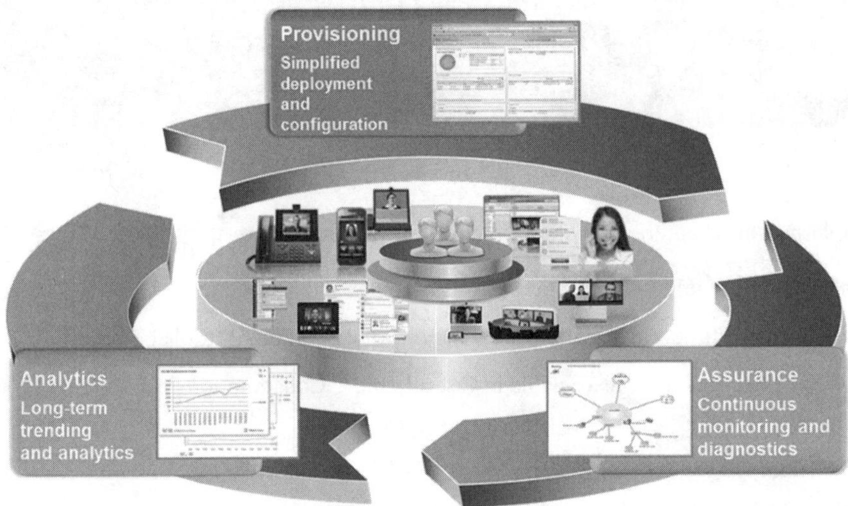

Figure 20-1 *Cisco Prime™ Collaboration Modules and Architecture*

Cisco Prime™ Collaboration removes management complexity and provides automated, accelerated provisioning, real-time monitoring, proactive troubleshooting, and long-term trending and analytics in one integrated product. The solution delivers a premier operations experience through an intuitive user interface and optimized operator methodology, including automated workflows that ease implementation and ongoing administration.

Provisioning

- This module accelerates Cisco Collaboration Systems site rollouts and dramatically reduces time to perform user moves, adds, changes, and deletes (MACD).
- This module also removes complexity and helps enable delegation to help desk personnel, which can lower operating expenses.

Assurance

- This module helps ensure reliable service delivery through proactive fault detection and rapid isolation using purpose-built diagnostic tools.
- This module expedites operator resolution of service quality issues before these issues impact end users.

Analytics

- This module helps administrators analyze trends for capacity planning, resource optimization, and quality of service.
- This module quickly determines the success of advanced, collaboration technology adoption to advance future investment decisions.

Complete Lifecycle Management

Figure 20-2 describes how the lifecycle management is done with Cisco Prime™ Collaboration.

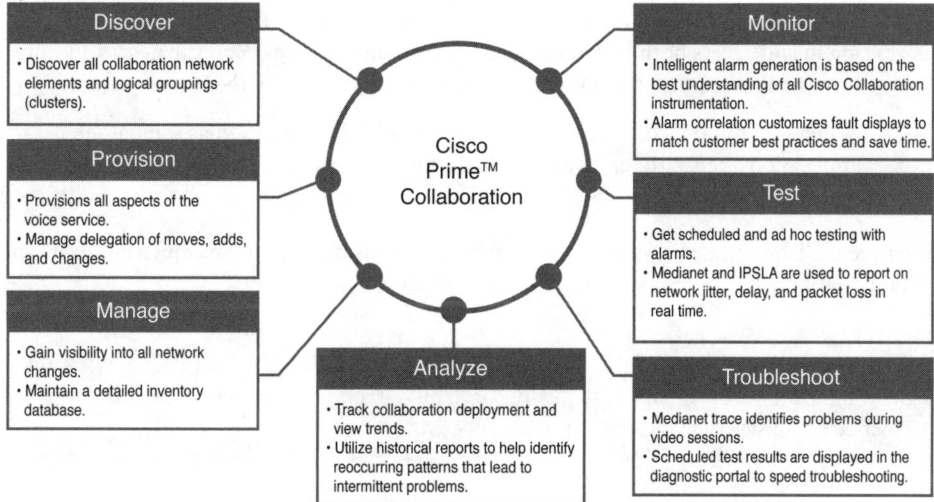

Figure 20-2 *Cisco Prime™ Collaboration Complete Lifecycle Management*

Cisco Prime™ Collaboration is a single product that is capable of managing all of your collaboration lifecycle needs. Cisco Prime™ Collaboration allows you to simplify and automate many day-to-day tasks as shown in the figure.

The Cisco Prime™ Collaboration menu controls navigation according to the stages in the lifecycle approach.

The graphical user interface (GUI) shows all menus because Cisco Prime™ Collaboration Provisioning and Assurance and converged:

- Home
- Design
- Deploy
- Operate
- Analyze
- Administration

You can use the GUI from each application separately or create a unified access. For example, if you access Cisco Prime™ Collaboration Provisioning directly, the menu might look different than when you use a unified access.

Cisco Prime™ Collaboration as a converged application combines the benefit of Assurance and Provisioning features. You can run Prime Collaboration as a converged application or as standalone applications.

- When you run the converged application, a single sign-on (SSO) is available to log in and access both Assurance and Provisioning features. You can access all Provisioning features from the Design and Deploy menus in the Home page.
- When you run the components of Cisco Prime™ Collaboration as standalone applications, separate logins are available for the Assurance and Provisioning features.

Prime Collaboration allows you to integrate the Provisioning and Assurance applications and configure the Provisioning system from Assurance using SSO.

Note In the converged mode, before you restart or shut down the Prime Collaboration Provisioning application, you must ensure that you detach it from Prime Collaboration Assurance and converge it after the restart process.

Cisco Prime™ Collaboration Standard and Advanced

Table 20-1 describes the features that are available in Cisco Prime™ Collaboration Provisioning versions of Standard and Advanced.

Table 20-1 *Cisco Prime™ Collaboration Standard and Advanced*

Feature	Standard	Advanced
Cluster support	Manages only one cluster of Cisco Unified CM and one cluster of Unity Connection	Manages multiple cluster with mixes of cluster revisions and cluster associations
Delegation of roles or role-based access control (RBAC)	Allows three levels of RBAC	Allows advanced RBAC and delegation.
Ordering workflow roles	No	Yes
Batch provisioning	Yes	Yes
Infrastructure templates	No	Yes
Application programming interface	No	Support for Northbound application programming interface (API)

Cisco Prime™ Collaboration Provisioning Standard manages only one Cisco Unified Communications Manager cluster and one Cisco Unity Connection cluster. The standard version supports only Cisco Collaboration Systems products in Version 10.0. Other differentiators are as follows:

- **Delegation of roles:** The standard version allows three levels of RBAC: system level, advanced ordering level, and basic ordering level. The advanced version allows advanced RBAC and delegation. Administrators with ordering privileges can be assigned to different domain user groups.
- **Ordering workflow roles:** The advanced version provides ordering workflow, including optional stages between placing an order and the actual provisioning of the order: approver, assigner, shipper, and receiver. The activity roles can be enabled or disabled, and assigned to different users for an efficient ordering workflow.
- **Batch provisioning:** The standard version allows you to deploy a large number of services by combining them into a single batch. Batch provisioning is available for a single cluster only. In the advanced version, a single provisioning batch can perform infrastructure and user provisioning across many Cisco Unified Communications Manager clusters, making Prime Collaboration batches global in scope.
- **Infrastructure templates:** Infrastructure templates are available only in the advanced version. Prime Collaboration Provisioning infrastructure templates can be created for Cisco Unified Communications Manager and Cisco IOS Software. These templates provide keyword support, which is not available in batch files, for repetitive tasks such as site rollouts. Templates can be scheduled for execution

at a later time and are tracked in the order tracking system for auditing or troubleshooting at a later time. These templates can leverage Cisco IOS prebuilt templates with keyword support.

- **API:** This feature is available only in the advanced version. The Northbound API is supported for integration with third-party management applications, HR systems, or other custom provisioning interfaces.

Automated System Provisioning

Table 20-2 describes the automated system provisioning with Cisco Prime™ Collaboration.

Table 20-2 *Cisco Prime™ Collaboration Automated System Provisioning*

Native Interface Provisioning	Cisco Prime™ Collaboration Provisioning
Multiple interfaces used	Unified: One interface
Admin determines process	Simplified: Business process- and user-oriented
Service activation takes more than 15–20 minutes	Rapid: Less than one minute to activate
Manual and duplicate entry errors	Accurate: Reduced manual and duplicate entry errors
No centralized tracking for changes	Tracking: Unified audit trail

With Cisco Prime™ Collaboration, you can automate provisioning. Provisioning is a web-based application based on the Java 2 Platform, Enterprise Edition (J2EE) architecture. Provisioning uses various interfaces to connect with Cisco Collaboration Systems applications, and does not need to deploy any agent software on those application platforms.

Provisioning uses open interfaces such as HTTP, HTTPS, AVVID XML Layer (AXL)–SOAP, SSH, and Telnet to remotely configure or query the applications that are being managed, as illustrated in Figure 20-3. Different levels of user access can be configured by the administrator.

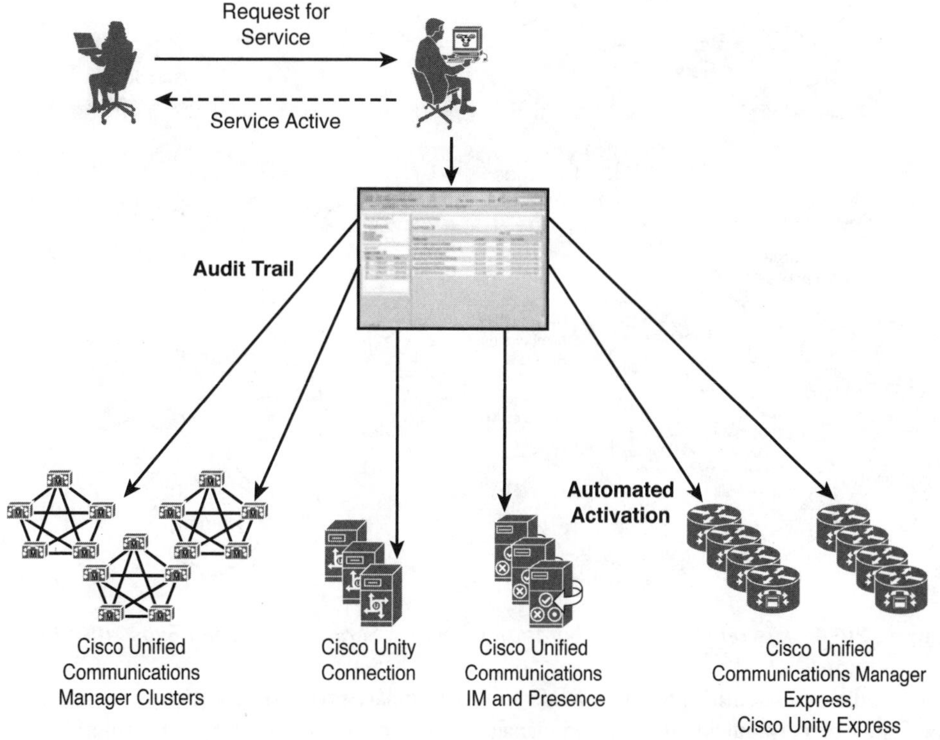

Figure 20-3 *Cisco Prime™ Collaboration Automated System Provisioning*

Domains, Service Areas, and Subscriber Types

Figure 20-4 describes an example of how you can combine domains, service areas, and different subscriber types for automated provisioning.

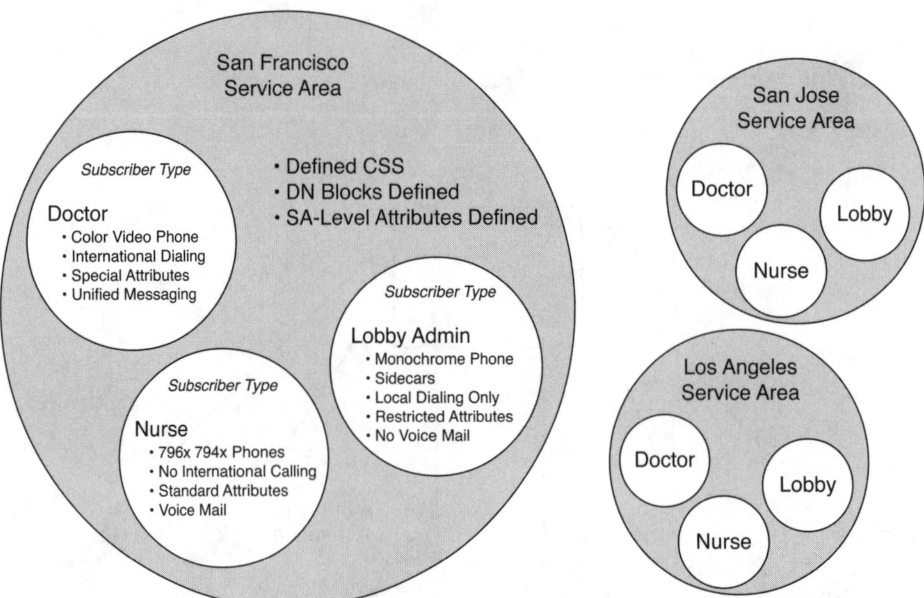

Figure 20-4 *Cisco Prime™ Collaboration Domains, Service Areas, and Subscriber Types*

Binding these entities together helps you to automate processes for groups, locations, and others to quickly deploy and manage the Cisco Collaboration Systems solution.

Domains

Domains are groupings of subscribers. For each grouping, one or more system users can be authorized to manage services for subscribers within that domain. In addition, rules or policies may be set on a domain; those rules and policies apply to services for subscribers in that domain. Common policies can also be applied on operations within a domain.

A user can manage more than one domain if the user is assigned the proper authorization role. All the user's services are provisioned in the services domain that you specify while adding the user.

Service Area

Service areas are groupings within a domain that are used to structure and manage the required IP telephony and messaging services across geographic, organizational, or technological boundaries. The service area typically acts as a service offering location and provides a template mechanism that determines the provisioning attribute values that are used during order processing. The service area determines the mappings from the business view of the service to the technology that delivers those services.

A service area also manages Cisco Unified Communications Manager (CUCM) partitioning and class of service by controlling the location, device pool, calling search space (CSS), and route partition assignments for any device that is provisioned into that service area. For example, on a service area that is associated to a CUCM, the service area defines the device pool, route partition, CSSs, location, and external phone number mask that the products will use within CUCM.

Subscriber Types

Subscriber roles control the products and services that a subscriber can order. The subscriber role also dictates the service areas that a subscriber is entitled to access.

Administration Levels

Figure 20-5 describes how different administrators can be set up to manage different domains.

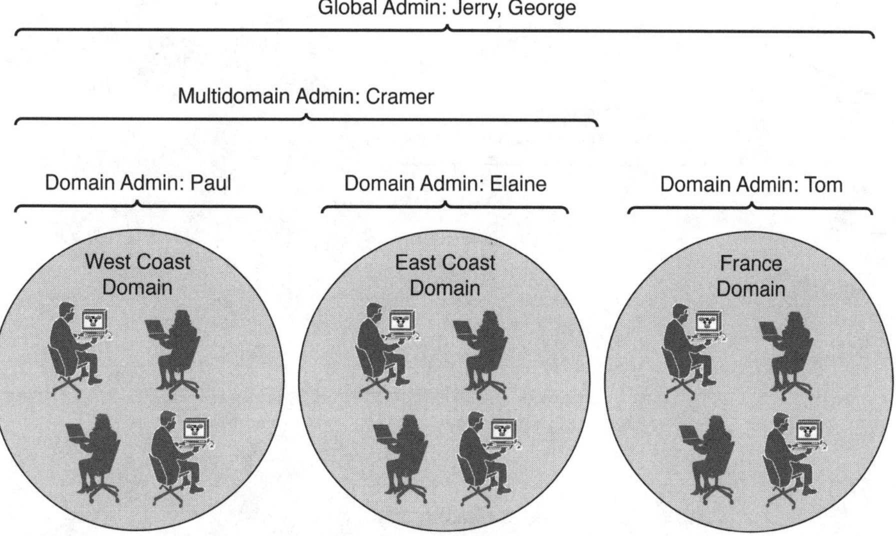

Figure 20-5 *Cisco Prime™ Collaboration Administration Levels*

Administrators can only see the subscribers and resources in the domains to which they are assigned, and assignments can be added or removed easily by a global administrator.

There is some additional granularity in basic and advanced roles that can be performed by different administrator types beyond what is shown in the figure.

There are preconfigured roles for administrators (for example, infrastructure management roles or workflow admin roles).

LDAP Import

Figure 20-6 illustrates the benefits of information synchronization from two LDAP servers to the Cisco Prime™ Collaboration server with different domains.

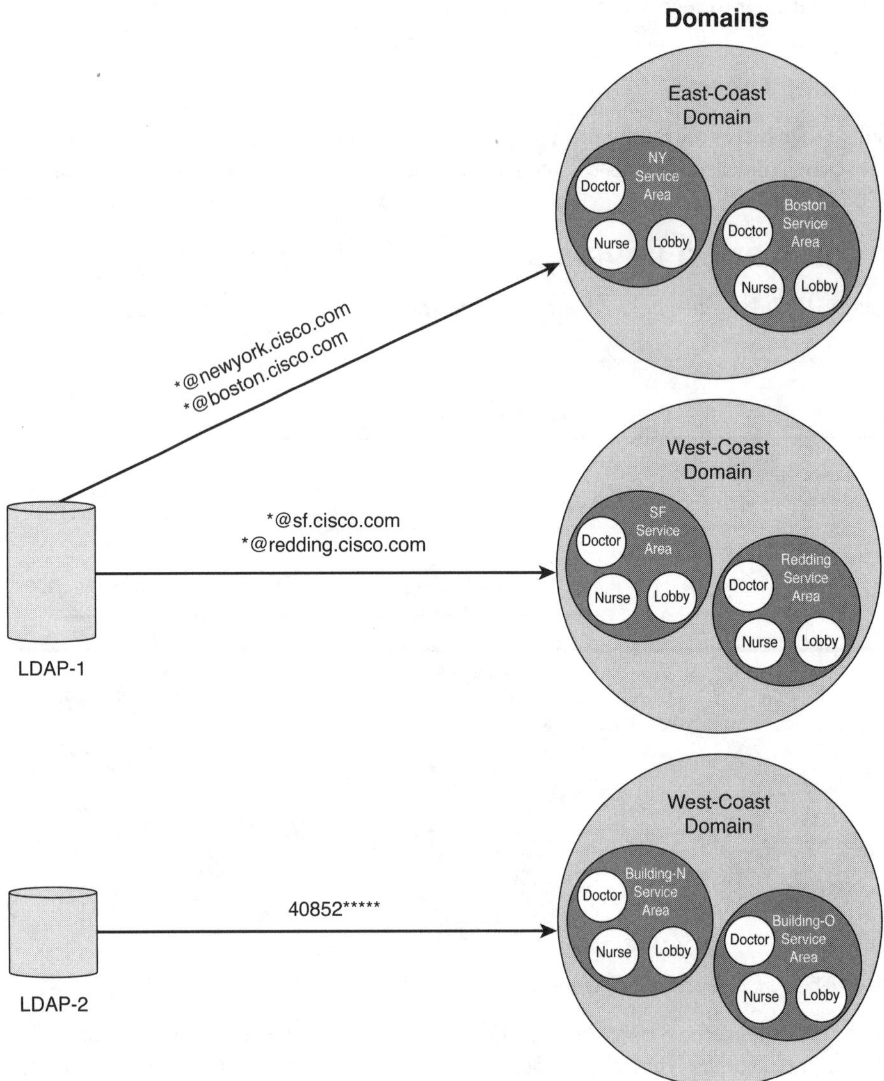

Figure 20-6 *Cisco Prime™ Collaboration Administration Levels*

Provisioning can use this information to create new subscribers, update existing subscriber information, or delete subscribers. You configure the LDAP server synchronization to determine which actions should be performed.

When provisioning new users in CUCM, you need to be sure that the user ID of the subscriber exactly matches the user ID in CUCM or the order will be rejected. Cisco Prime™ Collaboration can get Lightweight Directory Access Protocol (LDAP) subscribers from CUCM when CUCM is LDAP-integrated. This method is a pass-through method of synchronizing all LDAP subscribers that are known by CUCM.

With LDAP integration, Cisco Prime™ Collaboration can populate its subscriber database with user IDs directly from an associated LDAP source. A filter feature allows you to get only user IDs that belong in a specific domain, as opposed to importing the entire LDAP directory. An example of filtering is shown in the figure; for example, all users with the number 40852*****. Complex filters can be created based on the available fields in Active Directory.

There is an option that allows you to remove a user and their services from the Collaboration Systems network when a synchronization occurs and a user is no longer in the LDAP directory. Another option prevents a user from being deleted if they still have associated services. These optional settings can help remove unused services and free up directory numbers after employees leave a company.

Reports can also be generated showing the results of the import. Results can include new users, users that were removed, users who were deleted from CUCM, and users that need service cleanup before they are deleted.

If Cisco Prime™ Collaboration is used as the subscriber source, CUCM may not need to be LDAP enabled to ensure that only LDAP users are provisioned.

Subscriber Roles

Subscriber roles control the products and services that a subscriber can order. The subscriber role also dictates the service areas that a subscriber is entitled to access. Do not confuse subscribers with users. These two roles are different in Cisco Prime™ Collaboration.

The default subscriber types are as follows:

- **Employee:** This subscriber type is the default role that is assigned to new subscribers. The employee subscriber role should be configured to match the typical setup of employees in your organization. If you do not configure the employee subscriber role to meet your needs, you may not see all of the desired options in the employee subscriber record.
- **Pseudo:** This subscriber type is used to provision phones that do not have an associated user. Pseudo subscribers cannot be renamed or removed.
- **Executive:** This subscriber type is used for management of users with advanced communication requirements, for example video phones and international dialing.

These subscriber types exist in each domain in Cisco Prime™ Collaboration Provisioning. Each set of subscriber types can be customized in each domain by adding, removing, or changing these predefined subscriber types.

Deployment Aspects in Cisco Prime™ Collaboration

The following are the Day 1 and Day 2 activities, where Cisco Prime™ Collaboration helps you manage and automate these tasks.

- Day 1 activities:
    - Infrastructure configuration and batch provisioning
    - Unified Communication services
- Day 2 activities:
    - Subscriber management and services and self-care portal

Provisioning features include automated processes for Cisco Collaboration Systems initial deployments and for Day 2 move, add, change, and deletes (MACDs). An intuitive user interface provides a single view of a subscriber and the subscriber's services as well as a consolidated view of subscribers across the organization. With these capabilities, Cisco Prime™ Collaboration significantly accelerates site rollouts and dramatically reduces the time that is required for ongoing changes, resulting in exceptional productivity gains and lower operating expenses.

In addition, by significantly simplifying moves, adds, changes, and deletes, the solution facilitates delegation of these tasks. Delegation allows organizations to optimize IT resources and further reduce total cost of ownership. A self-care portal allows end users to control preference settings (for example, call forwarding, speed dials, and passwords, which helps create a better-quality user experience).

Cisco Prime™ Collaboration offers flexibility and awareness:

- **Multicluster:** Prime Collaboration can manage one or many clusters spread across one or many domain groups.
- **Multirevision:** Prime Collaboration supports multiple versions of Cisco Collaboration Systems applications concurrently.
- **Multi-application:** Prime Collaboration supports mixes of call processors and message processors; for example, CUCM Express with Cisco Unity, or CUCM associated with Cisco Unity and Cisco Unity Connection, for example, in different versions.
- **Service-aware:** When adding voice mail, Cisco Prime™ Collaboration sets forwarding and extension settings automatically. When adding presence, the line is associated to the user ID.

Day 1 Services Infrastructure

Cisco Unified Configurator for Collaboration or CUCC is a simple GUI-based configuration tool that helps partners with rapid deployment to increase margins and reduce operating expenses. CUCC is Day 1 configuration tool that shortens the UCM installation time and performs repeatable process to avoid common mistakes.

The following are the Day 1 deployment options allowing you to quickly integrate and set up the Cisco Collaboration Systems applications:

- Policy and service definitions
  - Create policies, policy-based service offerings, and subscriber types.
- Template-based infrastructure provisioning
  - Push dial-plan components and other common constructs to end system.
- Batch processing of total services for subscribers
  - Bulk-create initial subscribers and provision their services.

The Infrastructure Configuration page of Cisco Prime™ Collaboration enables you to browse the infrastructure configuration settings of a Call Processor and Unified Message Processor. Through this page, you can add, edit, or delete the configuration settings of a Call Processor and Unified Message Processor.

The configuration can be done from Cisco Prime™ Collaboration by selecting **Deploy > Infrastructure Configuration** and chosing the device (Cisco Collaboration Systems applications are called processors) you want to configure. Then select the parameter (for example, **Route Pattern**), as shown in Figure 20-7. Delete or modify existing route patterns or create new route patterns.

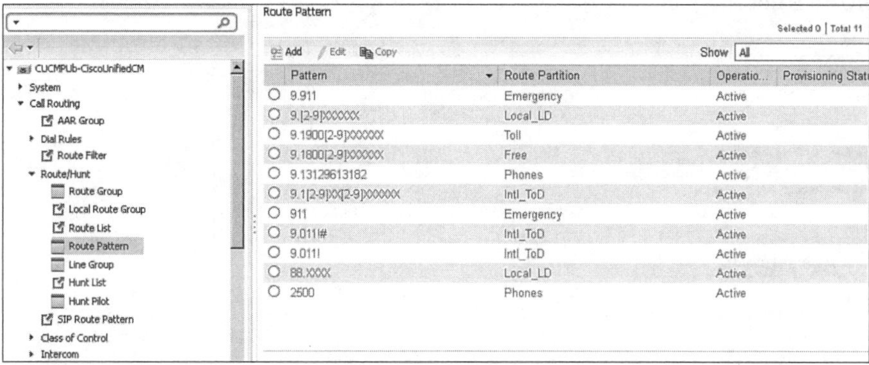

Figure 20-7 *Cisco Prime™ Collaboration Infrastructure Configuration*

Day 2 Services

When the Cisco Collaboration Systems applications are integrated and set up, the Day 2 work begins. You configure new users and maintain the user database including user phones and features.

In Cisco Prime™ Collaboration, choose **Deploy > User Provisioning.** Choose a subscriber, for example Fred Jones, as shown in Figure 20-8. In the service details section, you can view the services that are assigned to the user. By choosing New Service, you can add a new device or feature for a user. All orders are logged so that you can track the changes that are done in the system very easily. You can also add notes to a subscriber, which helps you remember certain information for users.

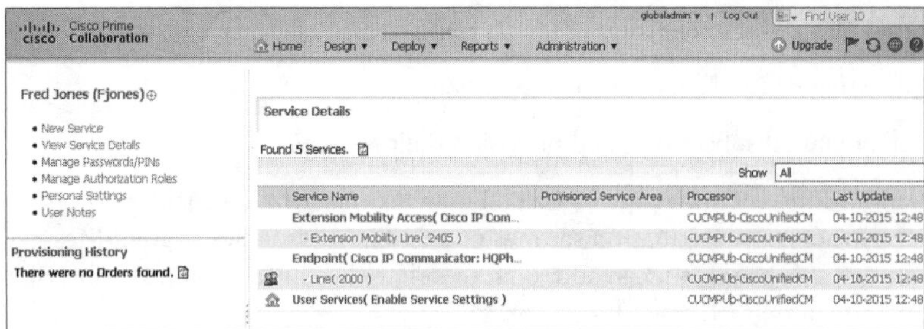

Figure 20-8 *Cisco Prime™ Collaboration User Provisioning*

Single Provisioning Interface

Figure 20-9 shows the orderable products (for example, a new phone and others). The figure does not show all options.

Figure 20-9 *Cisco Prime™ Collaboration Single Provisioning Interface*

As an example, for user Fred Jones, you can configure several different user services, as shown in Figure 20-10.

Endpoint Information	
*Endpoint Type	Cisco 9951
Device Description	
Protocol	SIP
MAC Address	
Use Dummy MAC Address	☐
Phone Button Template	Use System Default
Service Template	Not Selected

Figure 20-10 *Cisco Prime™ Collaboration User Device Configuration*

Based on the subscriber type, you will get a list of selectable phones for a user. Administrators can select new endpoints (like Cisco Jabber for Tablet and others) and assign telephony features, in the same way as they can for Cisco IP phones.

Cisco Prime™ Collaboration Dashboard

Figure 20-11 illustrates the Cisco Prime™ Collaboration dashboard.

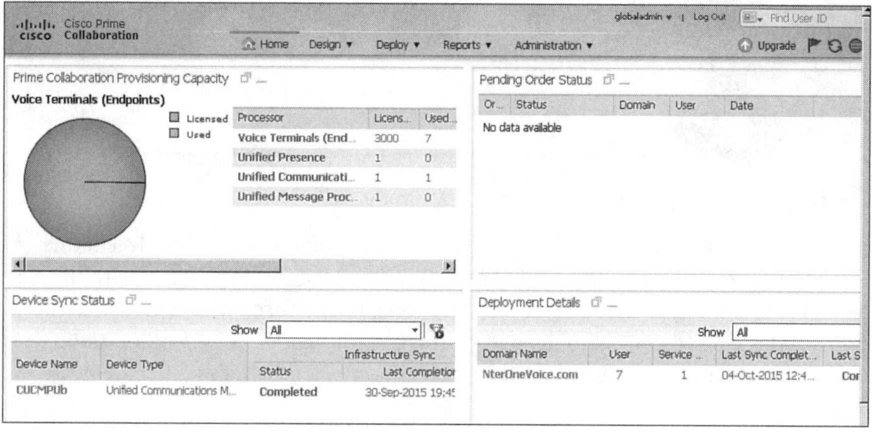

Figure 20-11 *Cisco Prime™ Collaboration Dashboard*

The Home dashboard allows you to view important statistics and details of the processors, pending orders, status of the device synchronization, domains and their deployment details, and users who are logged in as well as locked. The dashboards are available under Home.

You can see all of this information on a single page, instead of navigating through several pages. You can also click the links provided in the dashboard to view the relevant details.

A pie chart displays the details of the licensed and used voice terminals (phones). To view the pie chart, you must have Adobe Flash Player installed in your system. If it is not installed, you are prompted to install it.

Cisco Prime Telephone Self-Care

Figure 20-12 illustrates the Cisco Prime Telephone Self-Care portal and the options that a user can select and configure.

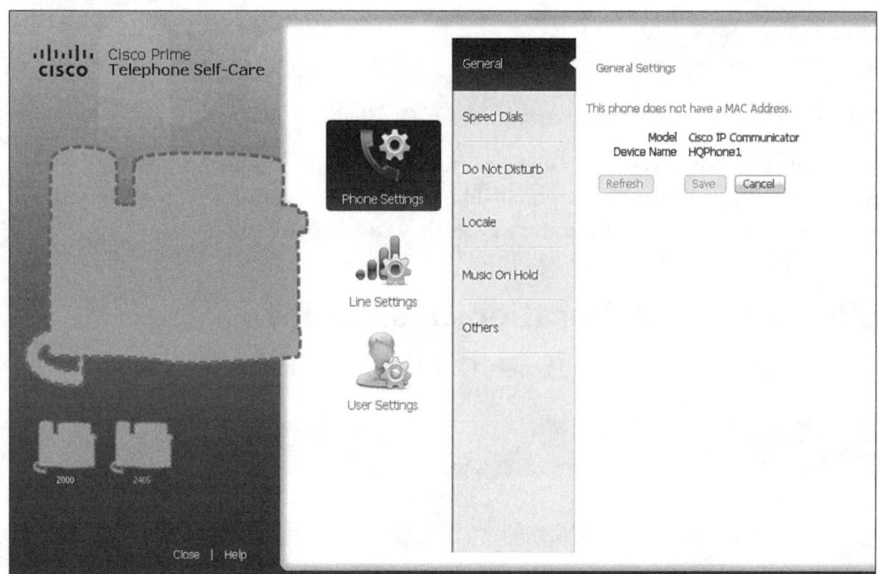

Figure 20-12 *Cisco Prime™ Collaboration Telephone Self-Care*

Figure 20-12 shows the phone settings of a user. To log in to Cisco Prime Telephone Self-Care, browse to the IP address of Cisco Prime™ Collaboration. Log in with the user credentials and configure the settings for the phone, line, or user. The options that the user sees and is able to configure depend on the Cisco Prime™ Collaboration setup. Users may configure speed dials, language settings, or enable services like Extension Mobility.

Figure 20-13 shows the line settings of a user. In the line settings, the user can configure call forward settings, caller ID, ringer notification and message waiting indicator (MWI), and others.

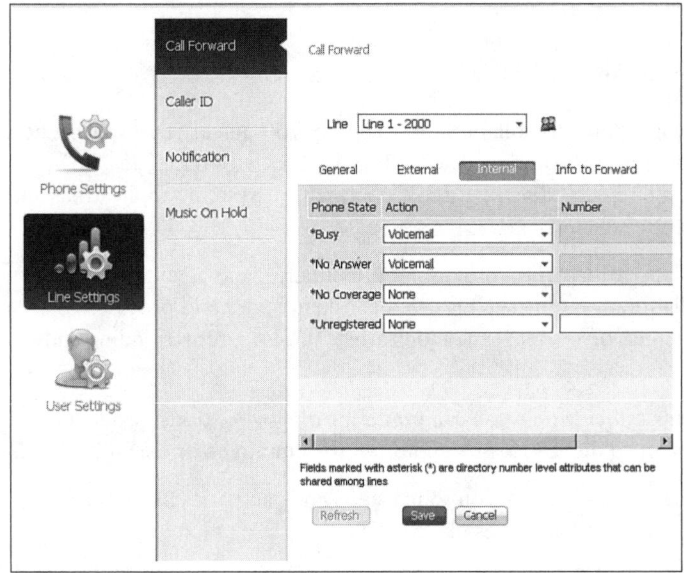

Figure 20-13 *Cisco Prime™ Collaboration Telephone Self-Care Phone Line Settings*

Figure 20-14 shows the user settings. In the **User Settings** area, select the Primary Device and set the PIN and password.

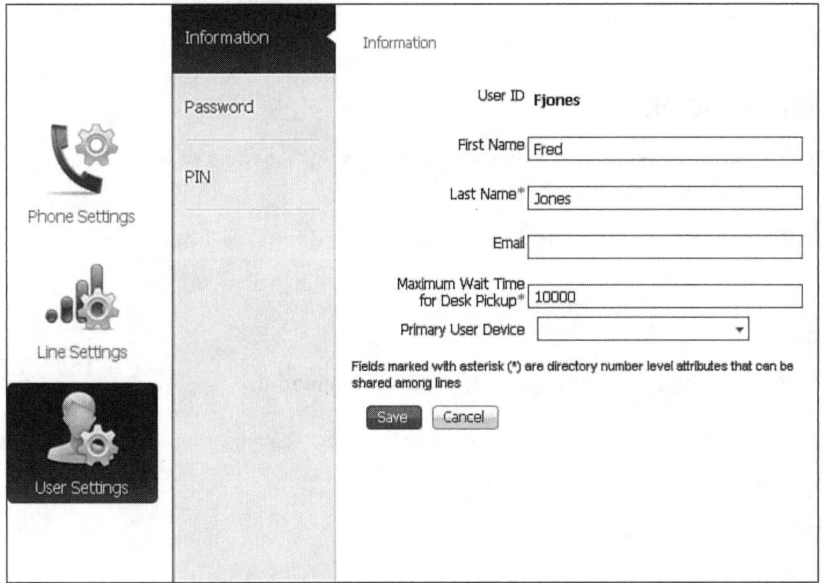

Figure 20-14 *Cisco Prime™ Collaboration User Settings*

Summary

This section summarizes the key points that were discussed in this chapter:

- Cisco Unified Configurator for Collaboration can help you quickly customize a new Cisco Collaboration Systems solution. The GUI tool works with templates, however, you need to have an understanding of Cisco Collaboration Systems applications and their configuration to use it.
- Cisco Prime™ Collaboration offers provisioning, assurance, and analytics modules. Cisco Prime™ Collaboration removes management complexity and provides automated provisioning, offers real-time monitoring, and long-term trending and analytics.
- With the default subscriber types, you can predefine a set of options, products, and features that you want to deploy, for example, for the employee or executive level.
- Cisco Prime™ Collaboration allows you to manage Day 1 activities like infrastructure configuration and Day 2 activities like MACD.
- Enable the Telephone Self-Care feature to allow users to configure device, line, and user settings in Cisco Prime™ Collaboration to free the administrator from daily configuration requests and to create a better-quality user experience.

The chapter described Cisco Prime™ Collaboration provisioning and how it can be used for Day 1 activities, like setting up the infrastructure, and Day 2 activities, such as daily moves, adds, changes, and deletions.

Review Questions

Answer the following questions, and then see Appendix A, "Answers to Review Questions," for the answers.

1. **Cisco Unified Configurator for Collaboration is used for Day 1 activities.**

   a. True

   b. False

2. **Which option is not a Cisco Prime™ Collaboration module?**

   a. Assurance

   b. Analytics

   c. Monitoring

   d. Provisioning

3. **To manage multiple Unified Communications clusters in different versions you need the Cisco Prime™ Collaboration Advanced license.**

   a. True

   b. False

4. **Which option is not a default subscriber type in Cisco Prime™ Collaboration?**

   a. Employee

   b. Executive

   c. Manager

   d. Pseudo

5. **Which service creates a phone with a line, including voice mail, and a set of voice services?**

   a. Endpoint Service

   b. Enhanced Endpoint Service

   c. User Service

   d. Advanced User Service

Chapter 21

Describing Video Infrastructure

Upon completing this chapter, you will be able to do the following:

- Describe the different layers of the collaboration infrastructure
- Describe the architectural evolution of the collaboration infrastructure
- Describe the migration from previous versions to Cisco Unified Communications 10.0
- Describe how to use Cisco Prime Collaboration Manager for video analysis
- Describe the high-level function of a Cisco Unified Communications Manager and Cisco TelePresence Video Communication Server implementation
- Describe the dual approach of integrating Cisco Unified Communications Manager and Cisco TelePresence Video Communication Server
- Describe the characteristics of the Cisco TelePresence Video Communication Server and show when to use it
- Describe the cluster limits and required resources for Cisco TelePresence Video Communications Server
- Present the call-processing terminology for Cisco Unified Communications Manager and Cisco TelePresence Video Communication Server
- Describe how Cisco Unified Communications Manager and Cisco TelePresence Video Communication Server are connected and the information flow between these systems
- Describe the dial plans in Cisco Unified Communications Manager and Cisco TelePresence Video Communication Server
- Describe conferencing in general
- Describe multiparty conference systems
- Describe the Cisco TelePresence Conductor functionality

- Describe the Cisco Jabber Video for TelePresence client, which was formerly known as Movi
- Describe the DNS SRV records for Cisco Jabber Video for TelePresence registration inside and outside the enterprise
- Describe how Cisco Jabber Video for TelePresence is autoprovisioned to register with Cisco TelePresence Video Communication Server
- Describe the simplification of the video endpoint portfolio

This chapter describes the layers of the collaboration infrastructure for video integrated solutions and explains the differences between Cisco Unified Communications Manager and Cisco TelePresence Video Communication Server (VCS) as the call-processing system. Cisco Jabber Video for TelePresence is described as a client that can be automatically provisioned and register with the Cisco TelePresence VCS only.

Cisco Collaboration Infrastructure

Figure 21-1 illustrates the different layers of the Cisco collaboration infrastructure.

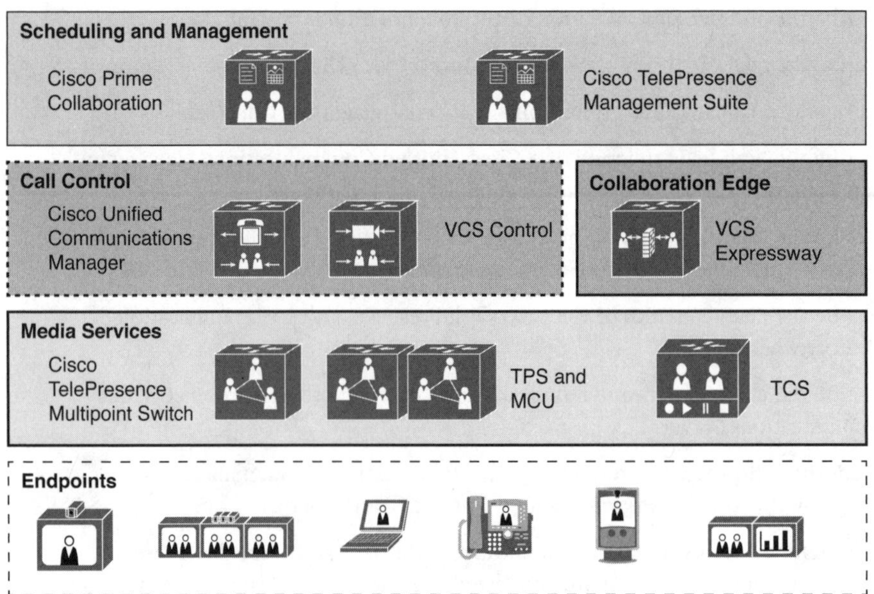

Figure 21-1 *Cisco Collaboration Infrastructure*

The scheduling and management layer comprises the following:

- **Cisco Prime Collaboration:** Cisco Prime Collaboration helps enable rapid installation and maintenance of Cisco Unified Communications and Cisco TelePresence components as well as the provisioning of users and services.

- **Cisco TelePresence Management Suite (Cisco TMS):** Cisco TMS offers complete control and management of multiparty conferencing, infrastructure, and endpoints, to centralize management of your entire video collaboration and TelePresence network.

The call control and collaboration edge layer includes the following products in addition to the Cisco Unified Communications Manager (CUCM):

- **Cisco VCS:** Cisco VCS Control provides video call and session control, registrations, and enhanced security for Cisco TelePresence conferences. Cisco VCS enables features such as routing, dial plans, and bandwidth usage control, while allowing organizations to define video call-management applications that are customized to their requirements.
- **Cisco VCS Expressway:** Cisco VCS Expressway allows video traffic to traverse the firewall securely, enabling rich video communications with partners, customers, suppliers, and mobile and teleworkers.

The media services layer consists of the following products:

- **Cisco TelePresence Multipoint Switch:** The Cisco TelePresence Multipoint Switch allows geographically dispersed organizations to hold Cisco TelePresence meetings across multiple locations reliably and easily.
- **Cisco TelePresence Server (Cisco TPS):** Cisco TPS provides high-quality, standards-based video conferencing for users of mobile, desktop, or room systems. It works with Cisco TelePresence Conductor to offer flexible and optimized conferencing.
- **Cisco TelePresence MCU series:** The Cisco TelePresence MCU series is a range of state-of-the-art multipoint control units (MCUs) that can grow with your business's video usage over the long term.
- **Cisco TelePresence Content Server (TCS):** Easily share knowledge using the Cisco TelePresence Content Server (TCS), which records Cisco TelePresence and third-party video conferencing meetings and multimedia presentations for live broadcast and on-demand access.

The endpoint layer includes the following types of endpoints:

- Cisco Jabber
- IP phones with video capabilities
- Collaboration desk endpoints with video capabilities
- Collaboration room endpoints
- Immersive TelePresence endpoints

Architectural Evolution

Figure 21-2 describes the components of the architectural evolution of the Cisco collaboration infrastructure.

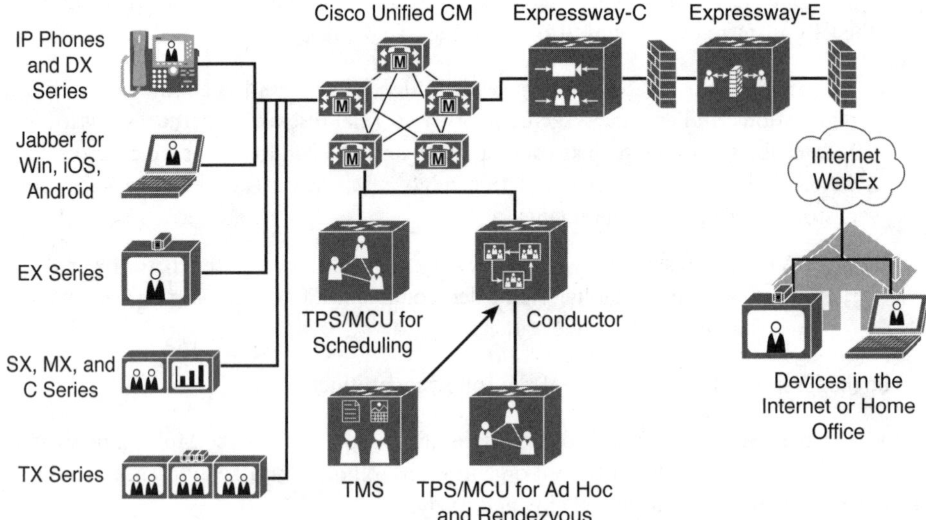

Figure 21-2 *Cisco Collaboration Architectural Evolution*

In 2010, at the close of the TANDBERG acquisition by Cisco, the state of the collaboration infrastructure was as follows:

- TelePresence and Cisco Unified Communications endpoints were typically deployed on separate call-processing clusters.
- There was limited interoperability between endpoints that were bridged using the Cisco TelePresence Server.
- A lot of product functional overlap existed in every category: endpoints, call control, B2B connectivity, bridging, scheduling, and management.
- Different dial plans existed, including numeric and alphanumeric plans.
- Different methods of provisioning, management, and monitoring were used.
- Features were not consistent across the portfolio.

In the years 2011 to 2013, both product lines grew together:

- Cisco TelePresence and traditional Cisco Unified Communications (telephony and standard definition video) are merged in a converged CUCM cluster. Former TANDBERG endpoints are predominantly still registered on Cisco VCS Control.

- Full native any-to-any interoperability is available between all endpoints and bridges. Ad hoc bridges are available with Cisco TelePresence Conductor on CUCM, and scheduled bridges are still registered on Cisco VCS Control.
- The functional overlap of products diminishes, and product roles are clarified, but consolidation is not yet fully realized.
- Both numeric and alphanumeric dial plans are now fully supported across most of the portfolio.
- Provisioning, management, and monitoring come together and Cisco Prime Collaboration grows in functionality.
- Consistency of features and user experience increases across the portfolio.
- New, compelling solutions like Cisco WebEx Enabled TelePresence extend the video solution.

Today, these product lines are merged and offer the following benefits for the customer:

- All endpoints and infrastructure are merged in a converged CUCM for call control with Cisco VCS Expressway (Control and Edge) for remote and mobile access (MRA) to CUCM. This convergence enhances B2B, WebEx, and cloud-enabled TelePresence connectivity and third-party interworking.
- Multiparty bridging for audio and video for all types of conferences is now trunked through CUCM. Cisco TMS scheduled resources are still separate from Cisco TelePresence Conductor ad hoc resources.
- Cisco Jabber is now available on Microsoft Windows, Mac OS X, iOS, and Android using Expressway. This availability provides access to CUCM and related Unified Communications services such as directories, presence, and visual voicemail without the need for a virtual private network (VPN).
- New applications like cloud-enabled TelePresence, video messaging, Cisco Contact Center Express remote experts, new enabling technologies like Cisco Jabber Guest and WebRTC, H.265, and scalable video coding (SVC) are available.
- Multiparty bridging for audio and video, for all types of conferences, is now consolidated under Cisco TelePresence Conductor with Cisco TMS for scheduling and meeting management.

Combined Model and Methods

This following points describe the environment of customers with an existing solution that is based on a Cisco Unified Communications version before Release 10.0 including Cisco TelePresence Video Communication Server (VCS) for video integration:

- Unified CM and VCS Control and Expressway
- TMS and Prime Collaboration

- IP phones, Jabber UC, Jabber Video (Movi), TC and TX series endpoints
- VPN-based and Expressway-based firewall traversal for RMA
- CUBE/Expressway for B2B calling
- CUBE for IP public switched telephone network (PSTN) trunking

These deployments should be migrated to Version 10.x to allow optimization of the existing solution and to follow the Cisco Validated Designs for Collaboration as follows:

- Migrate all endpoints to Unified CM 10.x
  - Prime Collaboration for endpoint provisioning and overall management
  - TMS for scheduling and conference management
- Migrate from Jabber Video (Movi) to Jabber UC 10.x
- Expressway X8.x for RMA and Expressway for B2B calling
- CUBE for IP PSTN trunking

You can find additional information at http://www.cisco.com/c/en/us/solutions/enterprise/validated-designs-collaboration/index.html.

High-Level Function of Collaboration Infrastructure

Figure 21-3 describes the high-level function of a CUCM and Cisco TelePresence VCS implementation.

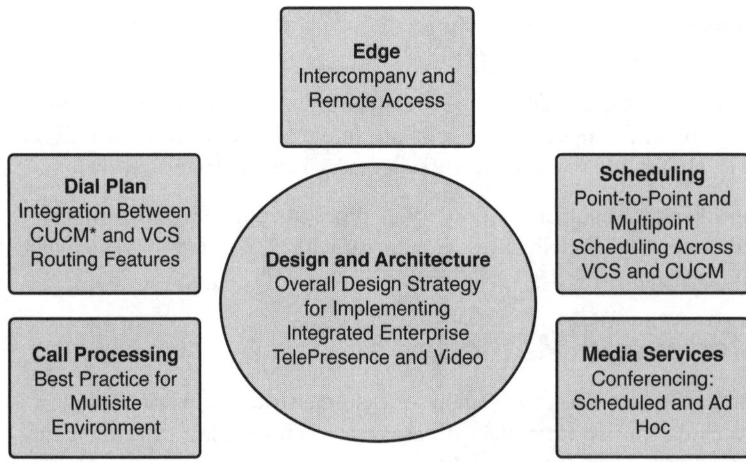

Figure 21-3 *High-Level Function of Collaboration Infrastructure*

Figure 21-3 shows the main high-level functions in the collaboration infrastructure that you must consider when integrating CUCM and Cisco TelePresence VCS.

Dual Approach

Figure 21-4 describes the dual approach of integrating CUCM and Cisco TelePresence VCS.

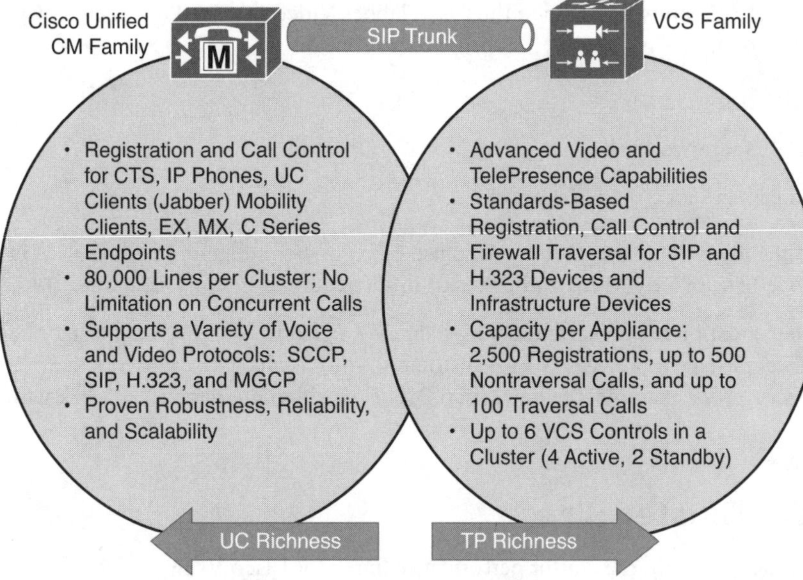

Figure 21-4 *Dual Approach of CUCM and VCS*

Cisco TelePresence VCS adds important telepresence enablement to a Unified Communications solution, as shown in the figure. Both systems have common areas (not shown in the figure), such as the following:

- Endpoint management
- Centralized dial plans
- Call detail records (CDRs)
- Security

Cisco TelePresence VCS Characteristics

The following points show the video-related features that were ported from Cisco VCS to CUCM to merge the call-processing systems:

- Video encryption
- Ad hoc conferencing using Multiway Add Participant and Join features
- Alphanumeric URI registration

- Secure firewall traversal using H.460.18 and 19
- TMS scheduling and management of EX, SX, MX, DX and C series endpoints on CUCM

The following features are exclusive to Cisco VCS and include the registration of H.323 devices, SIP-H.323 interworking, and the Cisco Jabber Video for TelePresence (Movi) client registration:

- H.323 registration
- SIP-H.323 interworking
- Cisco Jabber Video (Movi) support

However, the migration path for Movi is to use Cisco Jabber integrated with CUCM in phone mode or with CUCM IM and Presence in softphone or deskphone mode.

The recommendation for greenfield deployments is to plan for CUCM and not for the Cisco VCS deployment. For Cisco VCS customers, you should find a way to migrate to CUCM because, for example, the new Cisco DX series video phones do not work with Cisco VCS.

Cisco VCS Cluster Size

The following points are the cluster performance limits for Cisco VCS:

- 10,000 active users and redundancy for 5000 users
- Call limits per cluster are 400 traversal and 2000 nontraversal video calls
- OVA virtual resources for one large Cisco VCS server:
  - 8 vCPUs with a core speed of 3.2 GHz, 8-GB vRAM, 132-GB vDisk
  - 3 vNICs, each 10 Gbps

This performance data and the associated limits are based on 100 simultaneous interworked and encrypted calls at 768 kbps:

- The number of provisioned users on a single Cisco VCS cluster is 10,000.
- Cisco TMS can support 100,000 provisioned users.
- Users should be partitioned into groups to control how provisioning is sent to VCS clusters.

Interactive Connectivity Establishment (ICE) is a technique used in computer networking involving network address translators (NATs) in Internet applications of Voice over Internet Protocol (VoIP), peer-to-peer communications, video, instant messaging and other interactive media. Call signaling for nontraversal calls is performed only by Cisco VCS:

- In a call between Session Initiation Protocol (SIP) user agents (UAs), both SIP UAs have the same SIP contact address and source IP address.
- SIP calls are managed as ICE calls.

Call signaling and media routing for traversal calls are performed by Cisco VCS:

- Traversal calls are managed between instances of Cisco VCS Expressway (VCS-E).
- Cisco VCS manages IPv4-IPv6 interworking calls.
- Cisco VCS manages SIP-H.323 interworking calls.
- Back-to-back user agent (B2BUA) calls; for example, Microsoft Skype for Business integration.
- In a call between SIP UAs, one or both of the SIP UAs can have a SIP contact address that is different from the source IP address.
- Calls between an H.323 endpoint registered on Cisco VCS-E with H.460 traversal capability.

Call Control Terminology

Table 21-1 presents the comparison of call-processing terminology for CUCM and Cisco TelePresence VCS.

Table 21-1 *Call Control Terminology*

CUCM	Cisco VCS
Directory number (DN)	Device ID
Route pattern	Search rule
Translation pattern	Search rule or transform
Trunk	Neighbor or DNS zone
Cisco Unified Mobility	FindMe
Locations and regions	Link and pipes
Ad hoc conferencing	Multiway and Conductor

This table helps you distinguish between the terms that are used in the different call-processing systems.

Connecting CUCM and VCS Clusters

Figure 21-5 illustrates how CUCM and Cisco TelePresence VCS are connected and the information flow between these systems.

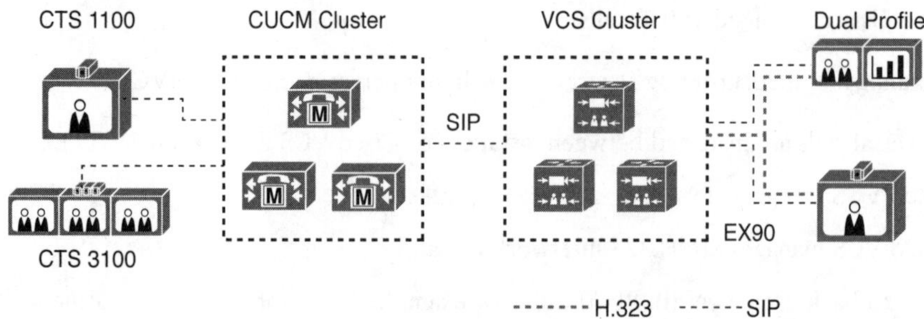

Figure 21-5 *Connecting CUCM and VCS Clusters*

With CUCM 10.x, the name or IP address of a server is replaced by the organization top-level domain (OTLD) in outgoing messages (for example, cisco.com). This change allows you to call john.doe@cisco.com instead of dialing john.doe@cucm1.cisco.com. The enhanced security support for 80-bit authentication tags was implemented for military customers to secure video communications.

In connecting CUCM with a cluster of Cisco VCS peers, there are two methods of providing Unified CM with the addresses of the VCS cluster peers:

- The trunk to the Cisco VCS specifies the DNS SRV address for the VCS cluster. Each peer should be set with an equal priority and weight in SRV records on the DNS server.
- The trunk to the Cisco VCS specifies a list of VCS peers as IP addresses. You can also set up multiple SIP trunks to each peer in the VCS cluster. This option is preferred when using flat dial plans.

When connecting VCS to a cluster of Unified CM nodes, VCS must be able to route calls to each Unified CM node. This routing can be done in the following two ways (in order of preference):

- Route calls using a single neighbor zone in VCS with the Unified CM nodes listed as location peer addresses.
- Route calls using DNS SRV records and a VCS DNS zone.

Note that both options ensure that the Cisco VCS-to-Unified CM call load is shared across Unified CM nodes.

Dial Plans

Table 21-2 compares the dial plans in CUCM and Cisco TelePresence VCS.

Table 21-2 *Dial Plans*

Address Scheme	Example	Cisco Unified CM Registration	Cisco VCS Registration
E.164	14081234567	Supported as directory number (DN)	H.323 E.164 registration
E.164-based URI	14081234567@cisco.com	Supported from CUCM 9 and higher	Supported H.323 ID and SIP URI
Alphanumeric URI	John.doe@cisco.com	Supported from CUCM 9 higher	Supported H.323 ID and SIP URI

In CUCM, the E.164 or +E.164 numbers are used for call routing. URI dialing is used in the Cisco VCS. Both dial plans are relevant:

- E.164 addresses allow easy integration with the PSTN and audio-only endpoints.
- URI addresses allow easier back-to-back communications using domain names and are generally more intuitive for end users.

CUCM and Cisco VCS do not share a database, so default routes are required between these systems. As an example, you dial jdoe@cisco.com on CUCM but cannot find the user on CUCM. The call is sent to Cisco VCS via the default route. There are two possibilities now. First, you find a match for jdoe@cisco.com, and you extend the call to the user phone. The second option is that Cisco VCS does not find a match and routes the call back. These systems will prevent looping after a certain number of hops.

In the past, E.164 was usually used in voice networks and H.323 and URI were used within SIP networks. In the future, collaboration services, instant messaging (IM), voice, video, and social communication will converge more and more. The endpoints and the infrastructure will need to support both address schemes to support scalable and consistent dialing.

Conferencing

Conferencing occurs when more than two participants join a meeting with a voice or video device. The challenge is to have a consistent user experience in voice or video conferences and to select the correct conference resource depending on the device, especially when mixing standard definition and high-definition video devices.

The Cisco focus for the future is Cisco ActivePresence using Cisco TelePresence Server instead of multipoint control units (MCUs) with lots of different layouts.

Ad hoc conferences are impromptu meetings; they are not scheduled beforehand and do not require an administrator to initiate them. Ad hoc conferences are suitable for smaller, on-the-fly meetings. A point-to-point call that is escalated to a multipoint call is considered an ad hoc conference.

Rendezvous conferences are also called Meet-Me, permanent, or static conferences. These conferences require that endpoints dial into a predetermined number and are often used for recurring group meetings that involve different endpoints each time.

Scheduled conferences provide a guarantee that endpoints and multipoint resources will be available at a certain time. Endpoints join manually or are automatically connected by the multipoint resource.

The Cisco TelePresence MCU 5300 series, for example, offers more than 50 layouts for continuous presence. All ports on this MCU also support advanced continuous presence.

The future trend is active presence supported by Cisco TelePresence Server. Cisco ActivePresence capability supports a full-screen immersive view of the primary speaker with an overlay of others who are participating in the call. ActivePresence is designed to maximize the large-scale immersive experience and is available on all ports of the Cisco TelePresence Server. The server interworks with Polycom RPX and TPX telepresence systems while preserving the full Cisco ActivePresence view. Four layout families are provided for single-screen endpoints, including panel-switched Cisco ActivePresence capability.

Up to 9 ActivePresence windows are supported on a single screen at one time. In a triple-screen system, a total of 27 ActivePresence windows are supported.

Multiparty Conferencing

Figure 21-6 illustrates some options of TPS.

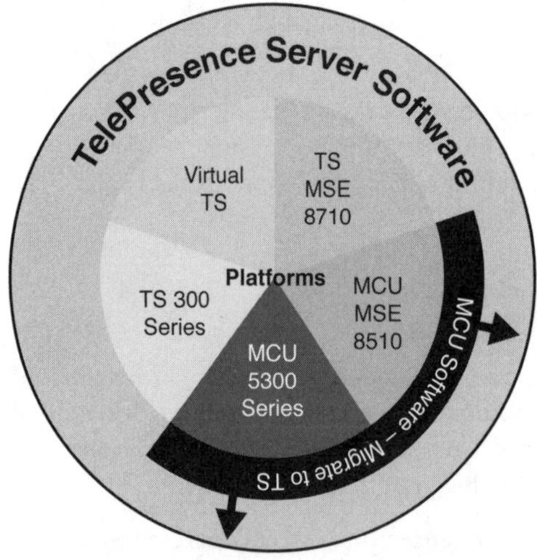

Figure 21-6 *Multiparty Conferencing*

With universal encoding, you can optimize the quality for users with different video qualities (for example, in a mixed video conference with participants using 360p, 720p, and 1080p resolution). In addition, the bandwidth is adapted between users with limited and slow Internet lines such as a 1-Mbps connection and users having 100 Mbps and more. Every single connection is transcoded to its best possible quality, forming a multiparty solution.

The following are guidelines for Cisco multiparty conferencing:

- Cisco TelePresence Server and Cisco TelePresence Conductor form a multiparty solution:
  - Any-to-any device connectivity, from mobile to immersive, bringing together video, web, and voice conferencing
  - Platforms to suit all deployment scenarios with a common application and industry-leading user experience
- MCU hardware platforms can run Cisco TelePresence Server software.
  - Customers migrate when appropriate

Cisco TelePresence Conductor

The following points summarize the Cisco TelePresence Conductor functionality:

- Improved user experience
  - Simple to use
- Zero downtime
  - Extended scale
- Enhanced conference size
  - Intelligent resource usage
- Any-to-any collaboration
  - Interoperable
  - Standards based

Instead of managing the MCUs directly with Cisco TelePresence VCS or CUCM, the MCUs are managed by Cisco TelePresence Conductor. There are two reasons for virtualizing and centralizing MCU management:

- You can have multiple MCUs, cascade them geographically, and define backup conference resources.
- Because pervasive video is complex and the call can happen anywhere in the organization, this approach allows optimal resources to be found depending on the device location.

For example, assume that there are three locations, one each in Asia, Europe, and America. When the Europe conference bridge is fully utilized, users should not get a failure message saying that there are no video resources available, or fall back to audio only. Cisco TelePresence Conductor manages this situation by automatically choosing an underutilized conference bridge, but always using local resources first, based on the location configuration. With preferences set, an overflow situation selects the next best conference bridge. Cisco TelePresence Conductor is best described as a centralized MCU controller.

Cisco TelePresence Conductor is mandatory for the new pervasive conferencing platforms such as Cisco TelePresence Server on a VM and TelePresence Server on the Cisco Multiparty Media 310/320.

Cisco Jabber Video for TelePresence (Movi)

Figure 21-7 illustrates the Cisco Jabber Video for TelePresence client, which was formerly known as Movi.

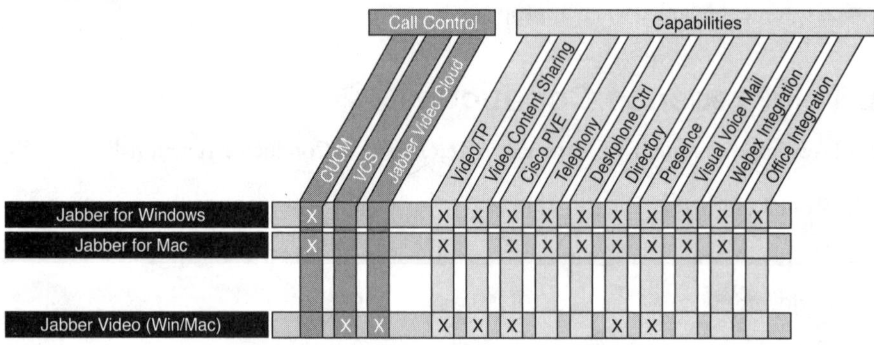

Figure 21-7 *Cisco Jabber Video for TelePresence (Movi)*

The presence functionality is limited to the Cisco TelePresence VCS cluster and only to video endpoints.

Cisco Jabber requires CUCM and Cisco Unified Communications IM and Presence to register and is a rich media-enabled client.

Cisco Jabber Video for TelePresence is a video-centric client that can only be registered with Cisco TelePresence VCS and can reach other clients on CUCM via a SIP trunk. There is also a cloud-based solution, where you can register the Cisco Jabber Video for TelePresence client as well. Cisco Jabber Video for TelePresence uses the Cisco Precision Video Engine technology, which is also used by the Cisco TelePresence EX60 and EX90 systems.

The software requirements to deploy Cisco Jabber Video for TelePresence are as follows:

- Cisco TelePresence VCS
- Cisco TMS

The provisioning option must be enabled on both products.

Cisco recommends using the Cisco TelePresence PrecisionHD USB Camera for Cisco Jabber Video for TelePresence on your PC for the best video and audio user experience.

To register, the client needs to locate the provisioning service and register with Cisco TelePresence VCS. You must set up the following to successfully register Cisco Jabber Video for TelePresence:

- SIP domain on the Cisco VCS with which the client will register
- DNS address of the primary VCS control cluster
- (Optional) DNS address of a Cisco VCS Expressway cluster

These settings can be preset by the administrator so that users do not have to set these parameters. In fact, if these settings are configured, users cannot change them.

DNS SRV Records

The following points summarize the DNS protocol:

- DNS service records, defined in RFC 2782, are a method to define a DNS record for a service instead of a specific host.
- The DNS SRV record resolves to one or more hostnames of servers and port numbers where the desired service may be found.
- It can be used to implement location-specific registration behavior.

For registration within the enterprise, set up the DNS SRV records for the client to register with the Cisco TelePresence VCS cluster, where the devices use round-robin registration according to the DNS settings shown as follows:

```
_service._protocol.domain TTL  class SRV priority weight port target
_sip._tcp.clustername.internal.com 86400  IN SRV 10 60 5060 server1.cisco.com.
_sip._tcp.clustername.internal.com 86400  IN SRV 10 60 5060 server2.cisco.com.
_sip._tcp.clustername.internal.com 86400  IN SRV 10 60 5060 server3.cisco.com.
_sip._tcp.clustername.internal.com 86400  IN SRV 10 60 5061 server1.cisco.com.
_sip._tcp.clustername.internal.com 86400  IN SRV 10 60 5061 server2.cisco.com.
_sip._tcp.clustername.internal.com 86400  IN SRV 10 60 5061 server3.cisco.com.
```

For external access, Cisco Jabber Video for TelePresence connects to the Cisco TelePresence VCS Expressway using firewall traversal:

```
_service._protocol.domain TTL  class SRV priority weight port target
_sip._tcp.express.external.com 86400  IN SRV 10 60 5060 server1.external.com.
_sip._tcp.express.external.com 86400  IN SRV 10 60 5060 server2.external.com.
```

Automated Provisioning with Cisco VCS and TMS

Figure 21-8 shows how Cisco Jabber Video for TelePresence autoregisters. Note that users can also be configured manually.

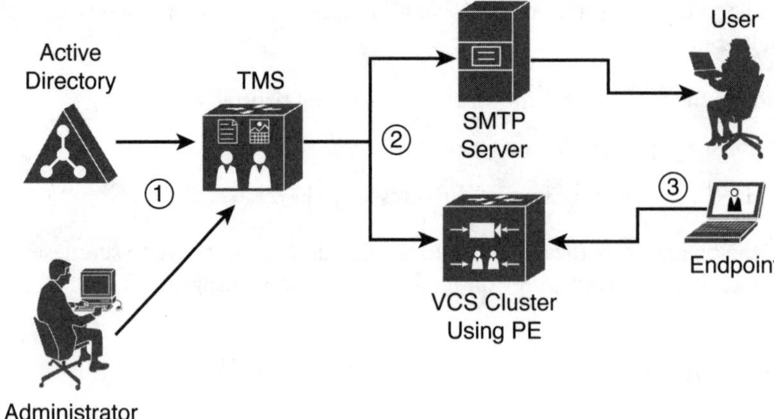

Figure 21-8 *Automated Provisioning with Cisco VCS and TMS*

In addition to Step 3, where the client successfully registers with Cisco VCS, the following happens:

- The endpoint registers to a Cisco VCS per the provisioning profile and the endpoint is ready for SIP calls.
- The endpoint subscribes to Cisco VCS for directory services.

Provisioning Extension characteristics are as follows:

- Provisioning of Cisco Jabber Video endpoints has evolved from provisioning agent to provisioning extension.
- Provisioning Extension is the only method for newer endpoints such as the EX series, C series, and Cisco Jabber Video starting in Cisco TMS Release 14.1 and later.
- Provisioning Extension is a feature activated on the Cisco TMS server and stores endpoint configuration data in an SQL database.
- Endpoints send SIP subscribe messages to the VCS, which retrieves the data from the Cisco TMS Provisioning Extension database and provides those settings to the endpoint.

Portfolio Simplification

Figure 21-9 describes the simplification of the video endpoint portfolio.

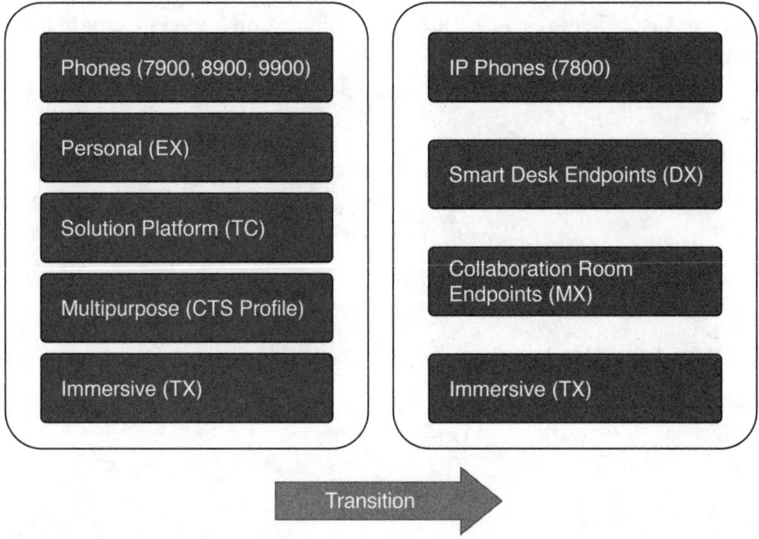

Figure 21-9 *Portfolio Simplification*

Because customers had difficulties in distinguishing among all the different video endpoints, Cisco simplified the video endpoint portfolio. Figure 21-9 shows the new video endpoint groupings. For more detail on collaboration endpoints, go to http://www.cisco.com/c/en/us/products/collaboration-endpoints/index.html.

Summary

This section summarizes the key points that were discussed in this chapter:

- CUCM is the main call control system to register all video endpoints. Cisco Jabber Video is the only exception and requires Cisco VCS to register.
- Cisco TMS is used for scheduled conferences. Cisco TMS can also be used to provision Cisco Jabber for video.
- MCU resource utilization can be optimized with Cisco TelePresence Conductor, especially when users have different resolutions and devices.

This chapter described the Cisco Jabber Video client and its registration with Cisco VCS. The CUCM and Cisco VCS call-processing systems were compared, and Cisco TMS was described as a scheduling and provisioning tool for Cisco Jabber Video.

Review Questions

Answer the following questions, and then see Appendix A, "Answers to Review Questions," for the answers.

1. **How many active Cisco TelePresence Video Communication Servers can you have in a VCS cluster?**

   a. 1

   b. 2

   c. 4

   d. 5

   e. 6

2. **How many vNICs are required on a Cisco TelePresence Video Communication Server?**

   a. 1

   b. 2

   c. 3

   d. 4

3. **What Cisco TelePresence Video Communication Server terminology matches the route pattern in CUCM?**

   a. Neighbor

   b. Search rule

   c. Transform

   d. None of the above

4. **Cisco TelePresence Server on Virtual Machine and TelePresence Server on Multiparty Media 310/320 can be deployed without Cisco TelePresence Conductor.**

   a. True

   b. False

Chapter 22

Describing Cisco TMS

Upon completing this chapter, you will be able to do the following:

- Describe the Cisco TMS modules and capabilities
- Describe the business needs for Cisco TMS
- Describe the resources that are required by Cisco TMS
- Describe the main Cisco TMS functions
- Describe the supported endpoints and infrastructure in a Cisco TMS environment
- Describe the scale and management scenarios in the Cisco TMS
- Describe conference call routing in Cisco TMS
- Describe port reservation in Cisco TMS
- Describe the call launch options that are provided by Cisco TMS
- Describe the calendaring options in the Cisco TMS
- Describe the Cisco TelePresence Conductor support
- Describe the recommended Cisco TMS scheduling deployment mode
- Describe how to add Cisco VCS endpoints to Cisco Unified Communications Manager for scheduling
- Describe the integration of Cisco TMSXE with Microsoft Exchange
- Describe the Cisco TMS Provisioning Extension features

This chapter provides a detailed description of the Cisco TelePresence Management Suite capabilities and scheduling options. Exchange Extension and web scheduling are also explained in detail.

Cisco TMS Introduction

Figure 22-1 illustrates the Cisco TelePresence Management Suite (Cisco TMS) modules and capabilities.

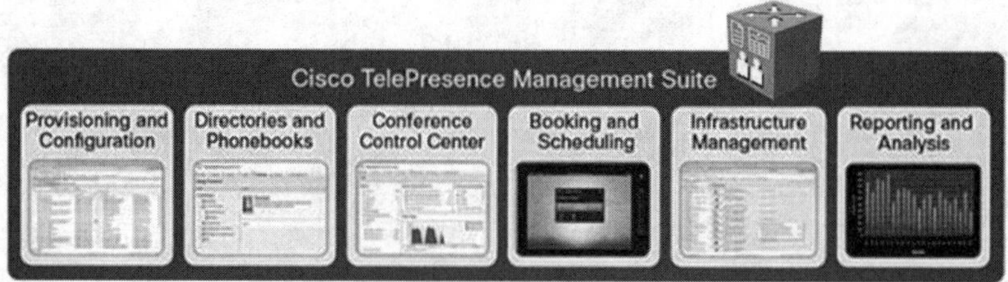

Figure 22-1 *Cisco TMS Components*

Cisco TMS Provisioning Extension supports provisioning and management of Cisco Jabber Video for TelePresence (formerly the Cisco TelePresence Movi application), Cisco Jabber for iPad, Cisco IP Video Phone E20, and Cisco TelePresence Systems EX60, EX90, MX200, and MX300.

Cisco TMS supports centralized phone book and directory services for Cisco and certain third-party H.323 and Session Initiation Protocol (SIP) endpoints. Import of directory records and synchronization with many data sources, including Cisco Unified Communications Manager, Microsoft Active Directory, H.350 Lightweight Directory Access Protocol (LDAP), gatekeepers, and file-based imports, is automatic.

Conference Control Center manages scheduled and unscheduled conference activity and monitors conference events for connectivity status, alarms, and changes.

Scheduling with Cisco TelePresence MCUs, Cisco TelePresence Servers, and Cisco TelePresence Conductor is supported. Variable-length PIN access controls on Cisco TelePresence MCUs and Cisco TelePresence Servers and participant access codes for Cisco WebEx Enabled TelePresence are supported to secure meetings.

Cisco TMS has a single management console for all Cisco and selected third-party telepresence devices, including endpoints, call control servers, Cisco TelePresence MCUs, Cisco TelePresence Servers, and other infrastructure.

Integrated application audit logging to monitor system changes is supported. Call-history reports for managed endpoints and infrastructure are provided. Scheduling activity reports include the user-based scheduling interface used, conference event logs, and conference reports.

Business Needs for Cisco TMS

Cisco TMS is used for resource management:

- Ad hoc user may use all multipoint control unit (MCU) capacity so customers cannot call in.

- This leads to unexpected and unwanted user experience.
- Oversubscription with booking cannot be prevented yet.
- Monitor the resource utilization to control usage.
- Adjust or enhance your MCU farms.

These scenarios describe unexpected and unwanted user experiences with video conference resources:

- Users want to dial in, but conference video resources are not available.
- Users want to dial in, but do not know the dial-in information, so in most meetings there are users that arrive late.
- Users do not know how to start a conference.

Cisco TMS helps resolve these issues:

- You can reserve resources for your conference.
- Cisco TMS simplifies the process to join a conference.

Cisco TMS Platform Overview

Cisco TMS can be virtualized. The supported operating systems to host Cisco TMS are as follows:

- Windows Server 2003 SP1 or later, 32 bit
- Windows Server 2003 R2 SP1 or later, 32 bit
- Windows Server 2008 SP2 or later, Standard 32 bit and 64 bit
- Windows Server 2008 R2 SP1 or later, Standard 64 bit (recommended)
- 4.0 .NET Framework Full (extended) version must be installed prior to running the Cisco TMS installer

The server operating system must be English, Japanese, or Chinese. Standard, Enterprise, and DataCenter editions are supported on both Windows Server 2003 and R2. Using the latest service pack is recommended for all versions.

For a large deployment, two virtual machines (VMs) are required, where one is the Cisco TMS server and the other is used for the Cisco TMS Extension for Microsoft Exchange (TMSXE). The VM resources for a large deployment vary slightly per VM:

- 4 vCPUs
- 8-GB vRAM
- 200-GB vDisk
- 1 vNIC with 1 Gbps

Testing was performed on a Cisco UCS C220 M3S platform. To fully utilize Cisco TMS, an external Microsoft SQL server is required. Use options keys for capacity or features to enhance the base version functionality.

Cisco TMS Overview

Figure 22-2 illustrates the main or core Cisco TMS functions.

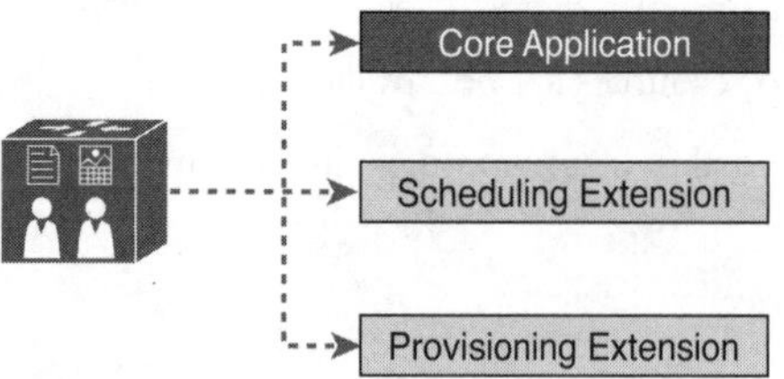

Figure 22-2 *Cisco TMS Overview*

Cisco TMS is the base system and can be enhanced with an extension to integrate with Microsoft Exchange or Lotus Notes to reserve video conference resources from the Microsoft or Lotus Notes calendar.

In addition, an application programming interface (API) can be used to book conference resources in Cisco TMS using different systems or applications. In addition, the Provisioning Extension can be used for endpoint registration and smart scheduling.

Endpoint and Infrastructure Support

Figure 22-3 illustrates the supported endpoints and infrastructure in a Cisco TMS environment.

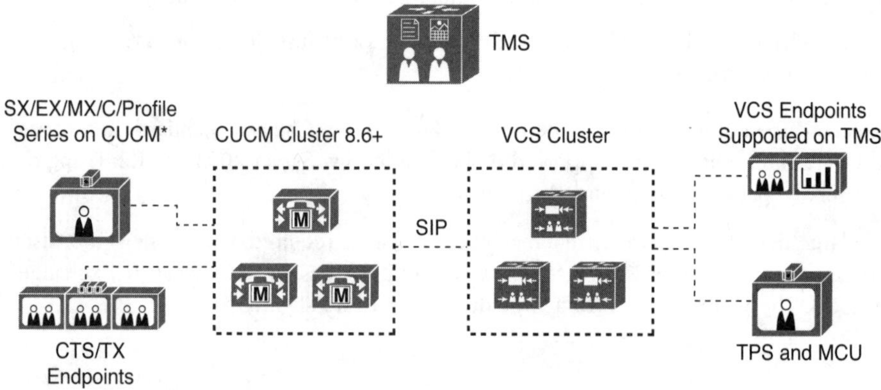

Figure 22-3 *Cisco TMS Endpoint and Infrastructure Support*

Cisco TMS Release 13.2 and later releases allow access to CTS and TX series endpoints for scheduling.

Cisco TelePresence SX, EX, MX, C, and Profile series endpoints that are registered on Cisco Unified Communications Manager can also be scheduled with Cisco TMS Release 13.2 and later releases.

Cisco TMS Scale and Management

Cisco TMS can support rapid, large-scale deployments of up to 100,000 telepresence users, endpoints, and soft clients across disparate customer locations, including up to 5000 direct-managed devices. The following are the limitations of TMS users:

- **Cisco TMS 14.3+:** Up to 5000 systems
- **Cisco TMSPE 1.x:** Up to 100,000 telepresence users

Cisco TMS has no direct communication with endpoints. Cisco TMS moves the configuration, for example, to the Cisco Video Communication Server (VCS).

For Cisco Unified Communications Manager customers, Cisco Prime Collaboration takes over the provisioning. New devices such as the Cisco DX series can only be registered with Cisco Unified Communications Manager. The Cisco Jabber Video for TelePresence migration path is to use Cisco Jabber for Windows, iOS, or Android with Cisco Unified Communications Manager and Cisco Unified Communications IM and Presence.

Cisco TMS Conference Call Routing

Figure 22-4 illustrates the conference call routing in Cisco TMS.

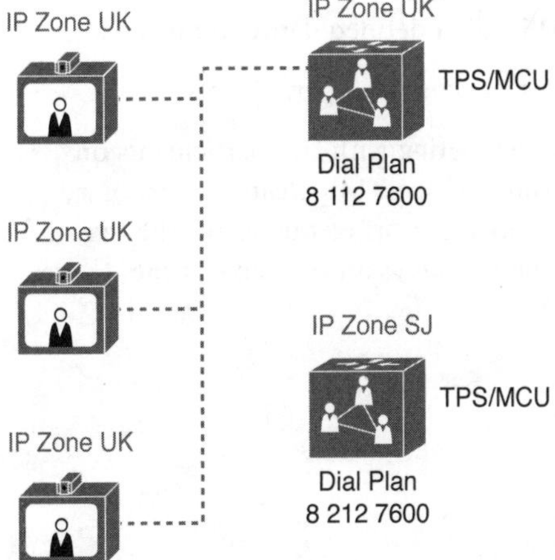

Figure 22-4 *Cisco TMS Conference Call Routing*

After setting up Cisco TMS, the first task is to configure IP zones. IP zones are logical groups in Cisco TMS. These groups are used for scheduling purposes.

In the figure, there are two IP zones: UK and SJ. The endpoints are grouped together with the MCU in the UK zone. When a meeting is scheduled, Cisco TMS sees that all (or the majority) of the participants are in the UK zone and selects a resource from the UK zone if a different zone is not specified. End users do not need to know which resources are used.

For the dial plan, specify a numeric ID base, numeric ID step, and numeric ID quantity. For example, if you specify the base ID 81127600, the ID step 1, and the ID quantity 31, 31 E.164 alias numbers are created and managed by Cisco TMS on the MCU. The lowest conference number available is selected. You cannot modify this behavior.

Cisco TMS Conference Port Reservation

Cisco TMS allows several methods to create meetings for voice or video.

- How it works:
  - Cisco TMS creates a temporary meeting on the Cisco TelePresence Server or MCU with the correct number of media ports.
  - Cisco TMS knows how many media ports each conference bridge has, and it will not let users overbook the system.
- Set up the port reservation:
  - On the MCU, enable media port reservation.
  - Specify the number of audio and video ports for reservations.
  - The conference is created by Cisco TMS with a defined date and time.
  - Optionally, limit the ports to the number of scheduled participants.

For example, suppose a user wants to schedule a meeting with five participants on Monday from 2:00 p.m. (1400) to 4:00 p.m. (1600). Cisco TMS creates a temporary meeting at the correct time with the correct number of port resources for the five users, as shown in Figure 22-5, assuming that the resources are available at the scheduled time.

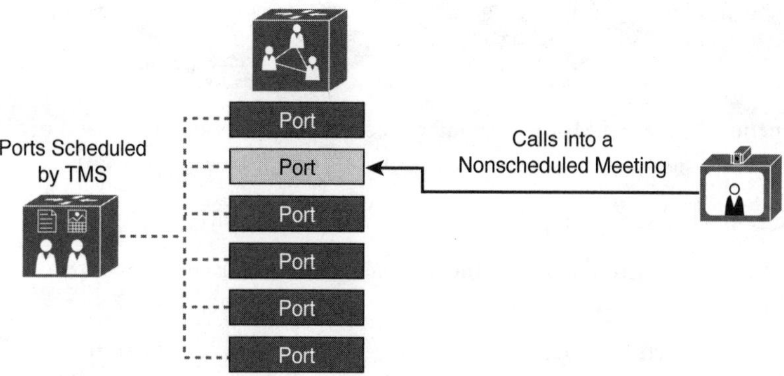

Figure 22-5 *Cisco TMS Port Reservations*

The setup steps takes you through the setup process and show you how to prevent MCU oversubscription.

An unscheduled call can use ports that are be reserved by Cisco TMS for scheduled conferences. In this case, oversubscription may occur. To prevent oversubscription, uncheck the **Allow Bookings** check box for the relevant multipoint control units. This action will create two multipoint control unit groups:

- The schedule-enabled MCUs are managed by Cisco TMS.
- Access is based on the best effort principle on the MCUs that are used for nonscheduled (ad hoc) conferences. Cisco TMS does not size ports on these MCUs, so overbooking can occur.

Specify the default setup buffer and default teardown buffer. These buffers specify how early a user can dial into a meeting, and how long the bridge remains open after the meeting ends is illustrated in Figure 22-6.

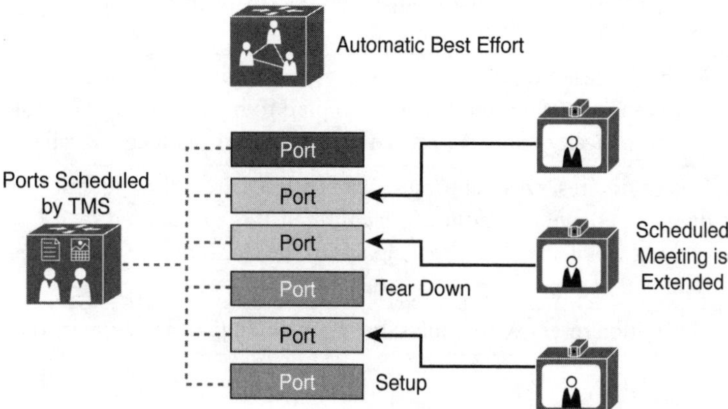

Figure 22-6 *Cisco TMS Port Reservation Considerations*

Note Ports are reserved for buffers during setup and teardown.

The Extend Scheduled Meeting Mode parameter specifies what happens at the end of the scheduled meeting time:

- **Off:** The meeting is disconnected.
- **Endpoint Prompt:** Prior to the end of the meeting, the user is asked whether the meeting should be extended.
- **Automatic Best Effort:** If resources are available, the meeting is extended by 15 minutes for a maximum of 16 times. However, if any of the endpoints in the conference have bookings within the next 15-minute period, the meeting is disconnected for all endpoints.

Note If a recording device is included in the meeting, and the recording device stays as the last party in the meeting, the call is extended without other participants left in the meeting.

Call Launch Options

Table 22-1 illustrates the call launch options that are provided by Cisco TMS.

Table 22-1 *Cisco TMS Call Launch Options*

Call Launch Option	Description
One Button to Push	Conference dial-in information is automatically presented on endpoints that support One Button to Push (OBTP).
Automatic Connect	Cisco TMS automatically connects all the participants at the specified time and date.
Manual Connect	At the specified time and date, the system listed as the video conference (VC) master will be prompted to begin the call. The call in automatically connected when the VC master initiates the call.
No Connect	This option reserves the rooms and generates the call route, but does not connect the route. The conference can be started by clicking Connect for the participants in the Conference Control Center.
Reservation	This option reserves the rooms, but does not initiate any connections.

One Button to Push (OBTP) can be used on the touch control, phone, or with a remote control. This option is the simplest for the user because the user does not need to know the conference number, ID, or a PIN. The user simply selects the correct meeting, pushes one button, and is connected to the conference. After the user pushes the button, a call is launched to the MCU to join the conference.

With Automatic Connect, the MCU dials the endpoints, and the user must answer the call to join the meeting. The default is to try three times to reach the endpoint. You can enable AutoAnswer to automatically connect the endpoint to the conference, but this approach may create "empty rooms" in your conference.

With Manual Connect and No Connect, an administrator must log in and start the meeting. With Reservation, only the room is reserved without a video endpoint.

Calendaring Options

The Cisco TMS scheduling extension products are as follows:

- The Cisco TMS Smart Scheduler interface, included with the Cisco TMS Provisioning Extension (Cisco TMSPE), allows simple, intuitive booking of single-instance and recurrent telepresence meetings.
- Cisco TMS supports Microsoft Exchange Server 2007 and 2010 calendar integration through the Cisco TMS Extension for Microsoft Exchange (Cisco TMSXE).
- Cisco TMS supports IBM Lotus Domino Server calendar integration through Cisco TMS Extension for IBM Lotus Notes (Cisco TMSXN).
- Custom-built scheduling interfaces for other calendaring products are supported through the Cisco TMS Extension Booking API (Cisco TMSBA).

Cisco TelePresence Conductor Support

Figure 22-7 describes the Cisco TelePresence Conductor support.

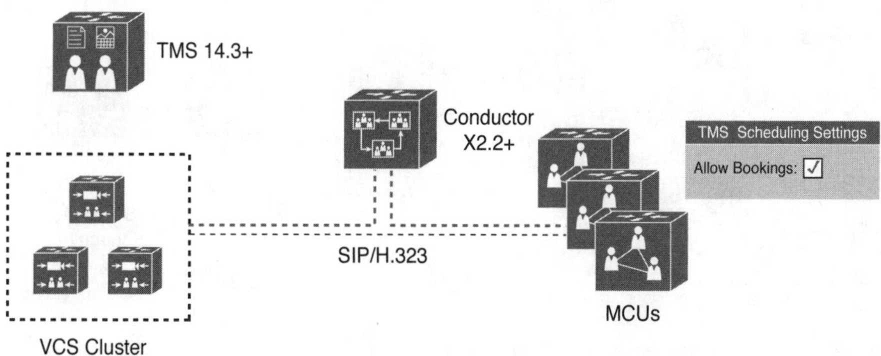

Figure 22-7 *Cisco TMS TelePresence Conductor Support*

In future versions, Cisco TelePresence Conductor can be connected with Cisco Unified Communications Manager, and Cisco TMS will be able to schedule conferences as well. With Cisco TelePresence Conductor, the conferencing management is virtualized, separated from the physical hardware, and managed centrally in Cisco TelePresence Conductor.

Limitations and recommendations for Cisco TelePresence Conductor include the following:

- Cisco TMS cannot properly reserve ports for meetings that are scheduled by Cisco TelePresence Conductor.
- As a result, conference resources are not assured.
- The recommendation for scheduled meetings is to directly manage and schedule the Cisco TelePresence Server and MCUs with Cisco TMS.

Recommended Cisco TMS Scheduling Deployment Mode

Figure 22-8 illustrates the recommended Cisco TMS scheduling deployment modes.

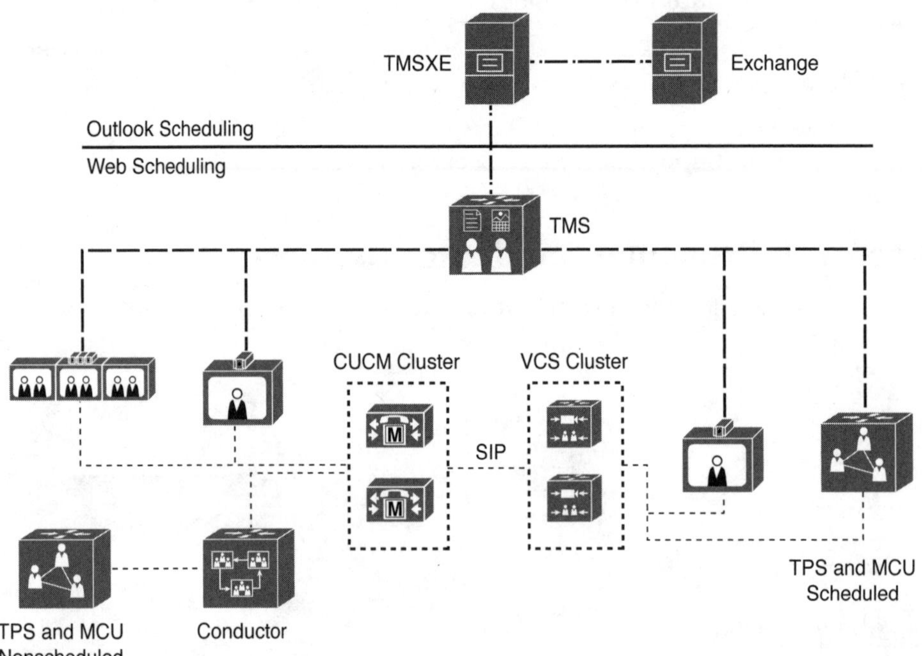

Figure 22-8 *Cisco TMS Scheduling Deployment Mode*

Cisco TMS directly manages MCUs and Cisco TelePresence Servers from a scheduling perspective. The Cisco TelePresence Conductor is used with Cisco Unified Communications Manager for nonscheduled conferences and for optimized resource utilization when devices with different capabilities are conferenced together.

The Cisco TMS Extension for Microsoft Exchange (Cisco TMSXE) is another layer for scheduled conferences.

Adding Cisco VCS Endpoints to Cisco Unified Communications Manager

The following steps summarize how to add Cisco TelePresence Video Communication Server (Cisco VCS) endpoints to Cisco Unified Communications Manager for scheduling:

1. Create an access control group with the following permissions:
   - Standard AXL API Access
   - Standard CTI Enabled
   - Standard SERVICEABILITY
   - Standard CCM Admin Users
   - Standard RealtimeAndTraceCollection
2. Create an application user for Cisco TMS:
   - Add the user to the access control group.
   - Assign all endpoints that you plan to add to Cisco TMS to the application user.

The application user is a service account that Cisco TMS uses to log in to Cisco Unified Communications Manager (CUCM) and to control video endpoints for scheduling.

In Cisco TMS, do the following:

- Add CUCM and specify the application user with its credentials.
- After integrating these systems, select the video endpoints from the received device list.

For Cisco VCS, do the following:

- Add the Cisco VCS endpoint to Cisco TMS with its IP address.
- Enter the administrator user credentials.

Integration of Cisco TMSXE with Microsoft Exchange

The following steps summarize the integration of Cisco TelePresence Management Suite Extension for Microsoft Exchange (Cisco TMSXE) with Microsoft Exchange. To add Exchange mailboxes, do the following:

1. Create a user mailbox for TMSXE.
2. Create a room mailbox for each endpoint.
3. Give the TMSXE user full access permission for each endpoint mailbox.
4. Configure the endpoint mailbox properties.
5. Configure the e-mail address in the endpoint configuration on CUCM.

Set the following on Microsoft Exchange for the endpoint mailbox:

- Automatically Accept Invitations (**True**/False)
- Remove the Private flag for All Meetings Accepted by the Mailbox (**True**/False)
- Delete Meeting Subject (**False**/True)
- Add Organizer to the Subject of a Booking (False/**True**)

Then start the TMSXE Configuration setup graphical user interface (GUI), which is in most cases on a standalone server, and specify the following:

- TMS server IP address, username, and password
- Exchange server IP address, username, and password, in addition to the e-mail address of the sender
- Add the video endpoints and map them to their e-mail addresses

Note Use the Cisco TMS display name as the mailbox name.

- Schedule a meeting and test the integration

Cisco TMS Provisioning Extension

Table 22-2 describes the Cisco TMS Provisioning Extension features.

Table 22-2 *Cisco TMS Provisioning Extension*

Benefits	Description
Provisioning scale	Simplifies management of up to 100,000 telepresence users across disparate locations and networks. Automated user account and phone book creation.
Intuitive meetings	Intuitive Collaboration Meeting Rooms (CMR). Configure personal CMR preferences.
Intuitive scheduling	Extend scheduling capability to everyone. Smart Scheduler simplifies the booking process for single and recurring telepresence meetings.
Endpoint support	Quick deployment with predefined templates. Low touch provisioning for C, E, EX, MX, and SX series endpoints and Cisco Jabber Video for Telepresence and iPad.

Note Smart Scheduler is a part of Cisco TMS Provisioning Extension.

Summary

This section summarizes the key points that were discussed in this chapter.

- Cisco TMS is the main application for scheduling video resources.
- Use Cisco TMSXE to use the Microsoft Outlook client to schedule video conferences on Cisco TMS.
- A booking API enables you to connect many applications to schedule meetings.

This chapter described the Cisco TelePresence Management Suite as the scheduling application with extensions for Microsoft Exchange or Lotus Notes integration to use legacy clients to set up conferences.

Review Questions

Answer the following questions, and then see Appendix A, "Answers to Review Questions," for the answers.

1. **Which option is not a Cisco TMS module?**

   a. Directories

   b. Provisioning

   c. Recording

   d. Scheduling

2. **Windows Server 2012 SP1 is a supported operating system for a Cisco TMS deployment.**

   a. True

   b. False

3. **Which option is not an extension for legacy calendar clients that is used for conferencing?**

   a. Cisco TMSBA

   b. Cisco TMSXE

   c. Cisco TMSXN

   d. None of the above

4. **Microsoft Exchange 2013 is supported with Cisco TMSXE for scheduling.**

   a. True

   b. False

5. **Smart Scheduler is deployed with Cisco TMSXE.**

   a. True

   b. False

Appendix A

Answers

Chapter 1

1. B
2. D
3. B
4. A
5. B
6. C

Chapter 2

1. A and D
2. F

Chapter 3

1. C and E
2. A
3. B
4. C

Chapter 4

1. B
2. B
3. B
4. C
5. A

Chapter 5

1. B and C
2. C
3. B
4. D
5. B and C

Chapter 6

1. B
2. B
3. B

Chapter 7

1. B
2. A
3. D
4. C

Chapter 8

1. A
2. B
3. C
4. B

Chapter 9

1. D
2. B
3. B
4. D
5. C

Chapter 10

1. C
2. A
3. B
4. C
5. D

Chapter 11

1. E
2. A
3. A
4. A and D
5. D

Chapter 12

1. C
2. E
3. A

Chapter 13

1. C
2. A
3. B
4. B
5. D

Chapter 14

1. B
2. B
3. B and E
4. D
5. A

Chapter 15

1. A
2. B
3. B
4. C

Chapter 16

1. B
2. A
3. E
4. A, C, and D
5. D

Chapter 17

1. B
2. C
3. B
4. B
5. C

Chapter 18

1. B
2. C
3. A
4. B

Chapter 19

1. B
2. A
3. C
4. B
5. A

Chapter 20

1. A
2. C
3. A
4. C
5. B

Chapter 21

1. C
2. C
3. B
4. B

Chapter 22

1. C
2. B
3. A
4. B
5. B

Glossary

AGC

Automatic gain control is an adaptive system found in many electronic devices. The average output signal level is fed back to adjust the gain to an appropriate level for a range of input signal levels. For example, without AGC the sound emitted from an AM radio receiver would vary to an extreme extent from a weak to a strong signal; the AGC effectively reduces the volume if the signal is strong and raises it when it is weaker.

API

Application programming interface. The means by which an application program talks to communications software. Standardized APIs allow application programs to be developed independently of the underlying method of communication. A set of standard software interrupts, calls, and data formats that computer application programs use to initiate contact with other devices (for example, network services, mainframe communications programs, or other program-to-program communications). Typically, APIs make it easier for software developers to create the links that an application needs to communicate with the operating system or with the network.

AvT

The Administration via Telephone application is a telephony-based interface that allows Cisco Unity Express that offers the following capabilities:

- Administrators can record new audio prompts or delete existing custom audio prompts without using a PC or sound-editing software, such as with the telephone user interface (TUI). These prompts can then be used in various Cisco Unity Express application scripts, such as the Welcome prompt in the default auto-attendant. The Emergency Alternate Greeting (EAG) is an option within the AvT that allows subscribers to record, modify, and enable or disable a special greeting to be played before the regular greeting, notifying callers of some temporary event or message.
- Administrators can rerecord existing prompts.

- Administrators can send broadcast messages. Subscribers who have the broadcast privilege can access a limited set of AvT capabilities.
- Administrators can record spoken names for remote locations and remote subscribers.

AXL

Administrative XML layer is a SOAP-based API that enables remote provisioning of CUCM.

BAT

Bulk Administration Tool. An application that performs bulk transactions to the database.

BHCA

Busy Hour Call Attempt is the number of telephone calls attempted at the busiest hour of the day (peak hour), and the higher the BHCA, the higher the stress on the network processors. BHCA is not to be confused with busy hour call completion (BHCC) which measures the throughput capacity of the network.

BHCC

Busy Hour Call Completion. The number of calls that a telephone system can complete during the busy hour of the day.

CAC

Call admission control is the practice or process of regulating traffic volume in voice communications, particularly in wireless mobile networks and in VoIP.

CFA

Call Forward All. A Cisco IP phone feature that forwards all calls to a given phone number.

CFB

Call Forward Busy. A Cisco IP phone feature that forwards call when the line is busy.

CFNA

Call Forward No Answer. A Cisco IP phone feature that forwards call if no one answers.

CFNC

Call Forward No Coverage. A Cisco IP phone feature.

CFUR

Call Forward Unregistered. A Cisco IP phone feature that forwards calls if the phone is unregistered to CUCM for any reason.

COBRAS

Consolidated Object Backup and Restore Application Suite (COBRAS) is a set of tools designed to allow administrators to backup all subscribers, call handlers, interview handlers, name lookup handlers, public distribution lists, and schedules and to restore some or all of that information onto another Unity or Connection server.

CoS

Class of service. An indication of how an upper-layer protocol requires a lower-layer protocol to treat its messages. In SNA subarea routing, CoS definitions are used by subarea nodes to determine the optimal route to establish a given session. A CoS definition comprises a virtual route number and a transmission priority field. Also called ToS (type of service).

CPU

Central processing unit. The hardware within a computer system or smartphone that carries out the instructions of a computer program by performing the basic arithmetical, logical, and input-output operations of the system.

CSS

Calling search space. A Cisco CUCM object that works with partitions to determine where calls can and cannot be made.

CTIQBE

The Cisco TAPI Service Provider (TSP) uses the Computer Telephony Interface Quick Buffer Encoding (CTIQBE) to communicate with Cisco CallManager on TCP port 2748.

DAS

Direct-attached storage is a local hard drive in a server.

DN

Dialed number is a number that a caller dialed to initiate a call (for example, 800-555-1212).

DN

Distinguished name. Global, authoritative name of an entry in the OSI directory (X.500).

DNS

Domain Name System. System used on the Internet for translating names of network nodes into addresses.

DSP

Digital signal processors are hardware based processors that designed to convert analog voice to digital voice over IP.

DTMF

Dual-tone multifrequency. Tones generated when a button is pressed on a telephone, primarily used in the United States and Canada.

EAG

Emergency Alternate Greeting (EAG) allows the Cisco Unity Express administrator to record an alternate AA greeting to be used in case of an emergency or other short-term event, such as a holiday or snow day.

ELM

Enterprise License Manager. This is a Cisco Collaboration Systems licensing feature that has been replaced by the Prime License Manager (PLM).

ESXi

VMware vSphere ESXi. ESXi is not an acronym. VMware's enterprise software hypervisor for guest virtual servers that runs directly on host server hardware without requiring an additional underlying operating system.

EWS

EWS provides access to much of the same data that is made available through Microsoft Office Outlook. EWS clients can integrate Outlook data into Line-of-Business (LOB) applications.

FCoE

Fibre Channel over Ethernet is a computer network technology that encapsulates Fibre Channel frames over Ethernet networks. This allows Fibre Channel to use 10 Gigabit Ethernet networks (or higher speeds) while preserving the Fibre Channel protocol.

G.711

A standard voice codec that describes the 64-kbps PCM voice coding technique. In G.711, encoded voice is already in the correct format for digital voice delivery in the PSTN or through PBXs. Described in the ITU-T standard in its G-series recommendations.

G.729

A standard voice codec that describes CELP compression where voice is coded into 8-kbps streams. There are two variations of this standard (G.729 and G.729 Annex A) that differ mainly in computational complexity; both provide speech quality similar to 32-kbps ADPCM. Described in the ITU-T standard in its G-series recommendations.

G2

Generation 2.

GDM

A GDM is associated with a group profile in the Cisco Unity Express configuration and does not have a login user ID or a PIN associated.

GMT

Greenwich mean time.

GSM

Global System for Mobile Communications.

HTTPS

HyperText Transfer Protocol Secure.

iLBC

Internet Low Bitrate Codec is a free speech codec suitable for robust voice communication over IP. The codec is designed for narrow band speech and results in a payload bit rate of 13.33 kbps with an encoding frame length of 30 ms and 15.20 kbps with an encoding length of 20 ms.

IMAP

Internet Message Access Protocol. Method of accessing e-mail or bulletin board messages kept on a mail server that can be shared. IMAP permits client e-mail applications to access remote message stores as if they were local without actually transferring the message.

IOPS

IOPS (Input/Output Operations Per Second, pronounced eye-ops) is a common performance measurement used to benchmark computer storage devices like hard disk drives (HDD), solid state drives (SSD), and storage area networks (SAN).

IPsec

IP Security. A framework of open standards that provides data confidentiality, data integrity, and data authentication between participating peers. IPsec provides these security services at the IP layer. IPsec uses IKE to handle the negotiation of protocols and algorithms based on local policy and to generate the encryption and authentication keys to be used by IPsec. IPsec can protect one or more data flows between a pair of hosts, between a pair of security gateways, or between a security gateway and a host.

iSCSI

Internet Small Computer Systems Interface. Works on top of the Transport Control Protocol (TCP) and allows the SCSI command to be sent end-to-end over local-area networks (LANs), wide-area networks (WANs), or the Internet.

ISR

An Integrated Services Router is a Cisco physical router with added technologies to make it into a voice gateway that specifies the elements to guarantee QoS on networks. For example, an ISR can be used to allow video and sound to reach the receiver without interruption. Every application that requires some kind of guarantee has to make an individual reservation.

IVR

Interactive voice response. Term used to describe systems that provide information in the form of recorded messages over telephone lines in response to user input in the form of spoken words or, more commonly, DTMF signaling. Examples include banks that allow you to check your balance from any telephone and automated stock quote systems.

JTAPI

Java Telephony Application Programming Interface. Sun Microsystems developed this call control model.

LDAP

Lightweight Directory Access Protocol is a protocol that provides access for management and browser applications that provide read/write interactive access to the X.500 Directory.

LPCM

Linear pulse-code modulation (LPCM) is a specific type of PCM where the quantization levels are linearly uniform. This is in contrast to PCM encodings where quantization levels vary as a function of amplitude (as with the A-law algorithm or the μ-law algorithm).

MACD

MACD is a common term referring to a request to create a new configuration.

MAN

A metropolitan-area network is a network that interconnects users with computer resources in a geographic area or region larger than that covered by even a large local-area network (LAN) but smaller than the area covered by a wide-area network (WAN).

MAPI

Messaging Application Programming Interface (MAPI) is a messaging architecture and a Component Object Model-based API for Microsoft Windows. MAPI allows client programs to become (e-mail) messaging-enabled, -aware, or -based by calling MAPI subsystem routines that interface with certain messaging servers.

MWI

Message waiting indicator is an audio or visual signal that a voicemail or other type of message is waiting.

NANP

The North American Numbering Plan (NANP) is a telephone numbering plan that encompasses 25 distinct regions in twenty countries primarily in North America, including the Caribbean and the U.S. territories. Not all North American countries participate in the NANP.

NAS

Network-attached storage is a file-level computer data storage server connected to a computer network providing data access to a heterogeneous group of clients. NAS is specialized for serving files either by its hardware, software, or configuration.

NAT

Network Address Translation. A mechanism for reducing the need for globally unique IP addresses. NAT allows an organization with addresses that are not globally unique to connect to the Internet by translating these addresses into globally routable address space. Also known as Network Address Translator.

NFS

Network File System. As commonly used, a distributed file system protocol suite developed by Sun Microsystems that allows remote file access across a network. In actuality, NFS is simply one protocol in the suite. NFS protocols include NFS, RPC, XDR, and others. These protocols are part of a larger architecture that Sun refers to as ONC.

NIC

Network interface card is a circuit board in a server that provides network communication capabilities to and from a computer system. A NIC is also called an adapter.

NTE

The named telephone events are carried as part of the voice stream and use the same sequence number and time-stamp base as the regular voice channel.

NTLM

NT LAN Manager. Also known as Microsoft Windows Challenge/Response, NT LAN Manager is the authentication protocol that is used on Windows systems and networks.

NTP

Network Time Protocol. A protocol that is built on top of TCP that ensures accurate local timekeeping with reference to radio and atomic clocks that are located on the Internet. This protocol is capable of synchronizing distributed clocks within milliseconds over long time periods.

OSI

Open Systems Interconnection. International standardization program created by ISO and ITU-T to develop standards for data networking that facilitate multivendor equipment interoperability.

OVA

An Open Virtual Appliance is merely a single file distribution of the same file package, stored in the TAR format.

OVF

An Open Virtualization Format is not only the name of the packaging format standard, but it also refers to the package when distributed as a group of files.

PAT

Port Address Translation. Translation method that allows the user to conserve addresses in the global address pool by allowing source ports in TCP connections or UDP conversations to be translated. Different local addresses then map to the same global address, with port translation providing the necessary uniqueness. When translation is required, the new port number is picked out of the same range as the original following the convention of Berkeley Standard Distribution (SD).

PCM

Pulse code modulation is a method used to digitally represent sampled analog signals. It is the standard form of digital audio in computers, Compact Discs, digital telephony and other digital audio applications.

PIMG

The Cisco Unity PBX IP Media Gateway (PIMG) is an 8-port, stackable integration device that emulates a digital or analog phone (station) on the PBX side and connects to the Cisco Unity server over a LAN or WAN using the Session Initiation Protocol (SIP).

PSTN

Public switched telephone network. General term referring to the variety of telephone networks and services in place worldwide. Sometimes called POTS.

QoS

Quality of service is a measure of performance for a transmission system that reflects its transmission quality and service availability.

RTMT

Real-Time Monitoring Tool. Runs as a client-side application; uses HTTPS and TCP to monitor system performance, device status, device discovery.

RTP

Real-Time Transport Protocol. Commonly used with IP networks. RTP is designed to provide end-to-end network transport functions for applications transmitting real-time data, such as audio, video, or simulation data, over multicast or unicast network services. RTP provides such services as payload type identification, sequence numbering, time-stamping, and delivery monitoring to real-time applications.

SAN

A storage-area network is a high-speed network of storage devices that also connects those storage devices with servers.

SCCP

Skinny Client Control Protocol is a proprietary network terminal control protocol originally developed by Selsius Systems, which was acquired by Cisco Systems in 1998. SCCP is a lightweight IP-based protocol for session signaling with Cisco Unified Communications Manager, formerly named CallManager.

SCSI

Small Computer Systems Interface. A set of parallel interface standards developed by the American National Standards Institute (ANSI) for attaching printers, disk drives, scanners and other peripherals to computers. SCSI (pronounced “skuzzy”) is supported by all major operating systems.

SDP

Session Description Protocol is a set of rules that defines how multimedia sessions can be set up to allow all end points to effectively participate in the session. In this context, a session consists of a set of communications end points along with a series of interactions among them.

SIP

Session Initiation Protocol. Protocol developed by the IETF MMUSIC Working Group as an alternative to H.323. SIP features are compliant with IETF RFC 2543, published in March 1999. SIP equips platforms to signal the setup of voice and multimedia calls over IP networks.

SIP

The Cisco ® ASR 1000 Series SPA Interface Processor (SIP), based on the Cisco I-Flex design, combines shared port adapters (SPAs) and SPA interface processors (SIPs), taking advantage of an extensible design that facilitates service prioritization for voice, video, and data (triple-play) services.

SLA

A service level agreement is a contract between a service provider (either internal or external) and the end user that defines the level of service expected from the service provider. SLAs are output-based in that their purpose is specifically to define what the customer will receive.

SMTP

Simple Mail Transfer Protocol. Internet protocol providing e-mail services.

SNMP

Simple Network Management Protocol. Network management protocol used almost exclusively in TCP/IP networks. SNMP provides a means to monitor and control network devices, and to manage configurations, statistics collection, performance, and security.

SOAP

Simple Object Access Protocol is an XML-based messaging protocol. It defines a set of rules for structuring messages that can be used for simple one-way messaging but is particularly useful for performing RPC-style (Remote Procedure Call) request-response dialogues.

SRE

The Cisco Services Ready Engine (SRE) modules are router blades for the second generation of Cisco Integrated Services Routers (ISR G2) that provide the capability to host Cisco, third-party, and custom applications.

SRST

Survivable Remote Site Telephony. Cisco Unified SRST provides Cisco Unified CM with fallback support for Cisco Unified IP phones that are attached to a Cisco router on your local network.

SRSV

Protect your communications with voicemail survivability for your organization's remote sites, such as branch offices or other small sites. When a remote site does not have access to your central voicemail system, as during a network service interruption, Cisco Unified Survivable Remote Site Voicemail provides voicemail backup services. This helps to ensure your remote site continues to have voicemail and auto-attendant service.

SSH

Secure Shell. Protocol that provides a secure remote connection to a route through a TCP application.

SSL

Secure Sockets Layer. Encryption technology for the web used to provide secure transactions, such as the transmission of credit card numbers for e-commerce.

TAC

Cisco Technical Assistance Center.

TIMG

The Cisco Unity T1 IP Media Gateway (TIMG) is a single-span, rack-optimized device that translates the digital voice channel of a T1 trunk into SIP for transmission over a LAN or WAN to the Cisco messaging system.

TRAP

Telephone Record and Playback.

TRC

Tested Reference Configuration.

TTS

TTS is a feature that converts written text to audible speech.

TUI

Telephone user interface represents the options available via the buttons on the phone (1-9, *, and #).

UCS

Cisco's server hardware platform.

URI

Uniform resource identifier. Type of formatted identifier that encapsulates the name of an Internet object, and labels it with an identification of the name space, thus producing a member of the universal set of names in registered name spaces and of addresses referring to registered protocols or name spaces. [RFC 1630]

VAD

Voice activity detection is a software application that allows a data network carrying voice traffic over the Internet to detect the absence of audio and conserve bandwidth by preventing the transmission of "silent packets" over the network.

ViQ

ViQ allows video callers to be queued within a call center.

VM

In computing, a virtual machine (VM) is an emulation of a particular computer system. Virtual machines operate based on the computer architecture and functions of a real or hypothetical computer, and their implementations might involve specialized hardware, software, or a combination of both.

VM-FEX

Cisco Virtual Machine Fabric Extender (VM-FEX) is a Cisco technology that addresses management and performance concerns in a data center by unifying physical and virtual switch management. The Cisco VM-FEX collapses virtual and physical networking into a single infrastructure.

VMFS

Virtual Machine File System. The VMware VMFS is a high-performance cluster file system that provides storage virtualization optimized for virtual machines.

VMO

Cisco Unity Connection ViewMail for Microsoft Outlook lets you send, listen to, and manage voice messages from Outlook. In the ViewMail for Outlook form, you use the controls on the Media Master to play and record voice messages.

VoD

Video on demand. System using video compression to supply video programs to viewers when requested via ISDN or cable.

VoH

Similar to music on hold, video on hold can play video for video callers waiting in a call center queue.

VPIM

Voice Profile for Internet Mail.

vSwitch

VMware vSphere Switch provides a centralized interface for virtual machine networking configuration.

VUI

A voice-user interface (VUI) makes human interaction with computers possible through a voice/speech platform in order to initiate an automated service or process. A VUI is the interface to any speech application.

VXML

VoiceXML is an application of the Extensible Markup Language (XML) which, when combined with voice recognition technology, enables interactive access to the Web through the telephone or a voice-driven browser.

WAN

Wide-area network. Data communications network that serves users across a broad geographic area and often uses transmission devices provided by common carriers. Frame Relay, SMDS, and X.25 are examples of WANs.

WebDAV

WebDAV (World Wide Web Distributed Authoring and Versioning) is the Internet Engineering Task Force (IETF) standard for collaborative authoring on the Web: A set of extensions to the Hypertext Transfer Protocol (HTTP) that facilitates collaborative editing and file management between users located remotely from each other on the Internet.

Index

A

B

C

D

E

F

G

H

I

K-L

M

N

O

P

Q

R

S

T

U

V

W

X-Y-Z